A HANDBOOK
on
PAUL'S LETTER TO THE ROMANS

The Handbooks in the **UBS Handbook Series** are detailed commentaries providing valuable exegetical, historical, cultural, and linguistic information on the books of the Bible. They are prepared primarily to assist practicing Bible translators as they carry out the important task of putting God's Word into the many languages spoken in the world today. The text is discussed verse by verse and is accompanied by running text in at least one modern English translation.

Over the years church leaders and Bible readers have found the UBS Handbooks to be useful for their own study of the Scriptures. Many of the issues Bible translators must address when trying to communicate the Bible's message to modern readers are the ones Bible students must address when approaching the Bible text as part of their own private study and devotions.

The Handbooks will continue to be prepared primarily for translators, but we are confident that they will be useful to a wider audience, helping all who use them to gain a better understanding of the Bible message.

Helps for Translators

UBS Handbook Series:

A Handbook on . . .

- Leviticus
- The Book of Joshua
- The Book of Ruth
- The Book of Job
- The Book of Psalms
- Lamentations
- The Book of Daniel
- The Book of Amos
- The Books of Obadiah, Jonah, and Micah
- The Books of Nahum, Habakkuk, and Zephaniah
- The Gospel of Matthew
- The Gospel of Mark
- The Gospel of Luke
- The Gospel of John
- The Acts of the Apostles
- Paul's Letter to the Romans
- Paul's First Letter to the Corinthians
- Paul's Second Letter to the Corinthians
- Paul's Letter to the Galatians
- Paul's Letter to the Ephesians
- Paul's Letter to the Philippians
- Paul's Letters to the Colossians and to Philemon
- Paul's Letters to the Thessalonians
- Paul's Letters to Timothy and to Titus
- The Letter to the Hebrews
- The First Letter from Peter
- The Letter from Jude and the Second Letter from Peter
- The Letters of John
- The Revelation to John

Guides:

A Translator's Guide to . . .

- Selections from the First Five Books of the Old Testament
- Selected Psalms
- the Gospel of Mark
- the Gospel of Luke
- Paul's Second Letter to the Corinthians

Technical Helps:

- Old Testament Quotations in the New Testament
- Short Bible Reference System
- New Testament Index
- The Theory and Practice of Translation
- Bible Index
- Fauna and Flora of the Bible
- Marginal Notes for the Old Testament
- Marginal Notes for the New Testament
- The Practice of Translating

A HANDBOOK ON

Paul's Letter to the Romans

by Barclay M. Newman

and Eugene A. Nida

UBS Handbook Series

United Bible Societies
New York

Books in the series of **Helps for Translators** may be ordered from a national Bible Society or from either of the following centers:

United Bible Societies
European Production Fund
D-70520 Stuttgart 80
Postfach 81 03 40
Germany

United Bible Societies
1865 Broadway
New York, NY 10023
U.S.A.

L.C. Cataloging-in-Publication Data:

Newman, Barclay Moon, 1931-
[Translator's handbook on Paul's letter to the Romans]
A handbook on Paul's letter to the Romans / by Barclay M. Newman and Eugene A. Nida.
p. cm. — (UBS handbook series) (Helps for translators)
Originally published: A translator's handbook on Paul's letter to the Romans. 1973.
Includes bibliographical references and index.
ISBN 0-8267-0160-4
1. Bible. N.T. Romans—Translating. 2. Bible. N.T. Romans—Commentaries. I. Nida, Eugene Albert, 1914- . II. Title. III. Title: Paul's letter to the Romans. IV. Series. V. Series: Helps for translators.
BS2665.5.N49 1994
227'.1077—dc20 93-39491
CIP

ABS-3/96-250-6,450-CM-10-102680

PREFACE

Those who are familiar with the preceding volumes in the series of Translators' Handbooks, published by the United Bible Societies, will note that in this Handbook on Romans there is a significant change in format, namely, the double presentation of the running text: first, in paragraph form, so as to facilitate the discussion of important features of the discourse structure; and second, in verse form, to call attention to some of the detailed problems of grammatical and lexical structure. This new arrangement of the running text has been strongly recommended by Translations Consultants, who have felt that a translator needs the running text presented in both ways if he is to use the Handbook efficiently.

As with other of the later volumes in this series, no attempt has been made to identify the particular language in which alternative renderings may occur, since the focus is upon the syntactic and semantic problems in question rather than upon those languages which may exhibit such features.

Since this is the first Handbook dealing with essentially expository discourse, it is inevitable that proportionately more attention has been given to the problems of discourse structure. The importance of the theological concepts in Romans and the existence of many different views with respect to the interpretation of certain key passages have resulted in significantly more detailed discussions of both interpretation and restructuring.

Special thanks must be extended to the members of the United Bible Societies Committee on Helps for Translators, who have carefully reviewed the manuscript of this volume and have made a number of helpful suggestions for important improvements.

Barclay M. Newman
Eugene A. Nida

January 1973

CONTENTS

TRANSLATING PAUL'S LETTER TO THE ROMANS

Doubtless Paul's Letter to the Romans is the most widely read book of the New Testament, except for the Gospels themselves. In fact, if the apostle Paul had written nothing else, he would still be recognized as one of the outstanding Christian thinkers of all time on the basis of this letter alone. What gives Romans this appeal? Why is it so highly valued?

Above all else, the appeal of Romans is its theology, especially its statement of "how God puts men right with himself...through faith, from beginning to end" (1.17). This is the heart of the letter, its very essence, and it forms the basis for all else that Paul says throughout the letter. Paul states this thesis in 1.17, and then develops his argument to show how all people, Jews and Gentiles alike, stand in need of being put right with God.

Paul first underscores the sinful condition of the non-Jewish world (1.18-32). He points out how its rebellion against God's revelation of himself in nature and in the human conscience has led to terrible distortions of the natural order and to the worship of "what God has created instead of the Creator himself" (1.25). The result of this is the revelation of God's wrath against "all the sin and evil of men whose evil ways prevent the truth from being known" (1.18).

The first part of the second chapter (2.1-16) speaks to both Jews and Gentiles. Paul has already demonstrated how the pagan corruption of life has brought down God's wrath. Now in these verses he indicates that Jews and Gentiles alike, whether or not they have committed these moral abuses, stand guilty before God's judgment: the self-righteous man, whether Jew or Gentile, will receive the same condemnation as the pagans described in 1.18-32.

In 2.17—3.20 Paul addresses himself directly to the Jews, indicating that the possession of the Law is of no advantage to them, unless they obey it. Theoretically, they should have had an advantage over the Gentiles, because "God trusted his message to the Jews" (3.2); but the Jews' unfaithfulness made void any advantage that they may have had. So then, the only valid conclusion is that the Jews are in no better condition than the Gentiles: "Jews and Gentiles alike are all under the power of sin" (3.9).

Having shown how all men stand in need of fellowship with God, in 3.21—4.25 Paul turns again to the subject of how God puts sinful men right with himself. It is through faith, and "has nothing to do with law" (3.21), as the example of Abraham indicates (4.1-25).

Chapters 5-8, though introducing a new section in the letter, are also primarily theological. Each of these chapters emphasizes from different perspectives what it means to be put right with God. In 5.1-11 Paul shows how all the graces of the Christian life grow out of a right relation with God, while in the last half of the chapter (5.12-21) he contrasts the old humanity with the new humanity and the way of death with the way of life.

There is a parallelism between chapters 6 and 7: Romans 6 affirms that sin no longer has power over the believer, and chapter 7 illustrates how the Christian is set free from the power of the Law. Chapter 8 serves as the climax to all that Paul has said in chapters 5-7: it is God's Spirit who enables the believer to conquer the power of sin (vv. 1-17) and to have hope in the glorious future that awaits God's people (vv. 18-30). This chapter concludes with an expression of thanksgiving for God's love in Christ Jesus (vv. 31-39).

Although Romans is primarily theological, it is also practical in that it shows that there is a relation between Christian theology and Christian living. To be put right with God lays certain demands on the life of the believer, and in a rather lengthy passage (12.1—15.13) Paul makes explicit some of the ethical demands of the Christian life. That Paul considers this an important part of his message can be seen by the fact that he follows this same pattern of "theology/practical application of theology" in all of his writings. Almost all of Romans 12, as well as 13.8—15.13, is nothing less than a series of applications of the meaning of Christian love in specific situations; and 13.1-7 indicates that the Christian has a responsibility toward the civil authorities, since God desires that his world be one of law and order.

For all else that Romans is, it is an intensely personal letter. It is not personal in the sense that Paul is addressing a congregation where he has served, but in other respects it is indeed personal. Paul begins by telling his readers that he has hoped to visit them on other occasions, but has been prevented from doing so (1.13), and he concludes by requesting them to pray so that he may "enjoy a refreshing visit" with them (15.32). And chapter 16 contains a series of personal greetings to members of their congregation whom he has met during his travels.

Besides mentioning his plans to visit Rome and to go on from there to Spain, in this letter Paul gives us an insight into his own personal situation. Paul knows of the dangers that he faces from the unbelievers in Jerusalem, and of the possibility that his service for the Christian fellowship may not be accepted by the believers in Judea (15.31). Moreover, if the parallel between Romans 1.1,5 and Galatians 1.1, 15 tells anything, there are intimations that the validity of Paul's apostleship is being questioned by some. This accounts for the stress that he places on his apostolic call at the outset of the letter. Paul is deeply concerned that he be recognized as a genuine apostle, so that his message will be accepted by the Christians at Rome; otherwise his mission to them and to churches beyond will be impossible, or at least severely limited.

Finally, chapters 9-11 are deeply personal. One might classify them as theological or philosophical, for in them Paul discusses the mystery of God's working in history, but essentially these chapters are personal. Paul himself is a Jew, and he loves his people. Why, then, have they failed to respond to the message about Jesus Christ? Is there any hope for them? Has God cast them off? Paul does not discuss this problem as an abstract issue, but as a matter that is of the utmost personal concern to him, and this is seen in the fact that at certain places in these chapters he is evidently more emotional than logical in his arguments.

Romans speaks as directly to the present generation as it did to the people of the first century A.D.; its evaluation of the human situation will be valid as long as men live in sinful rebellion against their Creator. And it will always have an appeal for men and women who are seeking to escape the power of sin and to be put right with God. In this regard, even the personal sections of this letter are important, because here we get a glimpse into the experiences of a man who was sinful like us, but who discovered the joy of the life of faith.

CHAPTER 1

1 From Paul, a servant of Christ Jesus, and an apostle chosen and called
by God to preach his Good News.
2 The Good News was promised long ago by God through his prophets, and
written in the Holy Scriptures. 3 It is about his Son, our Lord Jesus Christ: as
to his humanity, he was born a descendant of David; 4 as to his divine holiness,
he was shown with great power to be the Son of God by being raised from
death. 5 Through him God gave me the privilege of being an apostle, for the
sake of Christ, in order to lead people of all nations to believe and obey. 6 This
also includes you who are in Rome, whom God has called to belong to Jesus
Christ.
7 And so I write to all of you in Rome whom God loves and has called to
be his own people:
May God our Father and the Lord Jesus Christ give you grace and peace.

Greek letters of the first century A.D. normally began with the formula "writer to recipient, greeting," while Jewish letters generally began with "writer to recipient, may your peace be multiplied." One can readily see how Paul's letter to the Romans reflects such a customary formula, though he exercises freedom in further qualifying both himself and the persons to whom he is writing.

In Greek this introductory greeting consists of one sentence, and traditional translations have often attempted to make one sentence of it. Though this can be done without violating the grammatical rules of some receptor languages, the results are usually not only artificial but also stylistically "overloaded." For that reason in the TEV and in most other translations which aim at reproducing the closest natural equivalent, this relatively long sentence is broken up into several shorter sentences. In doing so, however, it is essential that the connection between the parts be carefully indicated. If one is to follow the progression of thought in this relatively complex sentence, careful markers of transition must be introduced. Basically, the sentence begins with statements concerning Paul and his relationship to the Good News. This immediately leads into statements concerning Jesus Christ, who is essentially the content of the Good News, as well as the one for whose sake Paul has become an apostle to all nations.

1.1 From Paul, a servant of Christ Jesus, and an apostle chosen and called by God to preach his Good News.

Since Romans is a genuine letter, the TEV tries to indicate this by beginning with from Paul (so also NEB and JB; Phillips begins with "this letter comes to you from Paul"). It was quite customary for a Jew of the first century A.D. to have both a Roman name and a Jewish name (see Acts 13.9). Paul was the writer's Roman and Saul his Jewish name, but he always refers to himself by his Roman name, and Saul is used only in Acts.

In a high percentage of languages it is necessary to employ a first person singular pronoun in relation to Paul. That is to say, one must employ a phrase such as "I am Paul" or "I, Paul." This is simply because in many languages one cannot speak of oneself in the third person, particularly not in this kind of introductory statement. To insist on using merely the third person in such languages could be quite misleading, since readers might assume that Paul, as the presumed writer of this letter, was speaking about some other Paul as an apostle of Jesus Christ.

In most languages which must introduce the first person singular pronoun, the normal practice is to say "I am Paul" or "I, Paul, am a servant of Jesus Christ," without making explicit reference in verse 1 to a writing or a letter. However, in some instances translators have taken a portion of verse 7 and incorporated it into verse 1—for example, "I, Paul, write to you in Rome"—since this is the normal manner in which, in the particular receptor language, letters may be introduced. If this is done, some repetition of the reference to writing must usually be included in verse 7, in order for the salutation to be properly introduced.

Paul speaks of himself as a servant of Christ Jesus, a phrase which appears in a number of translations as "a slave of Christ Jesus." It is true that the Greek word itself more nearly means "slave" in the modern sense of the word. On the other hand, it is quite possible that Paul took the meaning of this term from the Old Testament background where prophets, and sometimes worshipers in general, are referred to either as "servants of God" or as "servants of the Lord."

In a number of languages it is not possible to use a literal term "slave," since this often carries a very repugnant connotation, and hence a more generic expression such as servant is employed. In some languages, however, a clear distinction is made between a person who works for fixed wages and one who is a kind of "personal retainer," that is to say, a personal servant who is supported by his master but who has no fixed salary basis. It is this latter term which is to be preferred if a distinction must be made. In some instances one can only employ a generic expression such as "works for"—for example, "I, Paul, work for Jesus Christ." In still other instances the more personal relationship is expressed by "I am Jesus Christ's man." This would imply a habitual servant of someone.

Some translators attempt to represent carefully the different orders in the names "Jesus Christ" and "Christ Jesus." However, in a number of languages this cannot be done, and one order must be selected to the exclusion of the other. Where alternation is possible, the order in Greek can be followed; but where differences of order may be clumsy or misleading, one order must be employed throughout.

Paul further characterizes himself as an apostle, a term which is used in its more specialized sense to refer to the twelve, who were with our Lord during his earthly ministry (Luke 6.13), though it may also be used in a broader sense to include others (Acts 14.4, 14; Romans 16.7; 1 Corinthians 12.28; Ephesians 4.11). Although Paul is not one of the twelve, he considers his apostleship as equal with theirs (see 1 Corinthians 9.1-2), in the same way that he understands his gospel to be as authoritative as the message which they preach (see Galatians 1.11-12).

By the time one undertakes to translate the Letter to the Romans, no doubt a decision has been made about the appropriate equivalent for "apostle." However, in the case of languages which are only for the first time receiving a text of the Scriptures, it is very important to check constantly upon the appropriateness of such key terms as "apostle," "disciple," "prophet," etc. Although some persons have preferred to translate "apostle" in a more or less literal form as "one who is sent," it may be far more satisfactory to use some such term as "special messenger." Too often a phrase such as "one who is sent" simply implies "one who is sent away." The significance of the term "apostle" is that the individual has been sent with a particular commission to announce an important message.

The TEV takes chosen and called as qualifiers of apostle, while a number of translations understand "chosen" (literally "set apart") as a third qualification of Paul himself, distinct from servant and apostle. See, for example, the NEB "servant of Christ Jesus, apostle by God's call, set apart for the service of the Gospel." In Greek "called" comes before "apostle" (literally "a called apostle"), while "chosen" comes immediately after "apostle," so that either of these alternatives is possible as far as translation is concerned. The TEV understands "chosen" (a perfect participle in Greek) as action prior to "called," and for this reason the sequence of two qualifiers has been changed. From the context it is clear that the choosing and the calling have come from God, and the TEV makes this explicit (see also NEB).

In languages which employ primarily active expressions, one may restructure the phrase chosen and called by God as "God chose and called me." In some languages there are serious problems involved in the proper selection of a term for "called," for the meaning must not be "to yell at" or "to call to." A closer equivalent in some languages is "to commission" or even "to assign a task to."

To preach his Good News is literally "for the Good News of God." However, since God has been explicitly mentioned in the previous phrase, it is possible to refer back to him as "his" in this phrase. The phrase "for the Good News" in the present context evidently means "for the sake of preaching the Good News," though in other contexts this phrase (literally "Good News of God") may refer to the content of the proclamation. Paul uses the word Good News (Greek euangelion) some sixty times and the phrase Good News of God in 15.16; 2 Corinthians 11.7; 1 Thessalonians 2.2, 8, 9. Originally the Greek word referred to a reward for bringing good news, but in the New Testament the meaning is always good news itself and refers to the salvation that God has made possible through Jesus Christ. This salvation may be described as Good News, inasmuch as it produces joy or happiness in those who receive it. In verse 16 the TEV translates this same word by the technical Christian term gospel. For Paul the Good News is the message about Jesus Christ, especially the message about his death and resurrection.

Insofar as possible, it is useful to avoid a technical term for preach which suggests merely formal sermonizing. A more appropriate equivalent would be "announce" or "proclaim."

The phrase his Good News must be restructured in a number of languages since one cannot "possess" Good News. In this context it is the Good News which comes from God, since he is the source of it. In verses 2-3 it is clear that the Good News is about Jesus Christ, but comes from God. At the same time, it is impossible in some languages to speak of "Good News coming from God." Only animate beings may "come," but Good News may "originate with" or "be caused by."

1.2 The Good News was promised long ago by God through his prophets, and written in the Holy Scriptures.

In Greek the reference to the Good News is made by a pronoun (literally "which"), but it is necessary to transform this into a noun in the English discourse structure, inasmuch as this verse is made into a separate sentence rather than a dependent clause.

In the Greek text was promised appears with an indirect, or secondary, agent (through his prophets), and without the direct, or primary, agent specified (by God). Since it is obvious that God is the one who made this promise through the prophets, the TEV makes this explicit (see NEB "this gospel God announced beforehand"). For languages in which the active form is obligatory or much preferred, it is possible to restructure the first clause of verse 2 as "God promised the Good News long ago by means of his prophets." A far more complex problem, however, exists in reproducing an expression for indirect or secondary agent. In some languages one simply cannot say that "someone did something through (or by means of) someone else." The only way in which an indirect or secondary agent can be expressed is by a causative—for example, "God caused the prophets to promise long ago." If a causative expression is employed, "prophets" must also be made the subject of "writing"—for example, "and they wrote in the Holy Scriptures." There may, moreover, be certain serious difficulties involved in an expression such as written in the Holy Scriptures, since the writing actually was a part of the Holy Scriptures and not merely some marginal notes written in a book called the Holy Scriptures. In some languages, therefore, one must be quite explicit—for example, "written as a part of the Holy Scriptures" or "the prophets wrote this promise which became part of the Holy Scriptures."

Both in the Old Testament and in the New Testament prophets are primarily persons who speak on the behalf of God (Moses, David, and Solomon, along with others, are called prophets), and not merely persons who foretell the future. In the present context the emphasis is on the fact that what God promised through the prophets has come true. The Holy Scriptures is a reference to the Old Testament (see 2 Timothy 3.15 where this same phrase occurs). More often the Old Testament is referred to simply as "the Scriptures" (Matthew 21.42; 22.29; 26.54; John 5.39; etc.).

It is relatively easy to find a term for "holy" as applied to persons, since one may often use a phrase such as "dedicated to God." However, a satisfactory expression for "holy" in reference to the Scriptures may be far more difficult. One cannot employ an expression such as "spotless" or "clean" (which has been done in some languages), for this would apply merely to the condition of a page or book. In some languages a term for positive taboo is sufficiently generic so that it can be applied to the Scriptures; but in some instances the only satisfactory equivalent for "holy" in this kind of context seems to be a phrase relating the Scriptures to God—for example, "the Scriptures from God." At the same time, one must carefully avoid any expression which would make the Bible similar to the Koran, which, according to Islamic tradition, "descended from heaven."

1.3a It is about his Son, our Lord Jesus Christ:

In the statement it is about his Son, it refers back to the Good News, not to the Holy Scriptures as a whole (see JB "this news is about the Son of God").

In a number of languages is about must be rendered as "tells about," "speaks about," or even "describes."

The phrase our Lord Jesus Christ is introduced from verse 4 in order to show its connection with his Son and with the description that follows. Although neither the JB nor the NEB shifts this phrase from the following verse, they each make the relation explicit by the statement "it is about Jesus Christ our Lord."

Special care must be exercised in the use of so-called possessive relations with words such as Lord and God. In some languages, for example, one cannot say our Lord. One cannot, as it were, possess someone who rules over him. The closest equivalent in such languages may be "the one who lords (over) us" or "the one who rules us." Similarly, "our God" must be rendered in some languages as "the God whom we worship."

1.3b-4 as to his humanity, he was born a descendant of David; (4) as to his divine holiness, he was shown with great power to be the Son of God by being raised from death.

It is helpful to take the last half of verse 3 and all of verse 4 together, since the exegetical and translational problems are closely interrelated. As to his humanity (literally "according to the flesh") is taken by most commentators and translators in the same sense as by the TEV (NEB "on the human level"; JB "according to the human nature"). As a man Jesus was born (literally "became"; Galatians 4.4 uses this verb in the same way, literally "he became of a woman"). Our Lord is further qualified as a descendant of David (literally "from the seed of David"; NEB "he was born of David's stock"; JB "was a descendant of David"; Goodspeed combines this and the previous statement "who was physically descended from David").

The phrase as to his humanity is variously rendered in different receptor languages. The two principal equivalent expressions are "as a man" or "as far as his body was concerned." In some instances this is combined directly with the following phrase: "he had the same kind of body as the offspring of David." References to the lineage of David may be expressed as "he was a grandson of David" (in languages in which the term "grandson" is a generic term for any male descendant). On the other hand, David may be made the subject of such a phrase—for example, "David was his grandfather" or "David was his ancestor." Again, one may simply specify lineage: "he belonged to David's family." It is frequently, however, very difficult to translate literally he was born a descendant; such a passive phrase could be quite misleading.

As to his divine holiness (literally "according to [the] spirit of holiness") may be understood in either of two ways. (1) It may be understood along with the TEV as a reference to our Lord's own (divine) nature; that is, his "holiness" was the quality that most closely identified him with God (Goodspeed "in his holiness of spirit"; Knox "in respect of the sanctified spirit that was his"; JB "the spirit of holiness that was in him"). Or (2) it may be understood as a reference to the Holy Spirit (NEB "on the level of the spirit—the Holy Spirit"; RSV "according to the Spirit of holiness"; see also Moffatt). Some few interpreters take the phrase "spirit of holiness" as a reference to the Lord's own spirit which enabled him to "set apart" people for God. That is, the phrase is taken by them as a reference to the saving power or function of the Son of God, and not as a reference to his nature; however, no translation seems to go in that direction.

In support of the exegesis represented in the TEV there are at least two observations. (1) This phrase stands in formal contrast with as to his humanity, which definitely refers to one aspect of Jesus' person. (2) Paul nowhere else uses this phrase to refer to the Holy Spirit, and though some scholars maintain that Paul took it over as a set formula from Palestinian Christians, there is no clear evidence in the New Testament or in other early Christian literature that it was used of the Holy Spirit.

Though the phrase as to his divine holiness seems to be a particularly appropriate expression in English, it is extremely difficult to render such an expression in some other languages. An abstract such as "holiness" would rarely, if ever, have as an attributive an adjective such as "divine." Moreover, in many languages there is simply no attributive term such as "divine"; the closest equivalent would be "from God." Therefore, in some languages the closest equivalent of as to his divine holiness would be "as far as his being from God and his being holy is concerned." Some translators have followed a type of compromise rendering: "as far as his spirit, which was holy, is concerned."

The verb shown literally means "to set limits (or boundaries)," and so "define," "decide," "determine." It is quite often used of God's will and decision (Luke 22.22; Acts 2.23; 10.42; 17.26,31; Hebrews 4.7). In English translations the verb appears in a variety of renderings: "declared," "designated," "appointed," "marked out," "demonstrated," "installed," "proclaimed," and "foreordained." This passive expression was shown may be transformed into an active expression—for example, "God showed with great power that he was his Son."

With great power (literally "in power") is usually taken either with the verb as in the TEV (see Goodspeed "decisively declared") or as a qualifier of the Son of God (Moffatt "Son of God with power"; JB "Son of God in all his power"). Some translations make it independent (NEB "by a mighty act"), while Phillips connects it with the Holy Spirit ("marked out . . . by the power of that Spirit of holiness").

The phrase by being raised from death presents at least three problems. (1) The phrase may be taken either in a temporal sense, "from the time of the resurrection," or, as in most translations, in a causal sense. (2) Though this phrase (literally "resurrection of dead ones") may be taken as a general resurrection of the dead, most exegetes take it to refer to Christ's resurrection (RSV "by his resurrection from the dead"). (3) It is possible to understand this phrase either in an active sense (NEB "he rose from the dead") or in a passive sense, with God understood as the one who raised him from the dead (Moffatt "he was raised from the dead"; see also Goodspeed and Phillips). In light of the fact that Paul elsewhere in Romans speaks of God raising Christ from the dead (see 4.24; 6.4, 9; 8.11), it seems best to understand the present passage in a passive sense with God as the agent. This passive expression may be rendered as active, particularly if the preceding clause is transformed into an active expression. One may thus render the last part of verse 4 as "by the fact that God raised him from death" or "by the fact that God caused him to live again." In some languages one cannot be "raised from death," but one can be "caused to live again."

The mention of the Good News in the last part of verse 1 led Paul to a further statement about the Good News in verse 2, and this in turn led to a Christological statement in verses 3 and 4. Paul now returns to the theme of his apostleship which he mentioned in verse 1.

1.5 Through him God gave me the privilege of being an apostle, for the sake of Christ, in order to lead people of all nations to believe and obey.

Through him God gave me is literally "through whom we received." The plural pronoun "we" may refer to Paul and other apostles (it cannot include the Roman readers), or it may refer only to Paul's commission (so NEB and Moffatt). The phrase "we received" is translated in the TEV as God gave me, to show that it was from God that Paul received his commission. For languages which employ two forms of "we," inclusive and exclusive, the "we" in this instance should obviously be exclusive. However, Paul's repeated emphasis upon his particular commission as an apostle to the Gentiles would seem to favor greatly the use of "I" rather than "we" in this passage.

The expression of secondary agency in the phrase through him causes certain difficulties in a number of languages in which the only equivalent is some causative expression—for example, "God caused Christ to give me the privilege" or "God gave me the privilege; Christ did it."

The privilege of being an apostle is literally "grace and apostleship." Some understand "grace" and "apostleship" to refer to two separate events, the former to God's grace in Jesus Christ and the latter to God's call of Paul to be an apostle. Others take the two as a reference to a single event, that is to God's call of Paul to be an apostle (Knox "the grace of apostleship"; NEB "the privilege of a commission"; Moffatt "the favor of my commission"). Paul looked upon his apostleship as a special gift of God's grace (1 Corinthians 3.10; 15.10; Galatians 2.9). A similar construction appears in Acts 1.25 (literally "service and apostleship"), in which the second noun is used to qualify the first. There the meaning is "service as an apostle."

The phrase the privilege of being an apostle is difficult to render in some languages. In some instances the concept must be expressed in a paratactic relationship—for example, "God caused me to be an apostle; this is a privilege." The concept of privilege may be incorporated into the principal clause as "God gave me the good work of being an apostle." In other instances privilege is best expressed as "a special task" or even "the important commission" of being an apostle.

For the sake of Christ (literally "in behalf of his name") appears at the end of the verse in Greek, but it must be related to the whole purpose of Paul's call as an apostle, and for this reason the TEV places it here (note also the NEB). For the sake of Christ is equivalent in some languages to "in order that I might serve Christ," "in order that I might help Christ," or "for the benefit of Christ."

People of all nations refers to peoples from all nations; some take the Greek word in the more restrictive sense of "Gentiles" (Moffatt), "pagan" (JB), or "heathen" (Goodspeed). Believe and obey translates "obedience of faith." This is not "obedience to the faith" (Moffatt), but obedience that is caused by faith (NEB "to faith and obedience"; Goodspeed "obedience and faith"). Although "obedience" and "faith" are nouns in Greek, they describe events rather than objects, and so are better rendered by verbs.

The last clause in verse 5, introduced by in order to lead, reflects only a preposition in Greek. However, the relationship between the "apostleship" and the "obedience of faith" involves obvious purpose. Furthermore, in most languages one must make explicit the role of Paul with respect to the people of all nations, and for this reason the TEV makes this relationship explicit by means of the somewhat expanded rendering in order to lead people of all nations to believe and obey.

1.6 This also includes you who are in Rome, whom God has called to belong to Jesus Christ.

This also includes you indicates that the persons in Rome are among those whom God has led to believe and obey. Who are in Rome is not in the Greek text as such, though it is implicit (see the following verse), and the TEV makes this information explicit in this verse. This also includes you may be rendered in some languages as "you are also among them" or "you who are in Rome are also part of these people."

Whom God has called to belong to Jesus Christ is literally "called ones of Jesus Christ." It is possible to take the Greek to mean that Jesus Christ is the one who has called them, though in the New Testament the verbal adjective "called" generally implies that God is the one who has done the calling. The TEV assumes that God is the one who has done the calling, and that those who are called now belong to Jesus Christ (see also RSV "who are called to belong to

Jesus Christ"; NEB "you who have heard the call and belong to Jesus Christ"; JB "by his call [you] belong to Jesus Christ").

1.7 And so I write to all of you in Rome whom God loves and has called to be his own people:

May God our Father and the Lord Jesus Christ give you grace and peace.

This is the conclusion of the Greek sentence which begins in verse 1, and it contains the second part of the introduction to the letter, that is, Paul's greetings to the people in Rome. The TEV indicates this by and so I write to all of you in Rome, and the NEB by "I send greetings to all of you in Rome." Either "write" or "greet" satisfies the meaning implicit in the Greek (literally "to all who are in Rome").

Whom God loves translates the Greek genitive phrase "beloved of God." The Greek word "beloved" is used throughout the New Testament to indicate strong endearment; it is used specifically when the Father addresses the Son (Matthew 3.17; 17.5 and parallels).

Whom God... has called to be his own people is literally "called (to be) saints." The word "saints" (from the stem "holy") is not a description of the moral character of the Christians but refers to the fact that they belong to God (see NEB "his dedicated people"). In the same way that the Israelites in the Old Testament were God's people, so those who belong to Jesus Christ are also God's people. Paul indicates a close bond between himself and the Roman Christians: in the same way that God has called him to preach the Good News, so God has called them to belong to Jesus Christ (v. 6) and to be his own people (v. 7). As in verse 1, here also the verb called presents a number of difficulties in some languages, since the closest equivalent may indicate merely the process of calling to an individual. In this context an equivalent may be similar to "summon."

Grace and peace is a frequent formula in early Christian greetings and is the standard salutation in all of Paul's letters (see also 1 Peter 1.2; 2 Peter 1.2; Revelation 1.4). It combines the Christian concept "grace" with the Jewish "peace." "Grace" expresses God's love and mercy which he shows toward people who do not deserve it, while "peace" sums up all the benefits of God's gracious act, both in terms of a reconciled fellowship and of a wholeness of life, resulting in a calm and confident dependence on God. In many languages it is better to render these nouns by verbs. In Greek this last portion of verse 7 is literally "grace and peace to you from God...." In most languages there is no "third person imperative." Even in English such a rendering is quite unnatural, and for that reason the TEV employs may God our Father and the Lord Jesus Christ give you grace and peace. However, in a number of languages some introductory phrase must be employed with such a clause—for example, "I am asking God that..." or "I am wishing that...."

An adequate term for grace, particularly in this type of context, is not easy to find in some languages. The reference here is to God's gracious dealings with man, and therefore it is better rendered in some languages by a verbal expression—for example, "may God our Father and the Lord Jesus Christ show you mercy." In certain languages, however, a more idiomatic expression may be employed—for example, "so that you may experience the good heart of God our Father and the Lord Jesus Christ." Similarly, peace implies the experience of peace and hence likewise is frequently translated as a verb—for example, "cause you to know peace," or, idiomatically, "cause you to sit down in your hearts" or "cause your livers to be sweet."

Prayer of Thanksgiving

8First, I thank my God, through Jesus Christ, for all of you; because the
whole world is hearing of your faith. 9God can prove that what I say is true
—the God whom I serve with all my heart by preaching the Good News about
his Son. God knows that I always remember you 10every time I pray. I ask that
God, in his good will, may at last make it possible for me to visit you now.
11For I want very much to see you in order to share a spiritual blessing with
you, to make you strong. 12What I mean is that both you and I will be helped
at the same time, you by my faith and I by your faith.

The title Prayer of Thanksgiving is too highly generic for use as a title in some languages. A more appropriate equivalent may be "Paul Thanks God" or "Paul Prays to God, Thanking Him."

Paul continues to follow the letter form of the first century A.D. as he gives thanks for the Christians in Rome, prays to God on their behalf, and tells of his own personal plans. In this and the following paragraph (vv. 13-15) Paul attempts to establish a personal relationship with the Christians at Rome before going into a discussion of the theme of his letter (v. 16-17).

1.8 First, I thank my God, through Jesus Christ, for all of you; because the whole world is hearing of your faith.

First is never followed by "secondly," and so it must be taken in the sense of "first of all" (Moffatt; see NEB "let me begin" and Phillips "I must begin"). In some languages the equivalent of first may be "before I say anything else I want to say" or "I want to begin by saying."

The phrase through Jesus Christ is particularly difficult to render in some languages, since it represents some type of secondary agent but without specification as to the precise relationship implied. In some languages the appropriate equivalent would be "I am thankful to God; it is Jesus Christ who makes this possible."

As Paul writes he considers himself to be in the act of prayer, giving thanks to God for their faith (I thank is in the present tense in the Greek). Expressions of thanks may be highly idiomatic—for example, "I say to God I am happy in my heart" or even "I tell God how good he is."

Because the whole world is hearing of your faith forms the basis for Paul's prayer of thanksgiving. In Greek this is actually a passive expression (literally "your faith is being proclaimed in all the world"), which many translations transform into an active expression, as does the TEV (see Goodspeed "the news of your faith is spreading all over the world"; Twentieth Century "the report of your faith is spreading throughout the world"). Faith in the present context means "faith in Jesus Christ," and Paul seems to be stressing more the quality of their faith than the fact of their faith.

In many languages one cannot speak of the whole world is hearing, since the physical world cannot hear, only "people throughout the world are hearing." Moreover, in some languages one cannot say hearing of your faith. One can, however, "hear that you believe." For some languages some direct goal of believing is necessary and therefore one may say "hear that you believe in Jesus Christ" or "hear that you trust Jesus Christ."

1.9 God can prove that what I say is true—the God whom I serve with all my heart by preaching the Good News about his Son. God knows that I always remember you

God can prove that what I say is true . . . God knows that (see NEB "God is my witness . . . God knows how") translates "God is my witness . . . that." Both the TEV and the NEB repeat God knows in order to bring the object of the verb closer to the verb itself (in the Greek sentence order a long clause intervenes). Paul appeals to God, as to a witness in court, since God is the one who can testify or prove that Paul always thinks of the Romans when he prays.

The equivalent of prove in some languages is "show clearly" or "convince you."

The verb translated serve is always used in the New Testament of service rendered to God, and in some passages it may mean "worship" (see Luke 2.37; Acts 7.42; Philippians 3.3; Hebrews 9.9; 10.2).

With all my heart (literally "in my spirit") is translated in a variety of fashions: see JB "I worship spiritually" and NEB "I offer the humble service of my spirit." In the present context "spirit" refers to Paul's inner being (one might say to his total being), and for this reason the TEV translates with all my heart. In some languages the equivalent of with all my heart is "completely," "without in any way holding back," or "with all of my self."

By preaching the Good News about his Son is literally "in the Good News of his Son," but here Good News refers not to the content of the Good News but to its proclamation (see NEB "by preaching the gospel of his Son" and JB "by preaching the Good News of his Son").

I always remember you means that Paul always prays to God in behalf of the Romans. In this type of context remember must not be translated in such a way as to suggest that Paul had forgotten about the Romans. A more appropriate equivalent in some languages is "I always keep thinking about you" or "you are always in my mind."

1.10 every time I pray. I ask that God, in his good will, may at last make it possible for me to visit you now.

In Greek this and the preceding verse are one sentence and offer a variety of punctuation possibilities. However, none of the punctuation alternatives makes serious differences for translation.

Every time I pray translates a noun phrase in Greek (see RSV "always in my prayers").

God, in his good will, may at last make it possible may more literally be rendered "by God's will I may now at last succeed" (RSV). In his good will means "if it is God's will." In some languages it may be necessary to restructure the semantic content of a phrase such as in his good will—for example, "I ask that God will approve that I visit you now" or "I ask that God will think it is right that I visit you now." A form of condition may be introduced in a somewhat more paraphrastic manner: "I pray that God will make it possible for me to visit you if he wants me to."

To visit you (so NEB, JB) is literally "to come to you," but on the basis of 15.22-29 it is obvious that Paul plans to stop in Rome on his way to Spain; he does not plan to stay permanently in Rome. If in the choice of a word for visit it is necessary to imply some length of time, then probably a term which suggests several weeks to a few months would be most appropriate.

1.11 For I want very much to see you in order to share a spiritual blessing with you, to make you strong.

A spiritual blessing (literally "spiritual gift") may refer either to a gift, favor, or blessing from the Spirit of God, or to that which is related to one's (human) spirit. Most commentators tend to accept the former of these two interpretations. Paul further discusses this matter of spiritual gifts in 12.6-8.

The equivalent to an expression in order to share a spiritual blessing with you may be "in order that I may cause you to have a blessing from God's Spirit" or "in order that I may share with you the goodness that God gives by means of his Spirit."

To make you strong refers to spiritual, not physical strength. To indicate spiritual rather than physical strength, one may say "to make you strong in your hearts," "to make your spirits strong," or "to cause your real selves to be firm."

1.12 What I mean is that both you and I will be helped at the same time, you by my faith and I by your faith.

The Greek of this verse is difficult to translate, though the meaning is clear. Paul wants to avoid the implication that he looks upon his visit solely as a means of benefiting his readers: both you and I will be helped. The verb rendered helped is found only here in the New Testament, though a related verb is often used by Paul with the meaning "to encourage."

Because of the rather succinct nature of verse 12, it may be necessary to employ a somewhat expanded form—for example, "what I mean is that I will help to strengthen you and you will help to strengthen me." Similarly, the last clause may be rendered as "you will become strong because you know how I believe, and I will become strong because I know how you believe." In both instances it may be necessary to introduce some direct goal of my faith and your faith—for example, "how I trust Christ" and "how you trust Christ."

> [13]You must remember this, my brothers: many times I have planned to visit you, but something has always kept me from doing so. I want to win converts among you, too, as I have among other Gentiles. [14]For I have an obligation to all peoples, to the civilized and to the savage, to the educated and to the ignorant. [15]So then, I am eager to preach the Good News to you also who live in Rome.

1.13 You must remember this, my brothers: many times I have planned to visit you, but something has always kept me from doing so. I want to win converts among you, too, as I have among other Gentiles.

You must remember this is in Greek a double negative ("I don't want you to be ignorant"), which many translations render as a positive statement (see NEB "but I should like you to know" and Goodspeed "I want you to understand"). A typical equivalent of you must remember this may be "I want you to know this" or "be assured that." It is important to avoid a term which might suggest that the people had forgotten something.

The phrase my brothers may be rendered in two quite different ways: (1) by some generic kinship term such as "my relatives" or "my family" (if such a term may be employed for an extended in-group much larger than a family or clan), or (2) by some designation which specifies mutual faith—for example, "you who also trust Jesus Christ" or "you who are fellow believers" or "those who believe together with me." The use of "brothers" in this type of context is a clear reference to the Christian community, and one should employ as a translation the corresponding expression which has been generally adopted by the church in the receptor language in question.

Something has always kept me from doing so is in Greek a passive construction, meaning something like "I was always kept from doing so." The Greek is not clear as to whom or what has kept Paul from visiting the Romans, though it is possible that this is a Semitic idiom with God as the unexpressed subject. The most natural equivalent of this passive expression without specific indication of means of agent may simply be "I have not been able to...."

I want to win converts among you is literally "in order that I might have some fruit among you." The word "fruit" is often used figuratively of spiritual results (see John 15.1-8; Romans 6.21-22; Galatians 5.22; Philippians 1.11; 4.17), and the TEV takes it in the specific sense of "winning people to the Christian way." Other translations take it in a more general sense (see JB "that I might work as fruitfully among you"; Moffatt "to have some results among you"; and NEB "in the hope of achieving something among you").

In most languages it is impossible to render the final clause of verse 13 in a literal manner since "fruit" is rarely used in the sense of "result." It is therefore better to employ some such expression as the TEV, but one should be cautioned against translating win converts literally. A more natural equivalent in many languages is "cause people to believe" or "cause people to follow Jesus Christ."

Among other Gentiles is more literally "among the other nations" (see Segond) and is translated by the JB as "among the other pagans" and by the NEB as "in other parts of the world." The reference would seem to be to other Gentile (non-Jewish) peoples than those in Rome (see RSV "among the rest of the Gentiles").

1.14 For I have an obligation to all peoples, to the civilized and to the savage, to the educated and to the ignorant.

I have an obligation is literally "I am a debtor." It is difficult in some languages to speak of an obligation. In fact, the concept of "debt" is a far simpler expression to employ in this type of context. On the other hand, without special contextual conditioning the use of a term for "debt" might be taken literally—for example, "I am in debt to all people," a concept which should be avoided. In order to shift this metaphor to a simile, one may employ some such expression as "I seem to have a debt to all peoples" or "it is like I am in debt to all peoples." In some languages the figure of speech is somewhat shifted—for example, "I am a servant to help all peoples."

In the following categories, civilized... savage and educated... ignorant, Paul is clearly referring to all peoples, and the TEV makes this information explicit. In the first two expressions, civilized... savage (literally "Greeks... barbarians"), the distinction is not racial or national, but cultural. Paul is writing to Romans, who were "Greek" in terms of culture, and the Greeks called all other peoples "barbarians." The two terms, then, classify people who are considered either within or outside of the realm of civilized society. The next two terms, educated... ignorant, do not refer to innate intellectual capacities, but rather to degrees of learning.

It is not easy to find series of words which will properly contrast extremes of culture and education. In some instances one can only employ positive and negative features: "civilized and uncivilized," "educated and uneducated." In a number of languages there are no such general terms for cultural and educational advantages. However, there are almost always ways of talking about civilized versus uncivilized peoples, for there are no societies who do not look down on other societies as being less civilized than themselves. In some instances civilized people are spoken of as "those who live in villages," in contrast with "those who live in the forest." Educated people may be "those who can read," in contrast with "those who cannot read." In other situations, the civilized are "those who have chiefs," in contrast with people who are not led by chiefs, and the educated people are "those who know books," in contrast with those who do not. The translator must determine what in the local receptor language are those distinctive factors which designate contrasts of culture and education. It is interesting that in some instances the concept of civilization is very closely tied to religious beliefs—for example, the civilized may be "those who know the rules of God," while the uncivilized are "those who do not know God's rules."

1.15 So then, I am eager to preach the Good News to you also who live in Rome.

Eager must be understood in the sense of "readiness" or "desire."

The Power of the Gospel

[16]I have complete confidence in the gospel; it is God's power to save all who believe, first the Jews and also the Gentiles. [17]For the gospel reveals how God puts men right with himself: it is through faith, from beginning to end. As the scripture says, "He who is put right with God through faith shall live."

The title The Power of the Gospel may be recast as "The Good News Has Power" or "The Good News Is Powerful." In some instances the closest equivalent may be "The Good News Can Do Strong Things."

1.16 I have complete confidence in the gospel; it is God's power to save all who believe, first the Jews and also the Gentiles.

The first half of this verse serves as a transition from Paul's personal introduction to the Romans to his definition of the gospel in 16b and 17. I have complete confidence in is literally "I am not ashamed of." (The shame referred to is that which comes when one is disappointed by something he has trusted in.) Most translations render this literally, but Moffatt also transforms Paul's negative statement into a positive one: "I am proud of the Gospel." I have complete confidence in may be rendered as "I trust completely in" or, idiomatically, as "I rest my whole weight on" or "I lean against completely."

Paul equates the gospel (see vv. 1-2) with God's power to save all who believe (in Jesus Christ). Historically this message was proclaimed first to the Jews, but also to the Gentiles (literally "Greeks"). In this context "Greeks" does not refer to those who were Greek by nationality or culture, but to all persons other than Jews, and for this reason the TEV renders the term Gentiles. (See comments on v. 14.) In many languages the most appropriate term for Gentiles is "those who are not Jews; hence, the last phrase of verse 16 may be rendered as "first the Jews and then those who are not Jews."

In some languages it is impossible to speak of something being God's power. However, an object can be the means by which God can do certain things; therefore the second clause of verse 16 may be restructured as "by means of the gospel God can save all who believe" or "the good news is God's tool by which he can save all who believe."

In Greek to save is actually a noun phrase ("for salvation"), but an event is here spoken of and so a verb expression is accurate and more natural as an English equivalent (JB "it is the power of God saving all who believe"). Although the word "salvation" covers a wide area of meaning (in the early books of the

Old Testament it often denoted deliverance from physical danger), in this verse it refers to Christian salvation, the deliverance from the power of sin.

1.17 For the gospel reveals how God puts men right with himself: it is through faith, from beginning to end. As the scripture says, "He who is put right with God through faith shall live."

For the gospel reveals is in the Greek a passive construction, literally "for in it is revealed." For the gospel reveals may be rendered as "for the Good News shows" or "the Good News explains."

How God puts men right with himself represents the Greek phrase "the righteousness of God." In this context, however, "the righteousness of God" does not refer to God's own righteous character, but to his saving activity whereby he puts men in the right (as a judge declares a man innocent), or whereby he puts men in a right relationship to himself. Both Goodspeed ("God's way of uprightness") and the NEB ("God's way of right and wrong") indicate that this is a description of God's activity rather than of his character, but both of these translations do so with a rendering that sounds too impersonal. The JB renders this phrase by "the justice of God," but explains in a note: "the saving justice (cf. Isaiah 56.1) of God, 3.26, who fulfills his promise to save by giving salvation as a free gift." See further the comments on the verb (generally rendered "justify") in 3.24 below.

Traditionally, this reference to "the righteousness of God" has been explained as "forensic righteousness," that is to say, "God declaring men right." Accordingly, some translations employ "the gospel reveals how God declares men straight" or "how men have a straight heart." However, the theological focus at this point seems not to be so much on God's declaration of man's imputed innocence as on the fact that he puts men in a new relationship to himself. It is man's confidence in God which puts him in a new covenant relationship with God and thus establishes his "righteousness." The phrase in the TEV, puts men right with, seems to be particularly appropriate since it emphasizes this aspect of relation. It is not always easy to find a similar type of expression in other languages, and especially one which carries over a form such as right which has such a close relationship to "righteous" and "righteousness." In some instances translators use phrases such as "how God arranges people with himself as they should be," "how God brings men back to himself in the right way as they should be," or "how God makes men straight with himself."

Through faith, from beginning to end represents a rather ambiguous phrase in Greek, literally "from faith to faith." This expression is taken by some to mean "originating in God's faithfulness and resulting in man's faith," but it is more likely that it means "faith from start to finish." The NEB renders this as "starts from faith and ends in faith." In order to render satisfactorily the expression through faith, from beginning to end it may be necessary to recast rather radically the sets of semantic components—for example, "all this happened because people believed," "this is just a matter of people's believing," or "all that God does depends upon people's trusting throughout."

As the scripture says (literally "as it is written") is a reference to one passage of scripture, and not to the Old Testament as a whole.

He who is put right with God through faith shall live represents a quotation from Habakkuk 2.4 (see also in Galatians 3.11; Hebrews 10.38) and does not agree precisely either with the Hebrew text ("the righteous shall live by his faithfulness"), or with the Septuagint ("the righteous shall live by my faithfulness"), either in form or in meaning. Although it is possible that the traditional translation expresses the meaning (see the alternative rendering in the TEV, "he who is put right with God shall live through faith"), it is more likely that Paul means: "he who is put right with God through faith shall live." He who is put right with God translates the Greek, "the righteous (one)." Again, the meaning depends on the whole context of the letter, and while some see this as a moral attribute in man ("the upright [man]" of Goodspeed and JB; "the righteous [man]" of most translations), it seems rather that Paul is speaking of the man "who is put into a right relationship with God by faith" (see NEB "he shall gain life who is justified through faith"). Since in many languages it is difficult to employ the passive expression he who is put right with God, one may be obliged to use an active form: "the man whom God has put right with himself."

Through faith indicates instrumentality, often expressed as causative if faith is rendered as a separate verb of believing—for example, "the one whom God has put right with himself because he trusts God."

In some languages an expression such as shall live may mean merely continued physical existence. For this reason it is necessary in some instances to specify the kind of living referred to here as being exceptional—for example, "shall really live" or "shall truly live." The emphasis in this passage is clearly upon the quality of life, not upon mere continued existence.

The Guilt of Mankind

[18]God's wrath is revealed coming down from heaven upon all the sin and evil of men whose evil ways prevent the truth from being known. [19]God punishes them, because what men can know about God is plain to them. God himself made it plain to them. [20]Ever since God created the world, his invisible qualities, both his eternal power and his divine nature, have been clearly seen. Men can perceive them in the things that God has made. So they have no excuse at all! [21]They know God, but they do not give him the honor that belongs to him, nor do they thank him. Instead, their thoughts have become complete nonsense and their empty minds are filled with darkness. [22]They say they are wise, but they are fools; [23]instead of worshiping the immortal God, they worship images made to look like mortal man or birds or animals or reptiles.

The section heading The Guilt of Mankind may require some restructuring —for example, "All People Are Guilty," "All People Have Guilt Before God," "In God's Eyes No One Is Innocent."

The entire section (1.18—3.20) states the negative counterpart to 1.17, and at the same time lays the basis for what is said about God's righteousness in 1.17 and in 3.21-31. Paul indicates that both Gentiles (1.18-32) and Jews (2.1—3.20) are guilty and stand under the judgment of God's wrath. Consequently all need to be put into a right relationship with God, and this may be achieved only through faith.

1.18 God's wrath is revealed coming down from heaven upon all the sin and evil of men whose evil ways prevent the truth from being known.

God's wrath (2.5, 8; 3.5; 4.15; 5.9; 9.22; 12.19; 13.4, 5) does not refer simply to God's feelings (as might be suggested by Moffatt, Goodspeed, JB "God's anger"), but to his action in judging and punishing men for their sins (see NEB "divine retribution"). The close connection between God's activity of putting men right with himself and God's wrath is expressed through Paul by the use of the same verb in describing both of them: is revealed.

It is not easy to find an appropriate term for God's wrath. The literal translation of wrath may suggest far too much—"God's rage" or "God's anger." There is certainly a semantic component of anger in the biblical expression of wrath, but it is important to try to find some term which will avoid wrong connotations and at the same time focus upon God's act of judging. Some translations actually employ "God's judgment because of his anger" in an effort to represent both semantic components of wrath. In many languages one cannot speak of "wrath... coming down" since neither an emotion nor an event of judging can come down from heaven upon all the sin and evil of men. Hence a rather considerable restructuring of the semantic components of this first clause is usually necessary. An appropriate equivalent in some languages is "God has revealed how, in his anger, he will judge all the sin and evil of men." On the other hand, in some languages one cannot speak of judging sin and evil, because one can only judge people who are sinful and evil. Therefore one must say: "God has revealed how he will judge men for all the sin and evil which they have done."

Coming down from heaven (literally "from heaven") means that God himself sends his wrath down as judgment upon men's sins. Sin and evil, when taken together, are comprehensive terms. The first refers to wrong action against God, that is "impiety," "irreverence," or "godless action" (Romans 11.26; 2 Timothy 2.16; Titus 2.12; Jude 15, 18; see also the adjective in Romans 4.5; 5.6; 1 Timothy 1.9; 1 Peter 4.18; 2 Peter 2.5; 3.7; Jude 4, 15). The second describes wrong action against men, and so may be taken as "injustice," "wrongdoing," or "wickedness." The NEB combines these terms, and so translates "godless wickedness." When one can find in a receptor language terms which distinguish wrong in terms of actions toward God and those toward men, this is excellent. However, a far more general classification of evil is (1) the sin which is in men's hearts and (2) the sin which expresses itself in overt deeds. Since this distinction is not far removed from the distinction between sin and evil of the Greek text, it may be possible to translate sin and evil as "all the sin in their hearts and all the evil they have done."

Evil ways translates the same word rendered "evil" above. Truth refers to the truth about God, and the contrast is clear: God's wrath is revealed on those who keep the truth about him from being revealed. In many languages one cannot speak of "evil ways" doing something. Moreover, the passive expression being known must often be rendered as active. Therefore, this final clause of verse 18 may be recast as "who by the evil which they do prevent people from knowing the truth about God."

1.19 God punishes them, because what men can know about God is plain to them. God himself made it plain to them.

God punishes them is supplied from God's wrath in verse 18, to make clear the action implied by because. Men are punished because they sin even while knowing the truth about God. Is plain to them translates an aorist tense in Greek; Paul probably has in mind God's actions in creating the universe, which he looks upon as being one event. Is plain to them may be rendered as "can be clearly seen," "can be fully understood," or even "there is no uncertainty about what men can know about God."

What men can know about God is literally "what can be known about God," and the context of this knowledge is indicated in the following verse: his eternal power and his divine nature.

1.20 Ever since God created the world, his invisible qualities, both his eternal power and his divine nature, have been clearly seen. Men can perceive them in the things that God has made. So they have no excuse at all!

Ever since God created the world translates the Greek noun phrase "from the creation of the world." Paul qualifies what he means by the invisible qualities of God, that is his eternal power and his divine nature. Although these qualities are invisible, men can perceive them in the things that God has made. The noun rendered divine nature occurs only here in the New Testament; the corresponding adjective occurs in Acts 17.29; 2 Peter 1.3,4. The verb rendered perceive implies knowledge, understanding, and mental awareness. Since the Gentiles can perceive what God is like through the world that he has made, they have no excuse at all; and the Jews, who pass judgment on others, are in the same condition (see 2.1).

It is not easy to combine such expressions as his invisible qualities and have been clearly seen. How can what is not visible be clearly seen? In some languages, therefore, it is necessary to speak of "can be clearly known" or "can be fully understood." In a number of instances the specific qualities must actually precede the general statement about their being invisible. Hence the order of components in verse 20 may be changed as follows: "Ever since God created the world, people can clearly understand that his power never ceases and that he is truly God. These characteristics cannot be seen, but they can be known." The second sentence of verse 20 may then be translated: "People can know this about God because of the things which God has made." And the last sentence may be rendered: "As a result, they cannot have any excuse for what they have done" or "...there is no way in which they can defend what they have done."

1.21 They know God, but they do not give him the honor that belongs to him, nor do they thank him. Instead, their thoughts have become complete nonsense and their empty minds are filled with darkness.

Throughout the remainder of this chapter, most of the verbs are in the aorist tense, but the aorist does not necessarily indicate past time, and a past tense in English may imply that the action described has ceased. The force of the Greek aorist in this context is to indicate that these actions are typical of what men have done at all times throughout history; for the English reader the present tense is more natural in expressing such events. This is why throughout this passage the TEV uses the present tense, rather than the past tense, as most translations do.

They know God in Greek is actually a participle indicating concession, that is, "even though they know God" (see RSV). However, a number of translations do as the TEV does, and renders this by a finite verb (see JB "they knew God"). The knowledge referred to here is the recognition of God's existence, not the knowledge of a personal relationship with God. It is important in the selection of a term for know to indicate that this is knowledge about and not intimate relationship with. In some instances, therefore, one must employ a translation such as "they know about God" or "they are acquainted with who God is."

They do not give him the honor that belongs to him is rendered in the NEB by a more literal translation: "they have refused to honor him as God." In order to express the meaning of this clause appropriately, it may be necessary to say: "they refused to honor God as the one whom they really know he is" or "they refused to honor God; they did not say to him, You truly are God."

The clause nor do they thank him must be rendered in some languages as "and they do not say thank you to God" or "their hearts are not thankful for what God has done."

The verb rendered become complete nonsense occurs only here in the New Testament; the corresponding adjective occurs in a similar passage in 1 Corinthians 3.20 ("the thoughts of the wise are worthless") and elsewhere. Most translations render this phrase something like "they became futile in their thinking" (RSV). In languages in which thoughts is much more normally expressed as a verb, it may be necessary to restructure this clause as "when they think, they think nothing," "when they think, it has no value at all," or "they think complete foolishness."

Their empty minds is literally "their senseless heart." In such a context in English it is much more natural to use a plural rather than a singular, and for this reason the TEV uses the plural minds. Also, as is so often the case in the Bible, "heart" refers to the intellectual rather than the emotional capacity of the individual. The adjective rendered here empty means "stupid" or "without understanding" (see Matthew 15.16; Mark 7.18; Romans 1.31; 10.19). It is not easy to find an appropriate equivalent expression for this last clause of verse 21. In some languages the closest equivalent may be "their minds are empty, and their thoughts are dark," "since their minds are empty, they think only dark thoughts," or even "darkness covers (or fills) their empty minds." The attributive "dark" as a qualifier of "thoughts" does not refer to ignorance but to failure to think right or correctly about moral issues. Therefore one can translate as "they do not think as they should," "they do not think right," or even "their thoughts are all wrong." Terms such as "not right" or "wrong" should imply moral inadequacy, not simply technical incorrectness.

1.22 They say they are wise, but they are fools;

This verse relates back to the discussion of God's wrath; already God has caused men to begin to reap the results of their sins. In Greek they say they are wise is also a clause of concession, as is they know God in the preceding verse. Stylistically this may be handled in English by making the concession clause in Greek into the main clause in English, and by making the main Greek clause into an adversative clause in English. In Greek the words rendered wise and fools are at extreme opposite ends of the standards of measurement for people. Paul is saying that because the people have rejected God, they are exactly the opposite of what they think themselves to be.

Verse 22 may be rendered in some languages as "they pretended they had big minds, and they came down to no minds" or "they said their heads were wise, but their heads were only gourds."

1.23 instead of worshiping the immortal God, they worship images made to look like mortal man or birds or animals or reptiles.

Instead of worshiping the immortal God, they worship is literally "they exchanged the glory of the immortal God for." This, of course, is idolatry. To "exchange God's glory" for something else (see Psalm 106.20) is to give up acknowledging, praising, honoring, worshiping the true God, whose existence and being are revealed in his "glory," and to substitute idols as the object of worship. In this verse Paul makes an obvious contrast between God who is immortal and man who is mortal. Instead of worshiping may be rendered in some languages as "they give up worshiping" or "they no longer worship." Immortal is rendered in most languages as "who never dies" or "who always exists."

Images (here equivalent to "idols") actually translates a phrase in Greek (literally "in the likeness of an image"), which most translations render exactly as the TEV does. Images may be rendered simply as "likenesses," but in a number of languages one may use the equivalent of "fetish carvings" or "idols." Made to look like may be rendered as "which men make in order that they will look like" or "which men make so that they will seem like."

Not all languages distinguish neatly between birds, quadrupeds, and reptiles. In some languages the more usual expression is "animals that fly, those that walk, and those that crawl." What is important here is not the precise designation but the all-inclusive nature of these distinctions.

> 24 Because men are such fools, God has given them over to do the filthy things
> their hearts desire, and they do shameful things with each other. 25 They
> exchange the truth about God for a lie; they worship and serve what God has
> created instead of the Creator himself, who is to be praised forever! Amen.

1.24 Because men are such fools, God has given them over to do the filthy things their hearts desire, and they do shameful things with each other.

Beginning in this verse Paul describes the moral depravity which results from the rejection of God and the consequent worship of idols. Because men are such fools renders a strong transitional particle in Greek, which appears in the NEB as "for this reason" and in the JB "that is why." God has given them over is repeated in verses 26 and 28; it describes God's judgment in abandoning men to their own sinful resources. The implication is that God has deserted them and let them go their own way. The filthy things their hearts desire is a reference to the moral and spiritual depravity of man. This depravity results in the misuse of their bodies: they do shameful things with each other (see also vv. 26-27).

1.25 They exchange the truth about God for a lie; they worship and serve what God has created instead of the Creator himself, who is to be praised forever! Amen.

They exchange the truth about God for a lie may involve certain complications because of the semantic difficulty of "exchanging truth for a lie." It may be necessary to recast this clause as "they refuse to believe the truth about God, and accordingly they believe a lie," "they give up believing the truth about God, and they accept what is a lie," or "...what is untrue."

Worship and serve may be rendered as "worship and obey" or "worship and do reverence to." Serve translates the most general Greek term for religious activity in honor of a deity.

The contrast between what God has created and the Creator himself may be made explicit in some languages as "they worship and serve what God has made; they do not worship and serve the very one who made everything."

To be praised translates a Greek passive verbal adjective; it is used in the New Testament always of God, and describes the praise of worship that man should render to God. This may be looked upon as the conclusion of Paul's argument; he has proved his point, and now he presents a series of illustrations, adding no new information until verse 32.

Who is to be praised forever must be made somewhat more explicit in some languages—for example, "whom people should praise forever" or "who deserves that people should praise him forever."

In a high percentage of languages the terminal particle amen has been borrowed and therefore can be introduced in this type of expression. However, it is liable to be almost meaningless, since it will probably have been borrowed merely as a traditional device for indicating the end of prayers. A more appropriate equivalent in some languages may have a meaning such as "this is surely so" or "indeed this is true."

> [26]Because men do this, God has given them over to shameful passions. Even the women pervert the natural use of their sex by unnatural acts. [27]In the same way the men give up natural sexual relations with women and burn with passion for each other. Men do shameful things with each other, and as a result they themselves are punished as they deserve for their wrongdoing.

1.26 Because men do this, God has given them over to shameful passions. Even the women pervert the natural use of their sex by unnatural acts.

Because men do this is literally "because of this," and it has been rendered by such expressions as "for this reason" (RSV), "in consequence" (NEB), and "this is why" (Goodspeed, JB). In this verse any reference to men must, of course, be to "persons." In the present verse passions is equivalent to "lusts." The sin to which Paul has reference is homosexuality among women; homosexuality among men is referred to in the following verse. In most languages there is a perfectly proper manner of referring to homosexual activity. The reference to shameful passions may simply be translated by some generic term for homosexual relations, or it may require a very general expression such as "they have bad sexual desires" or "they have the wrong kind of sexual desires." This can then be followed by the two statements, the one referring to women and the other to men. The second sentence in verse 26 may simply be translated as "women have sexual relations with women, which is not the way it should be." This final phrase is simply a way of indicating the unnatural character of such acts.

1.27 In the same way the men give up natural sexual relations with women and burn with passion for each other. Men do shameful things with each other, and as a result they themselves are punished as they deserve for their wrongdoing.

The first sentence of verse 27 may be rendered in some languages as "in a similar way men give up sleeping with women and want to sleep with other men" or "...want to have men as their wives." Men do shameful things with each other may be rendered as "men have sexual relations with one another, and this is shameful" or "...this is bad."

They themselves are punished as they deserve is literally "the payment which is necessary" (see NEB "the fitting wage"), but in the present context "payment" refers to God's punishment upon them. In a number of languages the passive are punished must be changed into an active expression—for example, "as a result God punishes them."

Wrongdoing is literally "deceit" or "error" (see RSV), but the reference is to sexual perversion (see NEB, JB). For their wrongdoing may be rendered as "because of the evil which they have done" or "because of the bad way in which they have acted."

1.28

> [28]Because men refuse to keep in mind the true knowledge about God, he has
> given them over to corrupted minds, so that they do the things that they should
> not. [29]They are filled with all kinds of wickedness, evil, greed, and vice; they
> are full of jealousy, murder, fighting, deceit, and malice. They gossip, [30]and
> speak evil of one another; they are hateful to God, insolent, proud, and
> boastful; they think of more ways to do evil; they disobey their parents; [31]they
> are immoral; they do not keep their promises, and they show no kindness or
> pity to others. [32]They know that God's law says that people who live in this
> way deserve death. Yet, not only do they continue to do these very things, but
> they also approve of others who do them.

Verses 28-31 are a single sentence in Greek, but in most languages it is necessary to break the long sentence into shorter units. In doing so one must make certain that the connections in thought are carefully preserved.

1.28 Because men refuse to keep in mind the true knowledge about God, he has given them over to corrupted minds, so that they do the things that they should not.

This verse is the climax of man's fall from God: they refuse to keep in mind the true knowledge about God. The verb translated refuse to keep in mind basically means to reject something that one has put to the test. There is evidently a play on words in Greek between the verb refuse to keep in mind and the adjective corrupted, but this is difficult to carry over in translation. In the present context corrupted refers to a mind that no longer functions as it should; this does not imply insanity, but rather the lack of ability to make moral and spiritual distinctions. Phillips renders this phrase as "degenerate minds" and the NEB as "depraved reason."

Refuse to keep in mind may be rendered as "say, We will not think about" or "declare, We will not remember." The true knowledge about God may be rendered as "what men may know is true about God."

Has given them over to is not easily rendered in some languages. In fact, it must frequently be broken into two parts—for example, "he has let them go so that they will only think in bad ways" or "he has let them leave him, and now they only think in corrupted ways."

The concept of corrupted minds must be rendered in some languages by an idiomatic expression—for example, "a mind that is hungry for dirty words," "a mind that is completely twisted," or "a mind which has only stinking thoughts."

1.29-31 They are filled with all kinds of wickedness, evil, greed, and vice; they are full of jealousy, murder, fighting, deceit, and malice. They gossip, (30) and speak evil of one another; they are hateful to God, insolent, proud, and boastful; they think of more ways to do evil; they disobey their parents; (31) they are immoral; they do not keep their promises, and they show no kindness or pity to others.

Similar lists of sins appear in the New Testament at 13.13; 1 Corinthians

5.10,11; 6.9,10; 2 Corinthians 12.20,21; Galatians 5.19-21; etc. The specific sins mentioned do not necessarily represent distinct and separate qualities in each case; in some instances it is obvious that Paul has heaped synonyms together. Nevertheless, the translator must attempt, insofar as possible, to cover all of these areas of sin and wickedness with more or less equivalent terms. For wickedness and evil it may be necessary to employ simply one generic expression equivalent to "badness."

In a number of languages most of the nouns which identify evil activities must be expressed as verbs, so that greed must be rendered as "they want what others have" and vice as "they engage in badness with one another" or "they cause badness to one another."

Similarly, jealousy and murder may be translated as "they are very jealous of one another" and "they kill one another." Fighting is a Greek word which means "strife" or "party spirit," resulting in sharp argument and dissension. Deceit may be equivalent to "they deceive one another." Malice is a word which occurs only here in the New Testament and is defined as "the tendency to put the worst construction on everything." Malice may be rendered in some languages as "they are always thinking the worst of others."

Gossip may be rendered as "they say bad things about one another." This is substantially equivalent to the first evil mentioned in verse 30, and the same translation may cover both expressions. In some languages one may have idiomatic expressions for gossip—for example, "they harvest lies" or "they throw lies into the wind," with the implication that the lies will be carried far and wide.

The word rendered hateful to God (so also NEB) appears only here in the New Testament, and may possibly be taken as active: "haters of God" (RSV) or "enemies of God" (JB). Insolent may be rendered as "they insult one another." Terms such as proud and boastful may be translated in such a way as to indicate the difference between personal attitudes and outward behavior—for example, "in their hearts they think they are great and they are always telling people that they are great" or "their hearts are proud and their words are big." In some languages pride is expressed in a somewhat idiomatic form: "they think they are chiefs" or "they are always giving themselves power."

They are immoral is simply a highly generic expression to describe evil, and the word which follows, translated they do not keep their promises, apparently is a play on words with the preceding term. Failure to keep their promises may be rendered as "they do not do what they say they will do" or "they promise but do not perform." This may be rendered idiomatically in some languages as "they gamble with their words" or "their words have several layers."

The negative expression they show no kindness or pity may be rendered positively in some languages as "they go on handling others roughly."

1.32 They know that God's law says that people who live in this way deserve death. Yet, not only do they continue to do these very things, but they also approve of others who do them.

In the phrase rendered God's law, the Greek word is not the ordinary word for law, but one that may be understood as "God's decree" (RSV, Goodspeed; cf. NEB "just decree of God") or as "God's verdict" (JB).

Deserve death may often be rendered simply as "ought to die." Some languages may express this idea in an idiomatic manner: "the promise of death sits on them."

The contrast indicated by not only...but...also may need to be altered so as to shift the focus more precisely to the second part—for example, "and also they do what is even worse" or "and in addition they do something which is even worse than all the other bad they have done."

Showing approval may be expressed in some languages as "they are happy with those who do these things," "they say to those who do these things, You are doing all right," or "they take into their own hearts those who do such things."

CHAPTER 2

God's Judgment

2 Do you, my friend, pass judgment on others? You have no excuse at all,
whoever you are. For when you judge others, but do the same things that
they do, you condemn yourself. [2]We know that God is right when he judges
the people who do such things as these. [3]But you, my friend, do these very
things yourself for which you pass judgment on others! Do you think you will
escape God's judgment? [4]Or perhaps you despise his great kindness, tolerance,
and patience. Surely you know that God is kind because he is trying to lead
you to repent. [5]But you have a hard and stubborn heart. So then, you are
making your own punishment even greater on the Day when God's wrath and
right judgments will be revealed. [6]For God will reward every person according
to what he has done. [7]Some men keep on doing good, and seek glory, honor,
and immortal life; to them God will give eternal life. [8]Other men are selfish
and reject what is right, to follow what is wrong; on them God will pour his
wrath and anger. [9]There will be suffering and pain for all men who do what
is evil, for the Jews first and also for the Gentiles. [10]But God will give glory,
honor, and peace to all who do what is good, to the Jews first, and also to the
Gentiles. [11]For God judges everyone by the same standard.

The section heading God's Judgment must be transformed into a verbal expression in some languages—for example, "God Judges All Men" or "God Will Judge All Persons."

Some have thought that 2.1-16 contains a veiled polemic against Judaism, but in fact this is a description of God's judgment on both the Jews and the Gentiles (see 2.9-10). Paul has argued that the pagan corruption of life reveals God's wrath; he now points out that all persons, Jews and Gentiles alike, whether or not they have committed those moral abuses (1.18-31), are guilty before God's judgment. Paul insists that the self-righteous man, whether Jew or Gentile, stands under the same judgment as do the pagans, although he does not take up the specific problem of the Jews until 2.17—3.20.

Verses 1-11 are rather neatly structured into three principal parts. (1) The first begins with a question in verse 1 (in Greek this is only a statement, but it is structurally parallel to the question at the end of verse 3) and has its final answer in verse 3. (2) The second part begins with a question at the end of verse 3, and the final answer comes in verse 6. (3) Verse 7 begins the contrast between those who do good and those who do evil. Note that first good people are discussed, and then evil people (v. 8), with a further description of the suffering of evil men (v. 9), followed then by a statement of God's rewarding the good (v. 10). This chiasmus (that is, nonparallel or crossed arrangement) is summarized in verse 11, which also serves as a summary for the entire paragraph.

2.1 Do you, my friend, pass judgment on others? You have no excuse at all, whoever you are. For when you judge others, but do the same things that they do, you condemn yourself.

This verse begins with the same particle that was used in 1.24. Originally it meant something like "therefore," but many commentators believe that here its use is no more than a transitional particle.

Do you, my friend, pass judgment on others? is in Greek a statement which the TEV renders as a question in order to stress the emphatic nature of what Paul is saying.

The initial sentence in Greek is divided into two sentences in the TEV. The first is a question, Do you, my friend, pass judgment on others?, and the second is a statement, You have no excuse at all, whoever you are. In some languages the use of such a rhetorical question may be misleading. Obviously Paul is not asking people whether they pass judgment; he is simply stating that anyone and everyone who passes judgment has no excuse. A common and generally acceptable way of dealing with this type of structure is to employ a conditional clause—for example, "If you pass judgment on others you have no excuse at all, regardless of who you are."

My friend (literally "O man") does not appear as such in many modern translations. However, Romans not only reflects the letter form of the first century A.D., but in this chapter it has the form of a diatribe, a type of discourse used by preachers and philosophers of that century. The TEV seeks to maintain the continuity with this diatribe form; many modern translators feel that this form of address is redundant for the English reader, and so omit it.

In a number of languages, it is quite impossible to use an expression such as my friend. That would seem to be entirely too personal and imply that Paul was addressing his letter or remark to only one person. A plural form is sometimes acceptable, "my friends," but more often than not it is necessary to use an expression such as "you who judge."

You have no excuse at all is emphatic in the Greek sentence order. Have no excuse may be rendered as "have no word to oppose," "cannot save yourself from accusation," or even, in the form of direct discourse, "cannot say, I am not guilty."

In Greek pass judgment and judge are the same words; condemn comes from the same root as these two words, only it is a strengthened form. Whoever judges others condemns himself. In a number of languages there are two quite distinct words for judging. One implies purely objective evaluation and the other suggests strong condemnation. The first type of term would be relatively out of place in this kind of context, and hence it is the second which must normally be chosen for all three expressions: pass judgment, judge, and condemn.

The reference to the same things is to the various kinds of evil mentioned in 1.28-32. Do the same things may therefore be rendered as "act in such evil ways," "do so many evil deeds," or "behave so evilly."

2.2 We know that God is right when he judges the people who do such things as these.

We know introduces a general statement of truth acknowledged by all; in the NEB this appears as "it is admitted." Because of the very general character of an expression such as we know, it may be necessary to employ "we all know" or "all men know."

God is right when he judges refers to the standard of God's judgment. Some take this as a reference to God's impartial judgment (JB, Phillips), while others appear to accept the same interpretation as the TEV (NEB "God's judgment is rightly passed"; Goodspeed "God's judgment rightfully falls"). In some languages one must render this statement as "God is completely justified when he judges" or "God does right when he judges."

2.3 But you, my friend, do these very things yourself for which you pass judgment on others! Do you think you will escape God's judgment?

In Greek this verse is one sentence, a question. For the sake of carrying the force of Paul's statement for the English reader, the TEV divides this into two sentences, the first an exclamation, and the second a question. In the Greek the second you of do you think you is in the stressed position.

The rhetorical question Do you think you will escape God's judgment? must in many languages be changed into an emphatic negative, since this is not a request for information but a strong denial of the possibility of escaping. An appropriate rendering may therefore be "you certainly will not escape God's judgment," "you certainly will not be able to get away without God judging you," or "you will certainly not avoid God when he judges you."

2.4 Or perhaps you despise his great kindness, tolerance, and patience. Surely you know that God is kind because he is trying to lead you to repent.

In Greek this verse is also a question, and it is closely related to the one in verse 3. Here again the TEV divides a sentence into two parts. The verb translated despise may also have the meaning "take lightly" or "think lightly of" (NEB). His great kindness is literally "the riches of his kindness," a phrase which the NEB renders rather literally as "his wealth of kindness." The words rendered tolerance (only here and in 3.26 in the Greek New Testament) and patience are synonyms. If any distinction in meaning is to be sought, the first refers to God's act of holding back his punishment, while the second refers to God's willingness to endure man's rejection of him.

It is difficult in some languages to speak of "despising kindness" or "thinking lightly of kindness." However, one can despise a person or think lightly of God because he is kind. In the same manner it is possible to introduce kindness, tolerance, and patience primarily in terms of event words rather than merely as abstract nouns—for example, "you despise..." or "you think lightly of God because he is very kind and doesn't punish you right away and puts up with you for a long time." In some languages tolerance may be expressed in a figurative manner—for example, "has a big heart"—and patience may be "keeps on being the same regardless." In other languages patience may be "to have a soft heart." In still other languages tolerance and patience may be translated as "he is slow to judge and he carries you for a long time."

God is kind because he is trying to lead you to repent is literally "the goodness of God is leading you to repentance." Most scholars agree that "is leading" must be taken in the sense of "is trying to lead" (many translations "is meant to lead"). The NEB interprets "repentance" as "a change of heart."

Because of the general character of an expression such as you know, it is essential in most languages that you be plural throughout this passage, sometimes with an emphatic "all"—for example, "you all know."

A term for repentance must certainly focus upon the change in personality. Therefore "to change your hearts," "to have new hearts," or even "to think differently" may be satisfactory. On the other hand, one may have specific reference to a change of behavior—for example, "turn away from your sins" or "change and return to God."

2.5 But you have a hard and stubborn heart. So then, you are making your own punishment even greater on the Day when God's wrath and right judgments will be revealed.

But you have a hard and stubborn heart is actually a prepositional phrase to be taken with the verb you are making your own punishment even greater, and means something like "in keeping with your hard and stubborn heart." You are making your own punishment even greater is a word picture, the picture of a man treasuring up something for himself, only in this context it is punishment.

The sentence you have a hard and stubborn heart may be related to what follows as cause-effect—for example, "because you have a hard and stubborn heart, you are causing your judgment to be even greater." In many languages one must avoid an expression such as "hard" in connection with "heart," since the phrase "hard heart" frequently has quite a different meaning—"strong" or "brave," for example. In some languages the equivalent idiom for hard and stubborn heart would be "your ears have no holes" (that is to say, "you will not respond to reason"). It is this refusal to reason which is the basic meaning of hard and stubborn heart. In some languages the only satisfactory equivalent of this emphatic expression is "because you are so completely stubborn."

The word rendered punishment in the TEV is the word translated "wrath" elsewhere. The reference, of course, is to the punishment God brings because of his wrath. It is normally not difficult to find a word for punishment, but it is difficult in some languages to speak of "making your punishment greater." A more satisfactory equivalent may be "God will judge you more severely," "God will cause your punishment to be stronger when he judges," or "God will cause you to suffer even more when he judges."

Day is spelled with a capital in the TEV, inasmuch as in both Jewish and Christian thought this was a specialized term, referring to the final day on which

God would bring his wrath and punishment on all evil doers. The Day when God's wrath and right judgments will be revealed is in Greek a noun phrase, "in the day of wrath and the revelation of the righteous judgment of God."

The passive expression will be revealed may be transformed into an active with God as the agent—for example, "the day when God will show his anger and judge rightly." In some instances a reference to God's anger, without indicating that it is anger against sin, could prove to be inappropriate and out of keeping with the context. Therefore, one may say "God's anger against sin" or "God's anger because people have sinned."

2.6 For God will reward every person according to what he has done.

Although in Greek this verse consists of a relative clause, continuing the sentence begun in the previous verse, many modern translators make this into a separate sentence (Goodspeed, JB). "Who" of the Greek relative clause is rendered God by the TEV and "he" by many other translations. Paul lays down a thesis in this verse which becomes the basis for what he says in verses 7-11: that is, for God will reward every person according to what he has done (see Psalm 62.12). In English the transitional conjunction for seems appropriate at the beginning of verse 6, but this cannot be rendered literally "because" or "since" in view of the fact that the content of verse 6 is not a reason for what has immediately preceded, but merely a continuation of related events.

Although in English the word reward carries only positive connotations, the Greek word has both negative and positive connotations and may refer to payment for evil as well as for good. It is not easy to find a completely appropriate term for will reward. In general one must use some such term as "recompense" or "pay back," in order to suggest that what God will do for people is in direct proportion, or in line with, the manner in which they have acted. In verse 6 it may be necessary to employ plural references, rather than singular ones, in order to indicate that God's reward applies to all persons. Although every person is grammatically singular, it is semantically plural.

What he has done is literally "his works," a term which Paul defines in verses 7-10. Many feel that Paul is contradicting himself by the mention of God's rewarding every person according to what he has done, but it is clear that Paul himself sees no conflict between what he says here and his affirmation of "justification by faith" later. Here Paul is not speaking of the works by which one attempts to earn salvation, but rather of the sort of works that grow out of a right relationship already established with God. The "works" mentioned in verses 7 and 10 are the necessary outcome of a right relationship with God.

2.7 Some men keep on doing good, and seek glory, honor, and immortal life; to them God will give eternal life.

In Greek there is a formal contrast between this and the following verse, which the TEV expresses by some men... other men. The Greek phrase ("the endurance of doing good") is taken by many commentators as the sum total of a man's actions, and for this reason the TEV renders the phrase keep on doing good (see JB "always doing good" and Goodspeed "by persistently doing right").

It is difficult in some languages to speak merely of doing good. One must have some kind of indication of persons or objects who are benefited by such "doing good"—for example, "some men keep on doing good to other people." More specifically, this may be rendered in some languages as "keep on being kind to people," since this may be the most general way of characterizing proper behavior toward other people.

Glory and honor are concepts which are united both in Jewish and in Christian thought (see 1 Peter 1.7; Revelation 4.9). Glory is always a difficult term to express, though in the present context it must be taken along with honor and immortal life as qualifying various aspects of the eternal life which God will give at the end of time. To render glory by "renown" (JB "who sought renown") would seem to suggest a wrong emphasis, since "renown" is the praise which men give, whereas "glory" is the gift of God.

The Greek word translated immortal life is relatively rare in the New Testament; elsewhere it is also used as a quality of the eternal life that God gives (see 1 Corinthians 15.42,50,53,54; 2 Timothy 1.10).

In order to avoid wrong implications in "seeking" glory, honor, and immortal life, it is necessary in many languages to specify that these are direct gifts from God—for example, "seek for God to give them glory, honor, and immortal life." In a number of languages one cannot easily distinguish between glory and honor in this type of context, since both would be included in some such expression as "seek to have God give them honor" or even "seek to have God speak well of them." This is often the most general form of granting honor to a person. Frequently a phrase such as immortal life must be expressed as a verb—for example, "seek to have God...cause them to live forever" or "...cause them to have life which never ends."

God will give eternal life may also be rendered as a causative expression: "God will cause them to live endlessly" or "God will cause them never to cease to live."

2.8 Other men are selfish and reject what is right, to follow what is wrong; on them God will pour his wrath and anger.

(Please note that there are further comments on verse 8, in conjunction with verses 9 and 10 below.)

The contrast between some men (v. 7) and other men (v. 8) may be introduced in some languages with an adversative particle such as "but," "on the other hand," or "in contrast with these."

The word rendered selfish by the TEV (see NEB "who are governed by selfish ambition" and Goodspeed "self-seeking people") originally was a term used to describe persons who sought a political office for selfish purposes. However, it is possible that this word could also have the meaning of "strife" or "contentiousness" (see JB "unsubmissive" and Moffatt "willful"). This meaning may be rendered as "other men are always fighting with others" or "other men are always arguing against others" or "others only want their own way." Selfish may be rendered as "who always want to do just what they want to do," "who are always looking for their own benefit," or "who want everyone else to serve them."

In order to indicate that for Paul "truth" is a moral term and not merely an abstract idea, the TEV renders Paul's phrase "reject the truth" by reject what is right. In many languages what is right is rendered as "what they should do," thus implying moral obligation. In other languages the contrast with wrong is "that which is good." In many languages one cannot "follow what is wrong"; it is necessary to say "to do what is wrong" or "to continually do what is wrong."

2.8-10 Other men are selfish and reject what is right, to follow what is wrong; on them God will pour his wrath and anger. (9) There will be suffering and pain for all men who do what is evil, for the Jews first and also for the Gentiles. (10) But God will give glory, honor, and peace to all who do what is good, to the Jews first, and also to the Gentiles.

It may be helpful to consider these three verses together, since they have a common translational problem. The Greek text does not mention the source of wrath and anger (8), suffering and pain (9), and glory, honor, and peace (10). But Paul makes it clear that in each case God is the source, and for that reason the TEV supplies God will pour (8), there will be (9), and God will give (10). In the Greek text the series of nouns appears without verbs to relate them to particular agents, but for the English reader it is necessary to supply some sort of verb. Most English translations accomplish this by providing an impersonal verb (for example "...will come" or "there will be..."), but Paul is clearly speaking of that which is brought about by God himself.

In verse 8 wrath and anger are essentially synonyms, both describing the attitude of God towards those on whom his judgment falls. In many languages it is impossible to speak of "pouring out wrath and anger." One can, however, say "God will judge them in anger" or "God will be angry with them and judge them." By combining both "anger" and "judging," it is possible to reproduce something of the significance of the Greek terms translated wrath and anger. It is also possible to translate "God will punish" as an appropriate rendering of "pouring out wrath and anger."

Similarly, it is difficult to introduce terms such as suffering and pain without indicating who is the agent. Therefore, one may transform this expression into "God will cause them to suffer and to have pain."

For all men is literally "upon every soul of man," a Semitic way of speaking of all mankind.

The contrast between first applied to Jews and also applied to Gentiles should not be interpreted in a chronological sense—that is, that the Jews will suffer first and the Gentiles afterwards, or that the Jews were the first to do evil and the Gentiles afterwards. The emphasis here is simply one of priority in God's revelation or dealing with mankind, but this is difficult to indicate without distorting the actual meaning. For this reason, in some translations the contrast is made by a kind of collective expression "this includes both the Jews and the Gentiles." The order of "Jews" and "Gentiles" is only an indication of the underlying historical sequence.

2.11 For God judges everyone by the same standard.

This verse brings to a conclusion the thesis that Paul laid down in verse 6. God judges everyone by the same standard must be taken to indicate that God shows no partiality in dealing with men, whether they be Jews or Gentiles. Goodspeed renders this by "for God shows no partiality" and in the JB and NEB it appears as "God has no favorites." The clause God judges everyone by the same standard may be rendered variously in different languages—for example, "men are all the same in the eyes of God," "before God all people are equal," "God does not treat certain people better than other people," or even, "God does not say to one person rather than another, You are my special friend." The acceptability of such expressions depends, of course, upon their traditional usage and idiomatic significance.

12 The Gentiles do not have the Law of Moses; they sin and are lost apart
from the Law. The Jews have the Law; they sin and are judged by the Law.
13 For it is not by hearing the Law that men are put right with God, but by doing
what the Law commands. 14 The Gentiles do not have the Law; but whenever
of their own free will they do what the Law commands, they are a law to
themselves, even though they do not have the Law. 15 Their conduct shows that
what the Law commands is written in their hearts. Their consciences also show
that this is true, since their thoughts sometimes accuse them and sometimes
defend them. 16 And so, according to the Good News I preach, this is how it
will be on that Day when God, through Jesus Christ, will judge the secret
thoughts of men.

2.12 The Gentiles do not have the Law of Moses; they sin and are lost apart from the Law. The Jews have the Law; they sin and are judged by the Law.

In the previous verse Paul has concluded that all men, both Jews and Gentiles, are equal before God. However, there is one evident difference: the Jews possess the Law, and the Gentiles do not. Paul deals with this problem in verses 12-16. He points out that God has spoken to all men, some through the Jewish Law and some through the law of conscience, and so all men must answer to him. The Greek text of this verse reads literally: "Whoever sinned without having the law will be lost without having the law; and whoever sinned in the law will be judged by the law." But most commentators agree that Paul is contrasting the Gentiles who do not have the Law of Moses (see also NEB) with the Jews who have the Law, and this information is made explicit in the TEV.

They sin translates an aorist tense in Greek, and it is best taken as the expression of a truth that is valid for all times, rather than as an action that is past ("they sinned").

The logical connections in thought between the various clauses of verse 12 are not always easy to specify. In reality, do not have the Law of Moses is a nonrestrictive attributive to the Gentiles—for example, "the Gentiles, who do not have the Law of Moses, sin and are lost apart from the Law." This type of involved nonrestrictive clause is made a complete sentence in the TEV, the Gentiles do not have the Law of Moses. The expression they sin constitutes the temporal setting for the final part of this clause are lost apart from the Law—for example, "when they sin they are lost apart from the Law." In some languages this first half of verse 12 may be rendered as "whenever the Gentiles, who do not have the Law of Moses, sin, they are lost apart from the Law."

The phrase apart from the Law is difficult to express in some languages. In certain cases the closest equivalent is "even though they do not have the Law." But in some languages it is difficult to express concession implied by the conjunctive phrase "even though." The closest equivalent may be some adversative expression introduced by a conjunction such as "but"—for example, "they are lost, but the Law does not apply to them."

The expression the Law of Moses must be made somewhat more specific in some languages, as "the Law that came through Moses" or "the Law that was given by means of Moses." In order to indicate clearly that in the rest of this passage the same Law is being spoken of, one may use such phrases as "this same Law," "this Law," or even in some contexts the repetition of the entire phrase "the Law that came through Moses."

The second half of verse 12 may be rendered as "whenever the Jews who have the Law, sin, they are judged by the Law." However, in many languages one cannot speak of "being judged by Law." One can only "be judged by God on the basis of the Law," "be judged by what is written in the Law," or "be judged on the basis of what is written in the Law."

2.13 For it is not by hearing the Law that men are put right with God, but by doing what the Law commands.

Exegetically and translationally this verse presents no serious difficulties, though it is important to understand it in the light of Paul's total argument. The impact of Paul's argument is not to indicate that a man may be put into a right relationship with God through the keeping of the Law; rather he is arguing that the mere possession of the Law does not guarantee that a man is in a right relationship with God. Put right with God is literally "righteous beside God," but for the English speaker "righteous" indicates a moral quality, while Paul is speaking of a relationship with God.

The logical relations of the parts of verse 13 are difficult to express in some languages, especially in those in which one cannot speak about hearing the Law without specifically indicating who does the hearing. Moreover, a passive expression such as are put right may need to be changed into an active one. This means that the total form of verse 13 may require considerable recasting—for example, "God does not put people right with himself just because they have listened to the Law. Rather, he does this when they do what the Law says they should do." In some languages the passive expression may be retained but the expression of means by hearing the Law must be inverted—for example, "men are not put right with God merely by listening to the Law, but this does happen by their doing what the Law says they ought to do." In a number of languages, however, one cannot render literally what the Law commands, since only people can "command." One may need to translate the last part of this verse as "do what God has commanded in the Law."

2.14 The Gentiles do not have the Law; but whenever of their own free will they do what the Law commands, they are a law to themselves, even though they do not have the Law.

The Gentiles do not have the Law may need to be changed to the past tense, "the Gentiles have not possessed the Law," "the Gentiles did not receive the Law through Moses," or "the Law which came through Moses was not given to the Gentiles."

Of their own free will has been translated in a variety of ways: "instinctively" (Moffatt, Goodspeed), "by the light of nature" (Phillips, NEB) and "led by reason" (JB, with a note indicating "guided by conscience, not by revealed law"). In most translations this is rendered "by nature" (see RSV). The TEV understands Paul to be speaking of the free and inner response of a man to the conscience given him by God. This is a "natural" response, not because it is something that one does by instinct or by nature, but because it is a response of the divinely created conscience within man. An expression for their own free will is difficult to render in a number of languages. In some instances it is simply equivalent to "whenever they themselves decide," "whenever their own heart tells them to," or "whenever their innermost thoughts say they should."

The Law commands may need to be recast as "what is commanded in the Law" or "what the words written in the Law say that people should do."

They are a law to themselves must not be rendered in such a way as to imply that people can do whatever they want to do. A more appropriate equivalent is "they themselves show what should or should not be done" or "they have demonstrated that they know what should or should not be done."

In the last clause of verse 14 it may be again necessary to specify "the Law which comes from Moses"—for example,"even though they have not possessed the Law which came through Moses" or "even though the Law which came through Moses was not given to them."

2.15 Their conduct shows that what the Law commands is written in their hearts. Their consciences also show that this is true, since their thoughts sometimes accuse them and sometimes defend them.

When Paul says "they show," he evidently means their conduct shows, which may be rendered as "by what they do they show" or "by their behavior they indicate."

"The work of the Law" may be taken either in the sense of what the Law commands (see JB, Goodspeed, RSV), or with the meaning of "the effect of the Law" (NEB, Moffatt).

Written in their hearts may be rendered as "exists in their hearts" or "is found in their minds."

Show that this is true basically means "give testimony as a witness" (see NEB "their conscience is called as witness" and Goodspeed "their consciences will testify for them"). Paul gives three evidences to indicate that the Gentiles are a law to themselves, though they do not possess the Mosaic Law: (1) their conduct (2) their consciences, and (3) their thoughts.

It is difficult in many languages to distinguish between "heart" and "conscience." In some instances there may be a highly idiomatic expression for conscience—for example, "the little man that stands within" or "one's innermost." More frequently one must combine the concepts of both thought and heart—for example, "how they think in their hearts."

The pronoun this in the phrase this is true must refer back to the fact that what the Law commands is written in their hearts. It may be necessary to make this explicit by translating: "what they think in their hearts shows that what the Law commands is written there."

Their thoughts sometimes accuse them and sometimes defend them is a difficult clause in Greek, though most modern translations accept the same exegesis that the TEV follows. The Greek of this clause is difficult because there is no expressed object of the verb accuse or defend. It is possible to render this as the KJV does, "their thoughts the mean while accusing or else excusing one another"; but the question is whether Paul is speaking of a person's thoughts sometimes accusing and sometimes defending himself, or whether he is thinking of a person's thoughts sometimes accusing and sometimes defending someone else. In light of the rest of the verse, the former of these possibilities is probably better. Accuse and defend are expressed in some languages as direct discourse—for example, "sometimes their thoughts say, You did wrong, and sometimes their thoughts say, You did right."

2.16 And so, according to the Good News I preach, this is how it will be on that Day when God, through Jesus Christ, will judge the secret thoughts of men.

In Greek verses 15 and 16 form one sentence. This is how it will be refers back to the total content of the preceding verse, and is a stylistic device intended to show the relationship between verses 15 and 16 for the English reader. Most other translations use some stylistic device to show the relation between verse 15 (especially the last half; see NEB) and this verse, though both Moffatt and the JB conclude that verse 16 grammatically follows verse 13.

In rendering this is how it will be one may have to employ a completely restructured expression—for example, "this is just what will happen on the Day" or "the Day when God will judge will be just like what I have said."

In the Greek text the phrase according to the Good News I preach comes between the secret thoughts of men and through Jesus Christ, but all English translations restructure this for the English reader. In the NEB it appears as a separate statement at the end of verse 16: "so my gospel declares." According to the Good News I preach is rendered in some languages as "the Good News which I preach says that it will be just this way" or "the Good News which I preach agrees with this."

For the use of the word Day, see the comments on verse 5.

The secret thoughts of men is literally "the secrets of men" (RSV), but the reference is obviously to the innermost thoughts of men (NEB "the secrets of human hearts"). The secret thoughts of men may be recast as a verbal expression: "how men think secretly to themselves," "the secrets which men keep in their hearts," or "how people think in their hearts what no one knows about."

The Jews and the Law

[17]What about you? You call yourself a Jew; you depend on the Law and
boast about God; [18]you know what God wants you to do, and you have learned
from the Law to choose what is right; [19]you are sure that you are a guide for
the blind, a light for those who are in darkness, [20]an instructor for the foolish,
and a teacher for the young. You are certain that in the Law you have the full
content of knowledge and of truth. [21]You teach others—why don't you teach
yourself? You preach, "Do not steal"—but do you yourself steal? [22]You say,
"Do not commit adultery"—but do you commit adultery? You detest idols—
but do you rob temples? [23]You boast about having God's law—but do you
bring shame on God by breaking his law? [24]The scripture says, "Because of you
Jews, the Gentiles speak evil of God's name."

In many languages a title such as The Jews and the Law is relatively meaningless, especially since a coordinating conjunction such as "and" normally relates items which belong to the same semantic class, and Jews and Law are obviously not in the same class. Accordingly, a more appropriate title may be "The Relation of the Jews to the Law," "How the Law Affects Jews," or "What the Law Says about Jews."

Verse 17 stands in formal contrast to verse 12, and the entire section (17-29) is the counterpart to verses 12-16. In verses 17-20 Paul mentions the ways in which the Jews depend on the Law and boast about God. But he quickly points out that the Jews are guilty of the same sins of which they are accusing others, and by breaking the Law they are bringing shame on God rather than honor (21-24).

2.17 What about you? You call yourself a Jew; you depend on the Law and boast about God;

In Greek verse 17 introduces a series of "if" clauses, which are suddenly broken off in verse 20 without the conclusion being given. However, these "if" clauses are equivalent in force to an affirmative statement, and the TEV restructures them in this way for the sake of the English reader. The NEB employs the same translational technique, and both the TEV (what about you?) and the NEB ("but as for you—") bring out the intended emphasis in the Greek clause structure. The series Jew... Law... God is very significant: these terms describe at the same time both the national and religious heritage of the Jews, all of which was made possible by the divine choice.

The introductory rhetorical question What about you? cannot be reproduced as such in a number of languages, since it may imply that Paul had a number of uncertainties concerning the Jews. A more appropriate equivalent is sometimes "and now as for you who are Jews" or "with respect to the Jews."

You call yourself a Jew may be rendered as "you recognize yourself as a Jew" or "you say, I am a Jew." The clause you depend on the Law may be idiomatically rendered in some languages as "you hang to the Law" or "you lean on the Law." A more general way of expressing such a relation is "you trust the Law" or "you have confidence in the Law." In many instances, however, one must speak not directly of the Law but of possessing the Law—for example, "you have confidence because you have the Law" or "you are self-assured because the Law was given to you."

The expression boast about God can be misinterpreted, since it was not specifically boasting about God himself which characterized the Jews, but rather boasting about their particular relationship to God (see RSV "boast of your relation to God"). In some languages this may be equivalent to "boasting that God belongs to you," "boasting that you are God's special people," or "boasting that God favors you."

2.18 you know what God wants you to do, and you have learned from the Law to choose what is right;

What God wants you to do is in Greek literally "the will," a phrase current among the Jews when speaking of God's will in an absolute sense.

You know may be understood in the sense of "you are acquainted with" or "you have learned," emphasizing the results of having received the Law. In this way the first part of verse 18 becomes parallel to the second part.

To choose what is right (NEB "you know right from wrong"; Goodspeed, JB "can tell what is right") may have the force of proving what is best after one has put the various possibilities to the test (RSV "approve what is excellent"; Moffatt "with a sense of what is vital in religion"; Phillips "truly to appreciate moral values"). It is important, however, in introducing this clause to avoid implying that the Jews habitually chose what is right. A more appropriate wording may be "you have learned from the law how to choose what is right" or "... how one ought to choose what is right," suggesting that the Law forms the basis for teaching men how to choose the right, without necessarily implying that the Jews always do so.

2.19 you are sure that you are a guide for the blind, a light for those who are in darkness,

In a number of languages an expression such as you are sure that you are a guide for the blind must be rendered as "you confidently say, I am a guide for the blind." It is possible, however, that the metaphorical expressions guide for the blind and light for those who are in darkness may be wrongly construed by some readers. Accordingly, such phrases can be rendered as similes—for example, "that you can, as it were, serve as a guide for the blind"; and similarly, "to cause light for those whose hearts are in darkness" or "a light for those whose hearts cannot see because of the darkness." In some instances sure may be rendered idiomatically—for example, "your heart is very strong because you think you are a guide for the blind." In certain cases an appropriate equivalent is "you tell everyone that you are a guide for the blind." On the statement you are sure that you are a guide for the blind see Matthew 15.14 and Luke 18.9.

2.20 an instructor for the foolish, and a teacher for the young. You are certain that in the Law you have the full content of knowledge and of truth.

The word translated instructor (equivalent in the present context to "teacher") may also have the meaning of "one who punishes," a meaning which it does have in Hebrews 12.9, its only other occurrence in the New Testament. Some translators render this noun by a verb (Goodspeed "train the foolish"). The term foolish refers more to moral than to intellectual weakness, and for this reason renderings such as "ignorant" (JB) and "stupid" (NEB) may be misleading to the reader. The concept of moral weakness may be expressed in some languages as "those whose hearts are weak" or "those whose hearts are twisted."

The word rendered young (so also Goodspeed) may have the connotation of "immature" (NEB). The young may be rendered in some languages as "those who as yet have not learned" or "those who still need instruction."

Full content translates a word in Greek that is rendered "embodiment" in most translations. The only other place where this Greek word occurs in the New Testament is 2 Timothy 3.15, where it has the meaning of "the outward form." In the NEB this is rendered "the very shape (of knowledge and truth)."

Since in many languages the rendering of knowledge and of truth must be rather radically altered, the expression of full content may be indicated by an adverbial attributive—for example, "You are certain that because you have the law you know everything completely and what you say is absolutely true."

2.21-23 You teach others—why don't you teach yourself? You preach, "Do not steal"—but do you yourself steal? (22) You say, "Do not commit adultery"—but do you commit adultery? You detest idols—but do you rob temples? (23) You boast about having God's law—but do you bring shame on God by breaking his law?

In these verses Paul lists three sins which are also mentioned together in lists compiled by Jewish teachers: theft, adultery, and idolatry. The verbs teach and preach would refer to a context of a teaching and preaching situation, while the verb say should probably be understood as referring to a context of exegesis or interpretation.

In a number of languages the contrast between the four statements You teach... You preach... You say... You detest... and the following questions cannot be treated in the same way as in the TEV. The contrast must be preserved, but this can be done in other ways—for example, "you teach others but you ought to teach yourselves; you preach that people should not steal but you yourselves steal"; etc.

A translation of commit adultery should normally be the most general expression for illicit sex relations. In some languages this becomes quite specific and is often male oriented—for example, "you say, Do not sleep with other men's wives."

You detest idols may be translated as "you speak strongly against idols" or "you denounce those who worship idols." It is possible that in some languages there is no clear connection between the idols and their temples. It may, therefore, be necessary to say "you strongly denounce idols, but you rob buildings in which idols are kept" or "...buildings in which people worship idols."

The verb rendered rob temples (so most translations) may be taken in a more general sense, "to commit an irreverent act towards a holy place" (Phillips "how honest are you towards the property of heathen temples?"). It is extremely doubtful that this word should be taken with the meaning "to hold back one's gift from the (Jewish) temple."

God's law (v. 23) is literally "law," but the reference is to the law which God gave the Jewish people. The TEV makes this identification explicit (note JB "the Law"), in order to bring out the evident contrast with the statement that follows: but do you bring shame on God by breaking his law?

Bring shame on God may be rendered as "cause people to have disrespect for God" or "cause people to speak against God."

In many languages one cannot "break a law." One may, however, "disregard a law," "refuse to obey a law," or even "untie a law."

2.24 The scripture says, "Because of you Jews, the Gentiles speak evil of God's name."

The scripture to which Paul refers comes from Isaiah 52.5. The form in which Paul quotes it comes from the Septuagint; in the Hebrew the words because of you do not appear.

In a number of languages one cannot say the scripture says; only "people can say." An equivalent expression may be: "as it is written in the scripture," "the scripture has these words," or "these are the words of the writings."

The TEV makes the Greek expression "because of you" explicit as a reference to the Jews: because of you Jews, the Gentiles speak evil of God's name translates a Greek passive construction (literally, "the name of God is being spoken evil of among the nations"). Speak evil (NEB "dishonored") is generally rendered "blaspheme" in other translations wherever it appears in the New Testament. "Blaspheme" has a disadvantage of being a term which most readers do not understand unless they are familiar with biblical terminology; it is merely a transliteration of the Greek word blasphēmeō, a term which means, in contexts such as this, "to speak evil of God." In some languages it is confusing to say speak evil of God's name. The more natural equivalent is "speak evil of God." Since name is simply a symbolic substitute for God, it is frequently better to employ a more direct expression: "speak bad against God."

2.25

[25]If you obey the Law, your circumcision is of value; but if you disobey the
Law, you might as well never have been circumcised. [26]If the Gentile, who is
not circumcised, obeys the commands of the Law, will not God regard him
as though he were circumcised? [27]And so you Jews will be condemned by the
Gentiles, because you break the Law, even though you have it written down
and are circumcised, while they obey the Law, even though they are not
physically circumcised. [28]After all, who is a real Jew, truly circumcised? Not
the man who is a Jew on the outside, whose circumcision is a physical thing.
[29]Rather, the real Jew is the man who is a Jew on the inside, that is, whose
heart has been circumcised, which is the work of God's Spirit, not of the
written Law. This man receives his praise from God, not from men.

In this section Paul uses the style of a teacher, rather than that of a debater, as he did in the preceding section. Law and covenant, and covenant and circumcision, belong together, and the discussion of the Law leads naturally into a discussion of the value of circumcision. Circumcision, the sign of the covenant, is valuable only if one obeys the demands of the covenant set forth in the Law.

2.25 If you obey the Law, your circumcision is of value; but if you disobey the Law, you might as well never have been circumcised.

It is difficult in some languages to find a satisfactory term for circumcision. If the practice of circumcision is unknown, a descriptive expression often seems quite vulgar. If circumcision is known, direct references to such a practice may be taboo, especially in such contexts as the Scriptures. In general, there is a tendency to employ some kind of euphemism—for example, "the cutting of the skin" (without specifying what part of the skin is cut), "a mark in the flesh," or "a cutting of the body." In some instances an even more generic expression has developed by usage—for example, "the Jews cut them." This term might be regarded as being entirely too general in meaning, but which in at least one language it is used to refer specifically to circumcision. In any event, the practice of circumcision must be identified clearly in this type of context, but an explanation of precisely what is involved may be placed in a glossary with appropriate cross-referencing.

In some languages one does not obey the Law but "obeys what the Law says" or "does what the Law says one ought to do."

Your circumcision is of value may introduce problems because it may be necessary to use a verb in speaking of circumcision. The first two clauses of verse 25 may therefore be rendered as "if you do what the Law says you should do, it is good if you are circumcised" or "if you do what the Law commands, then the fact that you are circumcised will help you."

You might as well never have been circumcised (see JB "you might as well have stayed uncircumcised") is the meaning of Paul's statement "your circumcision becomes uncircumcision" (RSV).

You might as well never have been circumcised may be rendered in some languages as "it is just the same as though you had not been circumcised" or "your being circumcised is nothing."

2.26 If the Gentile, who is not circumcised, obeys the commands of the Law, will not God regard him as though he were circumcised?

The Gentile, who is not circumcised (see RSV "a man who is uncircumcised") is literally "the uncircumcision." Paul uses this word "uncircumcision" in three different senses, depending on the context: (1) the foreskin of the male, (2) the state of being uncircumcised, and (3) those persons who are uncircumcised, that is, Gentiles. In a similar fashion Paul sometimes uses "circumcision" as a reference to the Jews (see Romans 3.30; 4.9, 12; 15.8). The passive verb "be regarded" (RSV) is actually a Semitic way of speaking of God's action without mentioning the name of God. In order to make this information clear for the reader, the TEV renders the entire expression as will not God regard him as though he were circumcised?

Verse 26 involves several problems, not only because of the rhetorical question which completes the verse, but also because of the nonrestrictive attributive clause who is not circumcised. In some languages this expression must be a complete sentence, but clearly marked as contrastive—for example, "on the other hand, Gentiles are not circumcised; nevertheless, if they obey the commands of the Law, God will surely regard them as though they were circumcised." In this manner the logical relations between the various clauses is carefully preserved and the singular is changed to plural in order to indicate clearly that all such persons are involved.

2.27

It may be interesting to note that whereas the Greek text has 17 words, the TEV has 37 words in this verse. Moreover, in order to make this verse intelligible for the English reader, the TEV has to restructure it rather radically. By placing the TEV rendering of this verse side by side with that of the KJV, a rather literal rendering, the reason for the restructuring can readily be seen.

TEV	KJV
And so you Jews will be condemned by the Gentiles, because you break the Law, even though you have it written down and are circumcised, while they obey the Law, even though they are not physically circumcised.	And shall not uncircumcision which is by nature, if it fulfil the law, judge thee, who by the letter and circumcision dost transgress the law?

The main impact of this verse is to remind the Jews that they will be condemned by the Gentiles, and so the TEV isolates this main element and makes it into a separate sentence at the beginning of the verse. In the Greek you Jews is simply "you" (KJV "thee"), while the Gentiles is literally "the uncircumcision."

The first clause of verse 27 should not be interpreted as meaning that Gentiles themselves will condemn the Jews. It is the fact that the Gentiles obey the commands of the Law which serves as the basis for the Jews being condemned. This relationship may be expressed in some instances as "you Jews will be condemned because of the fact that the Gentiles themselves obey the commands of the Law." This provides an excellent basis for the contrast which follows: while they obey the Law, even though....

Because you break the Law must be introduced in such a way as to show clear contrast—for example, "but as for you Jews, you break the Law" or "but in contrast, you Jews break the Law."

The phrase "who through letter and circumcision" should be understood as in the TEV, even though you have it (the Law) written down and are circumcised (see Goodspeed "although you have it in writing, and are circumcised"). Most modern translations (JB, RSV, Moffatt, Phillips, Goodspeed) render the phrase "uncircumcision which is by nature" in the sense of physically uncircumcised. The NEB ("uncircumcised in his natural state") makes little sense, because all men, Jew and Gentile, are uncircumcised in their natural state. Paul's reference is, of course, to the Gentiles who are not physically circumcised.

If it is necessary to change are circumcised into an active form, one may employ either of two different possibilities: a direct agent-action expression, "you circumcise one another," or a type of substitute passive, "you receive circumcision" or "you receive cutting of the body."

Physically circumcised may be rendered as "literally circumcised" or "but in the skin."

Although the verb rendered will be condemned may have the more general meaning of "to judge" or "to pass judgment on," in the present context the judgment is one of condemnation, and for that reason the TEV makes this explicit (so also Goodspeed). The JB states that "(the Gentile) is a living condemnation of the way you (the Jew) disobey the Law," but in this context it would seem that Paul is referring to the final judgment, and for this reason the idea of "a living condemnation" seems to miss the point.

2.28-29 After all, who is a real Jew, truly circumcised? Not the man who is a Jew on the outside, whose circumcision is a physical thing. (29) Rather, the real Jew is the man who is a Jew on the inside, that is, whose heart has been circumcised, which is the work of God's Spirit, not of the written Law. This man receives his praise from God, not from men.

The Greek of these two verses is elliptical (that is, certain elements in the sentences must be supplied by the reader), but the TEV rendering captures the meaning that is assumed by most translators and commentators. However, there is one clause which is interpreted differently by a number of exegetes:

which is the work of God's Spirit, not of the written Law. In Romans 7.6 and 2 Corinthians 3.6 similar expressions occur, and in both of these passages it is agreed that the reference is to the Holy Spirit. But in the present passage a number of translations take Paul's expression (literally "in spirit not letter") to mean "spiritual and not literal" (so RSV, Moffatt, Goodspeed). The JB seems also to go in this direction with its rendering: "something not of the letter but of the spirit." The NEB agrees with the TEV in its interpretation: "directed not by written precepts but by the Spirit."

The transitional phrase after all introduces a conclusion and may be rendered in some languages as "in conclusion," "all this means that...," or "all that has been said adds up to...."

The initial question, who is a real Jew, truly circumcised?, must in many languages be changed into a statement. The equivalent may be "a man who seems to be a real Jew may not be one," "not everyone is a Jew who appears to be a Jew," "not all are Jews whom people think are Jews." Another equivalent may be "being circumcised does not really make a person a Jew" or "if a person is circumcised this does not mean that he is really a Jew." The second sentence in verse 28 may likewise need to be semantically restructured as "a man is not a Jew just because he has received cutting in his body" or "by being circumcised a man does not necessarily become a Jew."

The transitional particle rather beginning verse 29 is particularly important and may be emphasized in some languages as "quite the contrary," "in contrast with this," or even "but indeed."

A Jew on the inside may be rendered in some languages as "a Jew in his heart" or "a Jew in his inside being."

The clause whose heart has been circumcised is particularly difficult to render. One cannot usually speak of "cutting the skin of the heart." In fact in some languages one must simply drop the semantic association between "heart" and "circumcised." An equivalent may be "whose heart has been prepared" or "whose heart has been marked as belonging to God."

The conjunction which, introducing the clause which is the work of God's Spirit, not of the written Law, refers specifically to the "circumcision of the heart," but it likewise refers to the total concept of "being a true Jew." Since this final clause is primarily related to the preceding clause as a causative, it is sometimes necessary to make a separate sentence of this last portion of the first sentence of verse 29—for example, "God's Spirit is the one which causes this, the written Law does not cause it." If the pronouns "this" and "it" are not specific enough, it may be possible to say: "God's Spirit causes a person to be a Jew on the inside; the words of the Law do not cause this." In some instances an inversion of the order may be appropriate—for example, "on the other hand, the real Jew is the man who is a Jew on the inside—a person who has been made a Jew by God's Spirit and not by any written Law, since being a real Jew is a matter of the heart and not of the body." By contrasting "heart" and "body," one can indicate clearly the significance of "circumcised of heart."

On the other hand, if, as suggested above, the Greek expression which is literally "in Spirit not letter" is to be taken to mean "spiritually and not literally," this reference to circumcision can be rendered as "this is not something done to his body but something which happens to his heart" or "this does not mean a cutting of the body but a change in a person's spirit."

The phrase receives his praise is a kind of substitute passive, since it is God who is the agent of such praise. An active equivalent may be "it is God who praises such a man; it is not other men who do so." An alternative form may be "praise for such a man comes from God and not from men."

CHAPTER 3

3 Do the Jews have any advantage over the Gentiles, then? Or is there any
value in being circumcised? [2]Much, indeed, in every way! In the first
place, God trusted his message to the Jews. [3]What if some of them were not
faithful? Does it mean that for this reason God will not be faithful? [4]Certainly
not! God must be true, even though every man is a liar. As the scripture says,
"You must be shown to be right when you speak;
you must win your case when you are being tried."
[5]But what if our doing wrong serves to show up more clearly God's doing
right? What can we say? That God does wrong when he punishes us? (I speak
here as men do.) [6]By no means! If God is not just, how can he judge the world?
[7]But what if my untruth serves God's glory by making his truth stand out
more clearly? Why should I still be condemned as a sinner? [8]Why not say, then,
"Let us do evil that good may come"? Some people, indeed, have insulted me
by accusing me of saying this very thing! They will be condemned, as they
should be.

In this chapter the style of the diatribe or philosophical argument (see 2.1) continues. Whether Paul is dealing with actual arguments raised by his opponents or by arguments which he knows they might raise, the impact is still the same. It could possibly be concluded from Paul's arguments in the previous chapter that the Jews have no advantage over the Gentiles; but on the basis of the Old Testament Paul knows differently, and he now undertakes to prove that historically the Jews have stood in a much more advantageous position than the Gentiles.

3.1 Do the Jews have any advantage over the Gentiles, then? Or is there any value in being circumcised?

Over the Gentiles is not an actual part of the Greek text, but it is assumed in Paul's argument, and is made explicit in the TEV. Perhaps it should be noted also, that whereas the Greek has the singular "Jew," the TEV renders by a plural Jews, because in English discourse structure this is more natural. Or is there any value in being circumcised? means "What good does it do for the Jews to be circumcised?"

This first section in Romans 3 (vv. 1-8) involves a number of structural problems, primarily because of the question-answer structure. For languages in which rhetorical questions are permitted, this is a very effective means of highlighting an issue and then providing a satisfactory response. However, for languages which do not employ this rhetorical device, it is not easy to find an appropriate and satisfactory equivalent. While it is true that some languages do not permit a rhetorical question such as Do the Jews have any advantage over the Gentiles, then?, they do permit rhetorical questions which begin with some such introductory phrase as "Do you think therefore that... ?" or "Do you suppose that... ?" Such a question borders on the rhetorical type of interrogation, but it is often regarded as perfectly appropriate, since it would seem natural that Paul might himself ask his audience in Rome about their reactions to such issues. It is also possible to deal with such rhetorical questions by introducing them in another manner—for example, "Someone may ask, Do the Jews have any advantage over the Gentiles?" Placing the question into the speech of someone else frequently makes it completely admissible, and it is precisely this type of question which is important in a passage such as this, in which very definite responses to the question are included in the text.

It is not always easy to find a ready equivalent to the expression have any advantage over. However, there are always ways in which the same concept may be expressed, often in an idiomatic form—for example, "how do the Jews go ahead of the Gentiles?" or "how are the Jews lifted up higher than the Gentiles?" Any value in being circumcised? may be translated as "any good to be circumcised?" or "does it help at all to be circumcised?"

3.2 Much, indeed, in every way! In the first place, God trusted his message to the Jews.

It would seem from Paul's statement in the first place that he intends to list a series of advantages that the Jews have, but in fact he mentions only this one. However, in 9.4-5 Paul does mention other advantages of the Jews.

The emphatic response much, indeed, in every way! may need to be expanded somewhat by a repetition of part of the preceding verse—for example, "it certainly helps very much and in all ways" or "in everything indeed it helps very much." After this type of introductory statement, the phrase in the first place may be rendered as "the first way is that God trusted his message to the Jews."

God trusted his message to the Jews is a passive construction in Greek (see RSV "the Jews are entrusted with the oracles of God"). It may be helpful to note that the word rendered trusted is the verb which appears elsewhere in the New Testament with the sense of "to have faith" (in God or Christ). In 1 Corinthians 9.17 and 1 Thessalonians 2.4 the verb is used in a sense similar to its use in this passage.

God trusted his message to the Jews may be rendered as "God gave his message to the Jews to preserve." It is important to avoid the implication that God gave this message to the Jews for them to keep as a secret.

There is some question regarding the exact limitations to be placed on the meaning of his message (RSV, NEB "the oracles of God"; Goodspeed "the utterances of God"; Phillips "God's messages"; JB "God's message"; Moffatt "the scriptures of God"). Some take this to be a reference to the entire Old Testament, while others limit it either to special divine revelations as on Mount Sinai, or to the promises of God in the Old Testament. However, in light of the parallel passage in 9.4, it would seem best to take it in the larger sense of the entire Old Testament.

3.3 What if some of them were not faithful? Does it mean that for this reason God will not be faithful?

Although most modern translations understand the first verb in this verse in the same sense as the TEV, were not faithful, it is possible to take this verb with the meaning of "did not believe" (see Goodspeed "has shown a lack of faith"). The context seems to support the interpretation given by the TEV, since Paul is making a contrast between the Jews who were not faithful to the covenant they had made with God and God who was faithful in keeping the covenant. This seems quite evident from the choice of the Greek words which Paul uses in this passage.

This use of faithful in the first question of verse 3 may be understood either in the sense of "not preserving properly the message of God" or "not complying with the message of God." Evidently this latter interpretation is in focus. It is thus important that the preceding statement in verse 2 agree with this interpretation of being faithful in following out the implications of the message.

In languages which cannot employ a question at this point it is possible to use a statement, either "some of the Jews were not faithful" or "it is true that some of the Jews were not faithful." By means of the introductory expression "it is true" the structure of argument and counterargument is retained.

Does it mean that for this reason God will not be faithful? is literally "Does their faithlessness nullify the faithfulness of God?" (RSV). It is possible, on the basis of the Greek, to take this question to mean, "Does it mean that for this reason faith in God is useless?" but no modern translations take Paul's question in that sense. The Greek word rendered "nullify" in the RSV is used also in 3.31, and it is there translated in the TEV as do away with.

An introductory expression such as does it mean may be rendered in some languages as "do you think." If a question form cannot be employed in the second part of verse 3, one can always say "this does not mean that for this reason God will not be faithful" or "you must not think that for this reason God will not be faithful." The phrase for this reason may be made specific in some languages as "you must not think that God will not be faithful, just because some men are not faithful."

3.4 Certainly not! God must be true, even though every man is a liar. As the scripture says,

"You must be shown to be right when you speak;
you must win your case when you are being tried."

The introductory statement certainly not! may be reproduced in some languages as "indeed you must not think so" or "certainly that is not true." This same Greek expression is translated as by no means in verse 6.

In this verse Paul uses a third person imperative form (the RSV translates literally "Let God be true"), which must be taken in the sense of God must be true (so NEB; Goodspeed "God must prove true"; JB "God will always be true"). In the context the statement means that God will do what he has said he will do, he will keep his word.

In a number of languages one can speak of "a true word" or "speaking truly," but it is not possible to say that a person "is true." In rendering the statement God must be true one may have to introduce some verb of speaking—for example, "you may know that God always speaks the truth." It is inappropriate in some languages to introduce an obligatory element such as must in connection with speaking the truth, since this would imply that God is under some moral obligation to speak the truth rather than that by his very nature he always speaks the truth. This particular meaning of true is clearly contrasted in the following clause which speaks of other persons being liars.

Every man is a liar is an allusion to Psalm 116.11, while the scripture quotation in the last part of this verse is an exact quotation from Psalm 51.4 in the Septuagint. The scene described in the 51st Psalm is that of a court scene in which God always emerges victorious over his opponents because he is right.

As the scripture says is the same formula that appears in 1.17 and 2.24.

As in the case of the clause God must be true, the auxiliary verbs must in the two lines of quotation should be interpreted not as obligation but as certainty —for example, "you will certainly be shown to be right" and "you will certainly win your case." An active alternative to the passive expression must be shown may be "whenever you speak, everyone will certainly see that you are right."

In some languages it is not easy to find a satisfactory equivalent of the last statement of verse 4, since subjecting God to a court trial may seem quite inappropriate, and there may be no terms for trial which do not prejudge the guilt of one being tried. Accordingly, one may employ in some instances: "whenever you defend yourself you will show that you have done right" or "you will always win out against those who accuse you."

3.5 But what if our doing wrong serves to show up more clearly God's doing right? What can we say? That God does wrong when he punishes us? (I speak here as men do.)

The noun rendered doing wrong appears also in 1.18 (evil ways), 1.29 (wickedness), and 2.8 (what is wrong). Here it stands in formal contrast to God's doing right (literally "righteousness of God"). Although the phrase God's doing right is essentially the same phrase that Paul uses in 1.17, it is clear that Paul uses the phrase in a different sense in the present context. Whereas in the former passage it is used in the general Pauline sense of God's placing men in a right relationship with himself, here it refers to an attribute of God, specifically the fact that God is right and does what is right. The phrase God's doing right is translated in a variety of ways (Moffatt "the justice of God"; JB "his integrity"; NEB "God's justice"; Phillips "the goodness of God"; and Goodspeed "the uprightness of God").

This first question in verse 5 is particularly difficult to translate, primarily since it involves two kinds of events, our doing wrong and God's doing right, in which the one distinctly affects the other. Moreover, the expression serves to show up more clearly is often difficult, since there is no indication to whom God's doing right is shown up more clearly. It may, therefore, be necessary to recast this question in a somewhat different form—for example, "But what, if when we do wrong, people can see more clearly that God does right?" or "But what if, by our doing wrong, God's doing right is shown to people so that they can see it more clearly?" For languages in which this type of question presents difficulties, it is possible to change to a nonquestion form, by introducing some type of context such as "men may argue" or "some men may say"—for example, "But some men argue that when we do wrong people can see more clearly how God does right."

The question what can we say? is equivalent in some languages to "how can we answer this argument?," "what can we say in response?," or "is there an answer to this argument?" For languages in which such rhetorical questions are not possible, one can always say "but there is an answer to this argument."

The word rendered does wrong comes from the same stem as the word doing wrong in the earlier part of the verse.

When he punishes us is literally "bringing wrath on us," but in the present context the reference is to punishment (see NEB "to bring retribution upon us"; Goodspeed "to inflict punishment"; and Phillips "to punish us").

The question That God does wrong when he punishes us? may require some introductory phrase—for example, "Can we argue that..." or "Can we say...." Again, for languages which cannot employ such a rhetorical question, one may say: "Men may even argue that God does wrong when he punishes us."

By his statement I speak here as men do (see 6.19; 1 Corinthians 9.8; Galatians 3.15), Paul means that he is presenting arguments based on human wisdom. This statement is best understood as parenthetical (see NEB, JB, Phillips, and Goodspeed).

It may be necessary in rendering the verb do to make it somewhat more specific—for example, "I speak here as men ordinarily speak." Some type of modifier such as "ordinarily" may be required in order to indicate that this is not necessarily what men do on all occasions but what is their habitual practice.

For languages in which the rhetorical questions of verse 5 are changed into nonquestions introduced by some expression relating to the way in which people argue such issues, it is not necessary to introduce this parenthetical statement I speak here as men do, since in reality the contents of this parenthetical sentence have been, as it were, redistributed as introductory features to the earlier sentences of the verse.

3.6 By no means! If God is not just, how can he judge the world?

An expression such as by no means! may be rendered in some languages as "this cannot be" or "this is not true." However, if questions in verse 5 have been changed to statements, it may be more appropriate to translate: "one simply cannot argue this way" or "these arguments are completely false."

In this verse Paul raises a question (literally "how then could God judge the world?"), but the reference that he has in mind is unclear. Some take the question to mean "if God does not punish people, how can he judge the world?" while others take it as a reference to God's justice, if God is not just, how can he judge the world? (so NEB "if God were unjust, how could he judge the world?"). The reference in this verse is to the final judgment, and by the use of the world Paul means "all mankind."

It may also be necessary to change the final question in verse 6 to a statement—for example, "if God is not just, then he certainly cannot judge the world."

3.7 But what if my untruth serves God's glory by making his truth stand out more clearly? Why should I still be condemned as a sinner?

In this verse Paul deals with a question which he imagines his opponents can raise on the basis of his statement in verse 4. Paul imagines his Jewish opponents saying, But what if my untruth ("my unfaithfulness") serves God's glory ("serves to bring God greater honor") by making his truth ("his faithfulness") stand out more clearly? Why should I still be condemned as a sinner?

Though the meaning of verse 7 seems to be clear, it is extremely difficult to translate this verse adequately into some languages. There are two basic problems. The first has to do with the terms untruth and truth, and the second with the very complex relations between the various parts of the first question. My untruth is actually a causative agent for people recognizing more clearly God's glory, but this is done by the means of making his truth more conspicuous, in the sense of people thus being able to see it more clearly. Though the Greek text contrasts truth with untruth (or lie), the real significance is that of faithfulness verses unfaithfulness or, as in this context, righteousness versus unrighteousness. It is not "my speaking a lie which serves God's glory" but "my unrighteousness" or even "my sin," since in this context untruth is parallel to doing wrong introduced at the beginning of verse 5. The parallelism between the questions in verse 5 and verse 7 is evident. The meaning, therefore, may be given as "But what if my doing wrong enhances God's glory by making his doing right stand out more clearly?" Of course, when the contrast between untruth and truth can be preserved, one should attempt to do so, but in some languages "untruth" and "truth" can only be stated in terms of "when someone speaks a lie" and "when someone speaks the truth," and this is clearly not the central meaning in the present context.

Despite a shift of untruth and truth to the corresponding doing wrong and doing right, there are difficulties in stating precisely the relationships between the parts of the sentence. In fact it may be necessary to break up some of the parts into smaller or more isolatable units—for example, "But suppose that I do wrong. Do you think this helps God's glory because then people will see more clearly that he does right?" There is also a serious problem involved in translating serves God's glory. In some languages one can speak of "helping God's glory," "making God's glory conspicuous," or "lifting up God's glory." In other instances one can only employ a causative "causes people to see God's glory better," since in some languages one cannot speak of "enhancing God's glory" as this is an integral element of God's own nature. It cannot be increased or diminished; it can only be made more conspicuous or less conspicuous.

For languages which do not permit the use of such rhetorical questions as occur in verse 7, the questions may be changed into statements introduced by some such expression as "some men may argue" or "some men may say."

3.8 Why not say, then, "Let us do evil that good may come"? Some people, indeed, have insulted me by accusing me of saying this very thing! They will be condemned, as they should be.

If one accepts as valid the argument of Paul's opponents in verse 7, the natural conclusion will be let us do evil ("sin") that good ("honor to God") may come. Paul himself cannot accept this conclusion as valid, and affirms that those who accuse him of saying this thing will be condemned, as they should be.

This initial question in verse 8 may be changed into a statement by modifying the introductory portion—for example, "Therefore some people argue, Let us do evil as a way of honoring God."

Although Paul uses the first person plural "us" in the expressions "have insulted us by accusing us," commentators agree that Paul is here speaking about himself, and hence the TEV employs the first person singular me. The relation between the events insulted and accusing is essentially one of means and result: "by means of accusing Paul, they insulted him." This relation may be expressed in a number of languages by two paratactically combined sentences—for example, "Some people indeed have insulted me; they have accused me of saying this very thing" or "Indeed, some people have spoken bad about me; this is the very argument which they said I have used."

In the last part of this verse Paul literally says "their condemnation is just" (RSV). The TEV takes this as a reference to the condemnation which God will bring upon such people, they will be condemned, as they should be. Goodspeed has "such people will be condemned as they deserve!" but the JB ("but they are justly condemned") and the NEB ("to condemn such men as these is surely no injustice") apparently take this as a human condemnation. Moffatt ("such arguments are rightly condemned") and Phillips ("such an argument is quite properly condemned") seem to understand "they" as a reference to the arguments, rather than to the people who make the arguments.

Though in some languages one can be ambiguous as to the agent of the condemnation, in most languages that is not possible, especially if an active form of the verb "condemn" must be employed—for example, "God will condemn them just as he should." If one interprets the condemnation as being from persons, the subject may simply be changed: "people will condemn such accusations" or "people will condemn those who make such accusations."

No Man Is Righteous

9 Well then, are we Jews in any better condition than the Gentiles? Not at
all! I have already shown that Jews and Gentiles alike are all under the power
of sin. 10 As the Scriptures say:

"There is no one who is righteous,
11 no one who understands,
or who seeks for God.
12 All men have turned away from God;
they have all gone wrong;
no one does what is good, not even one.
13 Their mouths are like an open grave;
wicked lies roll off their tongues,
and deadly words, like snake's poison, from their lips;
14 their mouths are full of bitter curses.
15 They are quick to hurt and kill;

16 they leave ruin and misery wherever they go.
17 They have not known the path of peace,
18 nor have they learned to fear God."
19 Now we know that everything in the Law applies to those who live under the Law, in order to stop all human excuses and bring the whole world under God's judgment.
20 Because no man is put right in God's sight by doing what the Law requires; what the Law does is to make man know that he has sinned.

The section heading No Man Is Righteous may require certain modifications if a verb expression must be employed for Righteous—for example, "No Man Does What Is Right." However, it may be necessary to indicate something as to the general nature of such "right doing"—for example, "No Man Always Does What Is Right" or "No Persons Consistently Do What They Should."

3.9 Well then, are we Jews in any better condition than the Gentiles? Not at all! I have already shown that Jews and Gentiles alike are all under the power of sin.

The first part of this verse, Well then, are we Jews in any better condition than the Gentiles? Not at all!, presents several exegetical problems. (1) The Greek verb (one word in Greek, but ten words in TEV: are we Jews in any better condition than the Gentiles?) may be understood in one of three ways. Most scholars interpret this verb in the same sense as the TEV (see JB, NEB, Moffatt, Phillips), but Goodspeed understands it in precisely the opposite sense ("are we Jews at a disadvantage?"; see also the alternative renderings in the RSV and NEB). A third possibility of understanding this verb, though one not widely accepted, is represented in a footnote of the JB ("what excuse then can we [Jews] offer?"). The problem with this third possibility is that the words rendered well then would have to be taken along with the main verb (with the meaning "what excuse then are we offering"), and the answer to this would have to be "none at all" (rather than not at all, as in the Greek). (2) The words rendered not at all may also mean "not altogether" (see NEB note "not in all respects"). The final decision as to exegesis should be made on the basis of what seems to fit the context best, and the exegesis represented by the TEV, JB, NEB, Moffatt, and Phillips seems to be most in keeping with the immediate as well as the overall context.

In verse 1 of this chapter Paul raised the question whether the Jews had any advantage over the Gentiles. His answer was Much, indeed, in every way! Paul now returns to that question and approaches it from a different point of view. He points out that even though God did trust his message to the Jews (v. 2), the Jews and Gentiles alike are all under the power of sin. Viewed from this perspective, the Jews are not in any better condition than the Gentiles.

In addition to the complex exegetical difficulties involved in the first part of verse 9, there are a number of translational complications. In the first place, there is the transitional phrase well then, which is equivalent in some languages to "and now to return to the question," "and what is the conclusion?" or "what can we really say?"

In the second place, we in the expression we Jews must be taken as exclusive in languages which make a distinction between inclusive and exclusive first person plural. Paul is obviously not including all of his audience in Rome, and though presumably he may be including part of his audience (since there are no doubt Jews among the believers in Rome), it is preferable in this type of context to use the exclusive first person plural.

In the third place, in any better condition may be rendered in some instances as "have a better place" or "are in a better position" (the reference here is clearly not to a condition of health). However, since the relation here is primarily one involving God, it may be necessary to specify this—for example, "better as far as God looks upon us" or "better in the eyes of God."

In the fourth place, it may be necessary to change the question into a statement and incorporate the strong negative expression not at all as part of the initial statement—for example, "in summary then, we Jews are certainly not in any better condition than the Gentiles."

I have already shown is in the Greek text a plural ("we"), but once again Paul uses the plural form as a reference to himself.

The final sentence of verse 9 may be treated as a reason for the first sentence and thus be introduced by a conjunction such as "for" or "because"—for example, "because I have already pointed out that Jews and Gentiles...."

The phrase under the power of sin is difficult to express in some languages, especially since power is highly abstract and sin refers primarily to events, not to some object. In some languages, however, one may use a phrase such as "all are controlled by sin" or "sin controls all people." But in certain languages one cannot speak of sin controlling someone; it is only the desire to sin which can do this—for example, "all men are controlled by their desire to sin" or "men's desire to sin commands them."

3.10 As the Scriptures say:
"There is no one who is righteous,

(Please note that this verse is also treated in conjunction with verses 11 and 12 below.)

As the Scriptures say is the same formula as in verse 4 above. The reason for the difference in translation is that in this series of quotes (vv. 11-18) Paul is using various passages from the Old Testament as a summary of the entire content of its message. The accumulative effect of keeping all these verses together is seen in verses 19-20, that is, to indicate that all men have sinned and so are under God's judgment.

3.10-12 As the Scriptures say:

"There is no one who is righteous,
no one who understands,
or who seeks for God.
All men have turned away from God;
they have all gone wrong;
no one does what is good, not even one.

These verses come from Psalm 14.1-3 (parallel 53.1-3). In the Psalm the first and sixth lines read the same, but Paul has made a significant change by introducing into the quote the word righteous. This word appears neither in the Hebrew nor in the Septuagint, but it is a basic element in Paul's theology. For Paul this phrase would mean there is not a man who is in a right relation with God. It is significant that in verse 20 Paul summarizes his total argument from the scriptures by the quotation from Psalm 143.2: because no man is put right in God's sight by doing what the Law requires. To translate as the JB does ("there is not a good man left, no, not one") is to translate the Psalm rather than what Paul intends.

In view of the particular manner in which Paul uses righteous in this context, it may be necessary in some languages to use the phrase "right before God," "righteous in God's eyes," or "seen as righteous by God." This is certainly more than merely "doing right."

In a number of languages one cannot use an expression such as who understands without indicating something of the nature of what is or is not understood. The most neutral and contextually appropriate goal of such understanding is probably "what is right." Therefore one may translate: "There is not one person who really understands what is right."

The last clause of verse 11 must not be rendered in such a way as to imply that a person goes out looking for God in the same way that one would look for a lost coin. To avoid a wrong connotation one may have, in some languages, "seeks to be related to God," "seeks to be with God," or "wants to have God with him."

In the Psalm the phrase from God does not appear in the statement all men have turned away, but it is clearly implicit, and the TEV makes this information explicit for its readers.

The equivalent of the expression turned away from God is in some instances "do not wish to have God in their minds," "will not remember God any longer," or "have turned their backs on God." The verb rendered gone wrong (so RSV, Moffatt) literally means "to become useless" and appears in a variety of forms in various translations (Goodspeed "worthless"; NEB "debased"; Phillips "unprofitable"; JB "tainted"). The meaning of does what is good (so most translations) is to be preferred over the meaning "to show kindness" (NEB).

3.13 Their mouths are like an open grave;
wicked lies roll off their tongues,
and deadly words, like snake's poison,
from their lips;

The first two lines of this verse come from Psalm 5.9 (v. 10 in some versions, e.g. NAB). The first line is transformed from a metaphor (literally "their throat is an open grave") to a simile, their mouths are like an open grave. The last line of this verse comes from Psalm 140.3 and is connected in the TEV with the preceding line. Wicked lies roll off their tongues is literally "with their tongues they deceive"; while and deadly words, like snake's poison, from their lips goes back to "the poison of snakes is under their lips." The Psalmist is comparing the words of his enemies to the poison of snakes, and the TEV makes this comparison clear for its readers.

The figures of speech in this verse are difficult to translate in such a way as to make them meaningful. Their mouths are like an open grave can be understood in the sense that "their breath is so bad that it smells like a rotting corpse," but that is not the meaning of the passage. The focus here is rather upon the death which is caused by what men say. Accordingly, in some languages, the first line of verse 13 may be rendered as "by their words they cause death." One may, of course, employ in some languages an idiom such as "their mouths kill," but it must be perfectly clear in a receptor language that the mouth is to be regarded as the organ of speech and therefore it is by speech that men are killed or destroyed. The same type of problem exists in the second line of verse 13, since in some languages one does not speak of the tongue as being the instrument of speech. Some receptor languages identify speech with the lips, others with the mouth, still others with the throat, while some do use the tongue in this figurative sense. It may be necessary, therefore, to say "with the throat men speak wicked lies" or "with their lips men utter wicked words."

Deadly words are "words which cause death" or "...cause people to be killed."

3.14 their mouths are full of bitter curses.

This quotation comes from Psalm 10.7.

Their mouths are full of bitter curses may be equivalent in some languages to "they constantly speak bitter curses" or "they fill their mouths with curses which are bitter."

3.15-17 They are quick to hurt and kill;
they leave ruin and misery wherever they go.
They have not known the path of peace,

The Old Testament passages referred to in these verses are Isaiah 59.7-8 and Proverbs 1.16.

They are quick to hurt and kill renders a Hebrew idiom, which translated literally conveys little or no meaning for the average English reader (see NEB "their feet hasten to shed blood"). It may, of course, be necessary to specify the goal of hurting and killing—for example, "to hurt and kill people" or "to cause people to suffer and to kill them."

Verse 16 describes further the evil things done by these people; a translation such as "ruin and misery lie along their paths" (NEB) leaves the reader doubtful as to whether this is something that these people do or something that happens to them. They leave ruin and misery must be translated in many instances as a causative: "they cause ruin and misery," "they cause people to be destroyed and to suffer," or "they harm people and cause them to suffer."

Verse 17 must be taken to mean that these people never do anything to bring about peace with their fellowmen. Bringing about peace may be rendered as "cause people to know peace," "cause people to live in peace with one another," or "cause people to live together peacefully."

3.18 nor have they learned to fear God."

This quotation comes from Psalm 36.1. Both the TEV (nor have they learned to fear God) and the NEB ("and reverence for God does not enter their thoughts") translate dynamically, whereas most translations render literally a Semitic idiom which sounds odd to the English reader (note JB "there is no fear of God before their eyes").

The term for fear should indicate more than fright. There should be some indication of awesome respect. In some instances this may be expressed as "respect with trembling."

3.19 Now we know that everything in the Law applies to those who live under the Law, in order to stop all human excuses and bring the whole world under God's judgment.

It is generally agreed that the word Law in this passage refers to the entire Old Testament, the content of which Paul has summarized in verses 10-18. Paul reminds the Jews among his readers that the Law applies (literally "speaks") to those who live under the Law, that is, to the Jews; and so this means that the Jews themselves are guilty of the sins described in the previous verses. It has already been concluded that the Gentiles stand under God's judgment, and now the Jews also are shown to be guilty in God's sight, so the purpose of the Law is clearly to stop all human excuses and bring the whole world under God's judgment. In order to stop all human excuses (see NEB "so that no one may have anything to say in self-defence") translates another Semitic expression which is rendered literally by Goodspeed ("so that every mouth may be shut").

Everything in the Law may be rendered as "everything which is written in the Law" or "all the words of the Law." Applies to those may be translated as "speaks about those," "tells about those," or "relates to those."

The phrase under the Law is difficult to translate. In fact, rendered literally, it may convey a wrong meaning. For example, in some languages it indicates "the underworld" or "those who live in utter disregard of the Law." Under the Law may, however, be translated as "those who are obliged to keep the Law" or "those who bind themselves to behave according to the Law."

It is particularly important that the purpose clause beginning with in order to be related to the main verb of the first clause, namely, applies to rather than to any verb expression involved in the clause who live under the Law. In order to make this perfectly clear, one may have to translate: "the Law exists in order to stop all human excuses" or "...in order to prevent people from making all kinds of excuses."

The final phrase bring the whole world under God's judgment may be rendered in some languages as "cause everyone in the world to be subject to God's judgment," "cause that God's judgment will apply to all people," or "show that God will judge everyone in the world."

3.20 Because no man is put right in God's sight by doing what the Law requires; what the Law does is to make man know that he has sinned.

The scripture quotation in this verse comes from Psalm 143.2, with one significant addition: by doing what the Law requires. This phrase (literally "works of the Law") has reference to those things done in obedience to the Law and which may be looked upon in themselves as a means of establishing one in a right relationship with God.

Put right (in God's sight) renders the same verb that was used in 1.17 it will be further discussed in 3.24. Once again Paul reminds his readers that the purpose of the Law is not to give men salvation, but to make them know that they have sinned.

The basic relationship in the first part of verse 20 is that of result and means. By doing what the Law requires is the means of the first part of the sentence, though in a sense it is not the means, since no man is by this means put right in God's sight. This relationship may be expressed in some languages as "just because a man does what the Law requires does not mean that he is put right with God." In some languages this may be expressed as a condition—for example, "If a man does what the Law requires, that still does not mean that he is put right with God."

Since the second part of verse 20 is in contrast with the first, it may be necessary to introduce some adversative particle such as "but," "rather," or "on the other hand"—for example, "rather, the Law causes men to know that they have sinned."

How God Puts Men Right

21But now God's way of putting men right with himself has been revealed,
and it has nothing to do with law. The Law and the prophets gave their witness
to it: 22God puts men right through their faith in Jesus Christ. God does this
to all who believe in Christ, because there is no difference at all: 23all men have
sinned and are far away from God's saving presence. 24But by the free gift of
God's grace they are all put right with him through Christ Jesus, who sets
them free. 25God offered him so that by his death he should become the means
by which men's sins are forgiven, through their faith in him. God did this in
order to demonstrate his righteousness. In the past, he was patient and overlooked men's sins; 26but now in the present time he deals with men's sins, to
demonstrate his righteousness. In this way God shows that he himself is
righteous and that he puts right everyone who believes in Jesus.

27What, then, can we boast about? Nothing! And what is the reason for this?
Is it that we obey the Law? No, but that we believe. 28For we conclude that
a man is put right with God only through faith, and not by doing what the
Law commands. 29Or is God only the God of the Jews? Is he not the God of
the Gentiles also? Of course he is. 30God is one, and he will put the Jews right

with himself on the basis of their faith, and the Gentiles right through their faith. [31]Does this mean that we do away with the Law by this faith? No, not at all; instead, we uphold the Law.

The section heading How God Puts Men Right may require some slight modification—for example, "How God Puts Men Right with Himself" or "How God Causes Men to be Right with Himself."

Verse 21 introduces an important turning point in the letter. In 1.18—3.20 Paul has described in a negative fashion the sinfulness of mankind and the need that all men have for God. Now Paul makes a positive affirmation regarding what God has done to supply man's need of fellowship with him. Stated otherwise, the previous section (1.18—3.20) describes the wrath of God in judgment upon sin, while the present section (3.21—4.25) describes how God puts sinful men right with himself.

3.21 But now God's way of putting men right with himself has been revealed, and it has nothing to do with law. The Law and the prophets gave their witness to it:

But now is not merely a logical transition; it is also a temporal transition. For Paul all time is divided into two parts: the time before the revelation of the way in which God puts men right with himself, and the time after that. For similar transitions see 1 Corinthians 15.20; Ephesians 2.13; Hebrews 9.26. Paul indicates that the new age, the age of God's righteousness, has broken into the present age, the age of God's wrath. God's way of putting men right with himself translates the same expression used in 1.17 (literally "the righteousness of God"). Has been revealed translates a different verb from the one used in 1.17, though they are synonyms. What is important, however, is the fact that whereas the present tense was used in 1.17, the perfect tense is used here. This indicates a difference in focus. The former passage indicated how the Good News is presently revealing the way in which God puts men right with himself; the present passage points back to the one historical event (that is, the coming of Christ into the world) which forms the basis on which God puts men right with himself.

The passive expression has been revealed may, of course, be rendered active as "God has shown" or "God has revealed."

Paul further indicates that God's way of putting men right with himself has nothing to do with law, that is, with any sort of legalistic system. It seems better to understand law in this present context in the broad sense, as in the TEV (see also NEB "independently of law"), rather than to take it in the technical sense of the Jewish Law (see JB "outside the Law").

It may be necessary to restructure the clause it has nothing to do with law, in which law itself becomes the subject—for example, "the law has nothing to say about this," "the law is in no way related to putting men right with God," or even "the law is not the means of putting men right with God." However, an inversion of this clause must not negate the second sentence of verse 21 which indicates that, though the Law and the prophets are not the means for putting men right with God, they nevertheless gave witness to that means. In order to show this type of contrast, it may be necessary to introduce the final sentence of verse 21 with a particle such as "nevertheless" or "on the other hand"—for example, "nevertheless, the words of the Law and what the prophets said speak about this."

Paul further affirms that, even though God's way of putting men right with himself has nothing to do with any kind of legalistic system, the Law and the prophets (that is, the Old Testament) gave their witness to it.

On translating "law" (small l) in contrast with "Law" (a reference to the Old Testament Law) one can usually employ a plural expression such as "laws" or "regulations" or even "what one is obliged to do." Sometimes the general meaning of "law" may be indicated by the use of more than one term—for example, "It has nothing to do with laws and regulations," or even "Just because a man does what he should do does not mean that this is the way God puts men right with himself."

3.22 God puts men right through their faith in Jesus Christ. God does this to all who believe in Christ, because there is no difference at all:

In this verse Paul directs himself to the human side; that is, he tells what men must do in order for God to put them into a right relationship with himself. The answer is faith: God does this to all who believe in Christ. The last part of the verse serves as a transition to the following verse.

Though the first sentence of verse 22 seems to be somewhat of a summary of what is indicated at the end of verse 21, it would be wrong to translate in such a way as to imply that the first clause of verse 22 is a quotation from the Law and the prophets.

Through their faith in Jesus Christ is an expression of means, but in some languages this is normally communicated by a clause of cause—for example, "because they believe in Jesus Christ" or "since they trust Jesus Christ." If, however, a more specific indication of means can be employed, this should be done—for example, "by their trusting Jesus Christ" or "by means of their faith in Jesus Christ."

The expression there is no difference at all may require some expansion—for example, "there are no different ways in which God puts men right with himself." These words may also be taken as a reference to what follows, that is, to the lack of difference between Jews and Gentiles, since they are all sinners. In this case one may translate: "There is no difference at all between the Jews and the Gentiles. (23) All men have sinned...."

3.23 all men have sinned and are far away from God's saving presence.

In Greek verses 23-26 are all one sentence. This has been broken into several parts by the TEV for the sake of clarity.

There is a definite contrast in the tenses of the two verbs used in verse 23, have sinned and are far away. The expression which the TEV translates are far away from God's saving presence (literally "are falling short of the glory of God") may possibly be understood in another sense. "Glory" in this passage may refer not to God's saving presence, but to the likeness of God that each man is intended to bear but which has been forfeited because of sin. Most translations simply render this literally. Of the three modern translations that attempt to give meaning to this phrase, Phillips seems to have missed the meaning completely ("everyone falls short of the beauty of God's plan"), while the JB (see note in the JB) seems to go in the same direction as the TEV; the NEB ("are deprived of the divine splendor") seems to support the alternative interpretation explained here.

There are considerable difficulties involved in translating the expression far away from God's saving presence. One can, of course, say "far away from God who saves" and in essence this is the meaning of God's saving presence. "To fall short of the glory of God" may be rendered as "not to attain to the glory which comes from God" or "not to reach the glory which God gives."

3.24 But by the free gift of God's grace they are all put right with him through Christ Jesus, who sets them free.

By the free gift of God's grace (NEB "by God's free grace alone") is literally "as a free gift by his (God's) grace" (see JB "through the free gift of his grace"). The word free gift indicates that man contributes nothing toward being put in a right relationship with God, while the phrase "by God's grace" indicates that God supplies all that is necessary. In the phrase "by his grace" the possessive pronoun rendered God's in the TEV is in the emphatic position.

The expression of means in the phrase by the free gift of God's grace must be transformed into a verb expression in some languages, for example—"by means of God's showing his grace freely to people" or "because God shows his grace freely." This very emphatic expression may be reproduced in both a positive and negative manner, since free may need to be expressed as involving "no exchange"—for example, "since it is God who shows grace, and it is not an exchange gift."

Through Christ Jesus, who sets them free translates a noun expression in Greek "through the setting free in Christ Jesus." Although "setting free" is a noun in Greek, it describes an event rather than an object, and so is better rendered by a verb in English. This word is rendered in a variety of ways in the different translations—for example, "redemption" (RSV, NAB), "ransom" (Moffatt), "by being redeemed" (JB), "deliverance" (Goodspeed), and "act of liberation" (NEB). This particular word is used only once in the Septuagint (Daniel 4.34, which speaks of Nebuchadnezzar's recovery from his madness, "the time of my setting free came"), but other words derived from the same stem are used in a number of passages, especially in those which speak of God's setting his people free from Egypt. Although some of the Old Testament passages make mention of a price paid to effect the release, the emphasis is never on that aspect; the emphasis is rather on the result accomplished, that is, on the act of setting free. Paul uses this word once again in Romans (8.23), and it appears elsewhere in his writings in 1 Corinthians 1.30; Ephesians 1.7, 14; 4.30; Colossians 1.14. It is also found in Luke 21.28 and Hebrews 9.15; 11.35. In each of these passages the emphasis is upon the act of being set free, and in Ephesians 1.7 and Colossians 1.14 the setting free is specifically identified with the forgiveness of sins.

It may also be helpful to throw some further light on the verb translated put right. So far the verb has appeared three times in this letter (2.13; 3.4, 20), while its related noun form has appeared four times (1.17; 3.5, 21, 22). The verb itself is a causative stem, and means something like "to make right." The analogy that Paul has in mind is that of a law court. This then is not an ethical term, as though God's pronouncement made men morally upright or virtuous; rather it is used to indicate that God pronounces men acquitted or not guilty in his sight. In other words this is merely another term used to describe the way in which God forgives. The simplest way to express this idea in today's English is to say that God puts man into a right relationship with himself.

The serious difficulty of translation in verse 24 results from the two types of agents by which men are put right. God is, of course, the primary agent. He is the one who puts men right with himself. At the same time this verse specifies that it is done through Christ Jesus. In some languages the secondary agent must always be expressed by a causative verb—for example, "God causes Christ Jesus to put men right with God." In other instances, secondary agency is expressed by a paratactically combined clause which indicates the direct agent—for example, "God puts all men right with himself; Christ Jesus does this" or "God puts men right with himself; he did this by means of Christ Jesus, who sets them free."

This last phrase who sets them free is variously translated, depending upon the particular cultural context which is employed as a basis for the expression—for example, "he causes them to go out," "he causes them to be untied," or "he takes away the accusations against them."

3.25 God offered him so that by his death he should become the means by which men's sins are forgiven, through their faith in him. God did this in order to demonstrate his righteousness. In the past, he was patient and overlooked men's sins;

The verb rendered offered (RSV, Moffatt "put forward"; JB, Phillips "appointed"; NEB "designed") may be used with the special sense of "to offer as sacrifice" or even "to display publicly" (see Goodspeed "showed . . . publicly"). In 1.13 it is used in the sense of "to plan."

The phrase by his death (JB "to sacrifice his life"; NEB "by his sacrificial death"; Goodspeed "dying") is literally "by his blood," but "blood" is used in this passage in the same way that it is used in a number of other places in the New Testament, that is, to indicate a violent death. (See also the comments at 5.9.) The means by which men's sins are forgiven (see NEB "the means of expiating sin") is used in the Septuagint as a translation of "the mercy seat" that was a part of the covenant box (or ark), and so may also mean "the place where sins were forgiven" (see Hebrews 9.5, the only other occurrence of this word in the New Testament). Although this noun (and its related forms) is sometimes used by pagan writers in the sense of propitiation (that is, an act to appease or placate a god), it is never used this way in the Old Testament. There God never appears as the object of this noun (that is, the one who is placated), though God does appear as the subject with sin as the object, in which case the meaning is "God expiates (that is, forgives) sins." For this reason, the meaning of expiation (equivalent to TEV the means by which men's sins are forgiven) is a much more accurate translation than propitiation (see Moffatt and Phillips "the means of propitiation").

The Greek phrase "through faith" fits very loosely into the overall sentence structure, though it is generally agreed that it goes with the entire thought of the passage rather than with the words "in his blood" (TEV by his death). The TEV indicates this by making the object of "through faith" explicit (through their faith in him), while the NEB and the JB have placed "through faith" at the end of the sentence. As was mentioned earlier, verses 23-26 in the Greek text are one sentence, which the TEV makes into several shorter sentences. And in order to show the connection between the thought that follows and the earlier thought in this verse, the TEV introduces the second sentence with the words God did this. The verb to demonstrate (a noun phrase in Greek) includes in its meaning the idea of "to prove." To demonstrate his righteousness is taken by some translations (Moffatt, JB) to mean "to demonstrate his justice" (NEB). A major question, of course, is what does Paul mean by his use of "righteousness" in this context? If it refers to God's justice, then the thought is linked rather closely with what Paul says in verse 26, to demonstrate his righteousness. On the other hand, it is possible to understand the phrase to demonstrate his righteousness in light of what is said in the earlier part of verse 25 and so take it to mean "to demonstrate how God puts men right with himself." Moreover, this would have the advantage not only of carrying through the thought begun in the first part of this same verse, but also of tying in with what is said at the end of verse 26, in this way God shows...that he puts right everyone who believes in Jesus.

The concepts expressed in the first part of verse 25 are not only difficult, but the relations between the ideas are quite complex. The first sentence, particularly, involves a number of different relations of meaning. God offered him is the means for the purpose clause which begins with the conjunctive phrase so that. By his death is a phrase which indicates the means for the result he should become. By which men's sins are forgiven is another expression of means, and finally, through their faith in him expresses even an additional type of means. In order to express these relations in a fully intelligible manner one may have to semantically restructure this first sentence and to divide it into more than one sentence—for example, "God offered Christ so that he would become the one by whom men's sins are forgiven. Christ would do this by his death. By people's faith in Christ they would experience forgiveness," or "God offered Christ so that because Christ died he would cause men to have their sins forgiven; they would have their sins forgiven because they had faith in Christ."

In the second sentence of verse 25 the relations are not so complex; "God offered Christ" is merely the means to accomplish the purpose of showing how "he puts men right with himself."

God...was patient (literally "because of God's patience") comes from verse 26, where it concludes the clause begun in this verse. However, for English readers it more naturally comes first in the clause, and so it is placed there by the TEV (see also NEB "because in his forbearance he had overlooked the sins of the past"). Although it is possible that the verb rendered overlooked may instead mean "forgave" (see Phillips "by the wiping out of the sins of the past"), there seems to be very little support for that interpretation here. If Paul wanted to say that God had forgiven the sins of the past, he could easily have done so and made himself clear to his readers.

In the past may be translated in some instances as "before now," "up until now," or "in years that are gone."

In selecting a word for overlooked it is important not to imply that "God paid no attention to" or that "God was completely unaware of men's sins." Rather, one must indicate that God chose to pay no attention to such sins—for example, "God passed on as though the people had not sinned," "God refused to look at people's sins," or "God passed over sins."

3.26 but now in the present time he deals with men's sins, to demonstrate his righteousness. In this way God shows that he himself is righteous and that he puts right everyone who believes in Jesus.

The TEV uses the statement he deals with men's sins as a transitional device to make explicit the relation between the last part of verse 25 and the first part of verse 26: in the past, he...overlooked men's sins; but now in the present time he deals with men's sins.

God deals with men's sins may be translated as "God is concerned with men's sins" or "God does something about men's sins." Actually, in selecting a term for "is concerned with" it is important not to suggest that God was in the past in no way concerned with sin. It is only that he chose to overlook sin. It may, therefore, be necessary to point up the difference between the past and present by saying: "but now in the present time God does not overlook men's sins; instead he shows that he puts men right with himself."

To demonstrate renders essentially the same noun phrase in Greek that was used in the previous verse.

Paul's literal expression "so that he himself might be righteous" means, as the TEV indicates, in this way God shows that he himself is righteous (see NEB "showing that he is himself just"; JB "by showing positively that he is just"). He is righteous is perhaps best understood in the sense of "he does what is right."

3.27 What, then, can we boast about? Nothing! And what is the reason for this? Is it that we obey the Law? No, but that we believe.

In Greek Paul uses a further question ("through what kind of law?") in combination with an incorrect answer ("through [the law] of works?") and a strong negative response ("No!") to expand the answer (Nothing; literally "it was excluded") to his first question (What, then, can we boast about?). Then he gives the correct answer to the second question ("through [the law] of faith"). The TEV takes "law" to mean any sort of general rule or principle (see Moffatt, Goodspeed, NEB, RSV "on what principle?"), and considerably restructures the remainder of the verse. First, Paul's second question is made into a statement introducing an explanation (And what is the reason for this?). Then the two noun phrases ("through works" and "through faith") are transformed into verb phrases, while at the same time the idea of boasting is made explicit and the negative expression is rearranged: Is it that we obey the Law? No, but that we believe.

Even with the restructuring of verse 27, which is necessary to make the Greek text intelligible in English, considerable further restructuring may be required in some languages, especially in those which do not employ rhetorical questions together with answers. When questions and answers are excluded as a rhetorical device, one may translate as follows: "There is therefore nothing that a person may boast about, and the reason for this is that he is not put right with God because he obeys the law but simply because he believes." Even in instances where questions and answers may be employed in this very effective rhetorical structure of verse 27, it may be necessary to somewhat expand some of the expressions—for example, "What then can a man boast about? He can boast about nothing. Why can't he boast? Can he not boast because he obeys the Law and is in this way put right with God? No, indeed, he cannot, since he is put right with God not by obeying the Law but because he believes."

3.28 For we conclude that a man is put right with God only through faith, and not by doing what the Law commands.

And not by doing what the Law commands (see JB "and not by doing something the Law tells him to do") is literally "apart from the works of the Law," with "Law" understood as a reference to the Jewish Law.

In some languages means such as are expressed by the phrases through faith and not by doing what the Law commands may be expressed more specifically as cause—for example, "a man is put right with God only because he believes and not because he does what is commanded in the Law" or "...what God commands in the Law."

3.29 Or is God only the God of the Jews? Is he not the God of the Gentiles also? Of course he is.

It is important to point out that the argument here is a continuation of the one begun in verse 27. To Paul's question (What, then, can we boast about?) two answers are given. Paul says a man has nothing to boast about because (1) a man is put right with God only through faith, and not by doing what the Law commands; and (2) God is not only the God of the Jews, but he is also the God of the Gentiles.

There is a complex and subtle problem involved in the phrases the God of the Jews and the God of the Gentiles. This might appear to be the same kind of construction as so-called possessives "my God" or "our God" rendered in some languages as "the God in whom I believe" or "the God in whom we believe." However, it would not make sense to say "is God only the God in whom the Jews believe?" In some languages one must restructure this relation somewhat more explicitly as "is God related only to the Jews?" or "does God exist only for the sake of the Jews?" Quite naturally in languages for which such rhetorical questions are not possible, one must employ a statement—for example, "God of course exists for both Jews and Gentiles."

3.30 God is one, and he will put the Jews right with himself on the basis of their faith, and the Gentiles right through their faith.

This verse begins in Greek with a particle (eiper) that the NEB translates "if it be true" and that the RSV renders "since." This same particle appears in 8.9 as if, in fact and in 8.17 as for if. It indicates certainty (RSV "since") and not doubt, as may be implied by the NEB "if it be true." Since the particle in Greek suggests certainty, the TEV omits it translationally and begins this verse with the statement God is one. The Jews is literally "the circumcision" and the Gentiles is literally "the uncircumcision" (see comments on 2.26). Although Paul uses two different prepositions, one in reference to the Jews, on the basis of, and one in reference to the Gentiles, through, there is no significant difference in meaning between the two. Paul changes prepositions merely as a matter of style, and his argument is that Jews and Gentiles alike are put into a right relation with God only through faith.

Though the clause God is one might appear to be a general statement of monotheism, in reality it emphasizes that God is one and the same for both Jews and Gentiles. An equivalent in some languages may simply be "there is only one God for both Jews and Gentiles" or "God is the same for both Jews and Gentiles."

The phrases on the basis of their faith and through their faith may be expressed in some languages as means—for example, "by their trusting"—or as cause,—for example, "because they trust" or "because they believe." If it is necessary to specify a goal for terms of trust or faith, this may be "Jesus Christ" (see v. 22).

3.31 Does this mean that we do away with the Law by this faith? No, not at all; instead, we uphold the Law.

The verb translated do away with means "to make ineffective" and so "to render powerless" (NEB and Phillips use "undermine"; JB "make pointless"; Goodspeed "overthrow"). Do away with may be expressed idiomatically in some languages as "throw away the Law," "say that the Law is nothing," or "push the Law aside."

The final phrase by this faith may require some expansion—for example, "because people are put right with God on the basis that they trust him." A change from a question to a statement may be made by means of some such translation as "this does not in any sense mean that we are doing away with the Law by means of faith."

3.31

Uphold (NEB "we are placing law itself on a firmer footing") may also have the meaning of "to confirm" (see Goodspeed) or "to make valid" (JB "we are giving the Law its true value").

In verse 31 Paul uses the Law as a reference to the total religious system of Judaism, which finds its visible embodiment in the Old Testament. So Paul now turns to the Old Testament itself to prove that faith does not do away with the Law but rather upholds it. There is no other incident in the Old Testament likely to have more appeal to the Jews than the account of God's making the covenant with Abraham, and so in the following chapter Paul uses this passage in particular to establish his point.

CHAPTER 4

The Example of Abraham

4 What shall we say, then, of Abraham, our racial ancestor? What was his
experience? [2]If he was put right with God by the things he did, he would
have something to boast about. But he cannot boast before God. [3]The scripture
says, "Abraham believed God, and because of his faith God accepted him as
righteous." [4]A man who works is paid; his wages are not regarded as a gift,
but as something that he has earned. [5]But the man who has faith, not works,
who believes in the God who declares the guilty to be innocent, it is his faith
that God takes into account in order to put him right with himself. [6]This is
what David meant when he spoke of the happiness of the man whom God
accepts as righteous, apart from any works:

[7]"Happy are those whose wrongs God has forgiven,
whose sins he has covered over!
[8]Happy is the man whose sins the Lord will not keep
account of!"

The brief section heading The Example of Abraham may require expansion in one of two ways: either by adding some such element as "Shows the Importance of Faith," "Demonstrates how Important Faith Is," or by some modification in the rather technical term Example—for example, "The Story of Abraham Shows What Faith Does," "...How Important Faith Is," or "...How Essential It Is for a Man to Believe."

4.1 What shall we say, then, of Abraham, our racial ancestor? What was his experience?

Since Abraham was the father of the Jewish nation and was looked upon by them as being completely acceptable in God's sight, it will strengthen Paul's argument to point out that Abraham was put right with God through faith, rather than through obedience to the Law.

The translation of this verse is complicated by the presence of a textual problem. Some manuscripts omit altogether the words what was his experience? (see RSV, NEB, JB, NAB, Goodspeed). If these words are omitted, then the passage may be translated: "What, then, are we to say about Abraham, our racial ancestor?" Other manuscripts place these words (literally "what did he find?") in such a position in the sentence that they are connected with the phrase that the TEV renders racial (literally "according to the flesh"). In this case the words "according to the flesh" must be taken to mean something like "on his own," and the entire verse then rendered: "What did Abraham our ancestor accomplish on his own (that is, without God's grace)?" but apparently no modern translations follow this choice of text (Segond gives it as an alternative possibility, though accepting the same reading as the TEV in his text).

Most modern English translations prefer the shorter text, apparently assuming that the longer texts are the result of including a marginal note in the text. On the other hand, the Zürich Bible, Luther Revised, and Segond, along with the TEV, are in accord with the UBS Committee as to the Greek text. In favor of the UBS text is the diversity of manuscript evidence, which gives strong support to their choice of text, while the shorter reading has very little manuscript support.

Verse 1 presents a number of translational problems. In the first place, the rhetorical questions may need to be expressed as statements, "we should now speak of Abraham, our ancestor. The following was his experience" or "... this was what happened to him." However, a more difficult problem is involved in whether the inclusive or exclusive first person plural should be used in the phrase our racial ancestor. In his letter to the Romans Paul is obviously addressing an audience which is largely Gentile, as is clearly indicated in 1.6. Therefore it is necessary, in languages which do make a distinction in first person plurals, to use an exclusive form of "our" or to say "Abraham, the ancestor of the Jews." Similarly, the editorial we in the rhetorical question should be changed to "I" in a number of languages.

In a number of languages it is both confusing, as well as superfluous, to translate "according to the flesh," since a term for ancestor indicates specifically this kind of human relationship. Therefore, a term such as racial is often better omitted since it may constitute a misleading redundancy.

4.2 If he was put right with God by the things he did, he would have something to boast about. But he cannot boast before God.

According to certain rabbinic teachings of Paul's day, Abraham's faith gave him grounds to boast, not only before men but also before God. But it is Paul's intention to demonstrate through the following quotation from Scripture that Abraham had no grounds on which to boast before God.

The if clause of verse 2 may require some change, in view of the necessity in some languages of employing an active rather than a passive form—for example, "if God put Abraham right with himself by means of the things which Abraham did" or (as is more common in some languages) by an expression of cause: "if God put Abraham right with himself because of what Abraham did." In such inversions from active to passive it is essential that the appropriate reference to Abraham be clear.

The auxiliary cannot must be made somewhat more specific in some languages—for example, "he has no basis to boast" or "he has no reason to boast." Mere inability to boast is not sufficient in some languages.

4.3 The scripture says, "Abraham believed God, and because of his faith God accepted him as righteous."

The particle with which Paul begins this verse indicates that this is a continuation of the argument begun in the preceding verses. In some languages the most appropriate connective at this point would be an expression of cause—for example, "because the scripture says" or "the reason he cannot boast is that the scripture says."

Scripture (the reference is to Genesis 15.6) supports Paul's argument that God accepted Abraham as righteous only because Abraham believed God. Because of his faith God accepted him as righteous translates a passive construction in Greek ("it was counted to him for righteousness"). The agent indicated by the passive verb ("was counted") is God, and the subject ("it") is Abraham's faith. Thus the construction means that God accepted Abraham as righteous because of his faith. The phrase because of his faith may frequently be recast as a verb expression—for example, "because he believed God" or "because he trusted God." The term accepted may also be rendered as "regarded." This provides a basis for direct contrast with not regarded in verse 4. In fact, in some languages this may be rendered rather idiomatically as "looked at him as one who is," "counted him among those who are," or "put the mark of righteous on him."

4.4-5 A man who works is paid; his wages are not regarded as a gift, but as something that he has earned. (5) But the man who has faith, not works, who believes in the God who declares the guilty to be innocent, it is his faith that God takes into account in order to put him right with himself.

These verses are nothing other than an exegesis of the scripture quotation given in verse 3. Verse 4 is an illustration from everyday life: the man who works receives his wages from something he has earned, not as a gift. But despite the fact that matters of work and wages are commonplace, the semantic and syntactic construction of this verse may require considerable alteration—for example, "A man who works gets money for what he has done, but people do not say that his money is a gift; rather, they say that he earned it." The second clause of verse 4 may also be rendered as "but he does not think that his wages are something which the one who hired him gave him as a gift."

Verse 5 takes up where Paul left off in the previous verse. Here the contrast between "work and wages" and "faith and grace" is made clear. It is the faith of the believer that God takes into account, not the works of the man who tries to earn his own salvation. In these two verses there is a play on words which is almost impossible to introduce in a translation: regarded and takes into account are the same words in Greek. Declares... innocent renders the verb which is translated elsewhere to be put right with God. As indicated earlier, this verb was one which Paul took over from the law court; and he uses it to describe the man whom God had declared innocent in his court, and who therefore was in a right relation with God. In order to put him right with himself (literally "for righteousness") is actually a noun phrase, and has essentially the same meaning as the verb phrase just discussed.

The translation of verse 5 involves two principal problems. The first is in the rendering of works, and the second involves the rather extreme complexity of relations between the various events expressed in this rather long sentence.

One difficulty arises from the fact that there is an abrupt shift in the area of meaning of works from verse 4 to verse 5. In verse 4 work is to be understood in the ordinary sense of working for pay. In verse 5, however, the concern is not with work in the ordinary sense of physical activity but with "working for merit with God." In order to indicate this difference in the meaning of work in verse 5, some translators have transposed the first clause to follow the clause dealing with faith in God—for example, "the man who puts his faith in God rather than in his work" or "the man who trusts God rather than his work." This, however, still implies a rather specialized meaning for the word "work." Hence, in some languages "work" has been made quite specific—for example, "as for the man who does not work to gain merit with God" or "...to gain God's favor." But even in this instance it may be better to place the initial clause after the clause speaking of faith in God—for example, "as for the man who trusts God rather than trusting in what he does to gain God's favor."

Since there are seven different basic clause structures in verse 5, it is by no means easy to arrange them in such a manner that they will be clearly related one to another, particularly in languages in which words such as "faith" must be expressed as verbs, and in which the passives must be changed to actives. A proper treatment of the restrictive attributive clause who declares the guilty to be innocent complicates the picture even further, and in some instances the rearrangement requires certain radical shifts—for example, "But let us consider the man who trusts God rather than trusting in his works. God then takes into account the fact that this man trusts him and he says this guilty man is really innocent. In this way God puts the man right with himself." Or, "Let us think about the man who simply trusts God rather than trusting what he does to gain God's favor. It is God, of course, who can say this guilty man is innocent, and thus it is God who takes into account this man's faith in order to put the man right with God himself." As in all such instances of restructuring, it is essential that careful attention be paid to the pronominal reference in order to avoid misleading or awkward constructions.

4.6-8 This is what David meant when he spoke of the happiness of the man whom God accepts as righteous, apart from any works:

"Happy are those whose wrongs God has forgiven,
whose sins he has covered over!
Happy is the man whose sins the Lord will not keep
account of!"

The Jewish rabbis often used a method of exegesis by which they would appeal to two passages in which the same word occurred, and would use the second passage to throw light on the use of the word in the first passage. In Genesis 15.6 (quoted in v. 3 above) the writer used a word rendered accepted by the TEV. Paul uses this same word in verse 4, regarded as, and in verse 5, takes into account, and he now uses it again in verse 6, accepts. In the quotation from Psalm 32.1-2 (quoted in vv. 7 and 8) the word is used once more and is translated keep account of. By using a second scripture reference, Paul not only strengthens his argument based on the first scriptural proof, but also elaborates on it. That is, the quotation from Psalm 32 is intended to prove that the man whom God accepts as righteous, apart from any works, is a happy man. He is happy because God has forgiven his wrongs and has covered over his sins and not kept account of them.

It may be necessary to recast the clause when he spoke of the happiness of the man whom God accepts as righteous, because the happiness of the man may itself require expression as a separate clause—for example, "when he said the man whom God accepts as righteous is truly happy."

The final phrase apart from any works must normally be expressed as a complete clause—for example, "despite the fact that he had not worked to gain God's favor," "despite his not working in order to be accepted by God," or "despite his not having done anything so that God would accept him as righteous."

In speaking of works, Paul has reference to one's obedience to the commands of the Law by which one hopes to put God in one's debt, and so earn one's own salvation. This approach is, of course, opposite to what Paul talks about when he speaks about a man being put right with God through faith. Through works one seeks to earn salvation as the workman earns his wages; through faith one accepts salvation as a free gift from God, and so experiences God's forgiveness.

In the psalm that Paul quotes, the word rendered wrongs literally means "acts of lawlessness" (see NEB "lawless deeds") and is rendered "crimes" by the JB. It is not the usual word for sin, though it is used often in a way almost synonymous with the word rendered "sins." The word should be understood primarily in terms of one's attitude toward the commands of God, rather than toward the laws of society. For this reason Goodspeed renders "violations of the Law." The exclamatory form of the two clauses in verse 7 may be expressed in some languages as merely a strong affirmation—for example, "those whose bad deeds God has forgiven are truly happy. These are the persons whose sins have been covered." It is important in rendering verse 7 not to imply that there are two different kinds of persons who are happy—those whose evil deeds have been forgiven and those whose sins have been covered over. The two relative clauses are completely parallel and essentially synonymous; they simply reinforce each other.

In a number of languages it is necessary to avoid completely the expression of "sins being covered over," since this may be merely a way of talking about surreptitious sinning or hiding one's own sins. If one retains such an expression as covered over, it may be necessary to specify "covered over by God." It is frequently necessary, however, to change covered over to "blotted out," "removed," or "forgiven."

Will not keep account of may be rendered in a number of ways: "will not keep adding up," "will not keep marking down," or even "will not keep reciting each day."

> [9]Does this happiness that David spoke of belong only to those who are circumcised? No. It belongs also to those who are not circumcised. For we have quoted the scripture, "Abraham believed God, and because of his faith God accepted him as righteous." [10]When did this take place? Was it before or after Abraham was circumcised? Before, not after. [11]He was circumcised later, and his circumcision was a sign to prove that because of Abraham's faith God had accepted him as righteous before he had been circumcised. And so Abraham is the spiritual father of all who believe in God and are accepted as

righteous by him, even though they are not circumcised. [12]He is also the father of those who are circumcised, not just because they are circumcised, but because they live the same life of faith that our father Abraham lived before he was circumcised.

4.9 Does this happiness that David spoke of belong only to those who are circumcised? No. It belongs also to those who are not circumcised. For we have quoted the scripture, "Abraham believed God, and because of his faith God accepted him as righteous."

The rendering of this verse in the TEV is much longer than in the Greek text, because it is necessary to make explicit certain elements which the original readers understood clearly, but which would be easily missed by present-day readers. The question which Paul raises in this verse indicates an important transition in his argument, because according to certain Jewish rabbis the blessings described in Psalm 32 applied only to the people of Israel. Paul must now show that the happiness referred to in the psalm applies not only to the Jewish people but to the Gentiles as well. The TEV explains this happiness by the words that David spoke of in order to make clear the fact that Paul has reference to the quotation from the psalm made in the previous verse.

In translation it is often necessary either to transform rhetorical questions into statements or to make explicit the expected answer, as the TEV here does: No. It belongs also to those who are not circumcised.

We have quoted the scripture is literally "for we are saying." In this context the particle "for" is evidently used for the sake of furthering Paul's argument and of tying it to what he has previously said. In order to make his argument even stronger, Paul returns again to the passage in Genesis 15.6.

The initial rhetorical question and response may, of course, be rendered as an emphatic negative—for example, "This happiness that David spoke of does not belong merely to the circumcised" or "It is not merely those who are circumcised who experience this happiness that David spoke of." In some languages belongs...to may be more effectively rendered as "applies to" or "includes."

4.10 When did this take place? Was it before or after Abraham was circumcised? Before, not after.

When (so also JB) is literally "how" (RSV) and has been rendered "in what circumstances" by the NEB. Paul is not asking how God did this, as a literal rendering might imply; rather he is asking whether Abraham was circumcised or uncircumcised at the time, and so the nearest equivalent in English is when, since the next questions clarify fully the significance of this question.

Did...take place translates once again the word discussed in verse 6, and which appeared also in verses 3,4,5, and 8.

The rhetorical questions can, of course, be changed into positive statements—for example, "This took place before Abraham was circumcised, and not after he was circumcised." However, before and after may be variously expressed—for example, "This took place when Abraham was not yet circumcised;

it was not when he was already circumcised." It may even be necessary to be somewhat more specific in rendering the expression "this took place"—for example, "God accepted Abraham as righteous when he was not yet circumcised."

4.11 He was circumcised later, and his circumcision was a sign to prove that because of Abraham's faith God had accepted him as righteous before he had been circumcised. And so Abraham is the spiritual father of all who believe in God and are accepted as righteous by him, even though they are not circumcised.

In Greek verses 11 and 12 are actually one long, involved sentence. For this reason the TEV, along with most other modern translations, breaks this sentence into several smaller units. The first part of verse 11 is literally "and he received a sign of circumcision as a seal of the righteousness of the faith of the in-his-uncircumcision." "In his uncircumcision" has been rendered by the TEV as before he had been circumcised; but for the sake of the continuity of Paul's arguments, this information is also introduced in the first part of this verse: he was circumcised later. Moreover, since the word "seal" is in apposition to "sign," the TEV brings them together and interprets them to mean a sign to prove. In the JB these words are rendered "as a sign and guarantee." The NEB accepts the same exegetical point of view, but employs a more sophisticated expression: "the symbolic rite...as the hall-mark." If the initial clause he was circumcised later must be made active, only a reflexive construction can be employed, "he circumcised himself later" or "it was after God accepted him as righteous that he circumcised himself."

The TEV also transforms a number of other genitive phrases into unambiguous expressions. "Sign of circumcision" obviously means his circumcision was a sign. The next two "of" phrases ("of the righteousness of faith") are more difficult. We have already pointed out that the TEV takes the two terms "sign" and "seal" together to mean a sign to prove, and so it seems best to take these two phrases as the content of what this sign was intended to prove. In this context "righteousness" refers once again to God's activity of accepting men as righteous, while "faith" is a specific reference to Abraham's faith in God. So then the entire construction may be taken to mean (a sign to prove) that because of Abraham's faith God had accepted him as righteous. The last "of" phrase ("of the in-his-uncircumcision") has already been alluded to and is not difficult; "of the" refers back to "faith" and so is a reference to Abraham's faith that he had at the time he was uncircumcised.

In a number of languages the closest equivalent for sign is "a mark," or, more specifically, "a wound to show" or "a scar to show." The phrase because of Abraham's faith may be expressed as a complete clause—for example, "to prove that God had accepted Abraham as righteous because he trusted God." In some languages the final clause of the first sentence before he had been circumcised may seem unduly repetitious and redundant since the same information is expressed by the first clause he was circumcised later.

And so translates an infinitive expression in Greek which may either indicate purpose or result. If a choice has to be made, purpose is more natural. The connection of this sentence with what has preceded may be expressed in some languages as "and this happened to show that Abraham is...."

The word "father" is taken by the TEV to mean spiritual father, so as not to imply that Abraham was the literal ancestor of all who believe in God in the same way that he did (see JB "the ancestor of all uncircumcised believers"). The equivalent of spiritual father is in some languages merely "is like a father" or "may be thought of as a father." This removes the possibility of regarding Abraham as the actual ancestor of all who believe and thus restricting faith to Jews. In some languages the more appropriate equivalent for father would be "grandfather" or "ancestor." In still other languages a more idiomatic expression may be employed—for example, "the root" or "the headwaters."

Of all who believe in God is literally "of all those believing," but the reference is obviously to belief in God. In the phrase accepted as righteous by him (RSV "have righteousness reckoned to them") Paul once again uses the word translated accepted in verse 3.

4.12 He is also the father of those who are circumcised, not just because they are circumcised, but because they live the same life of faith that our father Abraham lived before he was circumcised.

The grammar of this verse is difficult, though the meaning is clear. Paul is saying that those who are circumcised (that is, the Jewish people) have Abraham as their father, not just because they are circumcised, but because they live the same life of faith. It should be pointed out that translations such as the NEB ("the circumcised as do not rely upon their circumcision alone") and the JB ("who though circumcised do not rely on that fact alone"), though consistent with the grammatical structure of this verse, do not seem to be consistent with what Paul is saying. These translations imply that those who are circumcised can rely on their circumcision in part ("not...alone") and also on their faith in part ("but also..."). Goodspeed is quite clear, "those circumcised persons who not only share his circumcision but follow our forefather Abraham's example...."

Live the same life of faith is literally "walking in the footprints of faith." The JB renders this "follow...along the path of faith," while the NEB has "walk in the footprints of the faith." The expression "to walk" is frequently used in the Old Testament as the equivalent of "to live a life."

They live the same life of faith cannot be rendered literally in most languages. One can, however, say in a number of instances "as they live they trust God," "they live by trusting God," or "they live constantly trusting God." That our father Abraham lived may then be rendered as "in the same way that our father Abraham lived." The full expression may then be translated as "they trusted God in the same way our father Abraham trusted and lived."

God's Promise Received through Faith

[13]God promised Abraham and his descendants that the world would belong to him. This promise was made, not because Abraham obeyed the Law, but

because he believed and was accepted as righteous by God. [14]For if what God promises is to be given to those who obey the Law, then man's faith means nothing and God's promise is worthless. [15]The Law brings God's wrath; but where there is no law, there is no disobeying of the law.

The section heading God's Promise Received through Faith may be rendered as "Because Abraham Trusted God He Received What God Promised." This, however, may produce a rather long and unnecessarily involved section heading, and one may simply use a title such as "God Makes a Promise to Abraham" or "God Makes a Promise to Those Who Trust Him."

In this passage Paul continues the theme discussed in verses 9-12. Just as Abraham was put right with God through faith, and not through obedience to the Law, so this promise of righteousness through faith extends to all people.

4.13 God promised Abraham and his descendants that the world would belong to him. This promise was made, not because Abraham obeyed the Law, but because he believed and was accepted as righteous by God.

The TEV (see also RSV and JB) restructures this verse rather considerably for its English readers; the NEB ("for it was not through law that Abraham, or his posterity, was given the promise...") follows very much the Greek word order. God promised Abraham and his descendants is literally "the promise to Abraham or to his seed." The noun phrase in Greek ("the promise to Abraham") must be restructured into a verb phrase for English readers; and so many modern translations render this by a passive verb construction (NEB "was given"; JB "was made"), while the RSV speaks of the promise coming to Abraham. The promise, of course, did not come on its own, it was given; and since God is the one who gave it, the TEV makes this information explicit: God promised.

In Hebrew to speak of one's "seed" is to speak of one's descendants, and most translations render "his seed" by his descendants.

In some languages his descendants are simply "his children" or "his grandchildren." In other instances one may employ "those who followed after him" or "those who came down from him."

That the world would belong to him is literally "that he would be heir of the world." In biblical language the noun "heir" frequently means simply "one who receives or gains possession of something," without the necessity of a death involved, as the English word often implies. So then, the expression "heir of the world" merely means the world would belong to him. The reference is probably to Genesis 22.17-18 (see also 18.18), and it is interesting to note that the Hebrew text of Genesis 22.17 has "will possess" while the Septuagint reads "will inherit."

In view of the fact that the promise was made to both Abraham and his descendants, it may be necessary to employ the pronoun "them" at the end of this first sentence—for example, "that the world would belong to them" or "that they should inherit the world."

In Greek verse 13 is one sentence, and the words this promise was made, not because Abraham obeyed the Law appear first in the Greek sentence structure (literally "for not through law"). The force of this construction in Greek is to emphasize the words "for not through law." However, since the subject of the sentence in Greek is "the promise," it is more natural in English to introduce this information first, and then qualify it later. That is why so many modern translations, including the TEV, restructure the order of the Greek sentence. This promise was made may be shifted into an active form by saying "God made this promise" or "God promised Abraham."

Throughout Romans Paul uses the word "law" in a variety of ways, and it is not always easy to discern which particular meaning he has in mind in a given passage. In the present context the TEV understands "law" as a specific reference to the Jewish Law (so also Moffatt, Goodspeed, Phillips, and so it seems, the RSV), while the NEB ("it was not through law") and the JB ("was... on account of any law") take it in a more general sense. To be sure, it is in keeping with Paul's thought that no man can be put right with God through any sort of legalistic religious system, but in the present context he seems to be dealing specifically with the Jewish Law in this regard.

Obeyed the Law may be rendered as "did what the Law said he should do," "followed the words of the Law," or, negatively, "did not transgress against what the Law said."

But because he believed and was accepted as righteous by God (literally "but through righteousness of faith") renders essentially the same phrase discussed in verse 11 above.

It may be necessary to relate but because he believed and was accepted as righteous by God as "but because he believed and as a result was accepted as righteous by God," "... and therefore was accepted as righteous by God," or "... and hence God accepted him as righteous."

4.14 For if what God promises is to be given to those who obey the Law, then man's faith means nothing and God's promise is worthless.

For if what God promises is to be given to those who obey the Law is literally "for if the heirs are from the law." "Heirs" must be understood in the sense mentioned in verse 13; and "from the law" refers to persons who obey the (Jewish) Law. In Paul's literal expression "faith has been emptied," "faith" is certainly to be taken in the sense of man's faith, and the verb "to be empty" (NEB "faith is empty") must be taken in the extended sense of "empty of all meaning" (Moffatt), that is, means nothing. This same verb occurs in 1 Corinthians 1.17 (robbed of its power) and is used in 1 Corinthians 9.15 in combination with "boasting" (to turn my rightful boast into empty words; see also 2 Corinthians 9.3 that our boasting... may not turn out to be empty words). The Greek expression "the promise" refers, of course, to God's promise. The verb is worthless (JB "worth nothing"; Goodspeed "amounts to nothing") has as its basic meaning "to make powerless or inoperative," and is a favorite verb of Paul's, appearing some twenty-five times in his writings.

It is not easy to relate verse 14 to the preceding verse, and the introductory structure, as indicated by the TEV sequence for if what, is particularly complex. In some languages one may restructure this as follows: "But let us suppose that God promises to give to those who obey the Law; if that were the case, then a man's trust in God would have no value, and the fact that God had made a promise would not have any worth." In some instances man's faith means nothing may be rendered as "it is worth nothing if a man trusts God" or "it helps not in the least if a man trusts God." Likewise, God's promise is worthless may be rendered as "it means nothing at all that God had made a promise" or "God may have promised, but this is of no value."

4.15 The Law brings God's wrath; but where there is no law, there is no disobeying of the law.

Paul's first reference to Law in this verse is literally "the law," which is most naturally taken to mean the (Jewish) Law (see Goodspeed and Moffatt), though the NEB and the JB take it simply in a general sense of "law." The RSV seems also to take this as a reference to the Jewish Law, though the phrase "the law" is ambiguous inasmuch as "law" is not written with a capital. It is generally agreed that the second reference to "law" in this passage is a reference to law in general, and not to the Jewish Law in particular.

In a number of languages it is extremely difficult to distinguish between Law, as a specific reference to the Old Testament Law, and law in general. Capitalization may be of some assistance to those who read the text, but it has no value to those who merely hear the reading; and since many more people are likely to hear a text read than read it for themselves, capitalization is of limited value. In some languages this distinction may be made by translating Law (capitalized) as "the Law of Moses" or "the Law which came through Moses," while the more generic meaning of law (with lower case) may be translated as "laws" or "regulations."

The verb rendered brings (NEB, RSV; Goodspeed "brings down") has as its basic meaning "to bring about" (see Moffatt "produces"). Paul is here speaking of a reality, not of a possibility, and so the JB falls short of his meaning "involves the possibility of." However, the JB does give a footnote indicating that this means literally "for law brings." Although Paul merely says "wrath" the reference is to God's wrath (see also Goodspeed), and the TEV makes this information explicit. On the meaning of wrath see 1.18.

In most languages one cannot speak about the "Law bringing down wrath." However, a causative may be employed—for example, "the Law causes God's wrath" or "the Law causes God's judgment."

Disobeying (of the law) (JB "breaking the law"; NEB "breach of law"; Goodspeed "violation of it [law]") translates the word usually rendered "transgression," a word not in general use among speakers of American English. The final two clauses in verse 15 may be treated as conditional—for example, "but if there are no regulations, then one cannot disobey the regulations" or "if laws do not exist, then no one can violate the laws."

4.16

> 16The promise was based on faith, then, in order that the promise should be
> guaranteed as God's free gift to all of Abraham's descendants—not just those
> who obey the Law, but also those who believe as Abraham did. For Abraham
> is the spiritual father of us all; 17as the scripture says, "I have made you father
> of many nations." So the promise is good in the sight of God, in whom
> Abraham believed—the God who brings the dead to life and whose command
> brings into being what did not exist. 18Abraham believed and hoped, when
> there was no hope, and so became "the father of many nations." Just as the
> scripture says, "Your descendants will be this many." 19He was almost one
> hundred years old; but his faith did not weaken when he thought of his body,
> which was already practically dead, or of the fact that Sarah could not have
> children. 20His faith did not leave him, and he did not doubt God's promise;
> his faith filled him with power, and he gave praise to God. 21He was absolutely
> sure that God would be able to do what he had promised. 22That is why
> Abraham, through faith, "was accepted as righteous by God." 23The words "he
> was accepted as righteous" were not written for him alone. 24They were written
> also for us who are to be accepted as righteous, who believe in him who raised
> Jesus our Lord from death. 25He was given over to die because of our sins, and
> was raised to life to put us right with God.

In verse 15 Paul made a brief digression, referring to material that he will discuss more fully in 5.12-14 and 7.7-13. Now he returns to his main argument, that is, that promise and faith go together, and that these have their origin in God's grace (v. 16). He returns once again to the experience of Abraham to validate his argument (17-22), and then makes application of Abraham's experience to the life of believers generally (23-25).

4.16 The promise was based on faith, then, in order that the promise should be guaranteed as God's free gift to all of Abraham's descendants—not just those who obey the Law, but also those who believe as Abraham did. For Abraham is the spiritual father of us all;

This verse is closely related to verse 14 and is introduced in Greek by a phrase rendered "that is why" in several translations (Moffatt, Goodspeed, RSV, JB). However, it is possible that the English reader may fail to see that this verse relates back to verse 14, and so the TEV makes the relation explicit: the promise was based on faith (as a rendering of Paul's words "this is why on the basis of faith"). The NEB is very close to the TEV: "the promise was made on the ground of faith."

This introductory clause the promise was based on faith may need to be somewhat more explicit in some languages—for example, "God made his promise because Abraham trusted him" or "God's promise rested on Abraham's believing."

In the second clause of this sentence, in order that the promise should be guaranteed as God's free gift..., the words rendered God's free gift are in the stressed position in the Greek sentence structure. God's free gift is literally "grace," and it has been rendered in a variety of ways: "a free gift" (JB), "a matter of sheer grace" (NEB), "God's favor" (Goodspeed), and "God's gift"

(Twentieth Century). To all of Abraham's descendants is literally "to all the seed" (see v. 13 above).

It is by no means easy to relate the promise and God's free gift. In some instances this may be done by saying: "what God had promised would be shown clearly to be God's gift" or "what God promised would be clearly what God had given freely to all of Abraham's offspring."

The last clause of this sentence is translated in a number of different ways, but the meaning is clear. It is important that the translator realize that the words those who believe as Abraham did refer, not to the content of what Abraham believed, but to the fact that Abraham did believe God.

This similarity of faith may be expressed more effectively in some instances by using a verb for "trust"—for example, "who trusted God as Abraham trusted him."

Spiritual father is literally "father" (see v. 11 above). It may be of some value for the translator to see the contrasts in this verse and the previous verse: verse 15 speaks of law, disobeying the law, and of God's wrath; verse 16 speaks of God's promise, man's faith, and God's free gift.

The first person plural us in the phrase father of us all must, of course, be rendered as inclusive for those languages which do make a distinction between the inclusive and exclusive first person plural, since us in this context must include both Jews and Gentiles.

4.17 as the scripture says, "I have made you father of many nations." So the promise is good in the sight of God, in whom Abraham believed—the God who brings the dead to life and whose command brings into being what did not exist.

Since Paul has just concluded that Abraham is the spiritual father of us all (v. 16), it is important that he be able to base this judgment on a passage of scripture, and he finds the appropriate passage in Genesis 17.5: I have made you father of many nations. The word rendered nations is the word which Paul customarily uses in the sense of "Gentiles."

Though a number of languages employ a causative for an expression such as I have made you father (for example, "I have caused you to become father"), the same relationship may be expressed in other ways—for example, "many nations will be your children," "the people of many nations will call you their father," or, in direct discourse, "the people of many nations will say to you, You are our father."

In Greek all of verse 17 is a continuation of the sentence begun at the first of verse 16. Following the scripture quotation there is a phrase which is difficult to fit in grammatically with the rest of the sentence, and so it has been understood in several different ways. The phrase to which reference is made is translated by the TEV as in the sight of God and is related to the context by the inclusion of the words so the promise is good. Both Goodspeed ("the promise is guaranteed in the very sight of God") and NEB ("this promise, then, was valid before God") employ the same solution. On the other hand, a number of commentators understand this as a reference back to Abraham (see JB "Abraham is our father in the eyes of God"). Phillips relates this to the idea of faith, and so translates: "this faith is valid because of the existence of God himself," a conclusion which does not seem to be supported by other scholars. It is difficult to tell what this phrase means in the RSV, since the construction is ambiguous and almost impossible to relate grammatically to the remainder of the sentence.

It is extremely difficult to translate in some languages the promise is good in the sight of God. This would seem to imply that God saw the promise as good, but since God himself had made the promise, such a relationship would appear to be strange. Accordingly, in some languages, the closest equivalent is "the promise is good because of God," "because of who God is, his promise is valid," or "his promise has strength." The phrase in whom Abraham believed may then be rendered as "this is the God in whom Abraham believed."

Paul's words "calls into existence the things that do not exist" (RSV) are to be taken as a reference to God's creative power: whose command brings into being what did not exist. Viewed from Paul's perspective, the man who believes turns his attention away from himself and to God, who is the source of all power and life.

Who brings the dead to life may be rendered as "who causes the dead to live again," "who causes the dead to come back to life," or "the one who causes those who were dead now to live."

The final clause of verse 17, whose command brings into being what did not exist, is difficult for two reasons. First, it must usually be translated as direct discourse following a verb such as command; and second, the content of the command is general rather than specific. Hence, two types of adaptations need to be made: first, to produce direct discourse, and, second, to employ more specific terms—for example, "and he commands, That which did not exist before must exist now." In some languages, however, one cannot speak of existence apart from perception. The closest equivalent of nonexistence is "what has never been seen" and to exist is "to be seen." Therefore, one may need to translate as "God commands, What people have never seen they can now see." In other instances the equivalent of exist is "live," and therefore one must translate: "God commands, That which never lived before lives now."

4.18 Abraham believed and hoped, when there was no hope, and so became "the father of many nations." Just as the scripture says, "Your descendants will be this many."

In Greek this verse begins with the relative pronoun "who," which is made explicit as a reference to Abraham by the TEV and others (so JB and Goodspeed). In this verse appears an idiomatic expression (literally "beyond hope on hope"), which is interpreted in substantially the same way by all translations, though expressed somewhat differently in each. In keeping with a number of other translations, the TEV transforms this noun phrase into a verb followed by a noun phrase: hoped, when there was no hope. In this context hoped is essentially the same as believed, and so what is meant is that Abraham continued to believe in

God even when all grounds for human hope were gone. Paul is here pointing out, of course, that Abraham became the father of many nations simply because he believed and hoped in the one who said to him, Your descendants will be this many.

In many languages it is particularly difficult to find a satisfactory term for "hope," largely because of the combination of somewhat diverse components expressed by this same term. Essentially, hope combines the components of "confidence," "waiting," and "favorable outcome," and is expressed by a phrase in some languages, "to await expectantly for good," "to wait with confidence for good," or "to wait in one's heart for desired things." To combine hope with an attributive phrase such as when there was no hope makes this first sentence of verse 18 even more complex. This may be rendered, however, in some languages as "waited in confidence when there was no reason for him to wait this way." In some languages believed and hoped are combined as "in expecting he believed strong against the thing that made him doubt."

4.19-21 He was almost one hundred years old; but his faith did not weaken when he thought of his body, which was already practically dead, or of the fact that Sarah could not have children. (20) His faith did not leave him, and he did not doubt God's promise; his faith filled him with power, and he gave praise to God. (21) He was absolutely sure that God would be able to do what he had promised.

These verses are intended to use a specific illustration from the life of Abraham to show how he believed and hoped when there was no more hope. In Greek these three verses are one sentence, and as one can readily understand, they have to be rather radically restructured in order to sound natural in English. From an exegetical point of view, these verses are not particularly difficult, and therefore they require only a few comments. The emphatic element in the Greek sentence structure is a clause rendered but his faith did not weaken.

Almost one hundred years old may be rendered in a number of different ways—for example, "he was not yet one hundred years old," "he lacked only a little of being one hundred years old," "he had one hundred years not yet," or "in a little while he would be one hundred years old." An expression such as "he was not yet one hundred years old" might seem to focus upon "youngness" rather than "oldness," but in many languages "almost" can only be expressed in terms of "not yet" or "not quite."

His faith did not weaken may be rendered positively as "his trust in God continued strong." The clause when he thought of his body may be made somewhat more emphatic as "even when he thought of his body," or, in the form of direct discourse, "even when he thought to himself, My body is practically dead," or "even when he said to himself, My body is dead, as it were, almost." The final clause the fact that Sarah could not have children is, of course, also a part of Abraham's thought and therefore may be incorporated as part of the direct discourse—for example, "even when he said to himself, My body is almost dead and my wife Sarah cannot give birth to children," "... cannot have a baby," or "... cannot produce a baby from her womb."

His faith did not leave him, and he did not doubt God's promise is literally "he did not doubt the promise of God by unbelief" (see NEB "never doubted God's promise in unbelief"). It is interesting to observe what other modern translations in English do with this passage. The RSV, which often employs a formal translation, renders this passage rather dynamically: "no distrust made him waver concerning the promise of God"; while Goodspeed, which often uses very contemporary English, renders: "he did not incredulously question God's promise."

In a number of languages one cannot speak of "faith leaving a person." One may, of course, "no longer trust" or "give up believing," so that an equivalent may be "Abraham did not give up believing" or, expressed positively, "Abraham kept on believing." In some languages it is difficult to express doubt about a promise except by means of some direct discourse—for example, "he did not say, God's promise is impossible" or "he did not reason in himself, What God has promised cannot possibly happen." Because of the relation of verse 20 to verse 19, it may be appropriate to introduce the two expressions with regard to faith and doubt with some such connective as "moreover" or "furthermore."

The clause which the TEV renders his faith filled him with power is understood in this same sense by most modern translations (see, for example, Phillips "he drew strength from his faith" and JB "drew strength from faith"); but some take it to mean either that Abraham grew strong in faith, or that his faith was confirmed and so strengthened (see Moffatt "his faith won strength").

Because of the contrast between the first and second parts of verse 20, one may introduce the latter part by some adversative conjunction—for example, "but rather his faith filled him with power." However, the expression his faith filled him with power may more frequently be expressed as "he became strong because of his faith" or "...because he trusted God."

In some languages praise to God can only be expressed as direct discourse —for example, "he said, God, you are wonderful" or "he said to God, You are great."

In verse 21 the Greek does not explicitly mention God (see NEB "in the firm conviction of his power to do what he had promised"), though many modern translations make the reference to God explicit: he was absolutely sure that God would be able to do what he had promised.

An expression such as he was absolutely sure may be expressed in some languages as direct discourse—for example, "he said to himself with confidence, God is surely able to do what he has promised me."

4.22 That is why Abraham, through faith, "was accepted as righteous by God."

It should be noted that the TEV rendering of this verse consists of twelve words (so also the NEB) while the Greek has only six words, one of which is a preposition and two of which are particles. However, the demands of communication require that the translation in English be rendered by more words than exist in the Greek text. The Greek begins with two particles which are rendered by the TEV that is why Abraham through faith. In the Greek sentence structure it is clear that these particles refer back to Abraham's faith, and so a number of other translations also make this connection explicit (see NEB "Abraham's faith"; Goodspeed, Moffatt "his faith"). Was accepted as righteous by God is a quotation from Genesis 15.6 and is so placed within quotation marks in the TEV. On this quotation see the comments on verses 2 and 9.

Through faith may be expressed in some languages as means—for example, "was accepted as righteous by God by means of his trusting God"—or more specifically as cause—for example, "was accepted as righteous by God because he believed."

4.23 The words "he was accepted as righteous" were not written for him alone.

In Paul's argument this verse is transitional. Paul has demonstrated on the basis of scripture that Abraham was accepted as righteous by God through faith, and now he begins to show how this applies also to everyone else who has faith.

4.24 They were written also for us who are to be accepted as righteous, who believe in him who raised Jesus our Lord from death.

As already pointed out, in Greek verses 23-25 form a single sentence. The TEV breaks the sentence here and renders the Greek conjunctions "but also" by they were written also. It is best to take the verb which Paul has used here (TEV are to be accepted as righteous) as an eschatological reference (that is, a reference to the final day of judgment) rather than as a timeless present. In this verse Paul also makes it clear that the same God who accepted Abraham as righteous is the one who accepts the Christian believer as righteous. Moreover, the Christian's faith is the same as that which Abraham had, for it is directed toward the God who is able to bring life out of death. Abraham believed in God who was able to bring life out of Sarah's dead womb; the Christian believes in God who raised Jesus our Lord from death.

The expression they were written also for us may be rendered more appropriately in some languages as "these words also apply to us" or "... speak to us." The future passive implied in the expression who are to be accepted as righteous may be rendered as "whom God will accept as righteous." The final relative clause, who believed in him who raised Jesus our Lord from death, may be understood as merely another attributive of us, or it may be understood in a somewhat causal sense—for example, "because we believe in God who raised Jesus our Lord from death," "... caused Jesus our Lord to come back to life," or "... to live again."

4.25 He was given over to die because of our sins, and was raised to life to put us right with God.

The first part of this verse, he was given over to die because of our sins, is an allusion to Isaiah 53.4,5; and it reflects a kind of Jewish parallelism (see RSV "who was put to death for our trespasses and raised for our justification").

The verb given over to die literally means "to give over" (see 1.24, 26, 28), but in this context the meaning is "to give over to die" (compare its use in 8.32 where the TEV translates by offered).

In Greek the same preposition is used in each clause and is ambiguously rendered by the RSV as "for." Most commentators appear to take the first "for" as retrospective or causal ("because of our sins"), though Goodspeed seems to take it prospectively ("to make up for our offenses"). On the other hand, the second "for" is usually taken in a prospective or final sense, to put us right with God (JB "to justify us"; Goodspeed "to make us upright"; Phillips "to secure our justification"; Moffatt "that we might be justified"). It is possible, though not as well in keeping with the context, to understand the second "for" as retrospective (see the alternative rendering in the NEB, "raised to life because we were now justified"). The translator should keep in mind that there is no separation in Paul's thinking between the significance of Christ's death and resurrection; they are inseparable events, because they both describe the mighty act of God by which we are brought into a right relationship with him and our sins are forgiven.

The passive expression he was given over to die may be rendered as active: "God gave Christ over to die," "God allowed Christ to die," or "God handed Christ over to people and they killed him."

Because of our sins is most frequently translated as "because we had sinned" or "because we had done evil." The passive expression was raised to life may likewise be made active with God as the agent—for example, "God caused him to live again in order that we would be put right with God," "... in order to put us right with God," or "... right with himself."

CHAPTER 5

Right with God

5 Now that we have been put right with God through faith, we have peace
with God through our Lord Jesus Christ. [2]He has brought us, by faith,
into this experience of God's grace, in which we now live. We rejoice, then,
in the hope we have of sharing God's glory! [3]And we also rejoice in our
troubles, because we know that trouble produces endurance, [4]endurance brings
God's approval, and his approval creates hope. [5]This hope does not disappoint
us, because God has poured out his love into our hearts by means of the Holy
Spirit, who is God's gift to us.

The section heading Right with God may be too fragmentary in some languages and thus must be somewhat amplified—for example, "God Puts Us Right with Himself" or "We Are Now Right with God."

Romans 5 begins a new section in the letter. This can be seen not only by the solemn conclusion of 4.23-25, but also by the content of chapter 5 itself. In 5.1-11 Paul indicates that all other gifts are contained in the gift of a right relation with God; then in the last half of the chapter (vv. 12-21) he contrasts the old humanity with the new and the way of death with the way of eternal life. Also contained within this chapter are themes that are developed later in the letter; for example, compare 5.1-11 with chapter 8, and 5.12-21 with chapter 6.

Paul began his letter by demonstrating that all persons, Gentiles and Jews alike, stand in need of being put into a right relation with God (1.18—3.20). Next, he indicated how this right relation with God was made possible (3.21-30). Then he demonstrated the truth of his argument from the experience of Abraham, bringing in the testimony from the Psalms as validation (4.1-25). Now, in chapters 5 through 8, Paul indicates some of the results of being placed in a right relation with God.

5.1 Now that we have been put right with God through faith, we have peace with God through our Lord Jesus Christ.

In Greek this verse and the next verse are one sentence. Now that we have been put right with God (two words in Greek) stands emphatic in the Greek sentence structure and relates closely to what was said in 4.25. There is, however, a serious textual problem in this verse and the choice of texts is not easy. As far as the written form of the Greek is concerned, there is a difference of only one letter, and evidently the spoken Greek of the first century A.D. did not differentiate in the sounds between the two letters involved. The difference in meaning is whether Paul said we have peace or "let us have peace." If Paul said "let us have peace," then it is best taken in the sense represented by the NEB ("let us continue at peace"). Otherwise it could imply that the person who has been put into a right relation with God might have the choice of deciding whether or not he wanted to be at peace with God. In Paul's thinking, however, to be in a right relation with God is to be at peace with God. On the other hand, in support of the reading we have peace is the observation that the entire passage (vv. 1-11) is written in the indicative (except for the possibility of two subjunctive forms in vv. 2 and 3). Moreover, the use of "but not only" (TEV and . . . also) is more in keeping with the indicative than it is with the subjunctive usage. Finally, it is easy to see how, as this passage was used in preaching, the indicative was changed to the subjunctive in order to make the passage into a type of exhortation to the church of that day. All in all, the context favors the reading of we have peace, though the manuscript evidence points the other way.

The introductory transition now that may, of course, be rendered as cause —for example, "because we have been put right with God." However, the expression through faith also introduces either means or cause, and the entire initial clause may be rendered as "since God has put us right with himself because we trust him."

Both in the Old Testament and in the New Testament the term peace has a wide range of meaning. Basically it describes the total well-being of a person's life; it was even adopted among the Jews as a formula of greeting. This term had such a profound meaning that it could also be used by the Jews as a description of the Messianic salvation. Because of this fact, there are times when it is used almost synonymously with the term rendered "to be in a right relation with God." Here the term appears to be used as a description of the harmonious relation established between man and God on the basis of God's having put man right with himself.

Peace with God is often expressed idiomatically—for example, "to have a still heart in the presence of God," "to sit down in one's heart with God," "to be beside God with a sweet liver," or "our hearts are glad in sitting beside God."

The phrase through our Lord Jesus Christ indicates secondary agency, which is expressed in some languages by a formula of cause—for example, "our Lord Jesus Christ caused us to be at peace with God" or "God caused us to be at peace with himself; our Lord Jesus Christ did it."

5.2 He has brought us, by faith, into this experience of God's grace, in which we now live. We rejoice, then, in the hope we have of sharing God's glory!

In Greek this verse begins with the statement "through whom we have obtained an entry," which is a kind of substitute passive construction. The TEV changes this to an active statement: he has brought us. The phrase by faith refers to the faith of the believers and not to the faith of the one who brought them. In order to avoid a misinterpretation of the phrase by faith, it may be necessary to employ an entire clause with the proper participants specified—for example, "because we believed in Christ, he brought us into the grace of God."

Into this experience of God's grace is literally "into this grace." Both the context and especially the use of the demonstrative pronoun "this" indicate that "this grace" is God's grace, and so the TEV makes the fact explicit (see also Goodspeed and NEB). A number of translators evidently feel that Paul's expression "this grace" (TEV this experience of God's grace) is inadequate for their readers, and so they try to make the meaning explicit (NEB "the sphere of God's grace"; JB "this state of grace"; Phillips "this new relationship of grace"). The problem is that grace, in the biblical sense, is not an object but an event in which God takes the initiative to offer himself and his salvation freely to man. The most perfect expression of God's grace is seen in the giving of his Son; moreover, God continues to offer himself and his salvation to the believer, and so what the believer continues to enjoy may then be described as an experience of God's grace.

Paul's word "stand" appears as live in the TEV, because it is more natural in English to speak of living an experience than of standing in one (see Goodspeed "that we now enjoy").

The rendering of he has brought us... into this experience of God's grace may require considerable restructuring—for example, "he caused us to experience God's grace," "he caused us to know how good God is," or "he caused us to see how God gives to us so freely." The final clause, in which we now live, may then be rendered as "and this is what we now experience" or "and this is what God is now doing for us."

The verb rendered rejoice has as its basic meaning "to boast" (see 2.17, 23), though it is generally agreed that the meaning here is "to rejoice" or "to be very happy." The problem is not with the meaning of the word in the present context, but rather with its grammatical form; that is, the first person plural indicative and the subjunctive of this verb are identical in form, so that the meaning may be we rejoice or "let us rejoice." On the basis of what we have said earlier (v. 1), the indicative seems to be more in keeping with the context. In the overall context Paul is not so much urging his readers to do and to be what they should as Christians; rather he is reminding them of what they already share because of their right relation with God.

A literal rendering of Paul's phrase "in the hope of the glory of God" is ambiguous in English, and so the TEV tries to make the meaning explicit: in the hope we have of sharing God's glory. Other translations also attempt to make the meaning explicit: JB "looking forward to God's glory"; NEB "in the hope of the divine splendor that is to be ours"; Goodspeed "in our hope of sharing the glory of God"; Phillips "the glorious things he has for us in the future." From reading these translations it is evident that all of them understand the phrase "the hope of the glory of God" in the sense of "the hope of sharing the glory of God." For a full understanding of this phrase it is necessary to examine more closely the meanings of the words hope and glory. For the English reader hope can have the idea of something that one wants to happen, though he is not certain that it is going to happen; but from the biblical point of view hope implies confidence in something which one knows is going to take place, though it has not yet taken place. That is to say, whereas for the English speaker hope may imply doubt, for Paul it implied certainty.

The meaning of the word glory is more difficult. Originally the word meant "heavy" or "weighty" and later came to be used in the specific sense of the revelation of some heavenly being, especially of God himself. So when Paul speaks of "the glory of God" he has in mind the revelation of what God is like, that is, God's own character. In 1.23 Paul used the phrase "they exchanged the glory of the immortal God," which is translated by the TEV as instead of worshiping the immortal God. In such a context "the glory of God" is a way of speaking of God himself. So in the present passage, when Paul speaks of sharing God's glory, what he means is that the believer will share in the likeness of God himself. The ultimate hope of the believer is that he will share in the divine qualities and attributes. This is simply another way of speaking of the total salvation experience; Paul has already spoken of it in terms of being put right with God and of enjoying peace with God.

We rejoice, then, in the hope may in some languages be equivalent to "we are very happy indeed because we hope." However, in keeping with the implications of this context, it may be possible to translate hope as "confidence"—for example, "we are very happy, then, because we have complete confidence that we will share in God's glory." The semantic components of hope, involving both confidence and expectation, are thus combined by employing an expression for confidence plus the future tense of "sharing."

It is not, however, easy to speak of sharing God's glory. One may say in some languages "to receive a share of God's glory" or "to receive from God the gift of his glory." The way in which one translates share is determined to some extent by the choice of a word for glory. In some cases this can be rendered as "brightness," but more frequently a better equivalent is something like "majesty" or "greatness." Therefore, a closer equivalent in some languages may be "to have a share of God's greatness," by which is meant some share in God's divine qualities.

5.3 And we also rejoice in our troubles, because we know that trouble produces endurance,

Paul introduces this verse with a formula (literally "but not only, but also") which is found elsewhere in his writings (5.11; 8.23; 9.10; 2 Corinthians 8.19). In the TEV this appears as and...also, while the NEB translates it "more than this," Moffatt "not only so," Goodspeed "more than that," and the JB "but that is not all." Because of the contrast in verse 3 compared with verse 2, it seems more appropriate to employ some kind of adversative particle or phrase—for example, "but in contrast," "but on the other hand," or "but...also."

On the problem of translating we rejoice, see verse 2.

The word translated troubles (so Goodspeed; NEB, JB, RSV "sufferings") originally applied to troubles brought on one from without. It is possible, though not necessary, to understand troubles in the specific sense of those difficulties that Paul and the early believers felt would come on them because they were living in the last age of time. It was a firm belief of the early church that the coming of Christ had inaugurated the end of time, and in light of their Jewish background they looked for the last days of history to bring suffering upon those people who were faithful to God.

Rejoice in our troubles may be rendered as "rejoice because of what we suffer." A meaning of concession ("rejoice even though we suffer") should be carefully avoided. Paul's attitude toward such troubles was far more positive.

Most modern translations render Paul's next term by endurance along with the TEV (so also in 5.4; see the comment at 2.7; in 8.25 and 15.4,5 it is rendered patience).

It is difficult in many languages to speak of experiences such as trouble, endurance, or approval as being agents of such events as produces, brings ... approval, and creates. The basic relation, however, is one of cause and effect, and this should be preserved in translation. Therefore, one may translate: "for we know that because we suffer we learn how to endure better" or "we know that we become better in enduring because we have suffered trouble."

5.4 endurance brings God's approval, and his approval creates hope.

The word rendered God's approval is a relatively rare term and is used in the New Testament in only three other places (2 Corinthians 2.9; 9.13; Philippians 2.22). This word is related to the verb used in 2.18, and it describes something that is put to the test and then is approved if it passes the test (see NEB "proof that we have stood the test"). In the present context both testing and approval are involved, and it is God who makes the judgment. For that reason it is proper to make the meaning of the term explicit, as God's approval. It is also possible to take this word in the sense of that which receives approval, in this context one's character (so RSV, Goodspeed, Moffatt). On the meaning of hope, see verse 2.

The relation between endurance and God's approval is likewise one of cause and effect. It may be rendered in some languages as "because we are better in enduring, God approves of us" or "God approves of us because we have learned how to endure." The same relation of cause and effect is to be found in the connection between his approval and hope. Therefore one may translate: "because he approves of us, we have hope." In some cases, however, one must make explicit certain components of approval—for example, "because God has tested us and seen that we are fit."

5.5 This hope does not disappoint us, because God has poured out his love into our hearts by means of the Holy Spirit, who is God's gift to us.

The word rendered disappoint is closely related both in form and meaning to the word used in 1.16 (there rendered I have complete confidence).

The relation between hope and "not being disappointed" may be expressed as condition and result—for example, "if we hope this way, we are never disappointed." The relation may also be expressed as cause and effect—for example, "because we hope in this manner, we are never disappointed."

God has poured out his love translates a phrase which is ambiguous in Greek. Literally it is "the love of God has been poured out." The Greek phrase itself may be a reference either to our love for God or to God's love for us. However, all translations in which the meaning is explicit render this as a reference to God's love for us (see Moffatt, Goodspeed, NEB; see also the note in the JB). This choice of meaning is supported by what Paul says in verse 8, but

God has shown us how much he loves us. Furthermore, not only is God's love mentioned explicitly in verse 8, but the illustration of his love begins in verse 6.

It is not uncommon to speak of God's Spirit as being poured out (Acts 2.17, 18,33; 10.45; Titus 3.6). This concept seems to go back to the book of Joel which speaks of God's Spirit poured out on men (Joel 2.28,29), and in other early Christian literature the verb "to pour out" is often used in speaking of gifts which come from above. Who is God's gift to us translates a passive expression in Greek (literally "who was given to us"), in which the implied agent of the action is God (NEB "he [that is, God] has given us").

It is quite impossible in most languages to speak of "pouring out love." In a number of instances one may, however, speak of "how greatly he loves us" or even "how much he has shown our hearts how much he loves us."

By means of the Holy Spirit must be expressed in some languages as a secondary agent—for example, "God has done this by means of the Holy Spirit" or "the Holy Spirit himself has shown how much God loves us."

The final clause who is God's gift to us may be rendered as "who is the one whom God has given to us" or "God himself gave us his Holy Spirit."

> 6For when we were still helpless, Christ died for the wicked, at the time that God chose. 7It is a difficult thing for someone to die for a righteous person. It may be that someone might dare to die for a good person. 8But God has shown us how much he loves us; it was while we were still sinners that Christ died for us! 9By his death we are now put right with God; how much more, then, will we be saved by him from God's wrath. 10We were God's enemies, but he made us his friends through the death of his Son. Now that we are God's friends, how much more will we be saved by Christ's life! 11But that is not all; we rejoice in God through our Lord Jesus Christ, who has now made us God's friends.

Verses 6-8 give the perfect illustration of God's love for us. This is followed in verses 9-11 by a return to Paul's earlier theme in the chapter, and an explanation regarding the significance of Christ's death on our behalf. There are some rather severe difficulties in the Greek text at this point, but these difficulties are not reflected in most contemporary English translations, and so, for purposes of this commentary, it is not necessary that they be discussed.

5.6 For when we were still helpless, Christ died for the wicked, at the time that God chose.

In this sentence the subject, Christ, and the main verb, died, are emphatic; they occur first and last in the structure, with all the other elements coming in between. The word rendered helpless (so also Goodspeed and JB) actually means "weak," but it is agreed that it has this meaning in the present passage (see NEB "powerless"; Phillips "powerless to help ourselves").

It is important that the translator realize that we are included in the group of the wicked, and not that we and wicked are set in contrast.

It is assumed by most translators and commentators that the phrase translated at the time that God chose is connected with the verb died. This phrase is related in meaning to the one in Galatians 4.4, when the right time finally came, and is rendered in a variety of ways in different translations. Perhaps the nearest thing to a literal rendering appears in the RSV, "at the right time" (Goodspeed "at the decisive moment"; JB "at his [Christ's] appointed time"). The NEB appears to connect this primarily with the time of our helplessness, though it does relate it also to the time of Christ's death ("for at the very time when we were still powerless, then Christ died"). However one translates this phrase, in this context it refers to the time that was within God's purpose and choice. This is the reason that the translation appears as it does in the TEV.

The principal difficulty in verse 6 is the occurrence of two expressions of time, both relating, but in different ways, to the main clause Christ died for the wicked. The first expression is a general term for time, equivalent in some languages to "during the time that we were still helpless." The second expression of time is quite specific (sometimes called punctiliar) and is translated as "at the specific time." In some languages the second expression of time is best treated as a separate sentence—for example, "while we were still helpless, Christ died for us who were wicked; he died just at the time that God chose." It may be necessary to introduce "us who were wicked" in order to make it perfectly clear that Christ died for the same persons who were still helpless.

An expression for helplessness may be "we could not help ourselves."

In rendering at the time that God chose, the idea of choosing a time may need to be expressed in quite a different manner from that of choosing an object. One may need to employ some other type of verbal expression—for example, "at the time that God decided" or "at the time that God decided was best." In these contexts "time" must refer to an occasion, not to time as a continuity or a continuation of events. In some languages the expression of occasion may only be rendered as "on the day that God chose," since "day" is also a generic expression for "occasion."

In the phrase for the wicked the preposition for must be taken with the meaning of "for the sake of," and not with the meaning "in place of." Moreover, it is valuable to realize that in the present passage Paul is not dealing so much with the theology of redemption as he is with the extent to which God went in order to show his love for sinful man. In most languages there is a well-defined way of introducing benefactives, that is to say, persons who are benefited by some particular action or event, introduced generally in English by the preposition for. However, in some languages benefaction is expressed specifically by a purpose clause with the verb "to help"—for example, "Christ died in order to help us who were wicked."

5.7 It is a difficult thing for someone to die for a righteous person. It may be that someone might dare to die for a good person.

Perhaps the basic distinction between a righteous person and a good person is that a righteous person is one who will, without bending, follow exactly what the law demands, while a good person is one who is not so much bound by legalistic requirements but who is willing to show mercy and kindness beyond what the law demands of him. Concerning Joseph the husband of Mary, it is said in Matthew 1.19 that he was a man who always did what was right (literally "he was a righteous man"). Jewish law demanded that he divorce Mary, since there were indications that she had had sexual intercourse with another man, and so he was prepared to obey the demands of the law. On the other hand, Barnabas is spoken of as a good man (Acts 11.24) since he was willing to show love and kindness and go beyond the limits of what was legally required.

For some languages there are problems involved in relating "difficulty" and "dying" in the first part of verse 7. In a strictly literal sense, "dying" would be no different whether one dies for a righteous person or for a good person, or, in fact, for anyone else. What is difficult here is the concept of a person dying for a righteous individual. As a result, this first sentence may be rendered as "it is very difficult to think of someone dying for a righteous person" or "it is difficult to imagine why someone would be willing to die for a righteous person." In this type of context righteous person may be rendered as "one who does what the law requires" or "one who follows the law." It is important to avoid a term which might suggest "one who is put right with God," since it was for this purpose that Christ himself died.

Might dare to die must be understood more in a sense of "might be willing to die." Specifically, it is a matter of willingness rather than literal daring. In order to bring out the full implications of good person, it may be appropriate to use some descriptive equivalent such as "a person who shows kindness to others."

5.8 But God has shown us how much he loves us; it was while we were still sinners that Christ died for us!

But God has shown us how much he loves us is literally "but God shows his own love for us." Several things should be said about this part of the verse. The verb rendered "shows" appears in 3.5 with the meaning "to show clearly." In Greek the verb appears in the present tense, which is to indicate for the readers that God's love for us is not limited to the past, but has its relevance for the present as well. It is interesting to note, in this light, that the verb used in verse 5, has poured out, is in the perfect tense in Greek as in English. In Greek this tense always throws emphasis on the relevance of a past action for the present. While it is difficult to communicate this shade of meaning in English (and probably in most other languages), it is better to keep the verb in the perfect tense, if that can be done. How much he loves us is variously rendered in modern translations. Both Moffatt and Goodspeed begin with "but God proves his love for us"; JB has "what proves that God loves us"; NEB has "that is God's own proof of his love towards us."

Although the word rendered wicked in verse 6 (guilty in 4.5) and the word rendered sinners in this verse are different terms, they are applied to the same persons. The first is a more specific term, generally rendered "godless" or "impious," while the second is a more generic term (see 3.7), generally rendered "sinner."

The contrast between verses 8 and 7 requires that some introductory particle such as but be employed. One may even have such an expression as "in contrast with this." The second part of verse 8 may be understood either as a description of the extent of God's love or the means by which God showed us how much he loves us. One may introduce this final portion by a conjunction such as "because"—for example, "because Christ died for us even while we were still sinners."

5.9 By his death we are now put right with God; how much more, then, will we be saved by him from God's wrath.

In verses 6-8 Paul has established the fact of God's love for the sinner. He now reminds the Romans of what this has meant for them in the past (it has put them into a right relation with God) and calls their attention to what it will mean for them in the future (it will save them from God's wrath on the final day of judgment). In typical Jewish fashion, Paul reasons from the greater to the lesser. If Christ was willing to die in order to bring men into a right relation with God (the greater), how much easier it will be for him to save us from God's wrath on the final day of judgment (the lesser).

The second aspect of verse 9 must be carefully introduced in order to indicate specifically the relationship between these two aspects of Christ's atoning work. This may be done in some languages by saying "if that is so, then obviously he will save us from God's angry judgment," "since that is so, then certainly Christ will save us when God will judge in anger."

By his death (see NEB "by Christ's sacrificial death"; JB "having died") is literally "by means of his blood." In the present passage "blood" is used of Christ's violent death, and so has the same meaning that it does in 3.25. When Paul speaks of "the blood of Christ," he is, of course, drawing from the language of the Jewish sacrificial system, which placed two emphases on the experience of the sacrificial death: (1) the initial, violent aspect of the death itself, and (2) the release of life for another purpose through the shedding of the blood (the Jews understood that the life of a person or animal was in his blood). In passages where the use of "blood" is on the initial, violent aspect of death, the TEV translates by death; while in passages where the emphasis is on the result of this experience in the lives of believers, the TEV employs the term blood. Though by his death is specifically the means by which God puts us right with himself, this is expressed in some languages as cause—for example, "because Christ died for us, we are put right with God."

Paul simply uses the word "wrath," but the reference is to God's wrath (see Goodspeed and JB "God's anger"); and by the use of the future tense, we will be saved, Paul indicates that the reference is to the expression of God's wrath on the final day of judgment (see NEB "from final retribution").

5.10 We were God's enemies, but he made us his friends through the death of his Son. Now that we are God's friends, how much more will we be saved by Christ's life!

This verse contains two parallel clauses, and so is similar in form to the structure of 4.25. The verse begins with an "if" clause, which in Greek is understood to be a condition true to fact, and so may be translated as a statement: We were God's enemies. The actual content of this verse is very parallel to the content of the previous verse. (1) He made us his friends is parallel to we are now put right with God. (2) Through the death of his Son is parallel to by his death of verse 9. Although in the earlier verse Paul literally said "by his blood," the thought is parallel to, and the meaning corresponds to, through the death of his Son. (3) Will we be saved carries the same force of will we be saved... from God's wrath. Saved in this verse also relates to the eschatological future in the same way that saved did in verse 9. (4) By Christ's life (literally "by his life") is equivalent in meaning to by him in the previous verse.

The meaning of now that we are God's friends (RSV "we were reconciled to God") may best be understood in light of the previous statement, we were God's enemies. The picture is that of men rebelling against God, their king, and finally being brought into peaceful terms with him. Paul uses this same verb in 1 Corinthians 7.11 to describe the reconciliation that takes place between a husband and wife who have separated. Elsewhere in the New Testament this verb is used only of the peaceful relation established between God and men through the work of Jesus Christ (2 Corinthians 5.18, 19, 20), and the related noun is used in the same way (Romans 5.11; 11.15; 2 Corinthians 5.18, 19). "To be made friends with God" carries the same meaning as "to be put right with God" of the previous verse; Paul is merely using two metaphors from different areas of life to describe what happens in the divine-human relation when men experience God's forgiveness.

We were God's enemies may be rendered as "we were angry with God," "we hated God," or "we would have nothing to do with God." And through the death of his Son may be rendered as "this happened because his Son died" or "by means of his Son's dying (we became God's friends)."

Now that we are God's friends indicates reconciliation, as indicated above, and expressions for reconciliation involve a wide difference of form due to the diverse cultural contexts in which reconciliation takes place—for example, "he caused us to snap fingers with him again," "he caused us to sit with him again," or "he caused us to eat with him again."

As in verse 9, the expression how much more may be rendered as "it is obvious then" or "it will surely be that."

It is not at all easy to indicate the means of our being saved by Christ's life. There is an obvious contrast with a statement concerning Christ's death earlier in the verse, but the parallelism involves merely the mention of Christ in verse 9. If this final clause must be put into an active form, one can probably best translate as "he will surely save us," but this does not do justice to the

Greek term for "life." In some languages this can perhaps be best expressed by "he will save us because he is alive."

5.11 But that is not all; we rejoice in God through our Lord Jesus Christ, who has now made us God's friends.

But that is not all translates the same transitional phrase used by Paul in verse 3, and...also. But that is not all may be rendered as "but there is still more," "but in addition to all this," or "but add also."

The Greek of this sentence is rather difficult. The phrase we rejoice represents a participle, whereas one would expect some finite verb form such as appears in verses 2 and 3. However, the meaning is not difficult, and most translations render this participle by a finite verb form. No new thoughts are introduced; as in verse 9, so here, Paul emphasizes the present reality of one's experience, now.

The expression we rejoice in God is difficult to render literally and at the same time provide any real sense. In many languages the closest equivalent is "we rejoice because of God" or even "God causes us to rejoice." The phrase through our Lord Jesus Christ expresses secondary agency which may be expressed in some languages as "God caused this by means of the Lord Jesus Christ," "our Lord Jesus Christ made this possible," or "...caused this to be." The final relative clause describes Christ as the agent of this process, and all of verse 11 may be somewhat restructured as follows: "There is even more; God has caused us to rejoice because it was our Lord Jesus Christ who has now made us God's friends."

Adam and Christ

12 Sin came into the world through one man, and his sin brought death with it. As a result, death spread to the whole human race, because all men sinned. 13 There was sin in the world before the Law was given; but where there is no law, no account is kept of sins. 14 But from the time of Adam to the time of Moses death ruled over all men, even over those who did not sin as Adam did by disobeying God's command.

The section heading Adam and Christ may need to be somewhat restructured in some languages—for example, "Adam and Christ Are Compared," "Christ Is Compared with Adam," or even "The Differences between Adam and Christ."

At first glance this entire section (5.12-21) appears to be a digression in Paul's argument, but it actually serves to strengthen his point. By contrasting Adam, Law, sin, and death with Christ, grace, righteousness, and life Paul accomplishes at least two things. (1) He indicates that the age of salvation is inaugurated by the person and work of Jesus Christ; and (2) he indicates that the Law belongs to the past age and has no part in the work of salvation. The conclusion that Paul states regarding the Law (5.20-21) is very similar to what he has said in 3.20 and 4.15. In every way possible Paul attempts to indicate that the Law belongs to the past age and not to the present age of God's salvation.

5.12 Sin came into the world through one man, and his sin brought death with it. As a result, death spread to the whole human race, because all men sinned.

This verse begins with a transitional formula (RSV "therefore"), which both commentators and translators find difficult to handle. The question is whether it relates back to verse 11 alone, or to 5.1-11, or to the entire section of 1.17—5.11. Most probably it is to be taken in relation to the passage immediately preceding, 5.1-11. This transition is indicated by translators in a number of ways. The TEV handles it by introducing a new paragraph and a new section heading, Adam and Christ. The JB also introduces a new section heading and a paragraph beginning with the words "well, then." The NEB begins this paragraph with "mark what follows"; Goodspeed "it is just like the way"; Phillips "this, then, is what has happened"; and Moffatt "thus, then."

Paul's beginning point is the account in Genesis 1—3. It was traditional for the Jewish interpreters to relate closely the concepts of sin and death, and so what Paul introduces in this initial verse is in keeping with good Jewish theology. Paul indicates that Adam sinned, and as a result of his sin death came into the human race. However, it is important to realize that Paul does not make men guilty of Adam's sin or indicate that all men die because of the sin of Adam. Paul says rather that death spread to the whole human race, because all men sinned. The verb rendered sinned in this passage is an aorist, and some few have tried to interpret this as meaning that when Adam sinned all of his physical descendants sinned along with him. It must be admitted that a meaning similar to this could be arrived at on the basis of verse 19, but that is not the meaning of the present passage. In this verse Paul is saying that death became a universal experience because all men sinned.

Verse 12 poses a number of serious difficulties in languages which have no nouns for sin and death. In such cases one cannot say "sin came into the world" or "sin brought death." In almost all languages, however, one can speak of "evil deeds" or "doing evil," but in some languages it is quite impossible to speak of sin without relating such sin to specific events or actions. One may, accordingly, render the first sentence of verse 12 as "one man caused evil deeds in the world, and because he sinned he died." The second sentence of verse 12 also causes difficulty, since in some languages one cannot speak of "death spreading." The only equivalent may be "all human beings (or persons) must die."

There is some difficulty involved in relating the phrase as a result and the clause because all men sinned to the principal clause of the second sentence. In order to avoid the impression that Adam's sin caused all men to die, the phrase as a result may be translated as "and in this way" or "and hence." This second sentence may therefore be rendered as "and hence, finally, all persons have had to die because all persons have sinned."

5.13-14a There was sin in the world before the Law was given; but where there is no law, no account is kept of sins. (14) But from the time of Adam to the time of Moses death ruled over all men, even over those who did not sin as Adam did by disobeying God's command.

These verses are difficult to fit into Paul's argument, though as far as the exegetical matters relating to translation are concerned, verse 13 is not difficult. Most translators assume that the Law referred to in this verse is the Jewish Law, and so indicate this by using a capital "L"; however, the NEB takes law in a more general sense ("before there was law").

The first clause of verse 13 may be quite easily rendered by making "people" the subject of sin—for example, "before the Law was given, people in the world sinned." In order to make specific an interpretation of the Law as being the Law of Moses, one may say "before the Law was given to Moses" or "before God gave the Law by means of Moses."

The verb rendered account is kept was a term used in business and referred to the entering of accounts into a ledger. If, in the receptor language, this passive verb has to be rendered by an active one, then God is the one who did not keep account of sins.

Paul's reasoning is here difficult to follow. If no account is kept of sins, why then did death rule over all men from the time of Adam to the time of Moses? Somehow Paul seems to imply that no record could be kept of sin, unless it was sin against a specific command of God, such as the specific command given to Adam or the specific commands contained in the Mosaic Law. But even though all men did not sin as Adam did by disobeying God's command (that is, by disobeying a specific command of God; see NEB "by disobeying a direct command"), all men did sin. And since all men did sin, death ruled over all men. Fortunately, the translator does not have to answer all of these difficult questions; but in order to deal adequately with the meaning of the passage, he should at least know the basic problems involved.

Most translations take Paul's literal words (RSV "whose sins were not like the transgression of Adam") in a way similar to what the TEV does. The rendering of the NEB has already been given; Goodspeed has "who had not sinned as Adam had, in the face of an express command"; while the JB has "even though their sin, unlike that of Adam, was not a matter of breaking a law."

The expression from the time of Adam to the time of Moses may cause certain difficulties in some languages because of the necessity of recasting the relations and relating these to death—for example, "all the people who lived from the time Adam lived until the time Moses lived, all had to die"; or, in relation to the following clause, "all people who followed after Adam, and all those who lived until Moses lived, had to die, even those persons who did not sin just as Adam sinned when he disobeyed the very command which God had given him"; or "...when he disobeyed the very words that God had spoken to him."

Adam was a figure of the one who was to come. [15]But the two are not the same, because God's free gift is not like Adam's sin. It is true that many men died because of the sin of that one man. But God's grace is much greater, and so is his free gift to so many men through the grace of the one man, Jesus Christ. [16]And there is a difference between God's gift and the sin of one man.

> After the one sin came the judgment of "Guilty"; but after so many sins comes the undeserved gift of "Not guilty!" [17]It is true that through the sin of one man death began to rule, because of that one man. But how much greater is the result of what was done by the one man, Jesus Christ! All who receive God's abundant grace and the free gift of his righteousness will rule in life through Christ.

Paul's arguments throughout this passage are so interwoven that it is difficult to determine where to make the break. Some modern translations do as the TEV and initiate a new paragraph with 14b (JB, Phillips), while the NEB begins the new paragraph at verse 15. The intention of this paragraph seems to be to set out an analogy and a contrast between Adam and Christ.

5.14b Adam was a figure of the one who was to come.

Paul begins by saying Adam was a figure of the one who was to come. The word rendered figure is difficult to translate; the RSV has merely transliterated ("a type"). Several modern translations render this noun either by the verb "prefigure" (JB "Adam prefigured the One to come"; Moffatt "Adam prefigured Him who was to come") or by the verb "foreshadow" (NEB "Adam foreshadows the Man who was to come"; Goodspeed "Adam foreshadowed the one who was to come"). Phillips has "Adam, the first man, corresponds in some degree to the man who was to come." This word figure is used in a variety of ways in the New Testament and in other early Christian literature outside the New Testament. Paul himself uses it in 1 Corinthians 10.6 with the meaning of "example," and in 1 Corinthians 10.11 the adverbial form made from this root is used with the meaning of "by way of example." The best explanation of the precise meaning of this word in the present passage is to be found in the series of analogies and contrasts listed in the verses following (15-17).

For languages which lack a term for "figure," "type," or "foreshadow," one may employ terms denoting similarity—for example, "Adam was in some regards similar to the one who was to come." In some languages one must indicate both the similarity and the contrast—for example, "Adam was in some ways like and in some ways different from the person who was destined to come."

5.15 But the two are not the same, because God's free gift is not like Adam's sin. It is true that many men died because of the sin of that one man. But God's grace is much greater, and so is his free gift to so many men through the grace of the one man, Jesus Christ.

In Greek verse 15 begins with the clause rendered by the TEV because God's free gift is not like Adam's sin. However, in order to make clear the relation between this verse and the preceding sentence, and at the same time to show that the contrast is between the two persons (Adam and Christ), the TEV introduces verse 15 with but the two are not the same.

In many instances it may be preferable to say "but the two are different" rather than but the two are not the same. The use of "different" is often a more effective way of indicating the contrast.

In verses 13, 14, and 15 Paul uses three different words for "sin." In verse 13, there was sin in the world, he uses the more generic term, while in verses 14 and 15 he uses words which are almost synonyms and which are generally taken to mean something like "an act of sin."

God's free gift translates a word which in other contexts may mean simply "gift" (so Moffatt) or "free gift" (so RSV), but in the present context the reference is to "God's gift" (so Goodspeed). There is a certain aspect of Paul's usage of the word "sin" and of the word "gift" in this passage which is difficult to explain. Both of these have the same ending in Greek (-ma), and this ending often carries the force of effect or result. That is, a "sin" in this context is the effect or result of the disobedience to a command, while a "gift" is the effect or result of God's grace. If that is the case, then this part of verse 15 may be rendered: "but God's act of grace is not like Adam's act of sin" (see NEB). In some languages one may translate as "for the way in which God gives freely to men is not like the way in which Adam sinned" or "but God's manner of showing grace is different from the manner in which Adam sinned."

Paul next uses an "if" clause ("for if..."), but the force of this clause is to state that the condition is true, and so the TEV translates it is true that. It is agreed that where Paul uses many men in this verse the equivalent is "all men" (see verse 12, the whole human race, literally "all men").

It is true that is rendered in some languages as "you may certainly know that" or "it is a fact that." On the other hand, one may take the following clause, which states what is true, and place it at the beginning of the sentence, followed by the qualification—for example, "the fact that many men have died because one man sinned is true."

In verse 14b Paul made the statement that Adam was in some way like the one who was to come. Now Paul qualifies that statement by affirming that God's grace and the one who brought it are both greater than Adam's sin.

The second word for free gift in this passage is different from the word used earlier; its meaning is essentially the same, though it does not have the formal contrast to the word which Paul used for "sin" in the earlier part of the verse.

But God's grace is much greater may be rendered as "but the way in which God shows his grace is much stronger."

The last clause of verse 15 also presents a number of complications, since the expression and so is his free gift to so many men through the grace of the one man, Jesus Christ is essentially an elaboration of what has just been said, God's grace is much greater. One may, therefore, translate this final clause as "this is the way in which God has given so freely to so many men by the way in which the one person, Jesus Christ, showed grace."

5.16 And there is a difference between God's gift and the sin of one man. After the one sin came the judgment of "Guilty"; but after so many sins comes the undeserved gift of "Not guilty!"

In Greek this verse begins with a negative statement (see RSV "and the free gift is not like the effect of that one man's sin"), which is changed into a positive statement by the TEV and others (and there is a difference between God's gift and the sin of one man; see JB "the results of the gift also outweigh the results of the one man's sin").

This first sentence of verse 16 is essentially similar to the second clause of verse 15 and may, in fact, be translated in essentially the same way, though with perhaps slightly different wording in order to avoid an apparent duplication. But the closest equivalent may simply be "the way in which God gives freely to men is very different from the way in which one man sinned."

At this point the analogy with Adam breaks down. After his one sin came the judgment of "Guilty"; but after so many sins comes the undeserved gift of "Not guilty!" In this way Paul demonstrates the superiority of God's grace over Adam's sin. Grace had a much more difficult road to travel than sin had. To use an illustration from everyday life, it is much easier for an infection to spread than it is to cure the infection once it has spread throughout the body.

Many sins refers to the sins of those persons who lived after Adam, and not to the sins of Adam himself, and so confirms the judgment reached in verse 12 regarding the clause because all men sinned.

In relation to words such as sin, judgment, and gift, one may need to introduce participants and employ verb expressions—for example, "after Adam sinned God judged him as guilty; but after so many people have sinned God shows his grace to them by saying, You are not guilty" or "...God gives them what they do not deserve by saying to them, You are not guilty."

5.17 It is true that through the sin of one man death began to rule, because of that one man. But how much greater is the result of what was done by the one man, Jesus Christ! All who receive God's abundant grace and the free gift of his righteousness will rule in life through Christ.

This verse also contains an "if" clause which is assumed to be true to fact (see v. 15). Once again Paul follows a typical rabbinic method of argument, but here he goes from the lesser to the greater (see v. 9). The intention of this verse is to validate and to carry further the argument begun in the previous verse. The significance of the aorist tense of the verb "to rule" in the present context is to place the emphasis upon the initiation of the action, and so the TEV renders began to rule.

The first sentence of verse 17 may be treated in a manner similar to the second sentence of verse 15, with which it is parallel. The special complication in this sentence is due to the expression of both means and cause. The sin of Adam is indicated not only as a means by which death rules, but that one man (Adam) is indicated as the cause. In some languages it is necessary to combine the two ideas, since Adam must be made explicit as the subject of sin. Therefore, one may translate: "It is true that, because one man sinned, death began to control all men" or "...the power of death began to rule all men." In some languages in which one cannot speak of "death ruling," it is still possible to talk about "the power of death ruling." If neither of these possibilities exists, one may employ essentially the same expression as in verse 15, "all men had to die."

The last half of this verse is rather drastically restructured by the TEV. In Greek the last half of verse 17 is one clause, which the TEV divides into two sentences for the sake of clarity. The first of these sentences combines the first and last elements of this Greek clause ("how much more...through the one man Jesus Christ"). The JB maintains the same number of clauses as has the Greek, but its translation closely parallels that of the TEV at this point: "it is even more certain that one man, Jesus Christ, will cause...."

The TEV uses its second sentence to describe the result of what was done by the one man, Jesus Christ. Along with other translations, it makes explicit the fact that the abundant grace referred to is God's grace (see NEB).

The exclamatory sentence in verse 17 may be transformed into an emphatic positive sentence in some languages—for example, "but what the one man, Jesus Christ, was able to accomplish is so much greater" or "what the one man, Jesus Christ, did was so much more powerful than what happened because one man sinned."

The free gift of his righteousness is ambiguous and requires some further comment. The phrase may mean either (1) the gift that comes from God because he is righteous or (2) the gift of being put into a right relation with God. Though it is difficult to separate these two concepts, it is more probable that the latter is in focus in this passage. Only two translations make this reference explicit, and both seem to favor this interpretation (Goodspeed "gift of uprightness"; JB "the free gift...of being made righteous"). This exegesis, then, concludes that the free gift of his righteousness describes the initial experience of salvation in which one is put into a right relation with God, while the phrase will rule in life describes the ultimate and future goal of salvation. Perhaps Paul used this rather exotic figure, will rule in life, because of the mention of rule in reference to death earlier in the verse. Will rule in life is simply another way of saying "will have eternal life." That is made possible through Christ; the shorter phrase through Christ is used here because the full phrase by the one man, Jesus Christ has already been used earlier in this verse.

The rendering of the last sentence of verse 17 is particularly complex in some languages. It is difficult in some instances to speak of "receiving grace." People can only be the goal of God's showing grace or giving grace; therefore the first clause may be rendered as "all to whom God has shown his grace abundantly."

The expression the free gift of his righteousness may be either "to whom God has given freely because he is righteous" or "to whom God has given a gift, namely, putting them right with himself."

Will rule in life should not be translated in such a way as to imply that these persons will have power over other individuals as earthly rulers. Rather they will have spiritual strength, and this is sometimes expressed as "they will be strong in their lives," "they will live with strength," or "they will live overcoming."

Through Christ may be rendered as means or cause—for example, "by means of Christ" or "because of what Christ has done."

> [18]So then, as the one sin condemned all men, in the same way the one righteous act sets all men free and gives them life. [19]And just as many men were made sinners as the result of the disobedience of one man, in the same way many will be put right with God as the result of the obedience of the one man.
> [20]Law was introduced in order to increase wrongdoing; but where sin increased, God's grace increased much more. [21]So then, just as sin ruled by means of death, so also God's grace rules by means of righteousness, leading us to eternal life through Jesus Christ our Lord.

5.18 So then, as the one sin condemned all men, in the same way the one righteous act sets all men free and gives them life.

In this verse Paul compares the obedience of Christ and its results to the disobedience of Adam and its results. The particle translated so then indicates that the conclusion of the argument begun in verse 12 is now introduced. Exegetically this verse is not difficult except for the phrase rendered rather literally by the KJV as "unto justification of life." All commentators point out that the word rendered in the KJV as "justification" means "acquittal" in this passage. In fact, many modern translations make this meaning explicit for their readers (for example, RSV "leads to acquittal and life"; NEB "is acquittal and life"; Goodspeed "means acquittal and life"). "Acquittal" is simply a technical term used in law to indicate that a person is set free from the jurisdiction of the court. Hence the TEV renders the entire phrase as sets all men free and gives them life.

In some languages one cannot speak of "sin condemning all men" or "one righteous act setting all men free." This cause and effect relationship must be expressed by clauses in which both "sin" and "setting free" have their corresponding subjects—for example, "just as all men were condemned because one man sinned, in the same way all men are set free because one person acted in a righteous way."

Sets all men free may be translated as "God declares that all men are innocent," but this is accomplished by "what one person did which was righteous."

Gives them life may be rendered as a causative, "causes them to live."

5.19 And just as many men were made sinners as the result of the disobedience of one man, in the same way many will be put right with God as the result of the obedience of the one man.

As in verse 15, so here many men is equivalent in meaning to "all men."

Were made translates the same verb used in Acts 7.27 (who made you ruler and judge?). It is best understood in the sense of "make (someone) to be (something)." The phrase were made sinners has its parallel in will be put right with God (RSV "will be made righteous"). It is important to understand the context in which Paul is speaking. He looks upon Adam as the father of the human race and the one who introduced sin into the world. From this perspective many men were made sinners as the result of the disobedience of one man. Paul does not intend to imply that men are held responsible for the sin that Adam committed, as is made clear by looking at the other aspect of Paul's thought in this verse. Paul also affirms that in the same way many will be put right with God as the result of the obedience of the one man. In the same way that Adam is looked upon as being the head of the old human race, so Christ is the head of the new humanity. And as Adam's disobedience brought sin into the world and made it possible for every man to sin, so Christ's obedience makes it possible for every man to be put right with God. Yet Adam's sin not only introduced sin into the world, but it meant that all of his descendants were born into a race which had separated itself from God. So then, when Paul says that many men were made sinners as the result of the disobedience of one man, he has in mind two things: (1) Adam is the one who brought sin into the world, and (2) all men are descendants of Adam and are born into a race of people who are already separated from God. Jesus Christ stands in sharp contrast to Adam: by his obedience to God Jesus Christ brought "righteousness" into the world and so made it possible for every man to be put right with God.

The phrases as the result of the disobedience of one man and as the result of the obedience of the one man must both be transformed into clauses of cause in many languages—for example, "and just as people became sinners because one man disobeyed God, in the same way God puts people right with himself because the one man obeyed God." It may be necessary to specify that "the one man" is "Jesus Christ."

5.20 Law was introduced in order to increase wrongdoing; but where sin increased, God's grace increased much more.

For several verses Paul has been discussing the analogy and contrast between Adam and Christ. Adam brought sin into the world and so was responsible for the fall of mankind; Christ brought righteousness into the world and so made possible the redemption of mankind. Where, then, in this process does the Law fit in? Paul chooses a rather strong verb that shows dramatically the subordinate role of the Law in God's purpose. Paul says it was introduced into a situation created by sin. The NEB translates the verb was introduced as "intruded"; while Moffatt and Goodspeed render it by "slipped in" (in Galatians 2.4 the TEV renders this verb as slipped in). The word is specifically chosen in order to demonstrate that the Law has an inferior status and was added later. The Law was not given until the time of Moses, and it came to an end with Christ (see 4.13-16; 9.4). Paul states that the reason that the Law was introduced was in order to increase wrongdoing. The meaning of this statement is best discussed in connection with the following chapters, especially in connection with chapter 7. The Law increases wrongdoing both by indicating what wrongdoing is and by stirring up within persons the desire to rebel against the commands given in the Law.

The Law did fulfill its function—it did increase wrongdoing—but God's grace increased much more.

The passive expression law was introduced may need to be transformed into an active in some languages—for example, "God introduced the law," "God brought the law in," "God caused the law to come in," or "God caused the law to be given."

To increase wrongdoing may only be rendered in some languages as "in order to cause people to do wrong more." The final half of verse 20 may then be translated as "but when people sinned more, God's showing grace became more and more." Though the clause where sin increased seems to be an expression of place, it is essentially an expression of time and therefore may be more appropriately rendered as "when sin increased" or "when people sinned more."

5.21 So then, just as sin ruled by means of death, so also God's grace rules by means of righteousness, leading us to eternal life through Jesus Christ our Lord.

The concepts presented in this verse have been commented on in earlier passages. However, for purposes of translation the use of righteousness in this verse needs to be made clear. Righteousness is best understood in the sense of "God's putting men right with himself," which is understood as the beginning point and eternal life as the final point of the salvation experience. The meaning, then, is that God's grace rules us by putting us into a right relation with him and by leading us to eternal life (see 6.22) through Jesus Christ our Lord. The phrase through Jesus Christ our Lord must be connected in meaning both with the matter of putting men right with God and of leading them to eternal life.

The transition so then may be rendered in some languages as "to sum up everything," "finally we may say," or "as a conclusion."

Though in some languages one cannot say sin ruled, it may be possible to say "sin was powerful." By means of death would then be rendered as "because all people had to die." The second principal clause may thus be translated in a parallel fashion: "so also God's way of showing grace is powerful because he puts men right with himself" or "...by means of putting men right with himself."

The phrase leading us to eternal life may be rendered in some languages as a causative: "he causes us to live without end" or "he causes us to always live truly" (the addition of "truly" implying a qualitative distinction in an "unending life").

Through Jesus Christ our Lord may be expressed as means—for example, "Jesus Christ our Lord made this possible" or "...caused this to be."

CHAPTER 6

Dead to Sin but Alive in Christ

6 What shall we say, then? That we should continue to live in sin so that
God's grace will increase? 2 Certainly not! We have died to sin—how then
can we go on living in it? 3 For surely you know this: when we were baptized
into union with Christ Jesus, we were baptized into union with his death. 4 By
our baptism, then, we were buried with him and shared his death, in order that,
just as Christ was raised from death by the glorious power of the Father, so
also we might live a new life.

The section heading Dead to Sin but Alive in Christ is extremely succinct, and in order to translate it one might have to employ a rather long sentence. Under such circumstances, it is advisable to use only part of the section heading—for example, Alive in Christ, rendered possibly as "We Are Alive in Our Union with Christ," "We Are Alive because of Christ," or "We Truly Live because of Christ."

Chapter 6 takes up a point touched on in 5.20, in which Paul states that where sin increased, God's grace increased much more. Does this mean, then, that the Christian is to live a life of sin in order that the greatness of God's grace may be shown more and more? Paul has already dealt briefly with this matter on the basis of Jewish presuppositions (see 3.5-6), and he must now deal with the same problem on the basis of Christian ethics. What reason is there for the Christian not to live in sin if his sin serves only to increase God's grace? This is the question that Paul sets out to answer in chapter 6. The earlier part of the chapter maintains the thesis that the person who has been baptized into union with Christ has died as far as sin is concerned (6.1-14); while the latter half of the chapter maintains that the believer is no longer a slave to sin but a slave to righteousness. Paul continues his argument through chapters 7 and 8. In chapter 7 he affirms that the believer has been set free from the control of the Law in his life, a law which continually served to arouse sin within his mortal body. And finally, in chapter 8, he makes known the secret of the believer's power over sin, that is, the Holy Spirit.

6.1 What shall we say, then? That we should continue to live in sin so that God's grace will increase?

Once again Paul adopts the form of a philosophical argument (see 2.1) and imagines the questions which his opponents would present to him. As mentioned in the introduction to this section, 6.1 refers back directly to 5.20. No new thoughts are introduced here that have not been discussed in the previous passage, and so further comments are unnecessary. (God's grace is the meaning of Paul's term "grace.")

Where the technique of question and answer cannot be employed, one can transform the questions of verse 1 into a strong negative statement—for example, "We certainly should not continue to live sinning so that God will show his grace more and more" or "We should by no means continue to sin in our lives just so that God's showing grace will be greater and greater."

6.2 Certainly not! We have died to sin—how then can we go on living in it?

Paul's answer to the question he has raised is in the form of a very strong negative: Certainly not (see also 3.4,6 where the same reply is given).

Died (an aorist tense in Greek) points to a definite time in the past, and on the basis of the following verse Paul evidently has the moment of baptism in mind. As a general rule, the Greek simple future does not describe action in progress, and so Paul adds a particle to the verb tense here in order to describe the continuation of the action: how then can we go on living in it? (see Goodspeed and NEB "how can we live in it any longer?").

We have died to sin may be rendered as "we have died as far as sinning is concerned," "if it is a matter of sinning, then we are dead," or "we have seemingly died; sin cannot move us." It may be necessary to introduce some such expression as "seemingly" in order to indicate clearly that the "dying" is to be understood metaphorically. In some languages, however, died to sin must be rendered as "dead from sin," that is to say, "dead, and in this way separated from the power of sin."

The final question, how then can we go on living in it?, may be rendered as either a question, "how can we go on sinning in our lives?," or as a statement, "we must not go on living and continuing to sin."

6.3 For surely you know this: when we were baptized into union with Christ Jesus, we were baptized into union with his death.

Paul introduces verse 3 with a negative question (RSV "do you not know that?") that is much more naturally expressed in English by a positive statement. The TEV renders this as for surely you know this (so also Moffatt); the NEB and Phillips have "have you forgotten that"; in the JB it is rendered "you have been taught that."

The idea of one person being baptized "into" another person is almost impossible for the English reader to comprehend. There is much disagreement among the scholars regarding the origin of Paul's doctrine of baptism, but there is general agreement that the phrase "into Christ Jesus" means into union with Christ Jesus (so also NEB). A similar thought is expressed in Galatians 3.27. The same judgment must be made with regard to the parallel expression "into his death." It is best rendered into union with his death. The picture of being baptized into union with his death is a difficult one, but it is necessary in light of the way Paul develops his argument beginning with verse 5. For Paul, death not only brings the end to life, but it makes possible the entrance into a new kind of life, and this is the basis on which his argument is founded.

The introductory statement for surely you know this has as its content the rest of verse 3. A common equivalent is simply "for certainly you know that when we were baptized...."

The expression baptized into union with Christ Jesus is very difficult to express in some languages, and in most languages it is quite meaningless to say merely "baptized into Christ Jesus." In some instances one can translate as "baptized so that we might be one with Christ Jesus," "baptized so that we would be tied together with Christ Jesus," or "... linked with Christ Jesus." For this type of expression one should attempt to find a means of indicating the closest possible relation to another individual.

The last clause of verse 3 causes even greater difficulties. In some languages this can only be expressed as "when we were baptized we died together with him" or "when we were baptized we died in a way like he died."

6.4 By our baptism, then, we were buried with him and shared his death, in order that, just as Christ was raised from death by the glorious power of the Father, so also we might live a new life.

In this verse Paul indicates that baptism is not merely a picture, but an actual event in which the believer shares in Christ's death with him. By translating shared his death, the TEV makes clear the meaning of Paul's expression "unto the death." By his use of the definite article "the" before death, Paul indicates that the reference is to Christ's death (see Moffatt "in his death"; JB "joined him in death"). To render this either as "into death" (RSV) or as "and lay dead" (NEB) is to overlook an important aspect of what Paul is saying. He is stating that by baptism the believer somehow shares both in Christ's burial and in his death.

By our baptism may be appropriately expressed in most languages as "when we were baptized." If this must be made an active expression, it is usually possible to employ some indefinite subject—for example, "when people baptized us." In some languages baptism may be expressed more specifically as means, "by our being baptized."

The metaphor we were buried with him may be translated as a simile, "we were, as it were, buried with him" or "we were seemingly buried alongside of him."

The concept of shared his death may be difficult to express, but it is usually possible to employ some such phrase as "we also died" or "we died together with him." In some languages it is necessary to place death before burial —for example, "when we were baptized we died, as it were, together with him, and we were buried together with him."

The phrase "the glory of the Father," when used instrumentally, is merely a circumlocution for speaking of God's great power: by the glorious power of the Father (Phillips "by that splendid revelation of the Father's power").

It is possible to make the Father the subject of the expression raised from death and therefore translate as "just as the Father raised Christ from death" or "just as the Father caused Christ to live again." By the glorious power may be translated in some languages as "by his wonderful strength" or "by means of his power which is so glorious."

In some languages there is a special problem involved in translating the Father since "Father" may not occur without some indication of relationship or possession. One cannot simply say "with the Father" but must always have "his Father," "our Father," or some such designation of the Father as being related to someone else. In this type of context the most appropriate form is normally "our Father" (first person plural inclusive), since Paul would assume that the Christians to whom he is addressing the letter acknowledge God as a common Father.

"To walk in newness of life" is simply a Jewish way of saying "to live a new life"; it is not necessary to carry over the metaphor of walking as some have done (see NEB "so also we might set our feet upon the new path of life").

In many languages one does not live a new life but rather "lives in a new way." However, since this is the direct purpose of the Christian's being buried with Christ and sharing in his death, it may be important to invert the last two clauses of verse 4, or even to separate them completely—for example, "in order that we might live in an entirely new way, just as the Father raised Christ from death by his wonderful power" or "in order that we might live in a new manner. This is similar to what happened to Christ whom God caused to live again by means of his wonderful power."

> [5]For if we became one with him in dying as he did, in the same way we shall
> be one with him by being raised to life as he was. [6]And we know this: our old
> being has been put to death with Christ on his cross, in order that the power
> of the sinful self might be destroyed, so that we should no longer be the slaves
> of sin. [7]For when a person dies he is set free from the power of sin. [8]If we have
> died with Christ, we believe that we will also live with him. [9]For we know that
> Christ has been raised from death and will never die again—death has no more
> power over him. [10]The death he died was death to sin, once and for all; and
> the life he now lives is life to God. [11]In the same way you are to think of
> yourselves as dead to sin but alive to God in union with Christ Jesus.

6.5 For if we became one with him in dying as he did, in the same way we shall be one with him by being raised to life as he was.

Although the grammatical construction of this verse is difficult, its purpose is clearly to validate what Paul has said in the previous verse. The first part is literally "for if we have grown together in the likeness of his death." Modern English translations supply with him, to be taken with the verb "have grown together." And most modern English translations (with the exception of Goodspeed and Moffatt) understand "have grown together" as a means of indicating unity with him. So the TEV translates for if we became one with him; the NEB "for if we have become incorporate with him"; and the JB "if in union with Christ." The TEV transforms Paul's noun phrase "in the likeness of his death" into a verbal expression in dying as he did (see JB "we have imitated his death"). The contrast in the verb tenses (see also v. 8) is significant. Death is viewed as a past experience and the resurrection as a future experience; this is the same contrast between the past and future that was constantly maintained throughout chapter 5.

Became one with him is not easy to translate in some languages. There may be some such expression as "identify ourselves with him," but more frequently one must employ a more metaphorical expression: "to join up with him," "to share together with him," "to become close companions with him," or "to become just as though we were one person with him."

In dying as he did is an expression of means—for example, "by dying as he did." Similarly, by being raised to life as he was is also an expression of means, but in this instance God is the agent—for example, "by God causing us to live again even as he caused Christ to live again."

6.6 And we know this: our old being has been put to death with Christ on his cross, in order that the power of the sinful self might be destroyed, so that we should no longer be the slaves of sin.

Old being (Moffatt and Goodspeed "old self"; JB "our former selves"; NEB "the man we once were") is literally "old man" (see old self of Ephesians 4.22 and Colossians 3.9). Paul's reference, of course, is to the kind of person that the believer was before his conversion.

In some languages our old being may be rendered as "what we used to be," "the way in which we used to live," or "as far as our being what we used to be."

There are certain complications in translating put to death with Christ on his cross. In some languages it is best to take with Christ on his cross as being temporally related to the phrase put to death—for example, "what we used to be was, as it were, put to death at the same time that Christ was put to death on the cross," "...when Christ was crucified," or "...when people crucified Christ."

The power of the sinful self (NEB "the sinful self") is literally "the body of sin" (Goodspeed, Moffatt, JB "sinful body"). Here "body" is used as a means of speaking of one's total being, and so self seems to be a more adequate translation than "body." The TEV takes the phrase "the body of sin" with the extended meaning of the power of the sinful self; this assumes that Paul is speaking of the power that the sinful self holds over one's person rather than of the sinful self itself.

The power of the sinful self may be equivalent in some instances to "our strong desire to sin" or "we who desire strongly to sin." The passive expression might be destroyed can be made active, in which case God would have to be the agent—for example, "in order that God could destroy our strong desires to sin." In some instances "the old man" may be translated as "the old heart," and therefore one may render this clause as "in order that our old heart might be destroyed" or "in order that the old heart which sins might be destroyed."

There is a special complication in verse 6, since there are two purpose clauses. The first purpose clause depends upon our old being having been put to death with Christ, and the second purpose clause, so that we should no longer be the slaves of sin, is the purpose of "our sinful self having been destroyed." In some languages it may be necessary to make a break between the first and second purposes and recapitulate briefly—for example, "our sinful self has been destroyed in order that we should no longer be slaves of sin."

The expression the slaves of sin is rendered in some languages as "to have sin boss us," "to have sin command us," or "to do what sin says, just as slaves do what their masters say."

6.7 For when a person dies he is set free from the power of sin.

The verb is set free from is literally "is justified"; however, all modern translations understand the word in this context to have the same meaning that the TEV gives it (see also Acts 13.38).

From the power of sin is literally "from sin." Paul's thesis is that death releases man from all responsibilities and obligations, and by the phrase "from sin" he makes one application of this general principle. In this light Paul apparently means that when a man dies, sin no longer exercises control over his life. To assume, with the JB, that this means "he has finished with sin" because he has lost his "sinful body" is to assume that for Paul the body is something innately sinful, a thought that would be totally contradictory to his Jewish background. On the other hand, Paul does not seem to be arguing that "a dead man is no longer answerable for his sin" (NEB); this does not fit in with the overall logic of Paul's argument within this context. Paul's intent is to point out that when the believer dies with Christ, sin no longer exercises control over his life.

He is set free from the power of sin may be rendered as "sin no longer controls him" or "sin no longer commands him." One may express both the freedom and the control by saying: "he is now free, and sin does not control him." In all such passages which speak of a universal experience, it may be necessary to use a plural and to make the time general—for example, "for whenever people die they are set free and sin cannot control them."

6.8 If we have died with Christ, we believe that we will also live with him.

Even though Paul uses the future tense in this verse (as he did in v. 5), the believers' confidence in this future experience has relevance for his present life (see v. 11).

It may be necessary to change the metaphor we have died with Christ to a simile—for example, "if we have, as it were, died with Christ" or "if we, so one might say, died when Christ died."

6.9-11 For we know that Christ has been raised from death and will never die again—death has no more power over him. (10) The death he died was death to sin, once and for all; and the life he now lives is life to God. (11) In the same way you are to think of yourselves as dead to sin but alive to God in union with Christ Jesus.

In verse 9 Paul affirms that the post-resurrection life of Christ is different from his former life: death has no more power over him. Paul expands the meaning of this statement in verse 10, in which he applies the significance of the death-resurrection motif to Christ, and in verse 11 to the present life of the believers. In translating the first half of verse 10, the translator must be careful not to leave the implication that Christ himself was guilty of sin before his death. Paul introduces this remark (that is, the death he died was death to sin) so that he can draw an analogy between the experience of Christ and that of the believers. What Paul is saying is that though Christ once lived in a world where sin held domination over men's lives (though not over his own life), by death he was set free from this realm of existence. Paul also views Christ's death from a positive aspect. Not only does death free him from the world where sin has power over men's lives, but death is a means by which he enters into a world where he enjoys uninterrupted fellowship with God. That is the meaning of the life he now lives is life to God.

The clause death has no more power over him may be translated as "death does not command him," "death can never in the future command him," or "... control him."

It is extremely difficult to translate the death he died was death to sin without implying that Christ himself had sinned. However, it is important to avoid such an implication, since it would be completely contrary to this context and to Paul's teaching. It is sometimes possible to render this clause as "he died as far as sin is concerned," "he died and sin had no power," or even "there was no more power of sin against him." By the use of "against him" one does not imply that sin had power "over him," but simply that sin was a factor.

The phrase once and for all may be rendered as "this was true for all time," "this is always true," or even "he didn't have to die again."

The life he now lives is life to God may be rendered as "how he now lives is for God." It is almost impossible to preserve the parallelism of death to sin and life to God.

In verse 11 Paul makes an application of all that has preceded. For the exegesis of this verse it is necessary to note several points. The phrase dead to sin must be taken with the meaning of "dead as far as the power of sin to control your lives is concerned." Alive to God may be taken either to mean "you live your lives in order to please God" or "you live your lives in fellowship with God." In union with Christ Jesus (so also NEB; literally "in Christ Jesus") is a form of the favorite Pauline expression "in Christ." This expression is closely related to the one used in verse 3 (there literally "into Christ Jesus"). Although the theological implications of this term are profound and theologians have spent much time discussing its meaning, the basic component of meaning is that of union (or fellowship) with Christ Jesus, and it is best to bring this meaning out in translation. In any case, for English readers, as for readers of many other languages, the literal expression "in Christ Jesus" says practically nothing.

In union with Christ Jesus may be understood as the means by which men are alive to God, that is to say, "through their union with Christ Jesus." This phrase may, however, also express the circumstances which accompany a man's being alive to God; or in union with Christ Jesus may be taken as explanatory of what alive to God means—for example, "alive to God, that is to say, being in union with Christ Jesus."

[12]Sin must no longer rule in your mortal bodies, so that you obey the desires of your natural self. [13]Nor must you surrender any part of yourselves to sin, to be used for wicked purposes. Instead, give yourselves to God, as men who have been brought from death to life, and surrender your whole being to him to be used for righteous purposes. [14]Sin must not rule over you; you do not live under law but under God's grace.

6.12 Sin must no longer rule in your mortal bodies, so that you obey the desires of your natural self.

In this and the following verses (12-14) Paul reinforces the argument stated in the previous verses (1-11). Must no longer rule (so also NEB) translates a present imperative in Greek which has precisely the force that the TEV and the NEB bring out. In many languages a third person imperative is difficult to express, and it is often necessary to render "you must not let sin rule any longer in your mortal bodies." In Greek bodies is singular (see NEB "body"), but in English the plural makes better sense.

There are several complications in the first clause of verse 12. It may be difficult, for example, to employ the active expression sin must no longer rule, but one may be able to say: "your mortal bodies must not be controlled by sin" or "...must not be under the power of sin" or "...controlled by your desire to sin." However, in some languages it is difficult to speak of mortal bodies, since the only equivalent would be "bodies which die," while in some other languages one cannot say "bodies which die," since it is not the body but the person which dies. Nevertheless, one can translate mortal as "which have an end" or "which do not continue forever." The concept of bodies may be more effectively expressed in some languages as "inside of you," so that this first clause may be translated as "sin should no longer have control inside of you."

Of your natural self is literally "of it," and the antecedent is "your mortal body." However, it is better to translate in such a way as not to limit the idea of sinful desires to "bodily passions" (so JB; NEB "the body's desires"; Phillips "your lusts"). Such a rendering seems to limit Paul's idea too narrowly; he has in mind not merely one's bodily passions, but the whole range of sinful desires and intentions which place one over against God. Since Paul, as a Jew, can speak of the body as the totality of one's person, he can speak of "the desires of your mortal body" and cover a much larger spectrum than the English translation "bodily desires" would imply.

The conjunctive phrase so that introduces purpose, but with a causative relation—for example, "so as to cause you to obey the desires of your natural self," "obey what you yourselves desire," or "...what you as a human being desire."

6.13 Nor must you surrender any part of yourselves to sin, to be used for wicked purposes. Instead, give yourselves to God, as men who have been brought from death to life, and surrender your whole being to him to be used for righteous purposes.

The Greek verbs translated surrender and give come from the same stem, though their tenses are different. The first verb, a present tense, intimates that Paul considers the Roman Christians to be in the process of surrendering "part of themselves to sin"; so the meaning of this imperative is something like "stop surrendering any part of yourselves to sin" (see NEB "you must no longer put its several parts at sin's disposal"). The second of these imperatives is an aorist and suggests that they are now to give themselves once and for all to God.

Any part of yourselves (JB "any part of your body") and your whole being (JB "every part of your body") translate the same expressions in Greek. The TEV takes the first of the phrases in a distributive sense, focusing attention on the individual parts of the body, and then takes the second phrase as a summary expression of one's whole being, thus focusing attention on the body as a unit (so NEB and JB). Most translations render both phrases by the same expression, generally in a way similar to the rendering of the TEV.

To be used for wicked purposes and to be used for righteous purposes are literally in Greek "instruments of wickedness" and "instruments of righteousness." Note how the TEV transforms Paul's noun phrases into verb phrases. It is necessary to do this in many languages. (See also NEB "as implements for doing wrong" and "as implements for doing right.")

A term such as surrender may be rendered as "allow"—for example, "you must not allow any part of yourself to sin," "you must not permit any part of you to sin," or, as in some languages, "you must not give freedom to any part of yourself so that it may sin." If sin in such instances is rendered as the active process of sinning rather than the principle of sin, the phrase to be used for wicked purposes is simply a further explanation—for example, "that is to say, to be used to do evil" or simply "to do evil." When one can retain sin as an active principle, it is preferable to do so and thus translate the first clause as "you must not surrender any part of yourself to the power of sin." In this way one can preserve the parallelism with the second part of verse 13—for example, "rather, you must give yourself to God."

As men who have been brought from death to life may be best rendered in some languages as a separate sentence—for example, "you are like men who are no longer dead but alive" or "you are like men who were dead, so to speak, but whom God has now caused to live."

The last clause of verse 13 may be translated as "you must give yourselves completely to God so that he will use you to do what is right."

6.14 Sin must not rule over you; you do not live under law but under God's grace.

Verse 14 serves both as a conclusion and as a transition. It is a conclusion to Paul's argument in the first part of the chapter, and it serves as a transition to a more detailed discussion in the rest of the chapter and in chapter 7. In Greek sin must not rule over you is a future tense (RSV "sin will have no dominion over you"), but in the context its force is imperative. The reason that sin must not rule over the believer is that he does not live under law but under God's grace. Paul looks upon the law as giving sin a free hand and contributing to its strength (see 5.20-21). Moreover, law and sin are related not only on this basis, but on the basis that law is symbolic of man's strivings by his own efforts to put himself right with God. God's grace (literally "grace"), on the other hand, delivers a man from sin, because it depends not on the human will or on human strength, but on the divine activity.

The initial clause sin must not rule over you may be construed as a matter of permission—for example, "you must not permit sin to command you." The final clause of verse 14 may be regarded as the reason for not permitting sin to rule over a person—for example, "because you do not live under law but under God's grace" or "because you do not live by what the law tells you you must do, but by the goodness which God has shown you."

Slaves of Righteousness

[15]What, then? Shall we sin, because we are not under law but under God's
grace? By no means! [16]Surely you know that when you surrender yourselves
as slaves to obey someone, you are in fact the slaves of the master you obey
—either of sin, which results in death, or of obedience, which results in being
put right with God. [17]But thanks be to God! For at one time you were slaves
to sin; but then you obeyed with all your heart the truths found in the teaching
you received. [18]You were set free from sin and became the slaves of righteousness. [19]I use ordinary words because of the weakness of your natural selves.
At one time you surrendered yourselves entirely as slaves to impurity and
wickedness, for wicked purposes. In the same way you must now surrender
yourselves entirely as slaves of righteousness, for holy purposes.

The phrase Slaves of Righteousness is too likely to be understood as merely "Righteous Slaves." One may, therefore, expand this expression to read "We Are Slaves to Do What Is Right." A much more meaningful equivalent may be "We Are under Obligation to Do What Is Right."

6.15 What, then? Shall we sin, because we are not under law but under God's grace? By no means!

Paul's question, What, then?, reminds one of the question that he raised in verse 1, What shall we say, then? It is best to understand this, not as a rhetorical question, but as a question which he thinks might be asked by his opponents. Paul's argument—that the Christian lives under God's grace and therefore should not sin—could be reversed, and so he begins in this verse to protect himself against such an argument. Most commentators and translators assume that by the use of the word law in this verse Paul has reference to any command of God, and not merely to the Jewish Law. By no means translates the same expression that Paul used in verse 2.

If the question and answer technique cannot be employed as a rhetorical device, it is generally possible to use a strong negation—for example, "we must not sin, for we are not under law but under God's grace" or "since we are not under law but under God's grace, we must therefore not sin."

Under law may be rendered as "abide by law," "are controlled by law," or "are ruled by law." The choice of a term for under law must in some measure be determined by the corresponding term, under God's grace; this may be expressed in various ways—for example, "God's grace controls us" or "God's grace compels us."

6.16 Surely you know that when you surrender yourselves as slaves to obey someone, you are in fact the slaves of the master you obey—either of sin, which results in death, or of obedience, which results in being put right with God.

The question with which Paul introduces this verse (see RSV "do you not know?") is emphatic and expects a positive answer; for this reason the TEV has rendered the question by a statement: Surely you know that (see also NEB "You know well enough that" and NAB "You must realize that").

The total content of this verse is a bit difficult because Paul tries to include so much in it. The meaning, however, is clear and comes out essentially the same in all translations. The first half of the verse is a reflection on a custom prevalent in Paul's day, according to which a man would sell himself into slavery in order to survive; the second half of the verse (separated in the TEV from the first part by a dash) takes up the idea of slavery and applies it both to the concepts of sin and obedience. Obedience in this verse must be understood in terms of obedience to God.

One should note that Paul uses the word death in at least three senses in his writings: (1) the biological fact of death as the judgment of God upon all human life (Romans 5.12-14); (2) the "spiritual death" of all men in their pre-Christian state (see Ephesians 2.1; Colossians 2.13); (3) eternal death as the final judgment of God on the life of sin (6.16).

Surrender yourselves as slaves may be translated as "give yourselves to people to become slaves of them," "make yourselves slaves of others," or "cause yourself to be a slave to someone." Since, however, such a surrendering of one's self as a slave is, in this context, more a condition than a temporal event, it may be more effectively expressed in some languages by an "if" clause—for example, "if you surrender yourself to a person to be his slave, and as such obey him, you are, in fact, a slave of the master whom you obey." The second part of verse 16 may then be rendered as "you either obey sin and this causes your death, or you obey God and this causes you to be put right with him" or "...you obey God and as a result he puts you right with himself."

6.17 But thanks be to God! For at one time you were slaves to sin; but then you obeyed with all your heart the truths found in the teaching you received.

The initial exclamation, But thanks be to God!, must be expressed with a subject in a number of languages, "but we must thank God" or "but we can be most thankful to God." What follows in verse 17 is the reason for thanks being given to God.

At one time in the TEV means "formerly" or "once" (so most translations). It is added simply to emphasize the difference in time between this clause and the one which follows, where then is added for the same reason.

You were slaves to sin may be translated as "you were like slaves obeying sin" or "you were like slaves obeying your desires to sin." If sin cannot be treated in a personified manner, it may be necessary here, as well as in similar contexts, to relate slaves to the desire to sin rather than to sin as a general principle.

With all your heart (literally "from the heart") appears in other translations as "wholehearted" (NEB), "without reservation" (JB), and "sincerely" (NAB).

The truths found in the teaching is rendered in several ways: "standard of teaching" (Goodspeed); "pattern of teaching" (NEB); "rule of teaching" (NAB); and "creed" (JB). The word that the TEV translates as truths literally means something like "pattern" (the same word is used in 5.14); in this context it must be given the broadest possible meaning. The translator must be careful not to read into the term some carefully formulated doctrinal statement, as the word "creed" might suggest; Paul had in mind mainly ethical teaching.

Because of the difficulty of finding an adequate term for truths, one may translate this last part of verse 17 as "but then you became completely obedient to what you found in the teaching you received."

You received actually translates a passive construction in Greek (RSV "to which you were committed"; NEB "to which you were made subject"); but it is better to transform this into an active (note Goodspeed "that you received") for the sake of the English reader. Paul speaks elsewhere of teaching being handed over to people (see 16.17), though not of people being handed over to teaching, as the use of the passive in this verse implies. For this reason, the TEV takes the passive verb here to have a somewhat different force, you received (see JB "you were taught"; NAB "which was imparted to you"; and the alternative reading in the NEB "which was handed on to you"). On the other hand, if this is a true passive, the meaning is "the truths found in the teaching to which you were made subject." If this is to be taken as a passive, then there are two other important aspects that must be considered. First, God would be the implied agent of the passive voice; and second, in light of the overall theme, the idea of being "made subject" should be understood in the context of slavery. So then, if the verb is assumed to have a genuine passive force, the following translation will result: "the truths found in the teaching to which God made you slaves."

6.18 You were set free from sin and became the slaves of righteousness.

In Greek this verse begins with a participial phrase which is equivalent to a subordinate clause (see RSV "having been set free from sin"), but the TEV makes this into a coordinate clause: you were set free from sin.

You were set free from sin may be translated: "you were released from the power of sin" or "God set you free from the power of sin." Became the slaves of righteousness may be translated as "became slaves to do what is right." However, such an expression can be badly misunderstood, and it may be appropriate to introduce God at this point in parallelism with verse 22 (namely, slaves of God) and therefore read: "became the slaves of God in order to do what is right."

6.19 I use ordinary words because of the weakness of your natural selves.

At one time you surrendered yourselves entirely as slaves to impurity and wickedness, for wicked purposes. In the same way you must now surrender yourselves entirely as slaves of righteousness, for holy purposes.

I use ordinary words (JB "if I may use human terms"; NAB "I use the following example from human affairs") is the same expression used in 3.5, I speak here as men do, and is best taken as a reference to what Paul is going to say. The equivalent might very well be "let me use an ordinary example" or "let me use an example from everyday life."

Paul's use of the phrase the weakness of your natural selves is not intended here to have moral or ethical implications; it is only a reference to the fact that he believes these people incapable of understanding profound truths unless he uses analogies from everyday life. The phrase is literally "the weakness of your flesh"; it appears in the NAB as "your weak human nature" and in the JB as "your natural weakness." The NEB combines the two phrases: "to use words that suit your human weakness."

It is important to avoid, in the choice of a word for weakness, an expression which will apply only to physical weakness. In fact, it may be necessary to qualify "weakness" as "weakness of your understanding" or "weakness of the way in which you, as just a human being, understand things."

Yourselves entirely appears twice in verse 13 and is there translated first by any part of yourselves and then by your whole being.

Impurity and wickedness (literally "lawlessness"; in 4.7 translated wrongs) were two sins that the Jews generally accused the Gentiles of committing. The idea of wickedness is made emphatic in this verse by being used twice (wickedness, for wicked purposes). The word rendered impurity is used also in Romans 1.24 (there rendered filthy things). Paul also uses the word in 2 Corinthians 12.21; Galatians 5.19; Ephesians 4.19; 5.3; Colossians 3.5; 1 Thessalonians 2.3; 4.7. Outside of Paul's writings it appears only in Matthew 23.27.

Slaves to impurity and wickedness may be rendered as "slaves to do what is impure and wicked" or "slaves to do what is sexually and generally bad." "Sexually and generally" are simply ways of designating the focal components of impurity and wickedness.

Since purpose has already been expressed in relating wickedness to slaves, it is often difficult to add a further purpose (for wicked purposes), which is merely an emphatic amplification of the term wickedness. One may, therefore, translate wickedness as "to do all kinds of wickedness."

Holy purposes (NEB "a holy life") appears in Moffatt and Goodspeed as "consecration" and is a word that is normally rendered "sanctification" or "holiness" in most translations. It appears in Paul's writings here and in 6.22; 1 Corinthians 1.30; 1 Thessalonians 4.3,4,7; 2 Thessalonians 2.13; 1 Timothy 2.15; and outside Paul's writings in Hebrews 12.14 and 1 Peter 1.2. Basically the idea involved in this word is that of being dedicated or set aside to God, and in other than Jewish and Christian contexts the word has no connotation of purity of life. However, in biblical thought purity of life does become basic because the people who are set aside for the service of God are expected to take on the likeness and character of God. So in the present context the idea is either that of being set aside to God for the sake of achieving his holy purposes (TEV) or for the sake of "making for a holy life" (NEB). Attention should be called to the fact that the adverb now stands emphatic in the second sentence of this verse.

As in verse 18, slaves of righteousness may be translated as "slaves to do what is right."

The final phrase for holy purposes may be rendered as an explanation of righteousness—for example, "that is to say, to do that which is holy." But if one adopts the meaning of "consecration," it may be rendered better as "this is in order that you may be truly God's people" or "in order that you may be really dedicated to God."

> [20]When you were the slaves of sin, you were free from righteousness. [21]What did you gain from doing the things that you are ashamed of now? The result of those things is death! [22]But now you have been set free from sin and are the slaves of God; your gain is a life fully dedicated to him, and the result is eternal life. [23]For sin pays its wage—death; but God's free gift is eternal life in union with Christ Jesus our Lord.

6.20-21 When you were the slaves of sin, you were free from righteousness. (21) What did you gain from doing the things that you are ashamed of now? The result of those things is death!

In these two verses Paul once again reminds the Roman believers of the situation in which they lived before they came to Christ. The meaning of the word righteousness in this verse needs some attention. In verse 18 righteousness is evidently made parallel with the truths found in the teaching you received of verse 17. But what is the meaning of righteousness in verses 19 and 20? Righteousness in these last two instances is best taken in a way related to its use in verse 18. That is, the more general meaning of righteousness in these two verses is "doing what God requires," and in verse 18 the specific requirements that God makes are identified with the truths found in the teaching you received (from God). And because Paul speaks in this context of impurity and wickedness as the results of slavery to sin, so it is likely that the major emphasis in righteousness in this passage is on the moral and ethical demands that God makes on his people.

It is not easy to translate satisfactorily the clause you were free from righteousness. The most satisfactory equivalent in some languages is simply "you were not under obligation to do what God required."

What did you gain? is literally "what fruit did you receive?", a common figure for Jewish speakers, and it is translated in a variety of ways: NAB "what benefit did you then enjoy?"; NEB "what was the gain?"; JB "what did you get from this?"

The question in verse 21 may be changed into a statement, "You certainly did not receive any good from the things that you are ashamed of now" or "Those things which cause you to be ashamed now certainly did not benefit you at all."

The final clause, the result of those things is death, may be translated as "these things (or experiences) cause your death" or "doing such things causes people to die."

In verse 21 there is a problem of punctuation. The question mark may come at the point where it is in the TEV (so also RSV, Goodspeed); or the question mark may be placed earlier in the sentence (NAB "what benefit did you then enjoy? Things you are now ashamed of, all of them tending toward death" ; see also NEB, JB, and Moffatt).

6.22 But now you have been set free from sin and are the slaves of God; your gain is a life fully dedicated to him, and the result is eternal life.

Set free is in Greek a participle which the TEV renders as a finite verb (see also JB), with the result that only coordinate constructions appear in this verse. Paul was very fond of using subordinate clauses, but in English it is sometimes more natural to transform them into coordinate structures. If the agent of the passive verbs in this verse (have been set free...are) must be expressed, then God is the agent: "but now God has set you free from sin and made you his slaves."

You have been set free from sin can only be interpreted psychologically in some languages—for example, "you have been set free from the strong desires to sin" or "God has set you free, so you are not controlled by the strong desires to sin" or "...do not do what your desires to sin tell you to do."

In Greek were set free from sin and are the slaves of God are both aorist participles, referring to events that have already taken place. In fact, these events are best looked upon as having taken place simultaneously, even though the TEV suggests successive actions.

And the result is similar to the expression rendered result in the previous verse.

Your gain is a life fully dedicated to him is literally "you have your fruit/harvest for holiness," and it is translated by the RSV as "the return you get is sanctification." In the previous verse Paul used the word "fruit" to denote result or outcome, and the word "holiness" (RSV "consecration") is the word discussed in verse 19. The NEB translates "your gains are such as make for holiness"; and Goodspeed "the benefit you get is consecration."

In some languages one cannot say a life fully dedicated. One can, however, say "you have dedicated yourself completely" or "in all that you do you have dedicated yourself." Hence, this clause may be translated: "as a result, in all that you do you have dedicated yourself completely for his sake."

Paul affirms that the end result of a life fully dedicated to God is eternal life. Eternal life (see 2.7; 5.21; 6.23) is basically a qualitative concept, that is, the kind of life that one shares when he experiences a proper relation with God. In biblical thought the qualitative aspect is always foremost, though the meaning also becomes quantitative, that is, the kind of life that does not end.

6.23 For sin pays its wage—death; but God's free gift is eternal life in union with Christ Jesus our Lord.

In a sense this verse is a conclusion to all that Paul has said throughout this chapter. He brings together two contrasts: the contrast between death and life, and the contrast between wage and free gift. The man who lives in sin receives what he has earned—death; but the believer receives God's free gift—eternal life.

The principal difficulty in translating the first clause of verse 23 is that in so many languages sin cannot be personified as an agent which pays wages. The closest equivalent may be "when a man sins he receives the consequences, that is, death," "the result of having sinned is death," or even "because a man sins he will inevitably die." The relationship between sin and death is essentially cause and effect, and in some languages this relationship is expressed idiomatically—for example, "the wages for the sinful heart is the death way."

God's free gift is eternal life may be slightly recast as "God freely gives eternal life" or "God causes people to live without end as a free gift from him."

In union with Christ Jesus our Lord may be understood either as the means by which eternal life is made possible or as a qualification of the nature of eternal life, that is, life lived in union with Christ Jesus our Lord. These ideas are closely related, and it is doubtful if one can insist on any real distinction between the two in Paul's mind. The conclusion of this verse is similar to that presented in 5.21 and 6.11.

In some languages the most satisfactory translation of in union with Christ Jesus our Lord is "this means that we are in union with Christ Jesus our Lord" or "that is to say, we are closely bound to Jesus Christ our Lord." It is also possible to treat this final phrase as an expression of means (as indicated above) and to render the phrase as "our living without end is possible, because we are in union with Christ Jesus our Lord" or "by being in union with Christ Jesus our Lord, we can live unendingly."

CHAPTER 7

An Illustration from Marriage

7 Certainly you understand what I am about to say, my brothers, because
all of you know about law. The law rules over a man only as long as he
lives. [2]A married woman, for example, is bound by the law to her husband as
long as he lives; but if he dies, then she is free from the law that bound her
to him. [3]So then, if she lives with another man while her husband is alive, she
will be called an adulteress; but if her husband dies, she is legally a free woman,
and does not commit adultery if she marries another man. [4]That is the way
it is with you, my brothers. You also have died, as far as the Law is concerned,
because you are part of the body of Christ; and now you belong to him who
was raised from death in order that we might be useful in the service of God.
[5]For when we lived according to our human nature, the sinful desires stirred
up by the Law were at work in our bodies, and we were useful in the service
of death. [6]Now, however, we are free from the Law, because we died to that
which once held us prisoners. No longer do we serve in the old way of a written
law, but in the new way of the Spirit.

The section heading An Illustration from Marriage may be difficult to translate in a succinct manner, and accordingly one may need to add a term for Law—for example, "An Example Concerning the Law about Marriage." In some instances, one may use simply the expression "The Law about Marriage" or "The Law about Marriage and Our Relationship to Christ."

Paul has already discussed from several aspects the question of the meaning and significance of the Law (see 3.20; 4.14, 15; 5.20; 6.14). Now, in the first six verses of this chapter, he takes up that theme again; in verses 1-3 he uses an illustration from marriage to emphasize his point; and then in verses 4-6 he makes specific application of this illustration to the Christian life.

As a number of interpreters point out, there is a parallelism between Romans 6 and 7: chapter 6 speaks of freedom from sin while chapter 7 speaks of freedom from the Law. Since Paul looks upon both sin and the Law as ruling over the Christian, he finds a number of parallels between the power of sin and the power of the Law over the life of the individual.

7.1 Certainly you understand what I am about to say, my brothers, because all of you know about law. The law rules over a man only as long as he lives.

This verse follows closely the preceding verse (6.23). It is not without significance that Paul addresses his readers directly in this verse and again in verse 4 as my brothers. He introduces this section with an emphatic negative question (literally "do you not know?") which the TEV makes into a positive statement, certainly you understand (see Moffatt "surely you know"). As noted previously, my brothers may be translated either by a general term for kinship which would be applicable to the extended in-group of the church, or by an expression such as "fellow believers," since this is its significance in this type of context.

7.2

What I am about to say...because all of you know about law is literally "because I am speaking to those who know law." It may be that Paul is using "law" in a specific sense either as a reference to the Roman law or to the Jewish Law, though most commentators believe that he is simply referring to the idea of law in general. Paul is not speaking to specialists in the law (so JB "who have studied law"), but to persons who have some general knowledge about law (NEB "who have some knowledge of law"). It is true that his illustration from marriage is more closely in keeping with the Jewish Law, but for Paul the Mosaic Law represents a specific expression of what is right for human conduct in general (see 2.12-16).

It is important that the expression what I am about to say be translated in such a way as to refer specifically to what follows. In some languages the equivalent may be "what I will say now," "what you will soon be reading," or "what I say, which follows."

A generic statement concerning law may in many languages be better expressed as a plural—for example, "all of you know about laws" or even "...how laws are applied."

Rules over a man may be rendered in some languages as "controls a man," "says what he must do," or "puts a man under obligation."

7.2 A married woman, for example, is bound by the law to her husband as long as he lives; but if he dies, then she is free from the law that bound her to him.

Paul's transitional particle (literally "for," so KJV and Goodspeed) is rendered for example by the TEV (also NEB and NAB) and as "for instance" by the JB. An equivalent in some languages is "it is like this" or "this is what it means."

The law described in this verse more nearly conforms with the regulations of Jewish Law than of Roman law; but for Paul's readers the meaning of the example is clear: a married woman...is bound by the law to her husband as long as he lives.

The law that bound her to him is literally "the law of her husband," but the reference is simply to "the obligations of the marriage-law" (NEB). The reason for this rather strange sounding expression is that in antiquity the law was looked upon as giving the husband authority over his wife; in fact, the expression married woman is literally "the woman who is under the power of her husband."

A married woman...is bound by the law to her husband may be changed into an active expression and translated in a somewhat different way—for example, "the law ties a married woman to her husband," "the law unites a woman to her husband," or "the law says a married woman must stay with her husband."

She is free from the law may be expressed as "the law does not tie her any longer," "the law unties her," "the law causes her to be free," or "the law says, She is now free."

7.3 So then, if she lives with another man while her husband is alive, she will be called an adulteress; but if her husband dies, she is legally a free woman, and does not commit adultery if she marries another man.

In light of what Paul is going to say in verse 4, it is important that he bring in the idea of another man in verse 3. If she lives with (so also RSV) is perhaps the best way to render the expression Paul uses here (literally "if she becomes another man's"). The NEB expresses the same thought with a different level of language ("if...she consorts with another man"), while the NAB and JB have "if she gives herself to another." It may be pressing Paul's meaning too far to say "if she marries another man" (Goodspeed), although the phrase that the TEV translates if she lives with another man is the same as that translated if she marries another man later in this same verse.

If she lives with another man is most usually translated simply as "if she has relations with another man" or "if she sleeps with another man," as a specific indication of sexual relations. One can also employ an expression such as "if she goes to live with another man" or "...goes and stays with another man."

There are terms for an adulteress in nearly all languages, but in some instances the expression may be highly idiomatic—for example, "she becomes a dog," "she opens herself," or "she goes from door to door."

7.4 That is the way it is with you, my brothers. You also have died, as far as the Law is concerned, because you are part of the body of Christ; and now you belong to him who was raised from death in order that we might be useful in the service of God.

Verse 4 is transitional; here Paul begins to apply the meaning of the illustration from marriage. A number of ways may be used to translate the particle with which Paul introduces this verse: that is the way it is (TEV); "that is why" (JB); "in the same way" (NAB), etc.

Once again Paul uses a specific address, my brothers, making this verse emphatic in its argument. The pronoun you, which appears four times in this verse, must be taken as a reference to all of Paul's readers and not to the Gentiles alone. For that reason the pronoun we in the latter part of the verse should be inclusive in those languages which distinguish between the inclusive and exclusive forms.

That is the way it is with you may be translated as "this also applies to you" or "you are also involved the same way."

In you also have died, Paul employs an unusual form of the verb "to die," a passive form, but all translations take it in the same sense as the TEV. In Greek the verb rendered have died is an aorist tense, and expresses action at some definite time in the past, perhaps a reference to the baptismal experience of the believers. You also have died may, however, require a change from metaphor to simile—for example, "it is just as though you had died" or "you also have seemingly died."

Paul's use of the word Law in this verse is ambiguous, though the TEV (also JB, Goodspeed, Moffatt) takes it to mean the Jewish Law. Paul's analogy in this passage is not perfect; but his main concern is to emphasize the contrasts between death and new life, and this is the point at which his argument must be understood. He has compared the believer to a married woman; when her husband dies she is free to marry another man. The Christian is released from the Law (though the Law does not die), and this release from the Law is made possible by the death of Christ and by the death of the believer in connection with Christ's death. As death opens up the possibility for the married woman to have a new relationship in life, so the death of Christ makes a new relationship possible for the believer.

As far as the Law is concerned may be rather differently expressed in some languages—for example, "if you think about the Law," "if you consider the Law," or even "if you are talking about the Law."

The phrase translated because you are a part of the body of Christ (literally "by means of the body of Christ") is difficult. Some understand body in the sense of the church, which is elsewhere spoken of as the body of Christ (see 12.5; 1 Corinthians 12.27), while others take it as a reference to the death of Christ (see 6.6). Apparently the TEV follows the first of these possibilities (so also the NEB "by becoming identified with the body of Christ"). If the second of these possibilities is followed, then this passage might be rendered: "by the death of Christ you also have died as far as the Law is concerned."

In the same way that Christ's death freed the believer from the Law, so his resurrection makes possible a new relationship: and now you belong to him who was raised from death in order that we might be useful in the service of God. The understood agent of the passive voice (was raised from death) is God, that is, "God raised him from death."

That we might be useful in the service of God is literally "that we might bear fruit for God" (so most translations). Of all the translations normally cited in this volume, only the TEV and the JB ("to make us productive for God") have made the meaning of the metaphor explicit. The metaphor may have the specific meaning of "bringing others to God," but in the present context the emphasis seems to be more general, that is, simply living a life that is useful to God. In some languages, useful in the service of God may be expressed as "doing good for God's sake" or "doing good as a way of serving God."

7.5 For when we lived according to our human nature, the sinful desires stirred up by the Law were at work in our bodies, and we were useful in the service of death.

It is important to notice the parallels between verses 5 and 6, and at the same time their relation to what follows. Verse 5 describes the pre-Christian experience, and has its parallel in 7.7-25; verse 6 describes the present life of faith under the leadership of God's Spirit, and has its parallel in 8.1-11.

For when we lived according to our human nature is literally "for when we were in the flesh." A number of translations render this clause literally, though others try to make some meaning of it: "when we were unspiritual" (Moffatt); "while we lived on the level of our lower nature" (NEB); "for when we were living mere physical lives" (Goodspeed). In the present passage "life in the flesh" is life lived apart from the control of God's Spirit (see v. 6); it describes life lived according to one's own human nature, and which is under the law, sin, and death. In 8.9 (see also Galatians 5.24) Paul uses this phrase with the same meaning; while in a passage such as Galatians 2.20 the phrase has no sinful overtones, but merely describes human existence in general.

In many languages there is simply no general expression such as human nature. Accordingly, the first clause in verse 5 must be rather drastically modified as far as its form is concerned, but not in terms of its content—for example, "when we live just as we ourselves want to," "when we live just as people generally like to live," or "when we live just as most people desire to live." In this manner one can describe the attitudes of most people and thus signify what human nature is.

The sinful desires translates a genitive expression in Greek (literally "the desires of sin") and may mean either "desires which lead to sin" or sinful desires; most translations seem to take this in the same sense that the TEV does. The most common equivalent is, of course, "desire to sin," and in the larger context "the Law causes us to desire to sin."

Were at work in our bodies may be expressed as "the desires which are in our bodies" or "the desires which our bodies have" or "what we desire in our bodies."

We were useful in the service of death may be translated simply as "all we did ended in death." However, the underlying Greek expression may be understood also in the sense of "caused us to die"; that is to say, "the desires ...at work in our bodies killed us" or "because we had these desires... in our bodies, we died." This death must be clearly distinguished from "dying to the law" (v. 4). For this reason in some translations the future tense is preferred —for example, "all we do will end in death" or "these desires...will cause us to die."

Stirred up by the Law is the meaning of the phrase that Paul uses here; to change this into a negative expression (JB "quite unsubdued by the Law") is to miss the impact of what Paul is saying. He is not trying to indicate that the Law failed to control one's sinful desires, but rather that the Law encouraged one's sinful desires (see 7.8). An equivalent of stirred up by the Law may be in some languages "because there was the Law, our desires to sin came to life" or "... became strong."

7.6 Now, however, we are free from the Law, because we died to that which once held us prisoners. No longer do we serve in the old way of a written law, but in the new way of the Spirit.

As mentioned earlier, verse 6 brings in the contrast between the "once" and the "now."

We are free (the same verb used in verse 2) translates an aorist passive (literally "we were set free"), which points to a specific time in the past, perhaps to the act of confession at baptism. Again the understood agent of the passive voice is God, "God set us free." In some languages this may be expressed as "God untied us from the Law" or even "God erased the Law as far as we were concerned."

7.6

The pronoun, that which, refers to the Law, "to the Law which." We died to that which once held us prisoners (that is, the Law) must be expressed in essentially the same way as in the second sentence of verse 4, that is, died, as far as the Law is concerned.

Held us prisoners may be rendered as "caused us to be prisoners," "locked us up," or "tied us up," or, metaphorically, "put chains on us."

In Greek this verse is one sentence, and the second sentence of the TEV represents a clause which in Greek introduces the conclusion. The transition between these two sentences may be introduced by "as a result," "hence," or "therefore."

The object of the verb serve is God: no longer do we serve (God). Paul now contrasts the two ways of rendering service to God. It may be that the compound phrase in the old way of a written law is not clear for the reader. It is perhaps better to take written law in apposition with the old way, and so to understand the phrase to mean "in the old way that was made possible for us by the written law." The same may be said of the second phrase, in the new way of the Spirit; this may be rendered "in the new way made possible by the Spirit." A few translations understand Spirit to refer to man's own spirit (JB "in the new spiritual way" and NAB "in the new spirit"), though most commentators understand it to be a reference to the Holy Spirit.

The relations between the term way and the corresponding expressions a written law and the Spirit must in some languages be made more explicit—for example, "the old way, that is, the way which the written law told us we should live." The new way of the Spirit may be "the new way, that is, how the Spirit causes us to live."

Law and Sin

[7]What shall we say, then? That the Law itself is sinful? Of course not! But it was the Law that made me know what sin is. I would not have known what it is to covet if the Law had not said, "Do not covet." [8]Sin found its chance to stir up all kinds of covetousness in me by working through the commandment. For sin is a dead thing apart from law. [9]I myself was once alive apart from law; but when the commandment came, sin sprang to life, [10]and I died. And the commandment which was meant to bring life, in my case brought death. [11]Sin found its chance and deceived me by working through the commandment; by means of the commandment sin killed me.

The section heading Law and Sin may not convey a satisfactory meaning if translated literally. Accordingly, one may want to employ some such phrase as "The Law Causes Sin" or "The Law Induces People to Sin."

With this verse Paul introduces a new section in his argument. However, analysis of verses 7-25 is difficult, as can be observed by the number of different ways in which this section is divided in the various translations. The TEV divides this part of Romans 7 into two sections of two paragraphs each (the latter part of verse 25 is a short paragraph summarizing the argument), and this will form the basis for our discussion of Paul's argument. In 7-13 Paul is dealing with the problem of the relation between law and sin. He argues that even though sin used the Law as a means to attack him (vv. 7-11), the Law itself is holy and good (vv. 12-13). So then, it was not the Law that brought death to him, but sin working through the Law.

In the latter half of the chapter Paul continues on the assumption that the Law is good. But even though it is good, Paul is a mortal man, a slave to sin, and cannot do as the Law commands, even though he would like to (vv. 14-20). Then he continues, in typical Jewish fashion, and speaks of the two "laws" at work in man: the "law" which leads him to do evil and the "law" which leads him to desire to do good. As a result, he is an unhappy man and on his way to death (vv. 21-24). However, there is a way of release (v. 25), and this way of release is made possible by God's Spirit (chapter 8).

7.7 What shall we say, then? That the Law itself is sinful? Of course not! But it was the Law that made me know what sin is. I would not have known what it is to covet if the Law had not said, "Do not covet."

Paul's question, What shall we say, then?, indicates the beginning of a new section in which he once again uses the style of a philosophical argument (see 2.1).

In some languages the equivalent of the two initial questions would be "some people may argue, The Law itself is sinful" or "some people might insist that the Law itself is bad."

Of course not reflects a typical Pauline formula by which he rejects a statement as being not true; elsewhere in Romans it has been rendered as certainly not and by no means (see 3.4,6,31; 6.2,15; it will also appear in 7.13; 9.14; 11.1,11). An appropriate rendering in some languages may be "but of course this is not true" or "certainly the Law is not bad."

Once again throughout this passage Paul uses the term Law primarily in the sense of the Jewish Law, though he would probably intend a wider application and so to include any command that comes from God in any form whatsoever.

Know is used, not in the sense of theoretical knowledge, but to indicate a concrete experience. It will be helpful to expand this statement further. All men are selfish and inwardly rebellious against God. However, sin cannot be brought to light in such a way that it can be seen and measured apart from its rejection of a specific commandment of God. This is what Paul means by "knowing sin"; he rejected God's command and so became conscious of himself as a sinful being. He uses the specific example of the tenth commandment to illustrate what he means. He would never have known what it is to covet if the Law had not said, "Do not covet."

The word translated covet means literally "desire" and is sometimes used in the New Testament in a good sense (see Luke 22.15), but generally it is found with evil connotations. Paul is here following a rather typical Jewish viewpoint, which speaks of the three stages of desire, sin, and death (cf. James 1.15). Of course, this concept has its roots in Genesis 3.

Although Paul uses two different tenses for the verb know in this verse (the first an aorist, and the second a pluperfect with the meaning of an imperfect), it is doubtful if any special difference in meaning is to be understood. In fact, the verbs themselves come from different roots, but they are used synonymously here.

The particular significance of know in this context may be expressed in some languages as "really know." In most languages it is better to use an expression meaning "to experience." In certain languages, however, the concept of knowing may be expressed as "feeling" or "know by doing."

7.8 Sin found its chance to stir up all kinds of covetousness in me by working through the commandment. For sin is a dead thing apart from law.

In the phrase sin found its chance the word chance translates a term which originally was used by the military to mean "a base of operation." But in New Testament times the word was used frequently in a metaphorical sense with the meaning of "opportunity (to do something)." It should be noted that Paul clearly distinguishes between law and sin; law was not intended to be the means by which sin would launch its attack, but sin took advantage of this opportunity to attack man. Found its chance may be rendered as "found a way" or "discovered how."

To stir up all kinds of covetousness may be rendered as "to cause me to desire all kinds of things" or "to cause me to desire those things I should not want."

By working through the commandment may often be expressed as a separate sentence—for example, "sin did this by using the commandment" or "sin did this by reminding me of the commandment not to covet."

The meaning of the last sentence in this verse, for sin is a dead thing apart from law, is difficult. Paul seems to mean that apart from law sin is inactive, that is, powerless (see the related thoughts in 4.15 and 5.13). In some languages sin is a dead thing apart from law may be expressed as "if there is no law, sin has no power" or "where the law does not exist sin can do nothing."

7.9 I myself was once alive apart from law; but when the commandment came, sin sprang to life,

It is important to notice the range of Paul's argument in this passage. He begins by interpreting his own experience in light of the account in Genesis 3. But he also assumes that every other man's experience is similar to his own, and so what he says has relevance for all men in all periods of history.

Sprang to life (so Moffatt; JB "came to life") may also have the meaning "came to life again" (this seems to be the meaning of the RSV "revived"), though most commentators understand this verb in the same sense as the TEV. Here, as in the previous verse, law is the equivalent of a specific command from God.

The rendering of the phrase apart from law in the first clause of verse 9 may present certain difficulties, especially when it must be made into a complete clause—for example, "I myself was alive when there were no laws to tell me I shouldn't do certain things" or "I was alive so long as I did not know about the laws which told me, You must not do such bad things."

In a number of languages one cannot say when the commandment came. But one can say, for example, "when I came to know about a commandment," "when

I learned that I shouldn't do certain things," or "...that God said I shouldn't do certain things."

In this type of context sin sprang to life may then be translated as "sin became active," "sin began to have power," or "sin became strong," or "then I had a strong desire to sin."

7.10 and I died. And the commandment which was meant to bring life, in my case brought death.

And I died may need to be expressed as a simile—for example, "and, as it were, I died," since this is not a reference to physical but to spiritual death.

According to the Genesis account, obedience to the command of God meant that life would continue, whereas disobedience meant death would come. But Paul discovers that Adam's experience and his own are similar: the commandment which was meant to bring life, in my case brought death.

The commandment which was meant to bring life may be rendered as "the commandment which was supposed to cause me to live" or "the commandment which God intended to cause me to live."

The final expression, in my case brought death, must again be understood in a metaphorical sense and may be expressed in some languages merely as "caused me to die" (though obviously Paul was not physically dead), or as a simile "caused me, as it were, to die." In some languages, however, it may be more appropriate to speak of a "sentence of death"—for example, "caused me to be under the sentence of death" or "caused me to be condemned to die."

7.11 Sin found its chance and deceived me by working through the commandment; by means of the commandment sin killed me.

Found its chance translates the same phrase found in verse 8, and the exegesis of this verse is similar to that of verse 8. In the Genesis account the serpent plays the part of the deceiver; for Paul it is sin that deceived him. Found its chance and deceived me may be combined into a single expression, "found a way to deceive me."

By working through the commandment may be translated as "it used the commandment." Similarly, in the last clause, one may say "sin used the commandment in order to kill me."

12 So then, the Law itself is holy, and the commandment is holy, right, and good. 13 Does this mean that what is good brought about my death? By no means! It was sin that did it; by using what is good, sin brought death to me in order that its true nature as sin might be revealed. And so, by means of the commandment, sin is shown to be even more terribly sinful.

7.12 So then, the Law itself is holy, and the commandment is holy, right, and good.

In this verse Paul brings a final answer to the question raised in verse 7. In Greek the connection with the previous argument is clearly indicated by a particle (RSV "so"), and this has been indicated in the TEV by the use of the words so then.

There is no doubt that Paul's use of the word Law in this verse refers to the Jewish Law. The Law itself is holy (because it comes from God). The commandment is holy (it also comes from God), and right (it tells what God demands), and good (it has as its purpose to benefit man).

Expressions for holy, right, and good present a number of difficulties when applied to terms such as Law and commandment. Technically, law consists of a body of regulations which are enforced by society, while a commandment is a specific order which is enforced by the individual who gives it. However, in speaking of the Law and the commandments of the Old Testament, this distinction does not strictly apply; the commandments which were given by God became the Law of the people, and they were enforced by sanctions imposed by the society. In order to indicate the contrast between Law and commandment in this verse, one may speak of the Law as being the "laws" and the commandment as being "each commandment" or "each command."

In rendering the term holy in this type of context, one may have to employ a phrase such as "comes from God," since this may be the only way of indicating how a law may be "holy." The expression the commandment is...right may be expressed in some languages as "the commandment tells what is right" or "the commandment tells what one ought to do." And, though the commandment is... good may in some cases need to be rendered as "the commandment helps people," there is usually some type of expression for good which may be applied to commandments as well as to behavior.

7.13 Does this mean that what is good brought about my death? By no means! It was sin that did it; by using what is good, sin brought death to me in order that its true nature as sin might be revealed. And so, by means of the commandment, sin is shown to be even more terribly sinful.

What is good is merely another way of speaking of the Law.

Brought about my death may be rendered as "caused me to die." Again, one must make certain that this is understood in a metaphorical sense. If the question-answer construction must be altered, one may translate: "this does not mean that what is good brought about my death" or "...caused me to die."

By no means (see 7.7).

It was not the Law that brought death to Paul; rather sin used what is good (the Law) to accomplish this. The outcome was that sin's true nature was revealed (NEB "sin exposed its true character"; JB "but sin, to show itself in its true colors"). Paul is saying that one cannot see how evil sin is until he realizes that sin takes what is good, that is, a divine command, and uses this to bring death to men. By using the commandment (to bring death to men), sin not only shows its true nature as sin, but sin is shown to be even more terribly sinful (NEB "sin became more sinful than ever").

Its true nature as sin might be revealed may be translated as "in order that people might know exactly what sin is" or "in order that sin would be shown for exactly what it is."

In Greek this verse has two purpose clauses, one of which is clearly indicated in the TEV, in order that its true nature as sin might be revealed. The second purpose clause is indicated by and so. This second clause is parallel with the first, but it goes one step further to show how terribly sinful sin is. The purpose involved is God's purpose; and Paul intimates that the reason God intended for sin to be shown up in its true nature was so that he might destroy it (see 5.20).

Though the final sentence of verse 13 does indicate purpose, it may in this context be treated as result—for example, "and hence the commandment causes sin to become even worse" or "and so because the commandment says one should not sin, sin becomes even worse." In the latter instance, by means of the commandment is expressed as cause, if this is the only succinct way in which such expressions of means may be communicated.

The Conflict in Man

14 We know that the Law is spiritual; but I am mortal man, sold as a slave
to sin. 15 I do not understand what I do; for I don't do what I would like to
do, but instead I do what I hate. 16 When I do what I don't want to do, this
shows that I agree that the Law is right. 17 So I am not really the one who does
this thing; rather it is the sin that lives in me. 18 I know that good does not live
in me—that is, in my human nature. For even though the desire to do good
is in me, I am not able to do it. 19 I don't do the good I want to do; instead,
I do the evil that I do not want to do. 20 If I do what I don't want to do, this
means that no longer am I the one who does it; instead, it is the sin that lives
in me.

The section heading The Conflict in Man may be rendered as "The Fight that Goes On Inside Man," "The War Inside Ourselves," "The Trouble Within Us," or "The Divisions Inside Us."

7.14 We know that the Law is spiritual; but I am mortal man, sold as a slave to sin.

Throughout this entire section (vv. 14-25) Paul uses familiar Jewish terminology when he speaks of the two impulses, the good and the evil, which are constantly struggling for supremacy over man. He introduces his discussion with a general principle with which all his readers will agree: we know that the Law is spiritual.

In some languages there seems to be no term more difficult to translate adequately than spiritual. In some contexts it applies to the work of the Holy Spirit. In others it relates primarily to man's spirit, and in still others it seems to be so general as to suggest merely something of "divine origin." In this particular context the most satisfactory equivalent is, in some languages, "the Law is for our spirits but I am just a body" or "...I am a person with a body," in other words, a physical being. One may also translate, in some languages, "the Law concerns our spirits." However, in this particular context in which the emphasis of spiritual is in contrast with mortal man (or "a person of flesh"), it is probably better to relate "spiritual" to God but not specifically to the Holy Spirit. For that reason some translators employ the expression "the Law is from God" or "the Law relates to God."

On the other hand, Paul contrasts himself with the nature of the Law: I am mortal man, sold as a slave to sin. The word rendered mortal man by the TEV is obviously used in contrast with the word spiritual. But there is a question as to the exact contrast that is intended, and the problem is intensified by the observation that Paul uses "flesh" in at least two senses in his writings (mortal man actually translates an adjective made from the noun "flesh"). Sometimes "flesh" is used to describe human existence in its frailty, whereas at other times it is used to describe human nature in its sinful rebellion against God. Most translations evidently take the adjective translated mortal man in the latter sense, and so render the word either by "carnal" (RSV, Phillips), "unspiritual" (NEB, JB), or "weak flesh" (NAB). Goodspeed ("the Law is spiritual, but I am physical") takes "flesh" in the same sense as the TEV, that is, as a description of the physical aspect of human life apart from any evil connotations. So many translators understand this word to have overtones of evil in the present context because of its connection with what follows: sold as a slave to sin. However, this is not a necessary conclusion. It is equally acceptable to understand Paul to be speaking of himself as a mortal man, that is, a man who is exposed to all of the temptations that can come to one because he is a physical being, and who has now come under the power of sin.

The final phrase sold as a slave to sin is difficult to render in languages which cannot employ a passive without indicating agent, and in this type of context one certainly would not want to say "God sold me as a slave to sin" or "I sold myself as a slave to sin." Under such circumstances it is better to omit the concept of sold rather than to employ a rendering which would be wrongly understood. One may therefore simply translate as "I am a slave to sin" in the sense of "I am a slave who obeys sin" or "I have become like a slave, obedient to sin."

7.15-16 I do not understand what I do; for I don't do what I would like to do, but instead I do what I hate. (16) When I do what I don't want to do, this shows that I agree that the Law is right.

In these verses Paul is illustrating that his conscience proved to him that the Law is good. Once again the question is whether Paul is referring to the Jewish Law in particular or to law in general; translators are divided in their conclusions. In verse 15 Paul uses two different words for do, but there is no essential distinction in meaning. Also the word rendered right ("good" in most translations; "admirable" in NEB) is not the same word as that translated good or that translated right in verse 12. However, it is unwise to insist on any distinction in meaning.

I do not understand may need to be expressed in a somewhat emphatic form: "I do not really understand."

The clause I agree that the Law is right may be expressed as direct discourse in some languages: "I say, Yes, the Law is right" or "I answer, Yes, the Law is right."

7.17 So I am not really the one who does this thing; rather it is the sin that lives in me.

In this verse Paul speaks of sin as though it were some personal force that takes hold of a man's life and controls it.

So I am not really the one who does this thing may be rendered as "so I myself do not do this thing" or "so I am not the person doing this."

It may be necessary to specify precisely where sin lives within the person —for example, "the sin that lives in my heart." In this way sin is presented as essentially "the desire to sin."

7.18 I know that good does not live in me—that is, in my human nature. For even though the desire to do good is in me, I am not able to do it.

I know that good does not live in me must be specified in some languages as "I know that the capacity to do good does not live in me," "...the ability to do good...," or, as in some languages, "I know that my heart is not able to cause me to do good."

Human nature (literally "flesh") is the same term that Paul uses in verse 5; see also the discussion of mortal man in verse 14. A literal translation of this phrase (so Moffatt and RSV) means little or nothing; and to translate "in my physical self" (Goodspeed) seems to miss the impact of what Paul is saying. Although Paul does believe that sin may launch its attack against man through his body, he certainly did not think of one's physical being as evil in itself. Rather he seems to be speaking of that aspect of one's self which refuses submission to the Spirit of God (NEB "in my unspiritual nature"; JB "in my unspiritual self"). Evidently Paul is contrasting his human nature with the desire to do good that is in him. As pointed out earlier, this is in keeping with the Jewish belief in two impulses that try to control man's life, an evil impulse and a good impulse. The desperateness of Paul's situation is demonstrated by the fact that, even though he desires to do good, he is not able to do it.

For some languages in my human nature is equivalent to "in my heart," but in most instances a more appropriate expression is "in me as just a human being," "in me as just a man," or "in the man that I am."

The clause for even though the desire to do good is in me may be rendered as "even though I want to do good." This sentence of concession-result may be expressed in some languages as "For I want to do good, but I am not able to do so."

7.19-20 I don't do the good I want to do; instead, I do the evil that I do not want to do. (20) If I do what I don't want to do, this means that no longer am I the one who does it; instead, it is the sin that lives in me.

Verse 19 brings into sharper focus the thoughts of verse 15, while the same conclusion is reached in verse 20 as in verse 17.

> [21]So I find that this law is at work: when I want to do what is good, what is evil is the only choice I have. [22]My inner being delights in the law of God. [23]But I see a different law at work in my body—a law that fights against the law that my mind approves of. It makes me a prisoner to the law of sin which is at work in my body. [24]What an unhappy man I am! Who will rescue me from this body that is taking me to death? [25]Thanks be to God, through our Lord Jesus Christ!
>
> This, then, is my condition: by myself I can serve God's law only with my mind, while my human nature serves the law of sin.

7.21 So I find that this law is at work: when I want to do what is good, what is evil is the only choice I have.

Verses 21-23 are a summary of what Paul has been saying thus far in the chapter. The last half of the verse is rendered in a variety of ways in the different translations. The RSV attempts a literal translation ("evil lies close at hand"), but in so doing it fails to bring out the impact of what Paul is saying. For example, the verb that the RSV here translates "lies close at hand" is also used in the last part of verse 18 in the literal Greek clause "for the will (to do good) is present in me." The RSV translates this clause as "I can will what is right" and the TEV as the desire to do good is in me. That is to say, the verb used here and in verse 18 means not merely that something is near, but that it is within one's grasp and present within one's self. On the basis of this observation the TEV transforms this part of the verse to read what is evil is the only choice I have; this is also the basis for Moffatt ("but wrong is all that I can manage") and for the NEB ("only the wrong is within my reach").

The initial clause, so I find that this law is at work, involves several problems. First, one must indicate clearly that this is a type of summary statement, introduced by some such particle as "so," "therefore," or "hence." The term for law is best understood in this context as a "principle." This use of law has nothing to do with "the law of God." Where there are special difficulties in rendering a term such as "principle," one may say "hence I find that this is what is happening in me."

The temporal clause, when I want to do what is good, may also be treated as concessive—for example, "although I want to do what is good." The final clause, what is evil is the only choice I have, may be rendered as "I can only choose what is evil" or "the only thing I can do is to choose what is evil."

7.22 My inner being delights in the law of God.

Inner being (NEB and JB "inmost self"; Moffatt "inner self"; Goodspeed "inner nature") is also used by Paul in 2 Corinthians 4.16. In each case it refers to one's essential self, and is almost synonymous with the "I" that wants to do good and hates evil (vv. 14-17; 19-20). It is also to be taken as a synonym of the mind in verses 23 and 25. What Paul evidently has in mind is the inner being of man which has been transformed by God's grace and so attempts to do God's will. Paul may refer to it as his inner being and also as his mind, because this is the aspect of human personality which is not seen, whereas the part of one's self which can be seen in its involvement in sin is the outer self, that is the body (see vv. 23-24).

In a number of languages my inner being is simply "my heart." In some languages, the equivalent is "the man in my heart"; in others, "down deep in my heart."

Delights in the law of God may be rendered as "is happy because of the law that comes from God."

7.23 But I see a different law at work in my body—a law that fights against the law that my mind approves of. It makes me a prisoner to the law of sin which is at work in my body.

It should be noticed that Paul does not speak in this verse of his body as being evil, but rather of a law at work in his body which controls it and so subjects it to sin. He is not attempting to use psychological terminology, nor is he setting the body over against the mind as though one were evil and the other innately good. Rather, he is reflecting on his own experience and the experience of mankind in general, and is trying to point out that even though he approves of what is right, he is unable to do what is right in his own strength. Although he does not look upon the body as being sinful in itself, he does realize that the body is the battlefield where the struggle against desire, sin, and death is fought. And he realizes that he, like all other men, has become a prisoner to the law of sin which is at work in his body.

The use of law in verse 23 parallels its use in verse 21, namely, as "principle." If a translator can retain "law" in this type of context, it is useful to do so, since this may provide a key to other uses of "law," especially in the first two sections of this same chapter.

In my body may be best translated in some languages as "inside of me." Otherwise body might be understood only in the physical sense. In order to contrast this with the law that my mind approves of, it may be useful to translate the first sentence of verse 23 as follows: "But I see a different law operating in me—a law which is against the law that I approve of in my mind."

The law of sin may be rendered as "the law concerning sin" or even "the law which results in sin."

The final clause, which is at work in my body, must refer to the law and not to sin. In some languages one may say "it is this law which is in me."

7.24 What an unhappy man I am! Who will rescue me from this body that is taking me to death?

The exclamation what an unhappy man I am! may be rendered as "I am exceedingly unhappy," "I am not at all happy," or "I am indeed miserable."

Here Paul uses a phrase which is ambiguous (literally "this body of death"), which the TEV takes to mean this body that is taking me to death. The NEB and JB translate this phrase as "this body doomed to death" (see Goodspeed "this doomed body"), and the NEB gives an alternative rendering, "the body doomed to this death." This body that is taking me to death may be translated as "this body which is causing me to die" or "this body which will result in my dying." In some languages the expression "body of death" is rendered as "this old heart which is killing me."

7.25 Thanks be to God, through our Lord Jesus Christ!

This, then, is my condition: by myself I can serve God's law only with my mind, while my human nature serves the law of sin.

This verse has caused exegetes and translators considerable difficulty. Some feel that from a psychological point of view the last part of verse 25 ought to come immediately following verse 24 (so Moffatt), or that it ought to be omitted altogether. However, there is no textual evidence either for the rearrangement of these verses or for the omission of any part of the verse, and so the translator must try to render the text in the way that Paul has written it. In fact, it is not difficult to see how the first part of verse 25 follows readily upon the dramatic question that Paul raises in the last part of verse 24, Who will rescue me from this body that is taking me to death? Paul assumes that God is the one who will rescue him, and so he gives thanks to God for the victory that he knows will be his. The NEB ("God alone, through Jesus Christ our Lord! Thanks be to God!") and Moffatt ("God will! Thanks be to him through Jesus Christ our Lord!") have both made this bit of information explicit for the reader. This answer is clearly implicit in the text, and so is not beyond the bounds of what can be included in translation.

The TEV understands the latter half of the verse to be a summary and so translates the transitional particle by this, then, is my condition.

Because of the real possibility that the first part of verse 25 will be related to the clause in verse 24, that is taking me to death, rather than to the question, who will rescue me?, it is important to introduce the response in a way that will indicate clearly that it is God who will rescue—for example, "it is God through our Lord Jesus Christ, and thanks be to him" or "I do thank God that through our Lord Jesus Christ he will rescue me." The expression of secondary agency of through our Lord Jesus Christ may be introduced as "I thank God who will rescue me; our Lord Jesus Christ will do it."

The final paragraph of this chapter should be introduced by some type of summary expression—for example, "then," "in conclusion," or "to say it briefly." This... is my condition may be equivalent to "this is how I am" or "I am like this."

In Greek "I myself" is emphatic and the TEV carries this through, by myself I.

Although the word only does not appear in the Greek text as such, it is clearly implicit in what Paul says. He is contrasting the fact that it is only with his mind that he can serve God with the fact that his human nature serves the law of sin (see 7.5).

As in several places in this section, the contrast between the mind and human nature is presented. It is not always easy to discover precisely what set of terms should be used to indicate this contrast. For some languages it is "mind" versus "heart" and for others it is "mind" versus "body." In still other languages one may choose to have "thinking" versus "desiring"—for example, "I can serve God's law only with what I think, while with my desires I serve the law which leads to sin" or "...the law concerning sin."

CHAPTER 8

Life in the Spirit

8 There is no condemnation now for those who live in union with Christ
Jesus. 2For the law of the Spirit, which brings us life in union with Christ
Jesus, has set me free from the law of sin and death. 3What the Law could not
do, because human nature was weak, God did. He condemned sin in human
nature by sending his own Son, who came with a nature like man's sinful
nature to do away with sin. 4God did this so that the righteous demands of
the Law might be fully satisfied in us who live according to the Spirit, not
according to human nature. 5Those who live as their human nature tells them
to, have their minds controlled by what human nature wants. Those who live
as the Spirit tells them to, have their minds controlled by what the Spirit wants.
6To have your mind controlled by human nature results in death; to have your
mind controlled by the Spirit results in life and peace. 7And so a man becomes
an enemy of God when his mind is controlled by human nature; for he does
not obey God's law, and in fact he cannot obey it. 8Those who obey their
human nature cannot please God.

Life in the Spirit may be translated in some languages as "Living According to What the Spirit of God Says" or "Living by the Strength from the Spirit of God." It is usually difficult to employ a literal rendering of Life in the Spirit.

Although Paul discusses a number of individual topics throughout this chapter, his main concern is to emphasize the work of God's Spirit, who enables the believer to conquer the power of sin in his life (vv. 1-17) and to have hope in the glorious future that awaits God's people (vv. 18-30). Paul concludes the chapter with an expression of thanksgiving for God's love in Christ Jesus (vv. 31-39).

8.1 There is no condemnation now for those who live in union with Christ Jesus.

This verse is introduced with a particle (Greek ara) which indicates that Paul is drawing a conclusion on the basis of what he has previously said. The RSV renders this particle as "therefore" and the NEB as "the conclusion of the matter is this." The TEV, the NAB, and Phillips indicate this by the use of a section heading rather than by a translation of this particular particle.

In Greek the word for no is the first word of the sentence and is in the emphatic position.

Now (Greek nun) is more a temporal marker than an indicator of logical consequences (see RSV, NAB, Phillips). Paul is making a contrast between the life of the man dominated by his human nature and the life of the believer under the control of God's Spirit.

Since in some languages it is impossible to speak of condemnation without specifying who condemns, there is no condemnation may be rendered as "no one can condemn" or even "God does not condemn."

For those who live in union with Christ Jesus is literally "for those in Christ Jesus" (see 6.3).

Some ancient manuscripts add at the end of this verse the words "who do not walk according to the flesh" (equivalent to TEV who live...not according to human nature in verse 4), while other manuscripts add both this phrase and the phrase who live according to the Spirit. It is recognized by scholars that the addition of one or both of these phrases represents an ancient scribe's attempt to incorporate into this verse the ideas of verse 4, and so to make explicit what it means to live in union with Christ Jesus. In the UBS Greek text the omission of these phrases is rated as having the highest degree of certainty. However, since many translators continue to follow one or the other of the expanded texts, it may be useful to mention briefly some of the problems associated with such a translation. In some languages one can preserve the concept of walking by an idiomatic expression such as "who do not walk the flesh road but the Holy Spirit road." Other languages may employ some such translation as "who do not do what the body says but what the Spirit says" or "who do not respond to the old heart but to the Spirit."

8.2 For the law of the Spirit, which brings us life in union with Christ Jesus, has set me free from the law of sin and death.

There is a causal connection between this and the previous verse. Verse 2 gives the basis for affirmation that there is no condemnation now for those who live in union with Christ Jesus.

In the phrase law of the Spirit, the word law is used in a way similar to its use in 7.21,23. In fact, Paul uses the phrase law of the Spirit (rather than simply saying "the Spirit") because of his use of the same term in the previous chapter. Law of the Spirit possibly means for Paul something like "power of the Spirit" or "rule of the Spirit." However, for the sake of the relation of this expression to the previous chapter, it is important to use the same word in both places, provided, of course, that there is no distortion of meaning. In many languages one cannot speak of the law of the Spirit, but one can indicate something of the contrast between the action of the Spirit and that of sin and death by translating "being controlled by the Spirit has freed me from the control of sin and death" or "...has set me free, and therefore sin and death do not control me."

"Spirit of life" is taken by most commentators to mean the Spirit, which brings us life (see NEB "the life-giving law of the Spirit"). Which brings us life may be rendered as "which causes us to really live." It may be necessary to include an expression such as "really" or "truly" in order to indicate that this life is not merely a matter of human existence but has a distinctive quality.

Life in union with Christ Jesus indicates a special quality of life. One may therefore translate as "causes us to really live in union with Christ Jesus" or "causes us to really live, being joined closely to Christ Jesus."

Some Greek manuscripts read "you" (singular) in place of me of this verse, while still other manuscripts read "us." The use of the inclusive pronoun "us" was doubtless introduced by some scribe who thought that both Paul and his readers should be included, but the choice between me and "you" is not so easy. The UBS Greek text suggests me, though rating this a "C" decision, indicating a high probability of doubt regarding the original reading. Most modern translators appear to accept me, assuming that it is more probable that a scribe would have changed the text from me to "you," than the other way around.

Paul continues his play on the word law in the phrase the law of sin and death. He could just as easily have said, "the Spirit has set me free from sin and death." If one can retain law in this context, it may be possible to translate as "the law which declares sin and death," "the law which shows sin and death," or "the law which causes sin and death."

8.3 What the Law could not do, because human nature was weak, God did. He condemned sin in human nature by sending his own Son, who came with a nature like man's sinful nature to do away with sin.

A number of modern translators understand Law here as a specific reference to the Jewish Law (so JB, Goodspeed, Moffatt); others take the word in a more general sense (so NEB, NAB).

Human nature is literally "flesh." See the discussion on this in the previous chapter.

The first sentence in verse 3 may require alteration in the order of clauses —for example, "God accomplished what the Law could not accomplish because human nature was weak." Weakness must refer to moral weakness, not lack of physical strength.

In rendering he condemned sin in human nature, it is important to avoid the idea of "condemning sinful human nature." It is rather "his condemnation of sin that operates in human nature" or "sin that uses human nature."

Who came with a nature like man's sinful nature is literally "in the likeness of sinful flesh." There are at least two exegetical problems involved in the translation of this verse. First, does Paul use the word "flesh" in the sense of Christ's physical body or of his human nature? In light of the manner in which Paul uses "flesh" in the earlier part of this verse, it seems better to understand his meaning here to be human nature (so NEB). However, a number of translators take this as a reference to our Lord's physical body (so Goodspeed and JB).

The second exegetical problem involves Paul's use of the word "likeness" (Greek homoiōma). Here it is important to realize that the emphasis is on the identity that Christ shared with "sinful flesh" and not on his difference from it. That is to say, Paul is either declaring that Christ had a physical body exactly like the physical bodies of other men, or that Christ had a human nature exactly like the human nature of other men. As indicated above, the TEV accepts the latter of these two interpretations. Does this interpretation then imply that Christ was sinful like all other men? The answer is "no." Paul is only affirming that even though Christ possessed a human nature like that of all other men, he himself remained sinless because he never yielded to the impulses of this nature. This may seem a difficult point to comprehend, but it is easier to understand if one realizes Paul's intention in this passage. He insists that Christ must fully identify with fallen man if he is to conquer sin in the arena where all other men have been conquered by sin. And this would require that Christ assume not only a physical body like the body of all other men, but that he assume the same nature that all other men possess. Thus Paul declares that as Christ possessed the full nature of God (his own Son), so he possessed the full nature of man.

The expression of means in the phrase by sending his own Son may be rendered in some languages as "in order to do this (that is, to condemn sin) he sent his own Son." The clause who came with a nature like man's sinful nature is rendered in some languages as "who came to earth with a heart like the hearts of men who sin" or "he came having a body just like men's bodies which tend to sin."

To do away with sin translates a phrase which is sometimes used in the Old Testament with the meaning "sin offering." Some translators see in this phrase an emphasis on the aspect of sacrifice (NEB "as a sacrifice for sin"; Goodspeed "a sin-offering"), while other translators emphasize the result of this action (JB "God dealt with sin"; Moffatt "to deal with sin"; NEB alternative rendering "to deal with sin").

If it is necessary to restructure the phrase with a nature like man's sinful nature so that the resulting form involves a clause, it may then also be necessary to separate the final phrase to do away with sin and make it a complete sentence. Otherwise, this purpose may become confused with some aspect of man's sinning. An adequate translation in some languages may be "he came in order to do away with sin" or "he came in order to be a sacrifice for sin." However, such a translation could imply that he was a sacrifice for his own sins, and therefore it may be necessary to say "he came in order to be a sacrifice for the sins which others had committed."

8.4 God did this so that the righteous demands of the Law might be fully satisfied in us who live according to the Spirit, not according to human nature.

In Greek verses 3 and 4 are one sentence, and verse 4 begins with a conjunction that appears in the TEV and in the NEB as so that (JB "in order that") and may be taken either with the force of purpose or of result, the former being the more probable. The TEV makes a full stop at the end of verse 3 and reintroduces the subject (God did this) so that the reader can see immediately the relationship between the two thoughts.

Righteous demands (JB "just demands") is in the Greek text a singular (NEB "the commandment"; Goodspeed "the requirement"). The TEV, along with a number of other translations (Phillips, NAB, Moffatt, JB), has this word in a collective sense, and this accounts for the plural demands. The righteous demands of the Law may be rendered as "the righteous deeds which the Law demands must be done" or "what the Law demands, which is right."

The fact that the salvation event upholds the Law and does not contradict it (so that the righteous demands of the Law might be fully satisfied) is a familiar theme in the book of Romans (see 3.31; 6.13). The passive expression might be fully satisfied in us may be made active, "that we might fully accomplish" or "that we might do completely." An inversion of clauses may thus result—for example, "God did this so that we, who live according to the Spirit and not according to human nature, might do completely what the Law demands as just."

Who live according to the Spirit is literally "who walk according to the Spirit." "To walk" in Semitic thought is merely another way of saying "to live, to behave, to act."

Human nature again is literally "flesh." For equivalent translations of according to the Spirit, not according to human nature, see the discussion under verse 1.

8.5 Those who live as their human nature tells them to, have their minds controlled by what human nature wants. Those who live as the Spirit tells them to, have their minds controlled by what the Spirit wants.

Verse 5 takes up the thought begun in verse 4 and expands it. Exegetically the verse is not difficult; Paul is simply saying that the way in which one lives is determined by that on which one focuses one's thoughts. He is speaking of the contrast between a life which is controlled by one's own human nature and the life which is controlled by God's Spirit. The NEB implies that the contrast is between one's "lower nature" and one's "spiritual nature," but this does not seem to be what Paul means. In this verse, as in the following verses, the word mind(s) is used as a comprehensive term to refer to one's will and affections as well as one's reason.

In this verse, in the rest of the chapter, and in a number of other contexts, it may be necessary to translate Spirit (with initial capital letter) as "the Spirit of God" or "the Holy Spirit." Capitalization alone is usually not sufficient to indicate clearly to the hearer that the reference is to the Holy Spirit. This is especially true if the term for Spirit may be either completely neutral in connotation or possibly have the implication of an evil spirit when the context does not mark it otherwise.

For many languages the equivalent of human nature in this context is "the body"—for example, "those who live as their body commands have their minds controlled by what their body wants," "...what their body wants controls their thinking," or "...causes them only to think of that." Similarly, the second sentence of verse 5 may be rendered as "those who live as the Spirit tells them to live think only about what the Spirit wants," "what the Spirit wants controls what they think," or "...occupies all their attention."

8.6 To have your mind controlled by human nature results in death; to have your mind controlled by the Spirit results in life and peace.

In this verse Paul gives the outcome of the two ways of life. To have your mind controlled by human nature results in death is literally "the mind of the flesh is death." There is no verb connecting "flesh" and "death," and so one has to be supplied from the context. Most translations supply "is" and a number of others supply "means," while the TEV supplies results in. Although Paul is describing the present condition of the man of faith and of the man who lives apart from faith, his focus of attention seems to be on the final outcome of their lives, and this is why the TEV has supplied the verb results in. The same is true of the second half of this verse.

In many languages expressions of result may be effectively restructured as conditions—for example, "If you think only about what your body wants you will die, but if you think only about what God's Spirit wants you will truly live and have peace." In some instances there must be an agent of life and peace, and therefore one may translate as "God will cause you to live and have peace."

8.7 And so a man becomes an enemy of God when his mind is controlled by human nature; for he does not obey God's law, and in fact he cannot obey it.

This verse takes up the thought of verse 6a and gives the reason for the statement made there. For a literal translation of the first half of this verse, see the RSV: "for the mind that is set on the flesh is hostile to God." But when Paul uses the word mind in such a context, he is referring to the entire person, who is considered God's enemy. The JB expresses this thought by "that is because to limit oneself to what is unspiritual is to be at enmity with God." It is generally agreed that law in this verse must be understood in the widest sense possible and is therefore not limited to the Jewish Law in particular.

The clause when his mind is controlled by human nature may be best interpreted in some languages as condition—for example, "and so if a man thinks only about what his body wants, he becomes an enemy of God" or "...he fights against God."

And in fact he cannot obey it is literally "neither is it (the mind) able." Here also "mind" is equivalent to the entire person, and so appears in the TEV as he. At the same time the TEV makes explicit the meaning of "is not able": cannot obey it ("God's law"). The JB translates: "never could... submit to God's law."

8.8 Those who obey their human nature cannot please God.

Those who obey their human nature is literally "those who are in the flesh." This expression is similar to the one that Paul uses in verse 5, those who live as their human nature tells them to, though it seems to be a bit stronger and more emphatic. There can be no doubt that throughout this passage Paul uses "flesh" in more than a physical sense; therefore a translation such as Goodspeed ("those who are physical cannot please God") does not seem to convey Paul's meaning adequately.

The clause those who obey their human nature may be rendered as simply "those who only do what they themselves want." In this type of context "flesh" can only refer to the natural condition of a person and therefore to people as they ordinarily are.

Cannot please God is rendered in some languages as "cannot cause God to be happy" or "cannot do what God likes."

[9]But you do not live as your human nature tells you to; you live as the Spirit tells you to—if, in fact, God's Spirit lives in you. Whoever does not have the Spirit of Christ does not belong to him. [10]But if Christ lives in you, although your bodies are going to die because of sin, yet the Spirit is life for you because you have been put right with God. [11]If the Spirit of God, who raised Jesus from death, lives in you, then he who raised Christ from death will also give life to your mortal bodies by the presence of his Spirit in you.

The fact that verses 9-11 introduce a new section is indicated by two features: (1) Paul addresses his readers by you and (2) in each of these three verses he uses particles (Greek ei de) which are stronger than the particle used in verses 2,3,5,6 (Greek gar). In verse 9 of the TEV these particles are taken in combination with the Greek indefinite pronoun "someone" (Greek tis) and the whole phrase (ei de tis) rendered whoever; while in verse 10 ei de of the Greek text appears as but if and in verse 11 as if.

8.9 But you do not live as your human nature tells you to; you live as the Spirit tells you to—if, in fact, God's Spirit lives in you. Whoever does not have the Spirit of Christ does not belong to him.

The first part of verse 9 is literally "but you are not in the flesh but in the Spirit." As the TEV makes clear, Paul is here speaking of the contrast between the two ways of life: the way which is guided by one's own human nature and the way guided by God's Spirit. Paul does not distinguish between God's Spirit and the Spirit of Christ; in either instance it is God's Spirit, and one can only know the Spirit of God through Jesus Christ.

In a number of languages it is preferable to place the conditional clause first—for example, "if indeed God's Spirit lives in you, you do not live as your human nature tells you to." However, it may be important to indicate clearly the contrast between what your human nature tells you to and the fact that you live as the Spirit tells you to. In some languages live in this type of context may be translated as "do," since this would correspond more closely to being told how to live or behave—for example, "you do not do just what your human nature tells you to do, but you do what the Spirit tells you to do." However, if at all possible one should preserve terms for "life" or "live," since this concept does occur frequently in following verses.

In some languages it is difficult to speak about "having the Spirit," but one can often employ an expression such as "the Spirit of Christ lives in you." In this context the clause introduced by whoever is conditional, and therefore in many languages it is more commonly expressed by "if"—for example, "if the Spirit of Christ does not live in you, you do not belong to Christ."

8.10 But if Christ lives in you, although your bodies are going to die because of sin, yet the Spirit is life for you because you have been put right with God.

In the same way that Paul uses God's Spirit and the Spirit of Christ interchangeably, so also he can speak of Christ and the Spirit (v. 11) living in the believer.

The conjunctions although...yet introduce contrasting clauses in Greek, which are often expressed by "on the one hand...on the other hand."

Your bodies are going to die because of sin is literally "the body (is) dead because of sin." The TEV changes the singular "body" to the plural your bodies, because in English this is more natural. But this phrase does raise a problem of exegesis. What precisely does Paul mean by this expression? There are at least two possibilities: (1) Paul may be affirming that the Christian's body is dead, because it is no longer the instrument of sin (see 6.1-14). However, this interpretation is difficult, because it does not give a satisfactory explanation of the phrase because of sin. (2) It is more natural to understand "dead" in the sense of "physical death" (see 5.12-14). The TEV and most other translations seem to follow this second interpretation. And since the believers' bodies are not actually physically dead as yet, the TEV renders this phrase by a future tense: your bodies are going to die. There are some who want to take the phrase because of sin as a reference to Adam's sin (Moffatt "though the body is a dead thing owing to Adam's sin"), but it seems more probable that Paul is referring to the believer's own sins.

The clause structure of verse 10 is complex. Note that there is first a conditional clause beginning with if, then a concessive clause beginning with although, followed by an adversative clause beginning with yet, and finally a clause beginning with because. In some languages this construction is too heavy and it may be necessary to break it up, while preserving, of course, the meaningful relations between the parts. For example, one may translate: "But if Christ lives in you, the Spirit will cause you to live. You will do this even though your bodies are going to die because of sin; and Christ does this because you have been put right with God."

The last part of this verse (literally "but the Spirit [is] life because of righteousness") is also difficult. Paul may be referring to the human spirit (see TEV alternative "your spirit is alive") or to the Holy Spirit. The TEV takes the latter alternative, the Spirit is life for you. Throughout this entire passage (and definitely in verse 11) Paul is using the term Spirit as a reference to God's Spirit, and so it seems likely that in this verse also he is referring to the Spirit of God. The TEV takes Paul's term "righteousness" in the same sense in which Paul so frequently uses it: you have been put right with God.

8.11 If the Spirit of God, who raised Jesus from death, lives in you, then he who raised Christ from death will also give life to your mortal bodies by the presence of his Spirit in you.

In the clause he who raised Christ from death, the pronoun refers to God (see NEB "then the God who raised Christ Jesus from the dead"). It seems best to take this verse as an eschatological reference; that is, God's Spirit, which is presently living in the believers, will be the means by which God will give life to their mortal bodies at the end of time.

For some languages there is something of a problem in the repetition of the reference to the resurrection of Jesus, who raised Jesus from death and he who raised Christ from death. There is clearly no distinction in the implied reference to God as the agent, and the names Jesus and Christ are only stylistic variants. However, in some languages this double reference can be rather confusing. Some translators, therefore, have attempted to reproduce the same essential meaning by using in the second instance an expression such as "this same God." In the original the repetition was for the sake of special emphasis, and this emphasis can be preserved by making the repetition clearly emphatic.

The phrase mortal bodies may be translated as "bodies which will die." The phrase give life to your mortal bodies may then be rendered as "cause to live your bodies which will die." The final phrase by the presence of his Spirit in you may be translated in some instances as a separate clause: "he will do this by means of his Spirit which lives in you" or "his Spirit which lives in you will do this."

> [12]So then, my brothers, we have an obligation, but not to live as our human
> nature wants us to. [13]For if you live according to your human nature, you are
> going to die; but if, by the Spirit, you kill your sinful actions, you will live.
> [14]Those who are led by God's Spirit are God's sons. [15]For the Spirit that God
> has given you does not make you a slave and cause you to be afraid; instead,
> the Spirit makes you God's sons, and by the Spirit's power we cry to God,
> "Father! my Father!" [16]God's Spirit joins himself to our spirits to declare that
> we are God's children. [17]Since we are his children, we will possess the blessings
> he keeps for his people, and we will also possess with Christ what God has kept
> for him; for if we share Christ's suffering, we will also share his glory.

8.12 So then, my brothers, we have an obligation, but not to live as our human nature wants us to.

Verse 12 introduces a conclusion, so then, based on the argument presented in 8.1-11. So then (Greek ara oun) are the same words with which Paul drew his conclusion in 7.25 this, then, is my condition.

Paul strengthens his words by using a familiar form of address, brothers. The present experience of life and peace made possible by God's Spirit (8.6), and the promise of eternal life, which will be effective through God's Spirit (8.11), bring the believers under an obligation to God's Spirit.

We have an obligation is literally "we are debtors" (RSV, KJV), and it appears in the JB as "there is...necessity for us." Paul's intention is to stress as strongly as possible the believer's obligation no longer to live his life under the domination of his human nature. In a number of languages the only way of expressing obligation is to use some kind of verbal auxiliary meaning "must," but such a form makes it necessary to specify who are obligated to do what. For this context one may translate: "we must live as the Spirit of God tells us; we must not live as our human nature wants us to live" or "...as we want to live because of our human nature." The latter adaptation may be required in some languages since human nature may be spoken of as an instrument but not as a subject of "wanting."

The we in this context is, of course, inclusive.

8.13 For if you live according to your human nature, you are going to die; but if, by the Spirit, you kill your sinful actions, you will live.

Paul moves from the use of the first person we to the second person you, though in meaning these are the same; this also holds true for his use of the third person those who in the following verse. In verse 13 Paul uses a Greek form which is much stronger than the simple future (see RSV "you will die"), and for this reason the TEV translates his words by you are going to die. In the JB this appears as "you are doomed to die" and in the NEB as "you must die." The death referred to is, of course, not physical death, but rather the final death.

By the particles which he uses, Paul makes a strong contrast between the way of death and the way of life (for if... but if).

Kill your sinful actions is literally "kill the deeds of the body." Paul's meaning is easily understood. He is affirming that life lived under the leadership of God's Spirit will show itself in the way that one conducts himself.

The metaphor kill your sinful actions is a very forceful one and should be retained if at all possible. In some languages one may retain something of this figure, but in an altered form—for example, "cease your sinful actions as though you were killing them." In other languages one may have to eliminate the metaphor and employ a nonmetaphorical equivalent—for example, "stop completely your sinful deeds."

The phrase by the Spirit indicates agency, but it must often be expressed as "with the help of the Spirit." In some languages one may even have "but if the Spirit helps you to cease completely your sinful actions."

8.14 Those who are led by God's Spirit are God's sons.

In the same way that verses 12 and 13 are closely related (in the NEB and JB they form a separate paragraph), so verses 14 to 17 are a unit within themselves. Verses 12-13 indicate that obedience is demanded of the believer, while verses 14-17 take up the theme of obedience and indicate its joyful results.

Most translations render the verb in this verse as led by, though others use "guided by" (Moffatt and Goodspeed) or "moved by" (NEB and JB). Other languages may use "directed by" or "commanded by," but in some instances an active expression may be preferable—for example, "obey God's Spirit" or "follow God's Spirit." The verb chosen should imply voluntary submission to the leadership of God's Spirit.

In this verse Paul describes the believers as God's sons, while in verse 16 they are described as God's children. Both terms describe the natural relationship which exists between parent and child. One might argue that sons in contrast with children could imply status and certain privileges, but the shift from sons to children in these verses is essentially stylistic, and no significant differences of meaning should be attributed to the variation in terms.

8.15 For the Spirit that God has given you does not make you a slave and cause you to be afraid; instead, the Spirit makes you God's sons, and by the Spirit's power we cry to God, "Father! my Father!"

In Greek the first part of this verse includes a phrase that is equivalent to a passive (see RSV "for you did not receive the spirit of slavery to fall back into fear"), which the TEV transforms into an active construction. "You received" indicates that someone has given something, and the implied subject is God, God has given you. The phrase "spirit of slavery" is taken to mean "a spirit which brings about slavery." In this context "spirit" is taken as a specific reference to God's Spirit, for the Spirit that God has given you does not make you a slave. Finally, the phrase "into fear" implies result, and so the TEV renders cause you to be afraid. The phrase which the RSV renders "to fall back into fear" is literally "again into fear." Most translations make the idea of "again" explicit, whereas the TEV leaves this as an implicit item in the translation. The idea is that before the coming of God's Spirit the believers were slaves of fear, but now God's Spirit has released them from fear.

The TEV has the same sort of restructuring in the second clause of this verse (literally "but you received a spirit of adoption") as it has in the earlier part. The phrase "spirit of adoption" is again a reference to the Holy Spirit, while the genitive relation means that the Spirit (of God) makes you God's sons. Some translators make a full stop at this point (so RSV, Moffatt) and connect the remainder of this verse with the following verse. The reason for this is that Paul here uses a phrase which is ambiguous; it may mean either "by whom" or "in the time which." Most translators understand the phrase in the former sense, while those who take it in the latter sense connect it with what follows (see RSV "when we cry"). If the former interpretation is accepted, then the reference is clearly to God's Spirit and so the TEV renders this phrase as by the Spirit's power (see NEB "Spirit...enabling us to cry").

If in this verse one understands "spirit" in the sense of the human spirit, the rendering must, of course, be quite different. In some languages, for example, translators employ expressions such as "God has not given you a heart like a slave, thus causing you to be afraid, but he has given you a heart like a son, and therefore you can say to God, You are my Father." However, this type of interpretation seems to be far less satisfactory than one which recognizes the use of "Spirit" as a reference to God's Spirit.

Similar judgments may be made regarding an exegesis such as the NEB, which sees in the first part of this verse a reference to the human spirit ("a spirit of slavery") and in the second half of the verse a reference to God's Spirit ("a Spirit that makes us sons"). Although it is possible to understand these as contrasting phrases, this is contrary to Paul's usage of "spirit" throughout this entire passage. Throughout this chapter the focus of reference is God's Spirit, and it is unlikely that Paul would change in this one instance. Moreover, it is better to see these two halves of the verse as a contrast between what God's Spirit does and does not do, rather than a contrast between the activity of the human spirit and God's Spirit.

In this verse Paul uses two different words for Father, the one Aramaic and the other Greek. Most translators transliterate the former of these terms "Abba," and translate the latter "Father." It is doubtful that the average reader can fully appreciate what Paul has done, and so it seems best to translate both of these words as Father. The TEV qualifies the second term as my Father, which is supported by the observation that in Greek the word meaning "Father" is preceded by the article and so may be rendered as my Father or "our Father," depending on the context. In some languages there may be a distinct problem of number in using an equivalent of my Father. For example, if one uses a second person plural "you" throughout this verse or shifts to "we" in the last clause, it may be necessary then to say "you are our Father." However, one can introduce a singular by employing a preceding expression "each one of you" or "each one of us." As is already implied, it may be difficult to employ a double expression of "Father" as in Father! my Father! The more common equivalents involve several formal adjustments—for example, "each one of us may address God and say, My Father" or "we may all speak to God as our Father."

The phrase by the Spirit's power is best taken as causative—for example, "the Spirit causes us to say to God."

8.16 God's Spirit joins himself to our spirits to declare that we are God's children.

The verb which Paul uses in this verse (joins himself...to declare) occurs also in 2.15 and appears again in 9.1. In the present context the verb may mean either "to bear witness with" or else "to confirm another's witness." Most translators take it in the former sense. In some languages this meaning of "bearing witness with" may be translated as "God's Spirit says at the same time with our spirits" or "God's Spirit and our spirits both say."

8.17 Since we are his children, we will possess the blessings he keeps for his people, and we will also possess with Christ what God has kept for him; for if we share Christ's suffering, we will also share his glory.

Since we are his children is literally "but if children." In such a context the Greek word ei, usually rendered "if," does not imply doubt, as a literal translation into English might suggest. Rather it assumes that the condition stated is true, and so the TEV renders by since.

We will possess the blessings he keeps for his people is literally "(we are) also heirs." The word "heirs" is the same word which occurs in 4.13, 14. In the biblical sense "God's heirs" are those who will receive the blessings that God has for his people. Often in the Old Testament this phrase is used in reference to the people of Israel who were to receive the land which God had promised them, though the same expression is applied in a more general and in a more spiritual sense in other passages. Throughout the New Testament it should be understood in the broadest possible spiritual sense. A translation of this phrase should certainly not imply that God's people will receive something upon God's death.

8.17

It may be difficult in some languages to obtain a satisfactory noun for blessings. This may be translated as a verb and related as purpose to the expression of "keeping"—for example, "we will possess what God keeps for his people in order to bless them" or "...as a way of blessing them."

We will also possess with Christ may, in some languages, be translated as "we and Christ together will possess."

A satisfactory translation of kept may be rendered as "has stored up for," "has reserved for," or "has put aside for."

The word rendered if is the same word translated if, in fact in 8.9. It is a rather emphatic term and implies that Paul assumes that his statement represents the circumstances as they do in fact exist; that is, "since we do in fact share Christ's suffering, we will share his glory." In some languages it may be difficult to have a sequence of conjunctions such as for if. In such a circumstance it may be possible to place the conditional clause after the principal clause—for example, "for we shall share Christ's glory if we share his suffering."

The verb rendered share...suffering is used also in 1 Corinthians 12.26 but nowhere else in the New Testament. The verb share...glory appears only here in the New Testament. In this verse the word glory is used with the same sense that it has in 5.2. The theme of suffering and glory is a familiar one in New Testament thought. It is based on the conviction that the believers must follow the same route and receive the same reward that their Lord did.

In Greek the last clause of this verse, we will also share his glory, is actually a clause of purpose (see Goodspeed "in order to share his glory too"). In many languages the concept of sharing can only be expressed in terms of "doing something together"—for example, "if we suffer together with Christ we shall also have glory along with him." The concept of "suffering along with Christ" may need to be expressed by some form of comparison—for example, "if we suffer somehow as Christ suffered" ("somehow" is used to indicate that our suffering is not identical with his).

The final clause may then be translated as "then we shall have glory as he has glory." In some languages glory in this type of context may be expressed as "experiencing wonderfulness," "having that which is wonderful," or "having majesty such as he has."

The Future Glory

[18]I consider that what we suffer at this present time cannot be compared at
all with the glory that is going to be revealed to us. [19]All of creation waits with
eager longing for God to reveal his sons. [20]For creation was condemned to
become worthless, not of its own will, but because God willed it to be so. Yet
there was this hope, [21]that creation itself would one day be set free from its
slavery to decay, and share the glorious freedom of the children of God. [22]For
we know that up to the present time all of creation groans with pain like the
pain of childbirth. [23]But not just creation alone; we who have the Spirit as the
first of God's gifts, we also groan within ourselves as we wait for God to make
us his sons and set our whole being free. [24]For it was by hope that we were

saved; but if we see what we hope for, then it is not really hope. For who hopes for something that he sees? [25]But if we hope for what we do not see, we wait for it with patience.

The section heading The Future Glory may seem rather too abstract in some languages. It may therefore be rendered as "We Will Have Glory" or "Majesty Will Be for Us."

The entire section (8.18-30) is a testimony to the future glory that will be shared by God's people. Verse 18 serves to introduce the theme and to summarize the content of what Paul is going to say in the following verses. In verses 19-27 Paul brings together three pieces of evidence which point toward the future glory of the believers, and in verses 28-30 he indicates that this future glory has its basis in the eternal purpose of God. The first testimony that gives support to this promise of future glory is that of the eager longing of the creation itself (vv. 19-22). Paul affirms that the entire created order will be transformed, but this will take place only when God reveals his sons. A second evidence pointing to the future glory for God's people is his Spirit which God has given as the first of his gifts (vv. 23-25). A final witness to this future hope of glory is the work of the Spirit within the lives of the believers, as he enables them to pray in accordance with God's will and strengthens their hope (vv. 26-27).

8.18 I consider that what we suffer at this present time cannot be compared at all with the glory that is going to be revealed to us.

Paul introduces this verse with a conjunction that is rendered "for" in several translations (KJV, Goodspeed, NEB). Although it is difficult to decide on precisely what meaning Paul sought in this particular conjunction, most translators assume that its force can be properly maintained merely by introducing a new paragraph division at this point. It would appear that Paul is not making a logical conclusion on the basis of his previous argument, but rather that he is making a theological declaration in light of his own faith and hope. The verb Paul uses here is one of his favorite expressions and is rendered I consider by most translators. It is a verb which expresses strong assurance and not doubt; a translation such as "I think" may imply less than what Paul intends. "I am assured" or "I am certain" comes much closer to conveying his meaning.

In going to be revealed the understood agent of the passive voice is God, that is, God is going to reveal it to us. Revealed in this context indicates something Christians will experience, not merely something they will see with their eyes.

To us (NEB "for us") is the meaning that most translators apparently give to the prepositional phrase (Greek eis hēmas) that Paul uses here, though some see in this the force of "in us" (KJV). The most natural meaning of the Greek preposition eis (TEV to) would seem to be that of "to" or "for," although there are definite instances in the New Testament where it does have the force of "in." If the usual meaning is given to this preposition, the present passage indicates that at the end of time God will reveal his glory "to" or "for the benefit of" his people (note Segond "for us"). Otherwise, the focus is on the truth that at that time God's people will share in and reflect God's true glory. No dogmatic conclusion can be made, and translators may follow either exegesis.

Paul's contrast between the present time with its evil and suffering and "the coming age" with its glory that is going to be revealed reflects the Jewish and Christian belief in two ages. According to this belief the present age is characterized by the forces of evil exerting themselves and so causing sin and suffering. But the "coming age" is the age in which God's rule will be fully revealed and the power of evil destroyed. When this happens, all sin and suffering will cease, and men of faith will enjoy the benefits of God's presence.

In some languages it is not easy to compare such events as "suffering" and "the possession of glory." The closest equivalent may be "no one can say that what we suffer at the present time and the glory that is going to be revealed to us are the same." But such a rendering completely misses the significant contrast which Paul is trying to introduce. Therefore, it may be more satisfactory to emphasize the difference rather than the comparison—for example, "I consider that what we suffer at the present time and the glory that is going to be revealed to us are utterly different" or "...are so very, very different."

In order to highlight the fact that the glory is going to be experienced rather than merely seen, one may want to translate: "the glory that God is going to give us" or "the glory that God is going to cause us to enjoy."

8.19 All of creation waits with eager longing for God to reveal his sons.

In verses 19-21 Paul introduces a theme that is basic in Jewish thought, and he relates it to the Christian hope. According to the Genesis account, man and the world in which he lives are so closely bound together that man's sin brings a curse on the entire created order. According to Jewish thought, the reverse is also true; that is, when man is redeemed the universe in which he lives will share his destiny. Paul personifies the created order and depicts it as waiting with eager longing for that moment to take place. In keeping with his Christian conviction, Paul affirms that it will take place when God reveals his sons. The phrase that the TEV translates God to reveal his sons (so JB) is literally "for the revelation of the sons of God." The logic behind this translation is in the observation that "revelation" describes an event rather than an object. And so the phrase "revelation of the sons of God" means "God will reveal his sons."

The TEV also changes the structure of the first part of this verse rather radically. All of creation waits with eager longing is literally "the eager longing of the creation is waiting." The word creation refers to the entire created order (see NAB "the whole created world"; JB "the whole creation"; NEB "the created universe"), and so the TEV renders this word by all of creation. Moreover, the expression "the eager longing of the creation waits" means "the creation is waiting with eager longing." To translate in this way is much more natural in English, since we rarely speak of an abstract idea as waiting. Eager longing (NEB "eager expectation") appears elsewhere in the New Testament only in Philippians 1.20 (there rendered deep desire by the TEV). In translating all of creation, it is important to avoid merely designating "all people who have been created," since the Greek text refers to the entire created universe. In some languages the closest equivalent is "everything that God has created" or "all that God has created."

It may be necessary to shift somewhat the relation between wait and eager longing, since the expression eager longing is semantically more focal, that is to say, more crucial to this verse. Waits with eager longing may, therefore, be translated in some languages as "is longing eagerly as it waits for God to reveal his sons." Eager longing may be equivalent simply to "desires very much," "desires with rapid beating heart," or "desires with outstretched neck," to cite only some of the figurative expressions which may be used to convey the meaning of eager longing.

8.20 For creation was condemned to become worthless, not of its own will, but because God willed it to be so. Yet there was this hope,

The word translated worthless appears in the emphatic position in this sentence. Some translators see in the word the idea of "futility" (so RSV, NAB), others see in it the meaning of "frustration" (NEB, Goodspeed), while in the JB it appears as "unable to attain its purpose." In the New Testament this word appears elsewhere only in Ephesians 4.17 (TEV worthless; NEB "good-for-nothing"; JB "aimless") and in 2 Peter 2.18 (TEV stupid; NEB "empty"; JB "hollow"). In the Septuagint the word is often used in reference to heathen idols. The concept of worthless is rendered in a variety of ways in other languages—for example, "has no meaning," "has no use," "has no purpose," "is full of nothing" (that is to say, "empty"), or "to be as though it were nothing."

The verb rendered was condemned literally means "was made subject to." The tense is aorist, and commentators see here a specific reference to Genesis 3.17, when God brought his judgment against the earth because of Adam's sin. This reference to Genesis helps to explain the translation of but because God willed it to be so (literally "but because of the one who subjected it"). Some see in "the one who subjected it" a reference either to the sin of Adam (or the sin of man in general) or a reference to Satan. However, most commentators agree that the reference is to God, and some translators make this information explicit (so JB, Moffatt, Phillips; see alternative rendering in NEB).

The passive expression was condemned must frequently be changed into an active expression in which God is the agent. Under such circumstances, however, the term condemned is not necessarily the most satisfactory rendering. Some chose to use an expression such as "God decided that," "God determined that," or "God judged all creation as."

There is a difference of opinion as to how the latter part of this verse should be punctuated, and the decision that is made in this respect will also affect the translation of verse 21. (1) One may do as the TEV does and put a full stop after because God willed it to be so (literally "because of the one who subjected it"). (2) Or one may relate the last words of the verse, yet there was this hope (literally "on the basis of hope"), with the preceding words and so translate as the RSV does: "by the will of him who subjected it in hope." This problem also relates to verse 21, which begins with a word which may mean either "because" or "that" (in its latter meaning the word often introduces indirect discourse). The TEV, of course, translates this word as that, and so makes the passage read: Yet there was this hope, that creation....

The contrast between what creation did not want and what God decided may be expressed as "that is not what creation itself wanted but it was what God determined" or "that was not what creation decided but what God decided."

In many languages it is difficult to speak of hope without relating it in some way to the person who hopes. One may, therefore, translate the last clause of verse 20 as "nevertheless God had this hope" or "God looked forward in confidence."

8.21 that creation itself would one day be set free from its slavery to decay, and share the glorious freedom of the children of God.

The reference in this verse is eschatological, and the TEV makes this clear by introducing the words one day (so also Moffatt).

Once again the assumed agent of the passive verb, be set free, must be God. If God is made subject of the process of "setting free," the phrase from its slavery to decay may be rendered as purpose—for example, "God set free all creation so that it would not decay" or "...so that finally everything would not rot." In some languages being set free from slavery to decay may be expressed quite idiomatically—for example, "set free so as not to be worm food again." Slavery to decay is literally "slavery of decay," but most translators make the meaning of "to" explicit in this context; the NEB expresses it as "shackles of mortality."

Share the glorious freedom is literally "for the freedom of the glory." In such a context one would normally understand the genitive "of glory" to be equivalent to an adjective "glorious" (so Goodspeed, Moffatt, NAB). However, it is possible to understand the phrase "the freedom of the glory" with the meaning "freedom and glory" (JB; see NEB "liberty and splendor"). A number of translators render Paul's preposition "for" (TEV share) by a verb ("obtain" RSV, "enter upon" NEB, "enjoy" JB, "have" Goodspeed). In some languages glorious freedom may be rendered as "to be set free in a wonderful way" or "will be given the wonderful liberty."

8.22 For we know that up to the present time all of creation groans with pain like the pain of childbirth.

For we know renders essentially the same phrase that occurs in 2.2; 3.19; 7.14; 8.28. Generally this expression is used to introduce a fact of common knowledge.

Groans with pain like the pain of childbirth is literally "groans and is in birth pangs." Each of these verbs has a prefix meaning "with" added to the regular root. Commentators agree that the force of these prefixes is to indicate that the universe is groaning and having pains "in all its parts" (NEB), not that it is groaning and having pains "together with us (believers)." The TEV (so also Moffatt, JB, NAB) makes this information implicit without translating the prefixes by a separate word. To translate by "together" as the RSV (so also KJV, Goodspeed) conveys very little meaning. The expression all of creation groans with pain may require certain modifications, not only in focus but also in a shift from metaphor to simile—for example, "all of creation, as it were, has pain and is groaning" or "all of creation groans because it has pain, so to speak."

Like the pain of childbirth may be rendered as "just like a woman who has pain before giving birth to a child."

8.23 But not just creation alone; we who have the Spirit as the first of God's gifts, we also groan within ourselves as we wait for God to make us his sons and set our whole being free.

In this verse Paul adds the testimony of the believer to that of the created order. The verse begins with three words ("but not only"), which, as the commentators point out, mean but not just creation alone (RSV "and not only the creation"; JB "and not only creation"). In many languages one must, of course, fill out the ellipsis: "but it is not just the creation which is in pain and groans."

We (Goodspeed; NAB "we ourselves") is very emphatic in the sentence order, though it is difficult to retain the emphasis in translation (Moffatt has tried to reproduce the full emphatic force with "but even we ourselves...even we").

A literal translation of the phrase the Spirit as the first of God's gifts (in many translations "first fruits of the Spirit") is not easy, because it introduces a technical term from Jewish thought. First, it should be pointed out that the word "first fruits" is in apposition with "Spirit" (see NEB "the Spirit is given as firstfruits"). Second, "first fruits" is a technical term taken from the Jewish sacrificial system; it describes the first yield of the harvest or the first offspring of animals which had to be dedicated to God before the rest could be used. In the present context the word is used of that which God gives to man rather than that which man offers to God, and so the imagery has changed somewhat. Not only has the imagery changed, but in some places in the New Testament this word is used simply with the meaning of "first" (11.16; 1 Corinthians 15.23; 16.15).

There are passages also where this term appears to be the equivalent of another Greek word arrabōn, with the meaning of "guarantee" or "promise" (of something to come, so 1 Corinthians 15.20). Evidently the NEB here follows the latter interpretation, while at the same time attempting to maintain the imagery of harvest: "as firstfruits of the harvest to come." Moffatt and Goodspeed follow the same interpretation and also retain something of the imagery: "a foretaste of the future." The TEV accepts the meaning of "first" and somewhat demetaphorizes the imagery: the first of God's gifts.

It is difficult in some languages to speak of "having the Spirit." Rather, one has to say "we in whom the Spirit dwells" or "we in whom the Spirit lives." The qualifying phrase as the first of God's gifts may be restructured so that gifts becomes a verb—for example, "as the first thing which God gives us."

The clause structure of the second part of verse 23 is relatively complex, for not only is there a relative clause which modifies we, but there is an additional phrase which modifies Spirit, and this phrase must in some languages be changed to a clause. It may be important, therefore, to break the sentence after the expression we also groan within ourselves. A new sentence may then begin with as we wait.

God to make us his sons (so also NEB; Goodspeed "to be declared God's sons") is literally "adoption," which the RSV renders "adoption as sons." Though in Greek the word "adoption" is a noun, Paul's meaning usually comes across much more clearly when this noun is rendered as a verb phrase. The word "adoption" is the same word which Paul used in verse 15, but with a somewhat different emphasis. Verse 15 has reference to the present life of the believer, while the reference in verse 23 is eschatological, looking forward to our final acceptance into God's family. Some ancient manuscripts do not include the word "adoption," and it is omitted from the JB and the NAB. The evidence for its inclusion is not conclusive, but most modern translations do include it as part of the text.

In practically all languages there is some more or less formal way of expressing "adoption." It may be spoken of as "take us up as his sons," "consider us his sons," or "call us his sons." Where adoption is not a regular cultural practice, one may employ a descriptive equivalent such as "regard us as his sons."

And set our whole being free is literally "the setting free of our body" (on the word "setting free" see 3.24) and is actually in apposition with the clause that precedes it ("adoption as sons, the redemption of our bodies"; Moffatt "the redemption of the body that means our full sonship"). Both the TEV and the NEB make it coordinate with the preceding clause, while Goodspeed connects it in another way ("as we wait to be declared God's sons, through the redemption of our bodies"). Paul uses the word "body," either because he is thinking specifically of the final resurrection, or because he is using the word as the equivalent to "one's whole being." The TEV follows the latter of these alternatives. The expression our whole being may be quite difficult to render because it is so completely abstract. A language may have some such expression as "the whole of us" or "us in all of our parts," but a more common expression would be "every part of us" or "all of the different parts of us."

8.24-25 For it was by hope that we were saved; but if we see what we hope for, then it is not really hope. For who hopes for something that he sees? (25) But if we hope for what we do not see, we wait for it with patience.

In verse 24 the emphatic element is the phrase by hope. There is some discussion as to whether Paul means by hope or "in this hope" (RSV; see Moffatt "with this hope ahead"). In this context hope is close in meaning to "faith," and so the rendering of the TEV is more logical.

As most translators indicate, Paul uses the past tense of the verb "to be saved" in this verse: we were saved. To translate by a future tense is wrong (JB "we shall be saved"), and even the use of the present (see JB note "we are saved") is misleading. Paul sometimes uses this verb in a present tense (2 Corinthians 2.15), and more often in a future tense (5.9,10), but in the present passage he uses the past tense, since his focus of attention is on the beginning of the salvation experience. Although the Christian hope is a confident expectation that God will do what he says (see 5.2), it is still something that will not be "seen" until the final day. And even though the Christian is confident that his hope will finally be realized, he must wait for it with patience. The word rendered patience in this passage is also translated as patience in 15.4,5, but as endurance in 5.3. The word itself seems to have more of an active force than the English word "patience" suggests, and it may be more closely related to our concept of "endurance."

It is particularly difficult in many languages to use hope without indicating who hopes. It is particularly complex to use hope merely as an expression of means without indicating the participants. Therefore, the first clause of verse 24 may require some recasting—for example, "for the fact that we were saved was because we hoped," "for by our hoping we were saved," or "because we looked forward with confidence God saved us."

Since hope must frequently be expressed by some descriptive phrase such as "look forward to with confidence," this may require some modification in the last part of the first sentence of verse 24—for example, "but if we already see what we have been looking forward to with confidence, then we are not really looking forward to it at all." Similarly, the last sentence of verse 24 may be rendered as "for no one looks forward to something which he already sees" (in this way changing a rhetorical question into a statement). In line, then, with what has already been done in verse 24, verse 25 may be translated as "but if we look forward confidently for something which we do not see, then we do endure in our looking forward," "...we do look forward with endurance," "...steadfastly," or "...not moving at all." On the other hand, if hope is expressed by some highly idiomatic expression as, for example, "the power of the abdomen" (as it is in some languages), then quite naturally the structure of verses 24 and 25 will have to be considerably different.

> 26 In the same way the Spirit also comes to help us, weak that we are. For we do not know how we ought to pray; the Spirit himself pleads with God for us, in groans that words cannot express.
> 27 And God, who sees into the hearts of men, knows what the thought of the Spirit is; because the Spirit pleads with God on behalf of his people and in accordance with his will.
>
> 28 We know that in all things God works for good with those who love him, those whom he has called according to his purpose.
> 29 Those whom God had already chosen he had also set apart to become like his Son, so that the Son would be the first among many brothers.
> 30 And so God called those that he had set apart; and those that he called he also put right with himself; and with those that he put right with himself he also shared his glory.

8.26 In the same way the Spirit also comes to help us, weak that we are. For we do not know how we ought to pray; the Spirit himself pleads with God for us, in groans that words cannot express.

Verses 26 and 27 are closely related to verse 23 and also have a relation to verse 16. These verses contain the third witness to the glorious future of God's people (see vv. 19 and 22). In verse 22 Paul spoke of the groaning of the entire creation, and in verse 23 of the groaning of the believers; but now he speaks of the help which God's Spirit gives, and of the way that the Spirit himself pleads with God for us, in groans that words cannot express. Although Paul literally says that "the Spirit comes to help our weakness" (see NEB "comes to the aid of our weakness"), it is much more natural in English to say, as in the TEV, the Spirit also comes to help us, weak that we are (see JB "comes to help us in our weakness"). It is not certain just what Paul means by "our weakness," though one aspect of it is certainly that we do not know how we ought to pray. The NEB suggests "what it is right to pray for" as an alternative meaning of how we ought to pray, though no other translation goes in this direction. Although the final meaning of these two expressions ("what is right" and how we ought) is about the same, the structure of the Greek more nearly supports how we ought to pray.

In the same way may be equivalent in some languages to "also," "at the same time," or "in addition."

Weak that we are may be related to the preceding as "to help us since we are so weak," "to help us who are so weak," or "to help us—we are very weak." A literal translation of "weak" may imply mere physical disability, while an expression such as "not strong" may suggest some more spiritual failure; therefore "not strong" may be employed in the place of "weak." If some expression must be employed to qualify weakness, probably "trust" or "confidence" would be the most satisfactory—for example, "since we are so weak in trusting God."

Although the words with God are not in the Greek text, they are clearly implied and the TEV makes this information explicit. The Spirit himself pleads with God for us may be translated as "the Spirit asks God on our behalf," "the Spirit talks to God for us," or even "the Spirit prays to God for us."

The expression in groans that words cannot express (Goodspeed "with inexpressible yearnings"; Moffatt "with sighs that are beyond words") is difficult. It is possible to take that words cannot express in the sense of "unspoken words" (see NEB "through our inarticulate groans"). Paul uses a similar expression in 2 Corinthians 12.4, things which cannot be put into words, and it is quite likely that both expressions have essentially the same meaning. Although the majority of translations evidently take these groanings as coming from the Spirit, the NEB and Barclay explicitly identify them as the groanings of men. The context would seem to favor the former—that is, the Spirit stands in immediate communion with the Father and so needs no spoken words to express his thoughts. The clause that words cannot express is translated in a number of different ways—for example, "that no person can speak," "with groanings we cannot say how," "with groanings for which there are no words," or "with groanings that surpass what words can say."

8.27 And God, who sees into the hearts of men, knows what the thought of the Spirit is; because the Spirit pleads with God on behalf of his people and in accordance with his will.

As a Jew, Paul can speak of God in the third person without actually mentioning his name, and that is what he does in this verse: and God, who sees into the hearts of men is literally "and the one searching the heart." That God "searches" (that is, sees into) the hearts of men is a familiar Old Testament concept (see 1 Samuel 16.7; 1 Kings 8.39; Psalm 7.9; Proverbs 15.11; Jeremiah 17.9-10). In some languages it may be necessary to specify more clearly the relation between God, who sees into the hearts of men and the fact that God knows what the thought of the Spirit is. Since God knows what men are thinking, he therefore knows precisely the intent of the Spirit who prays on behalf of men with groanings which cannot be expressed in words. This relation of cause and effect may be expressed as "because God sees what men want in their hearts, he knows what the Spirit intends." One may also translate this as "God sees into the hearts of men and therefore knows what the thought of the Spirit is."

In the last clause of this verse the word translated because (so NEB) may have the meaning of "that." As interpreted in the TEV and most other translations this clause tells why it is that God...knows what the thought of the Spirit is. If the other alternative is followed, then the clause tells the content of what the Spirit thinks (see JB "that the pleas of the saints expressed by the Spirit are according to the mind of God").

In this last clause the pronoun "he" is made explicit by most translations as a reference to the Spirit.

His people (Goodspeed and NEB "God's people") is literally "the saints." (On this term see 1.7.)

The pronoun his (in accordance with his will) refers back to God (RSV "according to the will of God").

The last clause of verse 27 may be rendered as "for the Spirit speaks with God (or speaks strongly) for God's people and in just the way that God desires" or "...for the same purpose that God desires for his people."

8.28 We know that in all things God works for good with those who love him, those whom he has called according to his purpose.

Paul introduces this verse with essentially the same expression that he introduced verse 22. The translation of this verse is made difficult by the fact that a textual problem exists which radically alters the meaning of the text. Basically the possibilities are two, though a third also exists. (1) Some manuscripts do not include God as a subject of this verse. That means that all things (Greek panta) may be the subject of the sentence. If that is the case, then the verb must be taken with the meaning of "to work together" and the dative expression given the meaning "for those who love God." Thus, the following translation results: "for we know that all things work together for good for those who love God." The TEV, RSV, NEB, and JB give this as an alternative possibility; but no modern translation makes this a first choice. (2) Some manuscripts include God as the subject of this verse. In that case, the verb must be taken with the meaning "work in cooperation with (in order to accomplish something)," and the dative expression must mean "with those who love God." Thus, the following translation results: We know that in all things God works for good with those who love him. Modern translations, with the exception of the NEB and Phillips, follow this rendering. (3) The third possible understanding of this verse is represented by the NEB. It is possible to follow the Greek text which does not have God as the subject and to assume (on the basis of the previous verses, especially verse 27) that the Holy Spirit is the subject of this verse. If one accepts this possibility, the following translation results: "For we know that in all things God's Spirit works for good with those who love him" (see NEB "and in everything, as we know, he [the Spirit] co-operates for good with those who love God"). The choice of the text is not easy, though either of the two latter possibilities seems to be in keeping with Paul's thought as expressed elsewhere. To accept the first choice is to assume a somewhat fatalistic universe, in which God has already determined everything that is going to happen, so that men do not really have a choice between good and evil. To accept either of the other two alternatives assumes that we live in a world in which God has permitted the possibilities of good and of evil; and that even where evil results from the choice of wicked men, God is able to work with those who love him in order to bring good out of the circumstances.

If one chooses the less satisfactory interpretation, namely, "all things work together for good," a rendering may be "everything that happens is for the good of those who love God." However, if one follows the more desirable exegetical alternatives, one may translate as "in every experience which we have God works things out for good with us who love him" or "...God, together with us who love him, works so that what happens will be for good." On the basis of the third possibility listed above, the Spirit may be simply substituted for God, and the goal of the verb love will be God—for example, "in every circumstance the Spirit works together with those of us who love God, in order that what happens will turn out for good."

The last clause in this verse, those whom he has called according to his purpose, is in apposition with those who love him and serves to explain the previous clause. For whom he has called (literally "who were called") see the comments at 1.6. In biblical thought the idea of "calling" has reference to the realization of God's purpose within history. That is to say, the salvation event is never something that is looked upon as being by accident or chance; it is always related to the eternal purpose of God. The translator should be careful that the terms used in this verse do not in any way imply that God has called some and rejected others. When the New Testament declares that we are "called to be God's people," two emphases are intended: (1) the fact that we are believers is within God's eternal purpose and (2) our part in this experience (that is, our faith) is never more than a response to the call of God. All of this is to say that in the salvation event God has taken the initiative to come to man and to offer himself to man. Never is the implication given that God intends to accept some and to reject others. The New Testament affirms absolutely that it is God's will that all men would come to know him.

Those whom he has called according to his purpose may be equivalent to "the persons to whom God has spoken as a means of accomplishing his plan." Of course, if a first person plural is used in the preceding clause, it may be necessary to translate "we to whom God has called in order to do what he intends." The use of the first person plural may, in some regards, serve to avoid what might otherwise seem to be prejudicial judgment on the part of God.

8.29-30 Those whom God had already chosen he had also set apart to become like his Son, so that the Son would be the first among many brothers. (30) And so God called those that he had set apart; and those that he called he also put right with himself; and with those that he put right with himself he also shared his glory.

In these two verses Paul uses a series of five verbs to describe the divine purpose and action. Each verb differs in meaning from the others, yet each is related to and grows out of the one which it follows. The first two verbs (already chosen, set apart) refer back to God's eternal purpose before time began, while the next three verbs (called, put right with himself, shared his glory) describe the realization of God's purpose in history. Before these verbs are looked at in detail, it will be helpful to remind ourselves of what Paul is doing in this passage. Negatively, he is not developing a doctrine of predestination in which he looks upon God as arbitrarily choosing some and rejecting others. Positively, he is reflecting on his own experience and the experience of other believers, and he sees this in light of God's eternal purpose. In other words, Paul is saying that his own salvation and the salvation of others is a result of God's purpose and of God's grace; it did not happen by chance, and it was not something that the believer earned by his own merit. Therefore, up to this point Paul's basic emphasis has been to show that salvation is by God's grace alone and it is not due to any human effort. Now he emphasizes the other aspect of the salvation event, that is, that it is within the eternal purpose and intention of God.

The verb which the TEV has translated already chosen literally means "to know beforehand," and is used in Acts 26.5; Romans 11.2; 1 Peter 1.20; 2 Peter 3.17. Even though by definition this word means "to know beforehand," when used by a Jewish speaker there is a possibility of an extended meaning in light of the Old Testament use of the word "to know" (Jeremiah 1.5; Amos 3.2; Hosea 13.5). For example, the meaning of "to choose beforehand" is obviously what is intended in 1 Peter 1.20, and it seems quite possible that that is the intended meaning in this passage and in Romans 11.2. In this present passage Goodspeed translates the verb as "marked out from the first" while the JB renders by "chose specially long ago." The RSV, Phillips, and the NEB translate by verbs equivalent in meaning to "know beforehand," and Moffatt renders by "decreed of old." Several observations support the meaning of "to choose beforehand" as over against "to know beforehand" for this present passage: (1) although Paul is writing in Greek, his thoughts are conditioned by the Hebrew Old Testament, and the Hebrew verb "to know" implies much more than is conveyed by the same verb in English; (2) the meaning of "to choose beforehand" can be supported on the basis of 1 Peter 1.20, and apparently this is the meaning in Romans 11.2; (3) for English speakers at least, one can speak of knowing facts beforehand though not of knowing persons beforehand. In selecting an expression to translate had already chosen the closest equivalent may be "those whom God had designated beforehand" or "those whom God had selected out beforehand."

The verb that the TEV has translated set apart is also used in Acts 4.28; 1 Corinthians 2.7; Ephesians 1.5, 11. The meaning of "predestined" is indicated by the RSV, Goodspeed, and Moffatt. The NEB translates this verb as "ordained" in verse 29 and as "fore-ordained" in verse 30, while the JB translates the verb in both instances as "intended," and Phillips renders by "chose" in both passages. By definition this word means "to decide beforehand" and obviously has that meaning in Acts 4.28. In 1 Corinthians 2.7 and Ephesians 1.5 it appears to have the meaning of "to choose beforehand," and so would be essentially synonymous with the first verb that Paul uses in this passage. In the present passage the distinction between these two verbs seems to be as follows: the first verb (already chosen) points back to God's choice of these people as his own, while the second verb (set apart) indicates that God had in mind a definite goal for those persons whom he had chosen (that is, to become like his Son).

In selecting an expression to render set apart, it is important to avoid the implication of setting something apart because it is bad. Since the process of "setting apart" so frequently involves separating out inferior objects rather than superior ones, there is a tendency for an expression meaning "to set apart" to acquire a connotation which would be unacceptable in this context. One may contrast chosen with set apart by translating the first part of verse 29 as "for those whom God had already chosen he also designated to become like his Son." In some languages the process of designation may be expressed as "put upon them the need to become" or "marked them so that they would become."

The phrase to become like his Son has been translated in a number of different ways, but the meaning is clear and the TEV is true to what Paul intended (Goodspeed "to be made like his Son"; Moffatt "share the likeness of his Son"). Although the verb set apart speaks as though this action was already decided on before history began, the purpose indicated, to become like his Son, can only be accomplished at the end of history.

First literally means "firstborn" (so most translations; NEB, Goodspeed, JB "eldest"). In light of the Jewish use of this word, its primary component of meaning is that of priority ("first place") rather than of age ("firstborn"). In fact, it is quite possible that in New Testament times this word had come merely to mean "first."

The final purpose clause of verse 29, introduced by so that, is actually only a second purpose clause following the purpose expressed by to become like his Son. In some languages it may be necessary to mark this second purpose clause by reproducing part of the previous purpose clause—for example, "they will become like his Son so that his Son will be the first among many brothers" or "...first together with many brothers."

In the first part of verse 30 the TEV reverses the order of the verbs so as to draw attention to the new verb called. The New Testament often uses the verb "to call" as the way in which God approaches man, and this verb indicates that in the divine-human encounter the initiative is always with God. Once again it is important to realize that there is no intimation in this word that God did not call others; but when the Christian reflects on his own experience, he realizes that it is due to the fact that God has first come to him.

The verb put right with himself has been discussed earlier (see under 1.17). All five of these verbs which Paul uses are in the past tense, though it is difficult to see why he would use the past tense for the verb shared his glory. This verb must be taken as something which is still in the future, though it is looked upon as if it were already realized. The meaning of shared his glory is essentially the same as to become like his Son. That is, each one of these phrases emphasizes the fact that the ultimate goal for the Christian is to become like the God who revealed himself in Jesus Christ. In the present verse the word glory is used with the same meaning which it has in 3.23. It is difficult to express in some languages the concept of he also shared his glory with them. This may be expressed as "he gave them part of his majesty," "he gave them some of the wonderfulness which he had," or "he caused them to be glorious in some way similar to the way he is glorious."

God's Love in Christ Jesus

31 Faced with all this, what can we say? If God is for us, who can be against
us? 32 He did not even keep back his own Son, but offered him for us all! He
gave us his Son—will he not also freely give us all things? 33 Who will accuse
God's chosen people? God himself declares them not guilty! 34 Can anyone,
then, condemn them? Christ Jesus is the one who died, or rather, who was
raised to life and is at the right side of God. He pleads with God for us! 35 Who,
then, can separate us from the love of Christ? Can trouble do it, or hardship,
or persecution, or hunger, or poverty, or danger, or death? 36 As the scripture
says,

> "For your sake we are in danger of death the whole day long;
> we are treated like sheep that are going to be slaughtered."

37 No, in all these things we have complete victory through him who loved us!
38 For I am certain that nothing can separate us from his love: neither death
nor life; neither angels nor other heavenly rulers or powers; neither the present
nor the future; 39 neither the world above nor the world below—there is nothing
in all creation that will ever be able to separate us from the love of God which
is ours through Christ Jesus our Lord.

The section heading God's Love in Christ Jesus may be expressed in some languages as "Through Jesus Christ God Shows How Much He Loves Us" or "Jesus Christ Shows How Much God Loves Us."

This final section (8.31-39) is introduced by a favorite Pauline formula, what can we say?, which appears also in 3.5; 4.1; 6.1; 7.7; 9.14,30. The first five verses consist of a series of rhetorical questions that reach their climax in the Scripture quotation of verse 36, which is evidently intended to carry a great deal of weight, inasmuch as throughout the entire chapter Paul has made no quotation from Scripture. Verse 37 gives the absolute answer to the question raised in verse 35. The last two verses elaborate the answer given in verse 37 and form something of a hymnic conclusion.

8.31 Faced with all this, what can we say? If God is for us, who can be against us?

Paul's literal words ("with respect to these things") have been rendered by the TEV as faced with all this (NEB "with all this in mind"). The translation of this verse is not difficult, though it should not imply that no one will ever be against the Christian. Paul is merely saying, in an emphatic way, that all opposition to God's people will finally come to nothing, because God is on their side. The proof of God's concern for his people is introduced in the following verse.

The introductory rhetorical question may need to be changed into a statement, especially since this question is followed by another question—in fact, an entire series of questions given without response. Perhaps the closest equivalent of a statement is simply "in view of all this, our conclusion is as follows" or "on the basis of this, we may conclude."

The second question in verse 31 may likewise be changed into a statement —for example, "If God is for us, no one can prevail against us." Notice that it is necessary to introduce some concept of "prevail," since this is the clear implication in the question who can be against us?

There are many languages in which rhetorical questions may be used effectively, but if they are introduced, it is often necessary to provide an answer in the text. In such a case, the answer to the second question of verse 31 would be "no one." Similarly, the answer to the first question would be "much indeed." In languages in which an answer to a rhetorical question is required, it is important that it not be omitted. Otherwise, the statement which follows at the beginning of verse 32 might imply that God is against us.

8.32 He did not even keep back his own Son, but offered him for us all! He gave us his Son—will he not also freely give us all things?

He did not even keep back his own Son is evidently an allusion to the story of Abraham's sacrifice in Genesis 22.16. In the Septuagint account of that story the Greek translator used the same verb that Paul uses here (keep back, literally "to spare"), and the thought of Abraham is fresh in his mind from the earlier chapters of this letter. Offered means literally "to give over" and is used by Paul in 4.25 (given over to die), as well as in 1.24, 26, 28 (given them over). The TEV actually translates this verb twice in the present verse, in order to relate the various parts of the verse and to bring out the emphasis which Paul intends: he gave us his Son.

Did not even keep back is rendered in some languages as "did not prevent from suffering" or "did not cause him to evade suffering."

In order to indicate clearly the significance of offered it may be necessary to add "as a sacrifice," therefore: "he offered him as a sacrifice on behalf of all of us."

By the form which Paul uses in asking his question, will he not also freely give us all things?, he indicates that he does believe that God will freely give us all things.

8.33 Who will accuse God's chosen people? God himself declares them not guilty!

In some languages the initial question of verse 33 may be rendered by an expression such as "can" or "is able to"—for example, "who can accuse God's chosen people?" or "who can declare, The people whom God has chosen are guilty?" The answer to such a rhetorical question is "no one," and the second part of verse 33 is the reason for that—for example, "no one can accuse them, since God himself has declared them not guilty" or "no one can say, They are guilty, since God himself has said, They are innocent."

God himself declares them not guilty! may be taken as a question indicating irony on Paul's part—for example, "will God, who himself declares them not guilty, be the one to accuse them?" But this introduces an unnecessary complication into what Paul is saying, and no translators follow this in the text of their translations (see, however, the alternative rendering in the NEB). Declares them not guilty translates the same verb that is rendered elsewhere with the meaning "to be put right with God" (see under 4.5).

8.34 Can anyone, then, condemn them? Christ Jesus is the one who died, or rather, who was raised to life and is at the right side of God. He pleads with God for us!

Just as it was possible to translate verse 33 as two questions, it is also possible to translate verse 34 as two questions, rather than as a question followed by an affirmation—for example, "Will Christ Jesus condemn them? Will Christ Jesus, who died, or rather, who was raised to life and is at the right hand of God, and who pleads with God for us, be the one to condemn them?" However, once again this introduces an unnecessary complication into Paul's thought; and it is not likely that he would be using irony in a passage such as this.

If one retains the initial rhetorical question, Can anyone, then, condemn them? it may be necessary to introduce the answer, "No, no one." If this is not done, it might be wrongly assumed that Christ Jesus, who is mentioned at the beginning of the next part of the verse, is the one who is going to condemn God's chosen people. As in the previous verse, condemn may be rendered as "declare them guilty." As a statement, the initial question may be rendered as "No one, indeed, can condemn them" or "Therefore no one can condemn them." The introduction of "therefore" is legitimate, since this is the result of the fact that God himself has declared them not guilty.

Most translators take the verb was raised to life with a passive force, with God as the assumed agent (for example, "God raised him to life"); but a few take this verb to have a middle force, which indicates that Christ himself was the agent of the action, and so translate "rose from the dead" (Moffatt, JB, KJV). When Paul says that Christ is at the right side of God, he means that Christ has the place of honor and authority.

8.35 Who, then, can separate us from the love of Christ? Can trouble do it, or hardship, or persecution, or hunger, or poverty, or danger, or death?

Even though Paul uses a simple future in this verse ("will separate"), his meaning is best conveyed in translation by who, then, can separate us?

Although some manuscripts read "the love of God," most translators follow the manuscripts which read the love of Christ, and this is recommended by the UBS Greek text. It is clear that the genitive expression the love of Christ means "Christ's love for us."

The initial question, Who, then, can separate us from the love of Christ?, may be made a statement, namely, "No one can separate us from Christ's love for us," "No one can remove us from Christ's love for us," or "No one can keep Christ's love from reaching us." In some instances rather figurative expressions are employed for the idea of being separated from Christ's love—for example, "Who can take us out of the hand of Christ who loves us?" or "Who can tear us away from Christ's heart toward us?" There is, however, a difficulty involved in introducing this question by "who," since what follows are events, not persons. Therefore it may be necessary to translate: "What can separate us from Christ's love?"

The first word in the list that Paul uses is a very general term and is best translated by the English word trouble (so Goodspeed); "affliction" of many translations implies something totally different to the English reader. The second of these terms is almost synonymous in meaning with the first, and perhaps is best rendered by such words as hardship (so also NEB) or "difficulties." In 2.9 these two terms are rendered in the TEV as suffering and pain. A number of translations take Paul's word "famine" in a more general sense of hunger (NEB, Goodspeed, NAB; JB "lacking food"; Phillips "lack of... food"). Also the word "nakedness" is often given a more general sense (TEV poverty; Phillips "lack of clothes"; JB "lacking... clothes"; Goodspeed "destitution"). The last word that Paul uses is literally "sword," but in the present context it has the meaning of death, specifically a violent death. Persecution and danger, the third and sixth words in the list, are not difficult, though it should be pointed out that persecution does not necessarily imply official action and is perhaps best taken in a more general frame of reference. Danger is, of course, also a general term describing any sort of threat to one's life.

The principal difficulty in rendering the second portion of verse 35 is that terms for trouble, hardship, persecution, hunger, poverty, danger, death are often verbs or phrases which involve verb expressions. These are obviously not things but events. The possibility expressed by a question with the auxiliary can implies a condition, and therefore one may translate the second sentence of verse 35 thus: "If we are in trouble, if we suffer hardships, if people persecute us, if we have nothing to eat, if we have nothing to wear, if people threaten us, or even if we are killed, does this mean that Christ's love does not hold us?" The same sentence may, of course, be changed into a statement—for example, "Nothing can separate us from Christ's love; not even if we are in trouble, or if we suffer, or if people persecute us," etc.

8.36 As the scripture says,

"For your sake we are in danger of death
the whole day long;
we are treated like sheep that are going
to be slaughtered."

Paul sees in the Old Testament a witness, not only to Christ's sufferings, but to the suffering of his people, and he quotes from Psalm 44.22 as proof of this. We are in danger of death is literally "we are being put to death" (Goodspeed). In 1 Corinthians 15.31 Paul says "I die every day," but what he obviously means is I face death every day. The TEV assumes that Paul uses the verb "to be put to death" with a similar meaning in the present passage. The first clause in the quotation may be translated in some languages as "every day people threaten to kill us because of you."

Sheep that are going to be slaughtered is actually a genitive expression "sheep of slaughter," but there is no doubt regarding the meaning and the TEV has made the relation clear. An active equivalent of this passive expression may be "people treat us just like sheep which they are going to slaughter" or "people treat us badly, as they treat the sheep which they are going to kill."

8.37 No, in all these things we have complete victory through him who loved us!

This verse looks back to and answers the question asked in verse 35. Paul actually begins this verse with a conjunction (literally "but"), which must be given the force of no (so RSV, KJV, Phillips, Moffatt). The word translated we have complete victory (NEB "overwhelming victory is ours"; Phillips "we win an overwhelming victory") is used only here in the New Testament.

If verse 37 is understood clearly as an answer to the question in verse 35, there is no difficulty involved in the introduction of the initial particle No. It is too easy, however, in some languages for people to understand "no" as a negation of the immediate preceding statement about being treated as sheep which are about to be slaughtered. For this reason, in some languages verse 37 must begin with an adversative particle such as "but." This is particularly true if the question in verse 35 is made into a statement.

In all these things means "in every experience of life" or, as in some languages, "in everything that happens to us."

Him who loved us is perhaps best understood as a reference to the love of Christ in verse 35, and the aorist tense may be taken as a specific reference to the act of his death. On the other hand if him is taken to be a reference to God, then the force of the aorist would refer back to the time that God offered his only Son.

Through him who loved us, an expression of agency, may be expressed as "the one who loved us helps us be victorious" or "the one who loved us makes this so."

8.38-39 For I am certain that nothing can separate us from his love: neither death nor life; neither angels nor other heavenly rulers or powers; neither the present nor the future; (39) neither the world above nor the world below—there is nothing in all creation that will ever be able to separate us from the love of God which is ours through Christ Jesus our Lord.

In these two verses Paul uses a series of terms which may sound foreign to the English reader, though they are actually very closely related to concepts held by people who believe in astrology. Most, if not all, of the terms are technical terms denoting astrological powers which were thought to exercise control over man and his fate. Following the mention of death and life, the actual order in which Paul lists these in verse 38 is: angels, (heavenly) rulers, the present, the future, and (heavenly) powers. Angels, rulers, and powers may describe astrological forces, and it is highly probable that the present and the future fit into the same category. The TEV has slightly reordered the list, placing the present and the future together, so as to make the list sound more natural to the English reader. Moreover, a classifier, heavenly, has been placed before rulers and powers to indicate more accurately the nature of these forces, since if they were left unqualified the reader might think immediately of earthly rulers and powers.

It is not at all easy to find terms which will be meaningful in a receptor language, especially one in which there is no reflection of such belief in astrological powers. Furthermore, there are special difficulties, since some of these terms represent celestial objects (for example, angels and heavenly rulers), others are abstract (the present and the future), while still others refer to events (death and life). It may therefore be necessary in some languages to employ a number of different kinds of expressions. A translation of verse 38 may have the following semantically restructured form: "For I am certain that nothing is able to take us away from his loving us; it makes no difference whether we die or whether we live; angels, rulers, and powers in heaven are not able to separate us from his love, and what is happening now and what will happen in the future will not be able to separate us from his love."

The terms world above and world below are literally "height" and "depth." These also were technical astrological terms—the first referring to the highest position that a given star could reach and the second to the region below the horizon out of which the stars rise. To translate literally (even if one capitalizes the terms "height" and "depth," as Moffatt does) fails to convey the force of these terms to the English reader. The TEV attempts to come up with something that is nearest in meaning to what Paul had in mind, and so translates: neither the world above nor the world below.

The rendering of the phrases neither the world above nor the world below may be treated in a manner parallel to what has been suggested for the series in verse 38—for example, "neither the world that is above us nor the world that is below us can separate us from Christ's love." However, in many languages a more meaningful translation would be "nothing that is above the world and nothing that is below the world can separate us from Christ's love." Such a translation anticipates the following clause (there is nothing in all creation...) and may be connected to it by some such phrase as "in fact" or "that is to say"—for example, "in fact there is nothing in everything which has been created which will ever be able to separate us."

The phrase "the love of God in Christ Jesus our Lord" conveys little, if any, meaning to the English reader in this form. The TEV (along with other translations) tries to make Paul's meaning explicit: the love of God which is ours through Christ Jesus our Lord (see NAB "the love of God that comes to us in Christ Jesus, our Lord"; Goodspeed "the love God has shown in Christ Jesus our Lord"). This love of God...through Christ Jesus may be expressed in some languages as "God's love which he has shown by means of Christ Jesus our Lord," "God's love which we experience because of Christ Jesus our Lord," or "God's love which Jesus Christ our Lord has caused us to experience."

CHAPTER 9

God and His Chosen People

9 What I say is true; I belong to Christ and I do not lie. My conscience,
ruled by the Holy Spirit, also assures me that I am not lying. [2]How great
is my sorrow, how endless the pain in my heart for my people, my own flesh
and blood! [3]For their sake I could wish that I myself were under God's curse
and separated from Christ. [4]They are God's chosen people; he made them his
sons and shared his glory with them; he made his covenants with them and
gave them the Law; they have the true worship; they have received God's
promises; [5]they are descended from the patriarchs, and Christ, as a human
being, belongs to their race. May God, who rules over all, be praised forever!
Amen.

The conjunction and in the section heading God and His Chosen People may be somewhat misleading in some languages. In fact, in many instances a fully satisfactory title of this section may be "God's Chosen People" or "The People Whom God Has Specially Chosen." One may also employ "God's Relation to His People" or "...to the People of Israel."

Scholars agree that chapters 9-11 introduce a new major division in the letter; and although there is no grammatical marker of the relation between chapters 8 and 9, the connection is evident. In the first eight chapters Paul has been concerned to show that salvation has its source in the character and work of God; chapters 9-11 are concerned with the place of Israel within the framework of God's redemptive purpose. These chapters divide easily into three sections: 9.1-29; 9.30—10.21; and 11.1-32. Each section is a unity within itself, but at the same time it forms the basis for what follows. The entire division concludes with the doxology of 11.33-36. The first section (9.1-29) describes the absolute freedom of the divine choice, and unites the themes of God's mercy and of his hardening of those who reject him. The second section (9.30—10.21) speaks of the freedom and responsibility of men within the divine purpose, and shows how Israel rejected the call to faith by attempting to establish its own righteousness. The third section (chapter 11) shows how God accomplishes his act of salvation, despite the rebellion of men.

9.1 What I say is true; I belong to Christ and I do not lie. My conscience, ruled by the Holy Spirit, also assures me that I am not lying.

In Greek verses 1 and 2 form one sentence. It is agreed that "in Christ" has the force of "in union with Christ" (JB), and so the TEV renders this phrase as a finite statement: I belong to Christ. It is possible either to connect this phrase with what precedes, what I say is true, as most translations do, or to connect it with what follows as the TEV does (see also JB).

It is necessary to avoid the implication that what Paul declares as being true is merely the fact that he belongs to Christ. The content of what is true begins with verse 2. In order to avoid a wrong relation of ideas, it is possible to translate the first sentence of verse 1 as "what I say is true; I do not lie, because I belong to Christ."

The TEV attempts to make clear the meaning of Paul's phrase "in the Holy Spirit" and so translates as ruled by the Holy Spirit. The NEB renders this phrase "enlightened by the Holy Spirit" and Goodspeed "under the holy Spirit's influence."

Paul is here appealing to three witnesses (his own conscience, his union with Jesus Christ, and his union with the Holy Spirit) which assure him that he is not lying. The TEV (so also NEB and JB) makes this information clear, but a translation such as the RSV ("my conscience bears me witness in the Holy Spirit, 2 that I have great sorrow...") suggests that Christ is a witness to the fact that Paul is not lying, while his conscience and the Holy Spirit are witnesses to the fact that he has great sorrow in his heart. This does not seem to be what Paul is saying. Verse 2 actually introduces the content of the assertion in verse 1, to which Christ, his conscience, and the Holy Spirit bear witness that he is not lying.

The phrase ruled by the Holy Spirit may be translated as "which the Holy Spirit ruled" or "which the Holy Spirit controlled."

Assures may be rendered as "tells me with confidence," "says strongly," or even "says that it is surely true that I am not lying."

Conscience may be variously translated, depending upon the particular set of associations connected with certain terms or phrases—for example, "my heart," "my innermost," "that which speaks within me," or "the voice in my heart."

9.2 How great is my sorrow, how endless the pain in my heart for my people, my own flesh and blood!

Translators should attempt to make as clear as possible the relation between verse 2 and verse 1. In order to show this relation properly, it may be necessary in some languages to say "what is true is that I have great sorrow" or "it is true that my sorrow for my people is very great."

The last phrase in this verse (for my people, my own flesh and blood!) actually appears in verse 3 of the Greek text. However, Paul's sorrow is not for himself, but for his people, and so the TEV brings this phrase up to verse 2 to make this fact clear.

The double exclamation of verse 2 may be changed into a strong affirmation—for example, "My sorrow is very great and the pain in my heart for my people never ends; I speak of the people of my own tribe." It is quite impossible in most languages to employ a literal translation of my own flesh and blood, nor can one reproduce literally what the Greek has: "relatives according to the flesh." A far more appropriate equivalent is usually some expression as "my own tribe," "the people to whom I belong," or "the people with whom I am one."

9.3 For their sake I could wish that I myself were under God's curse and separated from Christ.

I myself is an emphatic construction in Greek and the TEV seeks to indicate the emphasis.

Under God's curse renders one word in Greek (RSV "accursed"; NEB "outcast"; JB "condemned"). In the Septuagint this translates a Hebrew word describing persons or things that could not be put to ordinary use, since they were set apart to God and so had to be destroyed. In Greek this word is anathema, and Paul says, literally, "I could wish that I myself were anathema from Christ." The TEV and others (RSV, JB, Goodspeed, Moffatt) indicate this statement as having two elements: under God's curse and separated from Christ. Others take it as having only one element: "outcast from Christ" (NEB) and "separated from Christ" (NAB). For the use of this word in the Septuagint, see such passages as Leviticus 27.28; Deuteronomy 7.26; Joshua 6.17-18; 7.12-13; Zechariah 14.11. In the New Testament this term occurs also in 1 Corinthians 16.22 and Galatians 1.8-9.

It is important that the introductory phrase for their sake be clearly related to what follows. This may be expressed in some languages as "if I could help them I would wish" or "in order to help them I would be glad to." In many instances it is best to treat this introductory statement as a condition of probability, certainly not of actual fact, since Paul is not stating that his being cursed by God would, in fact, be of benefit to his kinsman. Therefore, "if I could help them I would wish" or "if it would be of help to them I could wish."

That I myself were under God's curse may be restructured as "that God himself would curse me" or "that the curse from God's power would be upon me."

The last phrase, separated from Christ, may be translated as "no longer belong to Christ" or "no longer have a part with Christ."

9.4 They are God's chosen people; he made them his sons and shared his glory with them; he made his covenants with them and gave them the Law; they have the true worship; they have received God's promises;

In this verse Paul describes the status of the Israelites by a series of nouns, which are better rendered by descriptive phrases in English. For a literal translation of this verse see the RSV ("they are Israelites, and to them belong the sonship, the glory, the covenants, the giving of the law, the worship, and the promises"). The TEV translates "Israelites" as God's chosen people, because the emphasis in the present context is not upon their racial origin but upon the fact that God chose them to be his own people. It is important in the selection of a word for chosen to avoid the idea of favoritism. It is true that God "specially selected" his people, but one should not suggest that this means that he treated them as pampered favorites.

The remaining series of nouns, though introduced in Greek by the phrase "to them belong," actually describes things that God did for his chosen people, and so the TEV makes this connection explicit: he made...shared...made... they have...they have received. It should be noticed that the JB also makes this connection clear. On the term "sonship" (TEV he made them his sons) see 8.15, 23. In the present passage Paul seems to be referring to the specific time of the Exodus, when God chose Israel to be his people (see Exodus 4.22).

On the use of the word "glory" (TEV shared his glory with them) see 3.23;

5.2. In the present passage the reference is to the specific manifestations of God among his people, beginning with the Exodus experiences and culminating with his presence with them in the temple.

In some languages one can only translate shared his glory with them as "gave them part of his glory," but a more appropriate equivalent, considering the context, is probably "showed them his glory" or "showed them how glorious he was."

The use of the plural, covenants, has occasioned some difficulty, and some manuscripts have the singular "covenant." However, the plural is by far the more difficult reading and is preferred by the UBS textual committee. Paul may have reference to the several covenants that God made (with Adam, Noah, Abraham, and Moses), or else he may have reference to the Jewish tradition which distinguished three covenants that together made up the great covenant of the Exodus (the covenant made at Horeb, the one made in the plains of Moab, and the one made at Mounts Gerizim and Ebal). Although Paul interprets the purpose of the Law in a different way from that of many Jews, he still looks upon it as a privilege which God gave to the people of Israel. If at all possible, one should choose a term for covenants which will indicate that the initiative exists with God. In other words, the covenant is not a "bargained contract." In some languages a term such as "compact" may be appropriate, provided this indicates something good. However, in order to indicate clearly the initiative on the part of God, it is possible in some languages to say "he tied himself to them" or "he linked himself to them."

The true worship is literally "the worship," but the reference is to the Israelite temple service, which the Jews considered to be the only true way to worship God. The equivalent of they have the true worship may be expressed in some languages as "they worship God in a true way," "they know how to worship God truly," or "God has shown them how to worship him in the true way."

God's promises (literally "the promises") is doubtless a reference to the many promises of salvation and deliverance made by God throughout the Old Testament.

9.5 they are descended from the patriarchs, and Christ, as a human being, belongs to their race. May God, who rules over all, be praised forever! Amen.

Except for the last sentence in this verse, all of verses 3-5 is one sentence in Greek. The patriarchs were the noted ancestors of the Jewish race (in particular Abraham, Isaac, and Jacob) with whom God made his covenant. The culmination of all Israel's blessings is the fact that Christ, as a human being, belongs to their race. The term patriarchs can involve two important components: (1) they are ancestors, and (2) they are important. This may simply be expressed in some languages as "the great ancestors," "the ancestors from which each tribe comes," or "the great ancestors for which the tribes are named."

It is important to indicate that Christ is the last element in the series by which God's chosen people are related to him in a special way, but it is essential to avoid any implication that the people were descended "from the patriarchs and Christ." Moreover, to indicate that Christ is the last element in this series, it may be useful to begin the last clause as "finally Christ...." The Greek text literally reads "the Christ," which some translators take as a title rather than a proper name (NEB "the Messiah"). However, this is not a necessary conclusion, since in verse 3 Paul also uses the definite article "the" before Christ (there NEB has "Christ"), where apparently all translations render by a proper name.

As a human being is literally "as far as the flesh is concerned," but this only means "insofar as Christ was a human being" or "insofar as Christ was a man." The final phrase, belongs to their race, is often equivalent to "belongs to the same tribe" or "is a member of the same nation." Another means of expressing race may be "he is one with them."

Since the earliest New Testament manuscripts were without any systematic punctuation, it is necessary for scholars to punctuate the text according to what seems appropriate to the syntax and the meaning. Basically, the question is whether the doxology has reference to God (TEV May God, who rules over all, be praised forever!), or to Christ (TEV alternative rendering "And may he, who is God ruling over all, be praised forever!"). Although there are strong grammatical arguments to the contrary, the UBS textual committee prefers the reading represented in the TEV, principally on the basis that Paul elsewhere never calls Christ God. Most modern English translations prefer the rendering represented in the TEV (so RSV, NEB, NAB, Goodspeed, Moffatt), but some do prefer the rendering represented in the alternative rendering of the TEV (so JB and Phillips).

The passive expression may God...be praised forever must be translated in some languages as "all men should forever praise God who rules over everything."

> [6]I am not saying that the promise of God has failed; because not all the people of Israel are the chosen people of God. [7]Neither are all Abraham's descendants the children of God. God said to Abraham, "The descendants of Isaac will be counted as yours." [8]This means that the children born in the natural way are not the children of God; instead, the children born as a result of God's promise are regarded as the true descendants. [9]For God's promise was made in these words: "At the right time I will come back and Sarah will have a son."
>
> [10]And this is not all. For Rebecca's two sons had the same father, our ancestor Isaac. [11-12]But in order that the choice of one son might be completely the result of God's own purpose, God said to her, "The older will serve the younger." He said this before they were born, before they had done anything either good or bad; so God's choice was based on his call, and not on anything they did. [13]As the scripture says, "I loved Jacob, but I hated Esau."

By what Paul says in the first 5 verses of this chapter he brings into sharp focus a problem relating to God's promise. It is very evident that God gave a unique position to the people of Israel; does their rejection of Christ indicate that God has failed to keep his promise to them? It is to this question that Paul now addresses himself.

9.6 I am not saying that the promise of God has failed; because not all the people of Israel are the chosen people of God.

Although Paul uses the phrase "the word of God," his reference is clearly to the promise of God (JB "does this mean that God has failed to keep his promise?"). Paul argues that this is not true, because not all the people of Israel are the chosen people of God. This sentence might be literally rendered "not all those who descend from Israel are Israel" (JB), but it is evident that in this clause the word "Israel" is used in two distinct ways: (1) those who share a common racial ancestry ("those who descend from Israel") and (2) those who are the chosen people of God. Goodspeed attempts to make the difference clear by rendering "for not everybody who is descended from Israel really belongs to Israel"; NEB by "for not all descendants of Israel are truly Israel"; and the NAB by "for not all Israelites are true Israelites."

I am not saying that the promise of God has failed may be difficult to translate in some languages. It may be easier to say: "I do not say that the promise of God has not succeeded" or "...has not done its work" or even "...God has failed to keep his promise."

The clause of cause, because not all...are the chosen people of God, is particularly crucial in this verse, and great care must be exercised in translating it. This clause relates to the main clause, I am not saying, and not to the promise of God has failed. It may be necessary in some languages to break this verse into two sentences and to shift from a negative to a positive aspect—for example, "I am not saying that what God promised has not happened. What God promised has actually happened; because the people whom God has specially chosen include more persons than simply the people of Israel."

9.7 Neither are all Abraham's descendants the children of God. God said to Abraham, "The descendants of Isaac will be counted as yours."

The first part of this verse reads literally: "neither are all Abraham's descendants children." It is not clear whether Paul intends "children" to mean "Abraham's children" or "God's children." On the basis of the following verse, the TEV understands this to be a reference to the children of God (see also the NEB alternative rendering); others make it a clear reference to Abraham's children. But even if "Abraham's children" is intended, there should be some type of qualifier (NEB and JB have "his true children"). Since the initial clause of verse 7 introduces a further example of a special relationship of people to God, it may be useful to introduce this clause by a conjunction like "moreover" or "furthermore." There is a distinct problem in saying that "not all those who descended from Abraham are the children of God." Such a rendering might seem to be entirely too general, particularly in view of the fact that the people referred to are actually "children according to God's promise." It may be necessary, therefore, in some languages to render this phrase as "the true children of God," or "the children whom God promised to Abraham."

Having introduced the major point in his argument, Paul now appeals to scripture to strengthen it. The reference is to Genesis 21.12, and Paul quotes from this verse without any introductory formula except the conjunction "but" (see RSV). The TEV makes it clear that the promise is something that God said to Abraham, a fact which is not made explicit in most translations.

The descendants of Isaac will be counted as yours may be translated as "only the offspring of Isaac will be counted as your offspring" or "only those who belong to Isaac's family will be counted as your children."

9.8 This means that the children born in the natural way are not the children of God; instead, the children born as a result of God's promise are regarded as the true descendants.

The children born in the natural way (literally "the children of the flesh") is not a reference to the manner of birth (that is, to natural birth as opposed to caesarean birth, for example), but rather a reference to "physical descent" (so JB).

There are real difficulties involved in any type of literal translation of "the children of the flesh" or the children born in the natural way, since such expressions are likely to be misunderstood. In some languages one may render such a construction as "this means that not all of Abraham's children were to be considered the children of God" or "...not all the children of whom Abraham was father are to be considered God's children."

God's promise (so NEB) is literally "the promise," but the reference is to God's promise.

The phrase as a result of God's promise may be rendered as "because God specifically promised them"—for example, "but only the children born to Abraham, because God had specially promised them to him, are to be called Abraham's descendants" or "...true descendants." True descendants is literally "descendants," which the NEB takes to mean "Abraham's descendants." However, in the context the meaning seems rather to be that the children born to Abraham as a result of God's promise are "God's descendants" (see Moffatt "His true offspring").

9.9 For God's promise was made in these words: "At the right time I will come back and Sarah will have a son."

The initial clause for God's promise was made in these words may be restructured as "for this is what God said when he made the promise to Abraham."

The scripture quotation in this verse represents a rather free combination of Genesis 18.10 and 14. At the right time (NEB "at the time fixed"; JB "at such and such a time"; NAB "at this time") is shown clearly by the passage in Genesis to mean "at this time next year" (Goodspeed).

Sarah will have a son may be rendered simply as "Sarah will possess a son" or it may be translated as "Sarah will give birth to a son" or "Sarah will have given birth to a son."

9.10 And this is not all. For Rebecca's two sons had the same father, our ancestor Isaac.

Paul's intention in verses 9-13 is to show the absolute freedom of God's choice.

And this is not all may be equivalent in some languages to a mere conjunctive abverb or phrase, such as "moreover," "therefore," or "in addition to this."

9.11-12 But in order that the choice of one son might be completely the result of God's own purpose, God said to her, "The older will serve the younger." He said this before they were born, before they had done anything either good or bad; so God's choice was based on his call, and not on anything they did.

In Greek these two verses are one sentence, and it is in a different order from that of the TEV. In the TEV the sentence is restructured so as to make the meaning clearer for English readers. This arrangement makes it impossible to indicate a point where verse 11 ends and verse 12 begins.

But in order that the choice of one son might be completely the result of God's own purpose is actually the second element in the Greek sentence structure. A literal translation of this clause is difficult, but an analysis of it will help to explain the TEV rendering. The subject is "God's purpose" and the verb is "in order that it might remain." The subject is modified by an adjective phrase "according to choice." Thus the entire clause reads "in order that the according-to-choice purpose of God might remain." And the entire phrase, "the according-to-choice purpose of God," refers to the purpose of God which expressed itself in a particular choice, in this context the choice of one son. The verb "remain" has the force of "continue to be," so that the entire clause may be rendered: "in order that the purpose of God might continue to exist on the basis of the choice that he himself made."

Last in the Greek sentence is the clause God said to her, "The older will serve the younger," which comes from Genesis 25.23. Actually, God said to her represents a passive construction, "it was said to her," but God is clearly the agent of speaking.

Even with the reordering of clauses in verses 11 and 12 and the repetition of the expressions of choosing, there are still a number of difficulties involved in reproducing these verses in certain languages. In the first place, it may be necessary to place a purpose clause after the clause of means—for example, "God said to Rebecca, Your older son will serve your younger son. He said this in order to show that the choice of one son and not the other depended entirely upon God's own plan," or "... in order to show that God's selecting one son and not another was because God planned it that way," or "... God wanted it that way."

The clause he said this before they were born may need to be somewhat more specific because of the particular context—for example, "he said this to Rebecca before her children were born" or "... before she gave birth to her two sons."

Before they had done anything either good or bad may require slight modification in order to indicate that this is not any collective activity of the two—for example, "before either one had done anything, whether good or bad."

9.13

So God's choice was based on his call, and not on anything they did (the third element in the Greek sentence) is literally "not from works but from the one who called." The term "works" must be taken in the broadest sense possible (not as a specific reference to the works of the Law). "The one who called" is a Semitic way of speaking of God. The NEB translates this part of the Greek text as "based not upon men's deeds but upon the call of God"; Moffatt has "which depends upon the call of God, not on anything man does."

The transitional particle so must be rendered in some languages as "hence" or "thus, as it can be seen," since what follows is a conclusion.

It is extremely difficult in some languages to say God's choice was based on his call, since this would imply that God called one or the other of the sons before he had even made a choice. This, of course, is not what is intended. The text itself indicates simply that the selection of one son in preference to another is a matter of God's calling one rather than the other and not a matter of what either one of them did. It may be better, therefore, to translate: "what happened depended entirely upon God's calling one rather than the other; it did not depend on anything that either one had done."

9.13 As the scripture says, "I loved Jacob, but I hated Esau."

Once again Paul makes an appeal to scripture; this time to Malachi 1.2-3. The verb loved has the force of "chose," while the verb hated has the force of "rejected." In this type of context it seems particularly useful to employ such terms as "chose" and "rejected" rather than the literal loved and hated, especially since an equivalent of hated may give entirely wrong connotations in a receptor language.

That Paul intends this scripture quotation to have a special weight is indicated by the way in which he introduces it, as the scripture says, and by the fact that he himself makes no further comment on it.

> [14]What shall we say, then? That God is unjust? Not at all. [15]For he said to Moses, "I will have mercy on whom I wish, I will take pity on whom I wish." [16]So then, it does not depend on what man wants or does, but only on God's mercy. [17]For the scripture says to Pharaoh, "I made you king for this very purpose, to use you to show my power, and to make my name known in all the world." [18]So then, God has mercy on whom he wishes, and he makes stubborn whom he wishes.

Paul once again uses a question-answer type of philosophical argument (see 2.1), in which he imagines an opponent raising the objection that God is unjust. In reply Paul first gives the theological basis for his answer (vv. 14-18), to which he adds an illustration from everyday life (vv. 19-21). Next, he brings together the theological conclusions of what he has just said (vv. 22-23), climaxing them with a strong affirmation (v. 24). Finally, he illustrates the thesis stated in verse 24 with examples from scripture (vv. 25-29).

It is clear that in these verses Paul is not only emphasizing God's freedom, but his mercy as well. God is not obligated to do anything for sinful man, and what he does he does because he is merciful. If, on the other hand, he condemns sinful man, he is just, because that is precisely what man deserves. That is to say, the keynote of these chapters is not only God's freedom but his mercy as well.

9.14 What shall we say, then? That God is unjust? Not at all.

What shall we say, then? appears also in 4.1; 6.1; 7.7; 8.31; and not at all is the same form used in 3.4.

The question-answer pattern may be reproduced in a nonquestion form as "some people will argue that God is unjust but this is not true." Even for languages which employ the question and answer rhetorical forms it may be wise to combine as one the two initial questions—for example, "Then shall we say that God is unjust? By no means."

9.15 For he said to Moses, "I will have mercy on whom I wish, I will take pity on whom I wish."

The quotation in this verse is from Exodus 33.19.

... on whom I wish ... on whom I wish may be translated in some languages more effectively as conditional clauses—for example, "if I wish to have mercy on someone, I will; if I wish to take pity on someone, I will do so."

9.16 So then, it does not depend on what man wants or does, but only on God's mercy.

This verse introduces a logical inference, so then, drawn on the basis of the scripture quotation in the previous verse. The TEV rendering is somewhat different from a literal rendering of the Greek text, "So then, not of the one who wills or of the one who runs, but of God who shows mercy." The RSV translates: "So it depends not upon man's will or exertion, but upon God's mercy"; and the NEB: "Thus it does not depend on man's will or effort, but on God's mercy." All three translations take the verb "to run" in the more general sense of "to exert oneself" (TEV does; RSV "exertion"; NEB "effort"). Although the pronoun it does not appear in the Greek text as such, a good English translation of Paul's words almost requires this type of construction. In fact, many English translations use a construction very similar to that employed by the TEV (JB is an exception: "the only thing that counts is not what human beings want or try to do...").

In a number of languages one must specify what the pronoun it refers to. In the present passage, it has reference to God's choice. Therefore, one may render verse 16 as "hence, whether God chooses a person or not does not depend on what a man wants or does, but only upon the mercy which God shows" or "... is not because of what a man wants or does but only because God wants to show mercy." In this type of context "to show mercy" must be understood in a very broad sense of "do good to" or "to cause good for."

9.17 For the scripture says to Pharaoh, "I made you king for this very purpose, to use you to show my power, and to make my name known in all the world."

In order to make his argument even stronger, Paul appeals to a further passage of scripture (Exodus 9.16). The TEV takes the first verb in this verse (literally "I raised you up") to mean I made you king.

In some languages it is impossible to introduce direct discourse beginning with I (I made you king...) by the phrase the scripture says to Pharaoh, since the pronoun I would seem to refer to the scripture. Rather, one must have "for the scripture quotes God as saying to Pharaoh" or "for the words of God to Pharaoh occur in the scripture as" or "in the scripture God says to Pharaoh."

In this quotation God tells Pharaoh that he has two reasons for making him king: (1) to use you to show my power and (2) to make my name known in all the world. Since there are clearly two purposes, for this very purpose may have to be made plural—for example, "for these reasons" or even "for the following reasons."

To use you to show my power is literally "to show my power in you" (NEB "to exhibit my power in my dealings with you"; JB "to use you as a means of showing my power"). In some languages this may be rendered as "to cause you to show how strong I am" or "...to show to all how great my power is."

To make my name known in all the world (NEB "to spread my fame over all the world"; Moffatt "to spread news of my name over all the earth") may be translated as "to cause all people throughout the world to know about me" or "...to know my name."

9.18 So then, God has mercy on whom he wishes, and he makes stubborn whom he wishes.

This verse is similar to verse 16 in that it draws a conclusion on the basis of the previous scripture quotation, so then.

Makes stubborn is literally "harden." The RSV and JB render this with the sense of "to harden (someone's) heart."

As in the case of verse 15, the clauses whom he wishes may be translated as conditional since in a sense these clauses are conditional relatives—for example, "whomever he wishes." Therefore, one may translate as "if God wishes to show mercy on someone, he does so, and if he wishes to make someone stubborn, he does that."

Normally it is wise to avoid the idiom "to harden the heart." Even in European languages in which this phrase has been translated literally, the correct meaning of the Semitic idiom (which is basically "to make stubborn or obstinate") has not been accurately represented. Furthermore, in some languages "to harden the heart" would mean "to make a person brave," and this is obviously wrong.

God's Wrath and Mercy

[19]One of you, then, will say to me, "If this is so, how can God find fault with a man? Who can resist God's will?" [20]But who are you, my friend, to talk back to God? A clay pot does not ask the man who made it, "Why did you make me like this?" [21]After all, the man who makes the pots has the right to use the clay as he wishes, and to make two pots from the same lump of clay, one for special occasions, and the other for ordinary use.

The section heading God's Wrath and Mercy may be appropriately rendered in some languages as "God Both Condemns and Shows Mercy."

9.19 One of you, then, will say to me, "If this is so, how can God find fault with a man? Who can resist God's will?"

This verse is similar to verse 14 in that it also introduces questions which Paul believes can be raised by his opponents: "If this is so (that is, what Paul has just stated in verse 18), how can God find fault with a man? Who can resist God's will?" Paul deals with these questions in a way similar to that in which he dealt with the question raised in 3.5-6. He does not really answer the questions; he merely denies that a man has the right to raise them.

The TEV makes the pronominal references explicit: God for Greek "he" and God's for "his."

Since questions are introduced in verse 19, it may be necessary to say "will ask me" rather than simply will say to me. The conditional clause if this is so may require some expansion: "if this is the way God does things" or "if this is how God acts."

Resist God's will may be translated in some languages as "fight back against what God wants," "refuse what God wants," or "object to what God wants."

9.20-21 But who are you, my friend, to talk back to God? A clay pot does not ask the man who made it, "Why did you make me like this?" (21) After all, the man who makes the pots has the right to use the clay as he wishes, and to make two pots from the same lump of clay, one for special occasions, and the other for ordinary use.

The place of these verses in Paul's argument is to underscore the fact that a man does not have the right to question God's actions.

My friend (so also Goodspeed; cf. NAB) is literally "O man" (cf. 2.1).

But who are you...to talk back to God? may be rendered as "but who do you think you are that you can talk back to God?" or "but how is it that you think you are so big (or important) that you can talk back to God?" or "...that you can object to what God has decided?"

Has the right may be translated as "is permitted to" or "is allowed to." In some languages this may be equivalent to some form of the auxiliary "can" or "may," both of which in English express certain aspects of permission and possibility.

The phrases for special occasions and for ordinary use are rendered in a number of ways in different translations, but the contrast is between a pot that is reserved for some special function and one in everyday use.

> [22]And the same is true of what God has done. He wanted to show his wrath and to make his power known. So he was very patient in enduring those who were the objects of his wrath, who were ready to be destroyed. [23]And he wanted also to reveal his rich glory, which was poured out on us who are the objects of his mercy, those of us whom he has prepared to receive his glory. [24]For we are the ones whom he called, not only from among the Jews but also from among the Gentiles.

9.22 And the same is true of what God has done. He wanted to show his wrath and to make his power known. So he was very patient in enduring those who were the objects of his wrath, who were ready to be destroyed.

Verses 22-24 are one sentence in Greek. They present a number of exegetical problems. In fact, as far as the grammatical construction is concerned, they are perhaps the most difficult verses in the entire book of Romans. These verses are in the form of an "if" clause ("if such and such is true..."), but no conclusion follows. However, this is not an impossible construction to deal with, and similar constructions exist elsewhere in the Greek New Testament (see Luke 19.41,42; John 6.61,62; and Acts 23.9). The TEV understands this "if" clause to have the force of introducing a condition which is true to fact. On that basis, the TEV attempts to relate this clause to the context by the words and the same is true of what God has done. In some languages an appropriate equivalent may be "this illustration applies to what God has done" or "what God has done is similar to this," in which case a new paragraph may not be required or may not even be helpful.

A second problem is presented by a participle, which may have either a causal force ("because he wanted...") or the force of concession ("although he wanted..."). Some translators believe that Paul is trying to soften the force of what he has said, and so they follow the second alternative: "then what if God, though he wanted to display his anger and show his power, has shown great patience...?" (Goodspeed; see also Moffatt, JB, and the alternative rendering of the NEB). On the other hand, the causal force seems to fit the context better. That is, the entire passage would then be brought into line with the meaning of verse 17, and verses 22-23 would present two parallel reasons for God's patience in enduring those who were the objects of his wrath. The TEV (though changing the participle to a finite verb) follows this interpretation: he wanted to show his wrath and to make his power known. So... (similarly RSV, NEB, NAB).

Objects of his wrath is literally "vessels of wrath." Paul uses the word "vessel" in this verse because it is the same word that he uses in the previous verse (rendered pot in the TEV), and he is simply trying to maintain the connection between the two verses. The objects of his wrath are "those whom he was going to judge in his anger."

The participle translated ready is rendered "ripe" by Goodspeed (see

Moffatt "ripe and ready"), and in the present context may have the force of "deserve" (JB). To be destroyed is actually a noun phrase (literally "for destruction"). A number of commentators understand the force in the present context to be "eternal destruction," but such a conclusion does not seem necessary. The passive construction to be destroyed may need to be transformed into an active one. This will also require some shift in the relation of ready—for example, "whom God was ready to destroy." In the translation of ready it is important to avoid the implication that these objects of his wrath were prepared to be destroyed. It is a matter of temporal proximity to destruction and not preparation which is in focus at this point.

9.23 And he wanted also to reveal his rich glory, which was poured out on us who are the objects of his mercy, those of us whom he has prepared to receive his glory.

There is a textual problem at the beginning of this verse: the question is whether the verse begins with "in order that" or "and in order that." The latter of these possibilities ("and in order that") is to be favored, both on the basis of manuscript evidence and in light of the fact that it is obviously the more difficult reading. Furthermore, this form of the text tends to lend support to the causal interpretation of the participle discussed in verse 22. For that reason the TEV uses the words he wanted in each case.

His rich glory is literally "the richness of his glory" (so JB), but in a construction of this type the abstract noun should be interpreted as a qualifier of the noun which appears in the genitive. To reveal his rich glory may be rendered as "to show how very glorious he is."

In some languages one cannot say glory, which was poured out on us, since it is impossible to speak of glory being poured out on someone. But one can often say "glory, which he shared with us" or even change a clause into a complete sentence: "glory. He has given some of this glory to us."

Objects is literally "vessels" (see the comments on verse 22), but the reference is obviously to the people with whom God had shared his mercy (see verse 24), and so the TEV makes this information explicit by introducing a pronoun: us... those of us. The clause who are the objects of his mercy may be rendered in some languages as "to whom he has been merciful" or "to whom he has shown mercy."

The Greek verb rendered prepared actually has the force of "to prepare beforehand" (see NEB "from the first" and JB "long ago"). Paul identifies God's actions in history as the working out of his eternal purpose. Elsewhere in the New Testament this verb appears only in Ephesians 2.10, where it is rendered by the TEV as already prepared.

9.24 For we are the ones whom he called, not only from among the Jews but also from among the Gentiles.

As mentioned earlier, this verse is the continuation of the Greek sentence begun in verse 22. We are the ones whom actually has no grammatical antecedent in the two previous verses, but, as mentioned in the comments on verse 23, the reference must be to the word rendered objects. The JB, like the TEV, has already made this identification explicit in verse 23 ("people he had prepared for this glory long ago") and the JB again makes that identification explicit in verse 24 ("we are those people"; cf. NEB "such vessels are we").

The final phrases of verse 24, not only from among the Jews but also from among the Gentiles, may be rendered as "some of us are Jews and some of us are Gentiles" or "this includes some Jews and some Gentiles."

> 25 This is what he says in the book of Hosea,
> "The people who were not mine,
> I will call 'My People.'
> The nation that I did not love,
> I will call 'My Beloved.'
> 26 And in the very place where they were told, 'You are not my people,'
> there they will be called the sons of the living God."
> 27 And Isaiah exclaims about Israel, "Even if the people of Israel are as many
> as the grains of sand by the sea, yet only a few of them will be saved; 28 for the
> Lord will quickly settle his full account with all the world." 29 It is as Isaiah
> had said before, "If the Lord Almighty had not left us some descendants, we
> would have become like Sodom, we would have been like Gomorrah."

9.25 This is what he says in the book of Hosea,
"The people who were not mine,
I will call 'My People.'
The nation that I did not love,
I will call 'My Beloved.'

Beginning with this verse and going through verse 29, Paul introduces a series of Old Testament passages to validate what he has said in verse 24. That is, that God's call extends both to the Jews and to the Gentiles, though neither all of the Jews nor all of the Gentiles have responded to this call.

Paul says, literally, "in Hosea," but this is merely a Semitic way of saying in the book of Hosea. The quotation comes from the Septuagint of Hosea 2.23 with a few minor alterations. In the original context Hosea is addressing himself to the northern kingdom of Israel. Hosea has named his daughter "Without-Mercy" and his son "Not-my-People" (Hosea 1.6,9) to indicate the fallen condition of the northern tribes of Israel. Now Hosea is saying that God will show mercy to Israel and restore them, so that they will once again be his people. However, it is clear that Paul is applying this verse to the Gentiles.

In the introductory statement of verse 25 (This is what he says...), it may be necessary to specify that it is God who is speaking—for example, "this is what God says, as written in the book of Hosea" or "...as Hosea wrote."

It is not easy to translate idiomatically an expression such as The people who were not mine, I will call 'My People.' In some languages the closest equivalent may be "I will use the words My-People when I speak of people who are really not mine" or "I will give the name of My-People to those people who are not mine."

"Her" of the RSV is actually a feminine article in Greek; it is translated by the TEV and others (NEB, JB) as the nation. The TEV also transforms a passive construction in Greek ("the [nation] that was not loved") to an active construction: the nation that I did not love (see also JB). As in the case of the first line of the quoted passage, one may also employ for this second line some such translation as "I will use the name My-Beloved in speaking of a nation that I did not love," "I will use the words My-Beloved when I talk about the nation I did not love," or "I will use the words I-Love-You when I talk about the nation that I did not love."

9.26 And in the very place where they were told,
'You are not my people,"
there they will be called the sons of the
living God."

The quotation in this verse comes from Hosea 1.10; again it is applied by Paul to the Gentile situation. In the original context Hosea was contrasting the idols of other peoples with the Lord, who was the living God. The expression living God indicates that the Lord is the source of life, the one who gives life.

It may be necessary in verse 26 to make explicit who is speaking—for example, "and in the very place where God said, You are not my people, there the living God will call them his sons."

9.27-28 And Isaiah exclaims about Israel, "Even if the people of Israel are as many as the grains of sand by the sea, yet only a few of them will be saved; (28) for the Lord will quickly settle his full account with all the world."

It is best to take these two verses together, since the quotations in them come from Isaiah 10.22-23. These verses in Hebrew are very difficult, and the Septuagint, which Paul seems to be quoting rather freely, is also quite difficult. In fact, it is likely that the opening words of the quotation from Isaiah are modified on the basis of Paul's recollection of the passage just quoted from Hosea 1.10. Fortunately, for the purpose of translating the Romans text, verse 27 is not difficult. In the second clause of the quotation in this verse, the words only a few of them (most translations "only a remnant") are emphatic. The comparison included within a clause of condition is difficult to express succinctly in a number of languages. An equivalent may be "even if the people of Israel are very many, just like the many grains of sand by the sea."

Verse 28 is literally "for the Lord will do his word on the earth, completing and cutting short." This verse is difficult, but all modern translations suggest that it refers to God's judgment rather than to his promise of salvation. In the NEB this quotation appears as "for the Lord's sentence on the land will be summary and final," and in the JB as "for without hesitation or delay the Lord will execute his sentence on the earth." Goodspeed translates as "for the Lord will execute his sentence rigorously and swiftly on the earth," and the NAB has "for quickly and decisively will the Lord execute sentence upon the earth." A satisfactory equivalent in some languages is "the Lord will soon judge firmly all the people of the world" or "the Lord will quickly, and once and for all, judge all the people on the earth."

9.29 It is as Isaiah had said before, "If the Lord Almighty had not left us some descendants, we would have become like Sodom, we would have been like Gomorrah."

It is important to construe properly the meaning of before. This is not a reference to Isaiah's speaking before Hosea did. It is Isaiah speaking in anticipation of the judgment.

The scripture reference in this verse comes from the Septuagint of Isaiah 1.9. Lord Almighty is translated "Lord of Hosts" in most translations. This phrase was used in the Old Testament frequently as a name for God, and originally meant "Lord of the armies," a name which described the Lord's strength in battle. A translation such as "Lord of Hosts" conveys nothing to the English reader, and the nearest equivalent appears to be "the Lord, the Almighty." It may be translated as "the Lord who is all powerful," "the Lord who has all strength," or "the Lord who is the strongest of all."

Some descendants in this particular context may be translated as "some persons to continue the lineage" or "some persons of our same tribe."

In some languages it may be useful to employ a classifier with Sodom and Gomorrah—for example, "we would become like the city of Sodom; we would become like the city of Gomorrah." In other languages it may be necessary for stylistic reasons to coalesce these into one—for example, "we would become like the cities of Sodom and Gomorrah." At this point a brief marginal note, a cross reference, or an identification of the significance of Sodom and Gomorrah in a glossary is important.

Israel and the Gospel

[30]What shall we say, then? This: that the Gentiles, who were not trying to put themselves right with God, were put right with him through faith; [31]while the chosen people, who were seeking a law that would put them right with God, did not find it. [32]And why not? Because what they did was not based on faith but on works. They stumbled over the "stumbling stone" [33]that the scripture speaks of:

"Look, I place in Zion a stone
that will make people stumble,
a rock that will make them fall.
But whoever believes in him will not be disappointed."

The section heading Israel and the Gospel may be semantically restructured as "The Good News Is Also for Israel" or "The Good News Also Applies to the People of Israel."

It is possible to take verses 30-33 either as a conclusion to the previous chapter or as an introduction to Chapter 10. Paul begins with a rhetorical question (parallel to 9.14) as a means of emphasizing God's mercy towards the Gentiles and God's judgment on the Jews. Verse 32 gives the basis for God's action, and this is strengthened by an appeal to scripture in verse 33. Thus it is possible to look upon this scripture quotation as the climax to all of the passages quoted in 9.24-29. Then 10.1, with its solemn form of address, my brothers (see 1.13; 7.1,4; 8.12), would be taken as introducing a new section in the letter. However, most commentators and the section headings in many modern translations (see Moffatt and NAB; see also the note in JB) take these verses as an introduction to the following section. That is, in 9.6-29 Paul affirms God's faithfulness in keeping his promise, though his decision may appear arbitrary, while beginning with this passage Paul speaks in much less arbitrary tones concerning God's decision and offers some hope for the final salvation of Israel.

9.30 What shall we say, then? This: that the Gentiles, who were not trying to put themselves right with God, were put right with him through faith;

The introductory question may be conveniently transformed into a statement—for example, "this is what we are saying," "this is what we mean," or "this is the significance of what we are saying."

In Greek this verse reads, "What shall we say? That the nations who were not seeking righteousness attained righteousness, but the righteousness of faith." Here again the TEV changes the noun "righteousness" to a verb phrase meaning "to be put right with God." And the phrase "the righteousness of faith" is translated as were put right with him through faith.

It is possible to understand the last part of this verse and all of verse 31 as a second question, that the Gentiles . . . did not find it?, but few modern translations accept this interpretation (see NAB). If this is taken as a question, it is obvious that the intended answer is "yes."

Because of the necessity in some languages of changing passive to active expressions, one may restructure the clauses of verse 30 as "the Gentiles were not trying to put themselves right with God, but God put them right with himself because they trusted him" or ". . . by means of their trusting him."

9.31 while the chosen people, who were seeking a law that would put them right with God, did not find it.

The chosen people is literally "Israel" (see the comments on 9.4). The genitive expression "law of righteousness" must be taken to mean a law that would put them right with God (Goodspeed "a law that should bring uprightness"; JB "a righteousness derived from Law"). It should be noted that Paul does not say that the Jews made righteousness their goal but rather that their goal was a law that would bring them righteousness.

The conjunction while should not be understood in a temporal sense, but in the sense of "in contrast with this" or "but on the other hand." Similarly, the contrast between seeking a law and not find it may be expressed as an adversative clause—for example, "on the other hand, the chosen people were looking for a law that would put them right with God, but they did not find it." In this context, it may be necessary to employ a plural, "laws," in order to designate a body of laws and not merely some particular regulation.

9.32 And why not? Because what they did was not based on faith but on works. They stumbled over the "stumbling stone"

The initial question and why not? is particularly important at this point. One may, however, need to introduce it by some such expression as "someone may ask, Why did they not find the law?"

The second sentence of this verse (literally "because not from faith, but as from works") has no verb phrase, with the result that one must be supplied. The TEV translates this sentence as because what they did was not based on faith but on works, while the JB translates, "because they relied on good works instead of trusting in faith." The Greek text includes a particle (hōs = "as") which is used by Paul to indicate that this was the opinion of the Jews by which they thought they could be right with God, and so does not represent his own thinking. This is the basis for the NEB "because their efforts were not based on faith, but (as they supposed) on deeds"; the RSV translates this particle by "as if it were" ("because they did not pursue it through faith, but as if it were based on works"). This sentence may also be rendered, "they did not find these laws because they depended on what they were doing and not on trusting God."

Most translations render "stone of stumbling" as stumbling stone (so KJV, RSV, JB). Goodspeed translates this as "that stone that makes people stumble" (see Moffatt "the stone that makes men stumble"), while the NEB renders as "the 'stone.'" As can be seen from the following verse, this phrase comes from the Old Testament.

9.33 that the scripture speaks of:

"Look, I place in Zion a stone
that will make people stumble,
a rock that will make them fall.
But whoever believes in him
will not be disappointed."

This verse actually begins "as it is written (in scripture)." However, many translations attempt to make the relation between the stone and the passage in scripture explicit: "...stone" that the scripture speaks of (TEV), "...'stone' mentioned in scripture" (NEB, JB). The scripture quotation in this verse is taken from the Septuagint of Isaiah 28.16, combined with words from Isaiah 8.14. Isaiah 28.16 is quoted again in 10.11. If the speaker of these words must be identified, then God is the one speaking. From the context it is clear that Paul understands Christ to be this stone, and his function is necessarily twofold: to be the cause of rejection and of faith.

The Greek particle translated "look" is primarily designed to call attention to what is being said, and it is not a direct command to look at something particular. Therefore in some languages the equivalent expression would be "listen carefully" or "pay attention."

In rendering the expression a stone that will make people stumble one should avoid the impression that the stone is an active agent in the sense of moving about in such a way as to make people stumble. In many languages the more appropriate expression would be "a stone against which people will stumble" or "a stone which will cause people to trip and stumble."

One should also avoid the impression that God is placing in Zion both a stone and a rock. The two first lines of the quotation are parallel and refer to the same object. This identity may be expressed in some languages as "that is to say, a rock on which they will trip."

Whoever believes in him may be translated as "whoever trusts in him" or "if anyone trusts in him."

In some languages will not be disappointed may be translated as "will never have reason to be disappointed" or "I will never fail him."

CHAPTER 10

10 My brothers, how I wish with all my heart that my own people might
be saved! How I pray to God for them! 2I can be a witness for them
that they are deeply devoted to God. But their devotion is not based on true
knowledge. 3They have not known the way in which God puts men right with
himself, and have tried to set up their own way; and so they did not submit
themselves to God's way of putting men right. 4For Christ has brought the Law
to an end, so that everyone who believes is put right with God.

This chapter cannot be severed from the previous chapter, especially not from the words of 9.30-33. Paul begins this chapter (v. 1) as he did the previous one, with a prayer for the salvation of his own people. He affirms once again that the Jewish nation as a whole has sought in the wrong way to establish a right relationship with God (vv. 3-4), and then affirms that God's salvation is for all who will come to him through Jesus Christ (vv. 5-21).

10.1 My brothers, how I wish with all my heart that my own people might be saved! How I pray to God for them!

Literally, this verse could be rendered as follows: "Brothers, indeed the wish of my heart and my prayer to God for them is for salvation." The TEV renders the nouns "wish" and "prayer" and the noun phrase "for salvation" as verbs: *I wish*...*I pray*...*might be saved*. Moreover, the pronoun "them" has been made explicit, as with other translations: *my own people* (KJV "Israel"; JB "the Jews"). Finally, the Greek particle *men* (rendered "indeed" in the literal translation) has the force of strengthening the impact of Paul's wish and prayer; in the TEV this force is carried through by the word *how* (*how I wish*...!).

The exclamations introduced by *how* may be transformed into strong affirmations—for example, "I wish very much" and "I pray very much."

One must not assume that intensity of wishing can always be expressed by a phrase such as *with all my heart*. In some languages the equivalent is simply "I do wish very, very much" or "I wish most strongly."

It may be essential in some instances to indicate clearly that *my own people* refers not to Paul's personal family but to his race. Therefore one may use "my own people the Jews" or "the Jews, who are my own people."

There may be special problems involved in the passive expression *might be saved*. One would not want to make this an active by making God merely the subject of *saved*, as "that God would save my own people the Jews." That would imply that in some way God had not been sufficiently active in his desire or intent to save the Jews. One can, however, employ a type of substitute passive in a phrase such as "experience salvation," "experience how God can save them," or "experience God's saving them."

10.2 I can be a witness for them that they are deeply devoted to God. But their devotion is not based on true knowledge.

Deeply devoted to God appears in many translations as "a zeal for God." This phrase is similar to the way in which Paul spoke of himself in Acts 22.3, dedicated to God. The clause they are deeply devoted to God may be rendered in some languages as "they want very much to serve God" or "they are very anxious to please God." The manner in which one translates this expression will, of course, influence the manner in which one refers to it in rendering their devotion in the next sentence—for example, "but the way in which they seek to serve God is not based on true knowledge."

In the phrase not based on true knowledge (KJV "not according to knowledge"), the Greek "knowledge" is a strengthened form of the word, and so the TEV renders it as true knowledge. In Colossians the TEV translates the same word as knowledge (1.9, 10), true understanding (2.2), and full knowledge (3.10). Not based on true knowledge appears in other translations as "not enlightened" (RSV), "not an intelligent" (Goodspeed), "misguided" (JB), and "ill-informed" (NEB). In some languages not based on true knowledge is equivalent to "they do not understand correctly," "their understanding of how to serve God is not right," or "they have not judged as they should have just how they should serve God."

10.3 They have not known the way in which God puts men right with himself, and have tried to set up their own way ; and so they did not submit themselves to God's way of putting men right.

The concepts expressed in this verse have been discussed earlier, and the verse requires only a few exegetical comments.

They have not known is actually a participle in Greek. It has the emphatic position in the sentence, and its force is to explain further what Paul meant by the last sentence of the previous verse. In translating known it is important not to suggest that the Jews had never heard about how God puts man right with himself. The focus here is upon "their not having understood the way."

The way in which God puts men right with himself is literally "the righteousness of God," but it is clear that this means "righteousness that comes from God" (RSV).

Have tried to set up their own way may be rendered as "have tried to establish their own system," "have tried to find a way whereby they could do this themselves," "have tried to find a means by which they could make themselves righteous before God," or "...cause God to find them righteous because of what they themselves had done."

They did not submit themselves to God's way may be translated as "they did not accept God's way" or, in some instances, "they did not say about God's way of putting men right, This is what it should be."

10.4 For Christ has brought the Law to an end, so that everyone who believes is put right with God.

The TEV rather radically restructures this verse, which is literally "for Christ is the end of the law for righteousness to everyone who believes." The phrase "end of the law" is taken by some to mean "the goal of the law," and by a few to mean "the total content of the law." Most scholars believe that "the end of the law" is more in keeping with the total context. Since the reference is to the Jewish Law, Paul means that the coming of Christ has made unnecessary the continuation of the Jewish Law, that is, Christ has brought the Law to an end. In a number of languages to bring something to an end is "to cause it to cease" or "to cause it to no longer have value." This particular clause may be rendered in some languages as "Christ has caused the Law no longer to have strength."

The last part of this verse ("for righteousness to everyone who believes") is taken to mean so that everyone who believes is put right with God (JB "and everyone who has faith may be justified").

The Greek conjunction rendered so that may express either result or purpose. Here the implication seems to be result, that is, "Christ has brought the Law to an end, and as a result God puts right with himself those who believe."

Salvation Is for All

[5]This is what Moses wrote about being put right with God by obeying the
Law: "Whoever does what the Law commands will live by it." [6]But this is what
is said about being put right with God through faith: "Do not say to yourself,
Who will go up into heaven?" (that is, to bring Christ down). [7]"Do not say
either, Who will go down into the world below?" (that is, to bring Christ up
from the dead). [8]What it says is this: "God's message is near you, on your lips
and in your heart"—that is, the message of faith that we preach. [9]If you declare
with your lips, "Jesus is Lord," and believe in your heart that God raised him
from the dead, you will be saved. [10]For we believe in our hearts and are put
right with God; we declare with our lips and are saved. [11]The scripture says,
"Whoever believes in him will not be disappointed." [12]This includes everyone,
because there is no difference between Jews and Gentiles; God is the same Lord
of all, and richly blesses all who call to him. [13]As the scripture says, "Everyone
who calls on the name of the Lord will be saved."

The section heading Salvation Is for All may be restructured as "Anyone Can Be Saved" or "There Is No One Whom God Cannot Save."

10.5 This is what Moses wrote about being put right with God by obeying the Law: "Whoever does what the Law commands will live by it."

Paul now speaks of the two ways of seeking salvation, the way of the Law and the way of faith, and illustrates these from Old Testament passages.

About being put right with God by obeying the Law is literally "about the righteousness which is from the Law." Here again "righteousness" is taken to mean the act of being put right with God, while the phrase "which is from the Law" is best understood in the sense of "which comes from obeying the Law." It is obvious that Law here refers specifically to the Jewish Law.

This verse has a textual problem, and one solution is reflected in the TEV (cf. Moffatt, NEB, JB, NAB), while another solution is reflected in the RSV (cf. Goodspeed). The question is whether the words rendered in the TEV as about being put right with God by obeying the Law are to be taken as a part of what

Moses wrote, or as an introduction to the words which Moses wrote. If the solution of the RSV is followed, then the translation into current English would read: "Moses wrote, Whoever does what the Law commands in order to be put right with God will live by it." Although the manuscript evidence is fairly well divided, the solution of the TEV is favored, because its manuscript support is early and diversified, and because it is easier to see why the scribes would tend to make changes in one direction rather than in the other.

The pronoun this in the introductory expression this is what Moses wrote about being put right with God by obeying the Law refers to what follows, and in many languages it must be placed immediately before the direct discourse, or else the introductory expression must be rather radically modified—for example, "Moses wrote about how God puts men right with himself because they obey the Law [or "by their obeying the Law"]. He had this to say..." or "When Moses wrote about how people are put right with God by obeying the Law, he said...."

The quotation in this verse comes from Leviticus 18.5, but the words what the Law commands are not explicit in this quotation. However, in light of the first part of this verse, it is important to make this information explicit in a translation (note JB "when Moses refers to being justified by the Law, he writes: those who keep the Law will draw life from it").

The direct quotation "Whoever does..." is a general statement and may apply to any and all persons. As such, it may also be considered as a conditional—for example, "If a man does what the Law commands, he will live by it." However, the reference to the Law in the phrase by it, as an expression of the means by which a person lives, may require considerable modification in languages in which such an expression of means becomes the agent of a verb of cause—for example, "If a man does what the Law commands, the Law will cause him to live." One must avoid the meaning of "live in conformity to the Law," which could be the meaning of the English expression live by it.

10.6-8 But this is what is said about being put right with God through faith: "Do not say to yourself, Who will go up into heaven?" (that is, to bring Christ down). (7) "Do not say either, Who will go down into the world below?" (that is, to bring Christ up from the dead). (8) What it says is this: "God's message is near you, on your lips and in your heart"---that is, the message of faith that we preach.

These verses are best taken together, since in them Paul uses a passage from the Septuagint of Deuteronomy 30.11-14. He does not quote the entire passage, and he makes some changes in the form of what he does use. Moreover, as one would expect, Paul changes the context of these verses and makes specific application of the words to Christ. These words originally applied to the Law. Moses was telling the people of Israel that the Law was not too difficult for them —they did not have to climb up to heaven to get it or cross the sea to find it— but rather it was to be found in their hearts and confessed with their mouths. It is difficult to know why Paul chose this particular passage from Deuteronomy, but his use of it is clear. He is emphasizing the fact that God's salvation is immediately available in Jesus Christ, and that salvation cannot be and need not be sought after by human efforts. Fortunately, even though the theological implications of Paul's words are very profound, the translation of what he says here is not difficult. Some Jews of Paul's day believed that if enough people in the nation obeyed completely the Law, then God would send his Savior to them. Paul argues that God in his grace has already sent Christ down.

But this is what is said about being put right with God through faith is literally "But the righteousness (which comes) from faith speaks as follows." The NEB renders "but the righteousness that comes by faith says." However, the idea of righteousness saying something is a rather difficult concept for the average reader to grasp, and what Paul actually means is that "here is a passage of Scripture that has something to say about righteousness that comes from faith." Because of the relatively awkward introduction to direct discourse contained in the words this is what is said about, it may be necessary to employ the more common formulation, "this is what the Scriptures say about."

Do not say to yourself (literally, "Do not say in your heart") must often be translated as "do not ask yourself," since what follows is a question.

In rendering the phrase to bring Christ down one must not suggest that this is a reference to "demoting Christ" or "removing Christ from his rightful position in heaven." An appropriate translation in some languages may be "(that is to say, to go up into heaven in order to ask Christ to come down to us)."

In verse 7 Paul continues the analogy, but he refers to the world below ("abyss" in most translations) in place of "the sea" which occurs in the Deuteronomy passage. It is easy to see how Paul would use this analogy; his reference is to the resurrection of Christ, as he makes clear. The phrase world below may be rendered as "world of the dead."

The introductory expression in verse 8, what it says is this, may need to be somewhat more explicit in some languages: "this is what the scripture says," "the scripture says the following," or "the scripture contains these words."

In verse 8 God's message...that is, the message of faith that we preach is literally "the word of faith which we preach." In such a context "word" has the extended meaning of "message," and so the TEV makes this explicit as a reference to God's message (so also Goodspeed). God's message is "what God has said" or "the message which God has spoken." Message of faith means "the message which calls for faith." This meaning may be rendered as "the message which says that you should trust God."

It may not be possible to translate literally on your lips (Greek, "in your mouth") and in your heart. The implication is "you have already spoken it, and it exists in your heart" or "you have already spoken the words, and you have them on your mind." On the other hand, one may interpret on your lips and in your heart as potentiality---for example, "you can acknowledge this message with your lips and accept it in your heart."

10.9 If you declare with your lips, "Jesus is Lord," and believe in your heart that God raised him from the dead, you will be saved.

This verse is apparently intended to give the content of the message of faith. For this reason the particle with which Paul introduces this verse (Greek hoti) must have the force of "that" rather than of "because" (RSV) or "for" (Goodspeed). The TEV, JB, NEB, and Moffatt have taken hoti to have the force of "that," but because of the requirements of English style they have not rendered this word by any particular word in English.

Most translations render the first verb in this sentence as "confess"; in the TEV it appears as declare and in Goodspeed as "acknowledge."

It should be pointed out that Jesus is Lord was one of the earliest of the Christian confessions. Related to it is the affirmation that God raised him from the dead, the real basis for the belief that Jesus is Lord.

As indicated in the discussion of translation problems of verse 8, it is impossible to say in some languages declare with your lips. In some cases another figurative expression for the speech organs may be employed—for example, "declare with your mouth" or "declare with your throat." In other cases it may be simpler to employ "to declare" or "to say." However, merely "to say" may be entirely too weak, since the Greek itself implies "a declaration before others." In some languages the closest equivalent may be "to say before all" or "to say openly." Similarly, believe in your heart may be rendered in some languages as "believe in your liver" or "believe in your abdomen." In still other languages the equivalent is "believe sincerely" or "believe strongly."

The passive expression you will be saved may be rendered in this context as active: "God will save you."

10.10 For we believe in our hearts and are put right with God; we declare with our lips and are saved.

The verbs in this verse are impersonal in form (literally "one believes... one declares"). However, it is more effective in English to render them with a personal force: we believe...we declare (see JB). The parallelism in this verse is similar to that discussed in 4.25; it is wrong to separate the two clauses and to look for a different meaning in each. Paul is here speaking of two sides of the same thing, not of two different things.

In the first part of verse 10 believe in our hearts and are put right with God are related as cause and effect, that is to say, our being put right with God results from our believing in our hearts. Similarly, salvation is the result of declaring this faith with our lips. However, it is usually better not to express the relation of result too explicitly but rather to leave the relation implicit, as is done in the TEV; the relation between the events is assumed to be a normal and natural sequence. To make the results too explicit would tend to make the reader assume that belief and declaration are two quite separate types of activities leading to two quite different results. One might, therefore, paraphrase the relation as "belief leads to being put right with God and declaration of faith leads to being saved."

10.11 The scripture says, "Whoever believes in him will not be disappointed."

The scripture reference in this verse is to Isaiah 28.16 (see 9.33). In this particular verse Paul adds the word "everyone" to the Old Testament passage (TEV whoever) in order to bring out the emphasis he intends.

10.12 This includes everyone, because there is no difference between Jews and Gentiles; God is the same Lord of all, and richly blesses all who call to him.

In the word order of the Greek this verse begins with because there is no difference between Jews and Gentiles, a statement which serves as a transition between the thought of verse 11 and the last part of verse 12. The JB makes this transition clear by placing a comma, rather than a full stop, at the end of verse 11: "when scripture says: those who believe in him will have no cause for shame, 12 it makes no distinction between Jew and Greek: all belong to the same Lord...." Both the TEV and NEB make the relation explicit by picking up the word everyone at the first of verse 12 (TEV this includes everyone; NEB "—everyone: there is no distinction between Jew and Greek").

In the Greek of this verse the phrase Jews and Gentiles is in the singular ("Jew and Greek"), but in English the plural is more natural. For the use of "Greek" as the equivalent of "Gentile," see the comments on 1.16.

To say there is no difference between Jews and Gentiles may cause some complications, since Jews and Gentiles did differ in certain respects. The emphasis in this context is, of course, that the manner in which Jews and Gentiles are saved is the same. Therefore, it may be appropriate in some languages to translate: "for it is the same for both Jews and Gentiles" or "since Jews and Gentiles are saved in the same way."

God is the same Lord of all is literally "for the same (is) Lord of all." Most scholars take this as a reference to Jesus Christ, who in the context is referred to as Lord (see, for example, NEB "the same Lord is Lord of all"). However, it is possible that the reference is to God the Father, and the TEV apparently interprets the phrase in this manner. Translators may prefer to use an expression employed in some languages: "there is just one Lord for all."

There is an interesting contrast between this verse and 3.22. In the earlier passage Paul indicated that Jews and Gentiles were alike, since they had all sinned; in the present passage he indicates that they are all alike, because God is the same Lord of all, and richly blesses all who call to him.

Richly blesses may be translated as "is extremely good to," "gives many good things to," or "causes great good to." In many languages the appropriate equivalent of call to is simply "pray to." Otherwise the implication may be that people are "screaming at God."

10.13 As the scripture says, "Everyone who calls on the name of the Lord will be saved."

In this verse Paul introduces another scripture quotation with the word "for" (Greek gar). In order to indicate that Paul is quoting scripture again, the TEV has introduced the normal formula, as the scripture says.

In a phrase such as the name of the Lord, the reference is to the Lord himself, since in Semitic thought the name represented what a person was. The relative conditional clause everyone who calls on the name of the Lord may be translated as a condition in some languages, "if anyone calls on the name of the Lord he will be saved."

The passive expression will be saved may be rendered actively as "the Lord will save him."

> [14]But how can they call to him, if they have not believed? And how can they believe, if they have not heard the message? And how can they hear, if the message is not proclaimed? [15]And how can the message be proclaimed, if the messengers are not sent out? As the scripture says, "How wonderful is the coming of those who bring good news!" [16]But they have not all accepted the Good News. Isaiah himself said, "Lord, who believed our message?" [17]So then, faith comes from hearing the message, and the message comes through preaching Christ.

10.14-15 But how can they call to him, if they have not believed? And how can they believe, if they have not heard the message? And how can they hear, if the message is not proclaimed? (15) And how can the message be proclaimed, if the messengers are not sent out? As the scripture says, "How wonderful is the coming of those who bring good news!"

In verse 13 Paul has affirmed that everyone who calls on the name of the Lord will be saved. For Paul the Lord is Jesus Christ, and it is clear to him that the Jewish nation as a whole has not called upon the name of the Lord. Throughout the remainder of this chapter Paul deals with the question as to why it is that the Jews have not called upon the Lord. He does this by constructing a logical chain with five links in order to see where the failure lies. These five links are expressed in reverse historical order by means of four questions (call to...believed...heard the message...proclaimed...sent out).

In the second of these two sentences the message translates an unusual pronoun construction, a genitive rather than the expected accusative. This genitive construction is the object of the verb heard, and the TEV understands the construction to mean "to hear someone proclaiming" (that is, "to hear the message proclaimed by someone"). Most translations take this to mean "to hear about someone," and so translate in a manner similar to what the NEB has: "and how could they have faith in one they had never heard of?"

The four closely linked questions in these verses may even be acceptable in languages which reject certain rhetorical questions. The reason for this is that questions introduced by "how" may seem more like exclamations. However, these same questions can be transformed into strong statements: "But they certainly cannot call on him if they have not believed! And they surely cannot believe if they have not heard the message!" etc.

In some languages it is impossible to use a verb "believe" without some type of goal—for example, "believed about him" or "believed the words about him." Similarly, it may be necessary to specify to some extent the content of the message—for example, "the message about him."

The passive expression, if the message is not proclaimed, may be rendered as active, "if someone does not proclaim the message to them." Similarly, the passive expression if the messengers are not sent out may be rendered as "if God does not send out the messengers" or "if the churches do not send out the messengers."

The scripture quotation in verse 15 comes from Isaiah 52.7 and is closer to the Hebrew than to the Septuagint. By rendering this as How wonderful is the coming of those who bring good news! (see Goodspeed and Moffatt), the TEV demetaphorizes the literal rendering of this verse (RSV "How beautiful are the feet of those who preach good news!"). In Jewish thought one often spoke of a certain part of the body as representative of the whole person, depending upon what part of the body was in focus at the time, and in the present context "feet" is simply a way of speaking about the coming of someone. It is difficult in some languages to speak of a coming as being wonderful, but one can slightly alter the semantic arrangement and still preserve the same essential meaning—for example, "It is so wonderful that those who bring good news are coming."

10.16 But they have not all accepted the Good News. Isaiah himself said, "Lord, who believed our message?"

Now Paul begins to show where the chain has broken. God has sent the messengers, the messengers have proclaimed the message, the Jews have heard the message, but they have not believed or called on the name of the Lord to be saved. Paul verifies this by a further appeal to scripture; this time the passage is from the Septuagint of Isaiah 53.1.

It is important that the reference of they be perfectly clear. It must be the same as they in verse 14. In order to avoid confusion with messengers and those who bring good news, one may translate as "but not everyone has accepted the Good News" or "not everyone has believed the Good News." In some languages the closest equivalent may be "but not everyone has received the Good News into his heart."

10.17 So then, faith comes from hearing the message, and the message comes through preaching Christ.

This verse reinforces the argument that Paul has just presented and at the same time serves as a transition to his further arguments. The verse is literally "so then faith from hearing, but hearing through the word of Christ." The Greek is clear without a verb, but for the English reader it is necessary to supply a verb (TEV comes), as practically all translations do. Moreover, the TEV makes the object of hearing explicit: the message (Goodspeed "what is told").

Since the phrase from hearing the message indicates the means which leads to the result of having faith, this relation may be expressed in some languages as "by hearing the message, people come to have faith." In other languages means may be expressed in the same way as cause—for example, "because they hear the message, they come to have faith." In certain languages, however, the relation may be left implicit and expressed best by two events in normal sequence—for example, "so they first hear the message and then they believe."

In the second clause "the hearing" is again taken in the sense of "the hearing of the message," but here it is translated the message.

Finally, the phrase "word of Christ" means either "preaching about Christ" or "the message about Christ." The TEV takes it in the sense of "preaching about Christ" and so translates through preaching Christ (Goodspeed "through the message about Christ"). The NEB employs essentially the same exegesis as the TEV, though the form of expression is quite different: "we conclude that faith is awakened by the message, and the message that awakens it comes through the word of Christ."

As in the first part of verse 17, the second part also expresses the relation of means and result, that is to say, preaching Christ is the means by which the message comes. This relation may be indicated in some languages as "by someone's preaching about Christ the people hear the message" or "someone preaches about Christ and the people hear the message."

18 But I ask: Is it true that they did not hear the message? Of course they did
—as the scripture says:

> "The sound of their voices went out to all the world;
> their words reached the ends of the earth."

19 Again I ask: Did the people of Israel not know? Moses himself is the first one
to answer:

> "I will make you jealous of a people who are not a real nation;
> I will make you angry with a nation of foolish people."

20 And Isaiah is bolder when he says,

> "I was found by those who were not looking for me,
> I appeared to those who were not asking for me."

21 But concerning Israel he says, "I held out my hands the whole day long to
a disobedient and rebellious people."

10.18 But I ask: Is it true that they did not hear the message? Of course they did—as the scripture says:

> "The sound of their voices went out to all the world;
> their words reached the ends of the earth."

Paul now begins to direct himself specifically to those Jews who have rejected the Christian message. Once again the TEV supplies the understood object of the verb hear, namely, the message (Goodspeed and NEB "it," with "message" as the antecedent).

Of course they did is a strong emphatic particle in Greek; in 9.20 it appears as but. The question and emphatic response may be transformed into a strong statement: "but it is certainly true that they did indeed hear the message" or "but most certainly they did hear the message."

Since Paul introduces another scripture quotation here, the TEV makes the identification clear with the words as the scripture says. Paul quotes directly from the Septuagint of Psalm 19.4, and he uses this passage to prove that the Christian message has gone to all the earth.

There is a problem in the reference of their in the quotation cited from Psalm 19.4. In the manner in which Paul employs this quotation one may justify employing a translation such as "the sound of the voices of the messengers went out to all the people in the world."

If one translates literally the sound of their voices it might imply "meaningless sound." Something which might have meaning would be "the words of their voices," "the words which they spoke aloud," or "the words which they spoke with their mouths."

10.19 Again I ask: Did the people of Israel not know? Moses himself is the first one to answer:

"I will make you jealous of a people who are not
a real nation;
I will make you angry with a nation of foolish people."

In Greek the expected answer to Paul's question, Did the people of Israel not know?, is "Yes, they did know." Paul is saying that Israel not only heard the message (v. 18) but that they were capable of understanding it. However, as he points out from Deuteronomy 32.21, the people of Israel will be put to shame because they failed to believe, though the Gentiles did believe. In the passage in Deuteronomy, God, not Moses, is the speaker. The same thing is true concerning the passage quoted from Isaiah in the two following verses.

The introductory rhetorical question may be changed into a statement—for example, "The people of Israel certainly did know."

Jealous of a people may be expressed in some languages as "jealous because of a people." Jealousy is often expressed in rather idiomatic terms—for example, "to burn in your hearts," "not to want to look at," or "to see with dark eyes."

Since in the quotation of verse 19 Moses is represented as speaking on behalf of God (I certainly refers to God), it may be necessary in some languages to introduce the direct quotation in such a way that this relation is clear—for example, "Moses himself, speaking for God, is the first one to answer."

10.20-21 And Isaiah is bolder when he says,

"I was found by those who were not looking for me,
I appeared to those who were not asking for me."

(21) But concerning Israel he says, "I held out my hands the whole day long to a disobedient and rebellious people."

These verses come from Isaiah 65.1-2. The intent of verse 20 is to show how the Gentiles came to God, while the purpose of verse 21 is to remind the people of Israel of how they rejected God despite his pleas to them.

As in the case of verse 19, it may be essential to introduce Isaiah as speaking "on behalf of God." Only in this way can the reader properly understand who I is.

The verb found must be understood in the sense of "discovered," with the meaning of "discovered without looking for."

In the opening statement of verse 21, it is possible to introduce God as the speaker—for example, "But he tells us that God says concerning Israel."

If, as is often the case, adjectives such as disobedient and rebellious must be translated as verbs (for example, "to disobey" and "to rebel against"), it may be necessary to have some type of goal—for example, "All day long I held out my hands to a people who disobey me and who rebel against me."

In some languages the expression I held out my hands may have little or no meaning. In fact, it might mean "I was begging from them," obviously a wrong meaning. An appropriate equivalent in some languages is "I offered peace to," "I sought to be reconciled with," or "I sought to reconcile people to me."

CHAPTER 11

God's Mercy on Israel

11 I ask, then: Did God reject his own people? Certainly not! I myself am
an Israelite, a descendant of Abraham, a member of the tribe of
Benjamin. [2]God has not rejected his people, whom he chose from the beginning. You know what the scripture says in the passage where Elijah pleads with
God against Israel: [3]"Lord, they have killed your prophets and torn down your
altars; I am the only one left, and they are trying to kill me." [4]What answer
did God give him? "I have kept for myself seven thousand men who have not
worshiped the false god Baal." [5]It is the same way now at this time: there is
a small number of those whom God has chosen, because of his mercy. [6]His
choice is based on his mercy, not on what they have done. For if God's choice
were based on what men do, then his mercy would not be true mercy.

The section heading God's Mercy on Israel may be changed from a noun to a verb expression: "God Shows Mercy to Israel," "God Has Shown Mercy to Israel," or "...to the People of Israel."

In 9.6-29 Paul shows that God was perfectly free to reject Israel, while in 9.30--10.21 he is quick to remind his readers that Israel deserved to be rejected because they neglected the salvation that God offered them. Now in chapter 11 Paul comes once again to his original question: Did God reject his own people? He approaches this question in several different ways. First, he points out that God did not reject all of his people, and the failure of the Jews to respond to God's offer of salvation has been the means by which salvation has come to the Gentiles (vv. 1-12). Next, he reminds the Gentiles that their salvation is a result of Israel's rejection, and so they themselves should be careful not to turn from God in the same way as the Jews did (vv. 13-24). Finally, he affirms that God's rejection of his people is not final, and that God works according to a purpose that is too profound for any man to understand (vv. 25-36).

11.1 I ask, then: Did God reject his own people? Certainly not! I myself am an Israelite, a descendant of Abraham, a member of the tribe of Benjamin.

Paul strongly denies that God has rejected his people: Certainly not! (see 3.4,6,31; 6.2,15; 7.7; 9.14; and 11.11). This initial combination of question and response may be stated as a strong affirmation: "I declare then, God has certainly not rejected his people."

The next sentence, I myself ... Benjamin, has been taken in two different ways: (1) As a proof that God has not rejected his people (that is, Paul, himself a Jew, has not been rejected); or (2) as an expression of Paul's own feelings of horror at such an idea (that is, as a Jew, Paul could never imagine that God would reject his people). Most translations appear to support the former of these two interpretations, but the NEB appears to support the latter ("I ask then, has God rejected his people? I cannot believe it!").

An Israelite may be rendered as "a man from the nation of Israel" or "a person of the people of Israel." A descendant of Abraham may be translated as "a member of the family line of Abraham," "a person in the lineage of Abraham," or "Abraham was my ancestor."

11.2-3 God has not rejected his people, whom he chose from the beginning. You know what the scripture says in the passage where Elijah pleads with God against Israel: (3) "Lord, they have killed your prophets and torn down your altars; I am the only one left, and they are trying to kill me."

In these verses Paul makes a formal denial of the question raised in the previous verse: God has not rejected his people, a statement based on Psalm 94.14.

Whom he chose from the beginning (NEB "which he acknowledged of old as his own"; JB "the people he chose specially long ago"; Goodspeed "which he had marked out from the first") translates the same verb rendered had already chosen in 8.29. As a comparison of the TEV and Goodspeed with the NEB and JB clearly shows, the question is whether this choice took place before history began or whether it was a choice made in the course of history even though long ago. If one adopts the interpretation of a choice before history, the closest equivalent may be "whom he chose before he created the world." The alternative interpretation may lead to a translation such as "whom he chose long, long ago."

The passage quoted in verse 3 comes from 1 Kings 19.10, 14. The last part of this quotation literally reads "they are seeking my soul," which is merely a Semitic way of saying they are trying to kill me.

Passage may be rendered in some languages as "what the scripture says (in that part where Elijah pleads with God)" or "...(in the story where Elijah pleads with God)."

An equivalent of pleads may be "speaks strongly" or "speaks... and urges."

Torn down may be translated as "destroyed," "caused to fall down," or even "smashed."

I am the only one left may be rendered as "I am the only prophet who remains."

11.4 What answer did God give him? "I have kept for myself seven thousand men who have not worshiped the false god Baal."

What answer did God give him? (RSV, Goodspeed "but what is God's reply"; NEB "but what does the divine voice say") is an unusual expression, but its meaning is clear: it refers to a message (in this case specifically an answer) that God has given. This question cannot be preserved in a number of languages, since the answer immediately follows as a direct quotation and without an introductory statement. A change of the question to a statement may, therefore, serve a double purpose, not only in eliminating what may be an awkward rhetorical expression, but also in introducing the immediately following direct discourse—for example, "and this is the answer God gave him:...."

Most translations render the last part of this verse literally (see, for example, RSV "men who have not bowed the knee to Baal"). The TEV does two things to help the reader understand the expression: (1) the phrase "bowed the knee" is shown to mean worshiped, and (2) Baal is qualified as a false god. It is often necessary to add classifiers before certain proper nouns, especially in translating the Old Testament, because in the original cultural context these words were easily understood, whereas in the cultural situation into which they are being translated the meaning may not be clear.

In some languages it is difficult to speak of a false god or a "false prophet." The latter may be identified by a phrase such as "a person who pretends to be a prophet of God but who is not." One cannot speak of the false god Baal as "Baal who pretends to be a god but is not," but one can say "Baal, whom people thought was a god, but who was not" or "Baal whom people called a god but who was not a god." One may also employ in some instances a phrase such as "worshiped the idol Baal." In the context of the Bible the term "idol" identifies a false god.

11.5 It is the same way now at this time: there is a small number of those whom God has chosen, because of his mercy.

In this and the following verse Paul applies the scripture passages to his present situation. Small number is translated by most as "remnant" (a synonym to the words used in 9.27: only a few).

God has chosen, because of his mercy (see NEB "selected by the grace of God"; Goodspeed "selected by God's mercy") is literally "according to the choice of grace." The choice is God's choice and the grace is God's grace. In many contexts the nearest equivalent in English of the biblical concept of "grace" is mercy. The equivalent of because of his mercy may be "because he is so good to people" or "because he shows mercy so much."

11.6 His choice is based on his mercy, not on what they have done. For if God's choice were based on what men do, then his mercy would not be true mercy.

The purpose of this verse is to indicate that God's mercy is based on his own free choice and not on what men do. The verse is literally: "But if by grace, no longer from works, since the grace would no longer be grace." In English the introductory words "but if" may convey the possibility of doubt. However, this is a form that in Greek introduces a condition true to fact, and so the verse need not be introduced by "if" (see TEV, Moffatt, JB).

The subject of the verse is not explicitly expressed, though it is clear from the context that it is his (God's) choice, which most translations indicate by including a pronoun "it" (NEB "selected by the grace of God.... But if by grace, then it..."). It is obvious that the phrase "no longer on works" can be transformed to read not on what they have done. The second sentence in the TEV again picks up the idea expressed in the first half of the verse ("but if by grace"), and so translates: For if God's choice were based on what men do....

The clause his choice is based on his mercy may be rendered as "because he is so merciful, he selects as he does" or "God is so very merciful; therefore he selects as he does." In this way one can show clearly the relation between the fact of God's mercy as the basis for God's selecting persons as he does. The connection with the latter part of the first sentence of verse 6 may then be explained as "he does not select people because of what they have done."

In the second sentence of this verse, the word mercy is the same word used in the previous sentence.

There is some question regarding the force of the negative used in this sentence. The normal meaning is "no longer" (RSV "otherwise grace would no longer be grace"; Moffatt, NEB "grace would cease to be grace"). If the negative is taken in this way, then the force of Paul's argument would be as follows. Paul would be saying that God originally made his choice according to grace, but if he now changed the way that he worked and made his choice on the basis of what men do, then his choice would no longer continue to be made on the basis of grace. On the other hand, it is possible to take the negative to mean simply "not": then his mercy would not be true mercy (Goodspeed "his mercy would not be mercy at all"; JB "grace would not be grace at all"; NAB "grace would not be grace"). If this interpretation is followed, it means that Paul is not actually thinking in temporal terms, as we consider them; rather he is making the absolute statement that if God at any time had based his choice on what men do, then his mercy would not be true mercy.

In order to show clearly that what men do does not constitute the basis for God's choice, one may translate as follows: "For if God were to choose people because they had done certain things, then he wouldn't really be showing mercy" or "...the way in which he would be showing mercy would not be genuine."

7 What then? The people of Israel did not find what they were looking for. It was the small group that God chose who found it; the rest grew deaf to God's call. 8 As the scripture says, "God made them dull of heart and mind; to this very day they cannot see with their eyes or hear with their ears." 9 And David says,

"May they be caught and trapped at their feasts;
may they fall, may they be punished!
10 May their eyes be closed so that they cannot see;
and make them bend under their troubles at all times."

11.7 What then? The people of Israel did not find what they were looking for. It was the small group that God chose who found it; the rest grew deaf to God's call.

This verse sums up the contents of Paul's discussion in verses 2-6. What they were looking for is emphatic in the Greek sentence structure, though Paul does not explain what he means by this phrase. Nevertheless, in light of the context, it is clear that the Jews were looking for a way to be put in a right relation with God.

In some languages the introductory question What then? may be related to what follows as "obviously the people of Israel did not find what they were looking for."

It was the small group that God chose who found it is literally "the chosen found it" (RSV "the elect obtained it"). "The chosen" has reference to the "people that God chose," while the context (see v. 5) indicates that this was only a small number (v. 5) or a small group (v. 7), and so the TEV makes the information clear.

In indicating the contrast between the first and second sentences of verse 7, one may place a contrastive particle at the beginning of the second sentence —for example, "but a small group whom God chose found it."

Grew deaf is literally "were hardened" (RSV; NEB "were made blind"; Goodspeed "became callous"; NAB "became blind"). This is an aorist tense in Greek, and as can be seen from the various translations, its force is generally felt to be inceptive; that is, it places the emphasis upon the beginning of the action.

Not all authorities are agreed in regard to the significance of the passive in this passage. Normally in such a construction it would be assumed that God is the agent ("God hardened them"), and this observation is supported by what is said in verses 8-10. On the other hand, in light of what is said in verse 11, some hesitate to go this far. The TEV gives this passive a middle force, and makes clear what it was that they grew deaf to, that is, to God's call (the JB uses the passive and supplies an object: "the rest were not allowed to see the truth"). It is best to take this verb form as a genuine passive and to assume that the act of hardening is God's judgment upon these people who have refused him. That is what Paul seems to be saying in the verses following, but he evidently looks upon this action as one aspect of God's mercy. The passive relation in the final clause of verse 7 may be expressed as "God caused the rest of the people to become deaf to his call" or "...to be unable to hear his call."

11.8 As the scripture says, "God made them dull of heart and mind; to this very day they cannot see with their eyes or hear with their ears."

Verses 8-10 are intended to give scriptural support to what Paul has said in the last part of verse 7. The passage to which he has reference in verse 8 seems to be Deuteronomy 29.4, but it has been somewhat modified on the basis of Isaiah 29.10. Paul's genitive expression (literally "a spirit of numbness") means "a spirit which causes people to be numb." Moreover, "to give a spirit of numbness" means "to make numb." Since the numbness referred to is of a spiritual nature, the TEV renders the entire clause as God made them dull of heart and mind (Goodspeed "God has thrown them into a state of spiritual insensibility"). Dull of heart and mind may be rendered as "not able to feel or think," "not able to sense or understand," or simply "not able to comprehend."

To this very day is an expression found quite often in Deuteronomy; it is apparently intended to be emphatic in the present verse, and for that reason the TEV places it at the beginning of the clause.

Expressions such as see with their eyes or hear with their ears seem utterly redundant and repetitious in many languages. What else could one employ for seeing except the eyes or for hearing except the ears? In some languages one can only translate "and up to this very day they cannot see or hear." However, the statement must be taken in a somewhat figurative sense, and so one may want to use terms which imply mental activity—for example, "they cannot perceive or comprehend."

11.9-10 And David says,

"May they be caught and trapped at their feasts;
  may they fall, may they be punished!
May their eyes be closed so that they cannot see;
  and make them bend under their troubles at all times."

The scripture quotation in these verses is basically from the Septuagint of Psalm 69.22-23, with allusions to Psalm 35.8. In Greek these verses appear as a third person imperative, a form which is difficult to translate into English. The traditional translation is "let . . . ," but the modern English equivalent is more nearly "may . . . ." May they be caught and trapped at their feasts is literally "may their feast [singular] become a snare and a trap," but in general the plural, feasts, is preferable.

It is impossible in many languages to employ a third person imperative representing a request or supplication. In such languages it is necessary to be explicit about the fact of supplication, and frequently one must indicate precisely who is supplicated and who is to act accordingly. Hence, it may be necessary to change the form, though not the content or meaning, of these supplications by rendering them as "I pray to God that he may catch and trap them at their feasts." For all of the passive expressions which follow, God may be made the subject: "that God may punish them" or "may God cause their eyes to be closed." It is God also who is the agent of the causative expression, "that God may make them bend."

On the basis of a literal translation of the first line in the quotation, it is impossible to determine whether the snare and trap are something they are going to be caught in themselves or something in which they hope to catch others. That the former is the case is made clear by the last two words in the second line of the Greek text, "for them." The word "snare" is difficult for English readers, and if this verse is to be translated literally the more general term "trap" should probably occur before the less well-known word "snare."

In order to make the meaning of the first line of the quotation clear to the reader, the TEV does several things. First, it provides in the first line the information that these people are to be the ones who are to be caught and trapped. Second, in order to avoid the difficulty of the simile ("become a snare and a trap"), it transforms these nouns into verbs. Finally, it uses a more generic term, caught, in the transfer from the noun "snare" to the verb "be snared."

Similar transformations are made in the second line of the quotation. In Greek the second line is a continuation of the first, and the meaning is "may their feasts become a trap." The word "trap" (some translations "stumbling-block") technically refers to the stick over which one trips in order to spring a trap, but it is here used simply as a synonym for the two words in the previous line. In order to show the connection between this line and the previous line, the TEV repeats the verb may they and transforms the word "trap" into a verb, fall.

May their eyes be closed so that they cannot see is literally "may their eyes be darkened so that they cannot see," which the NEB renders as "may their eyes become so dim that they lose their sight" and the JB as "may their eyes be struck incurably blind." The TEV interprets what is literally "bend their backs for ever" (so RSV) to mean make them bend under their troubles at all times (see Goodspeed "make their backs bend forever under their burden").

In some languages it is not possible to say make them bend under their troubles, since bend under is not applicable to such experiences as troubles. In some languages one may say that "troubles cause people to bend down," but it is more likely that a satisfactory equivalent will be found in some such expression as "cause them to suffer because of their troubles."

> [11]I ask, then: When the Jews stumbled, did they fall to their ruin? By no means! Because they sinned, salvation has come to the Gentiles, to make the Jews jealous of them. [12]The sin of the Jews brought rich blessings to the world, and their spiritual poverty brought rich blessings to the Gentiles. How much greater the blessings will be, then, when the complete number of Jews is included!

Paul began Chapter 11 by raising the question Did God reject his own people? In answer to this question he pointed out that God had never completely rejected his people but had always shown mercy towards those few who responded to him. In these two verses Paul takes up essentially the same question, but he now approaches it from a different angle.

11.11 I ask, then: When the Jews stumbled, did they fall to their ruin? By no means! Because they sinned, salvation has come to the Gentiles, to make the Jews jealous of them.

I ask, then is the same formula with which Paul introduced verse 1.

When the Jews stumbled, did they fall to their ruin? is literally "did they stumble in order to fall?" The TEV makes the pronominal subject of this sentence explicit, the Jews (so also JB). As the commentators point out, the verb "to fall" is a biblical expression for final destruction (NEB "complete downfall"; NAB "forever fallen"; JB "fallen for ever"; Goodspeed "absolute ruin").

By no means! is the same answer Paul gave to his question in verse 1 (Certainly not!).

As in so many instances, an initial question and response may be turned into a strong affirmation—for example, "I declare therefore that though the Jews stumbled, they did not fall completely" or even "...fall with no chance to get up." In order to indicate something of the absoluteness of the fall to which Paul refers, one may employ a number of different types of expressions—for example, "fall and not recover," "fall and stay always fallen," or "fall and never be able to rise again."

The last part of this verse literally reads "but by their fall salvation to the

Gentiles, in order to make them jealous." The fall referred to is the rejection of the Christian message, and the TEV transforms the noun phrase, "by their fall," into a verb phrase, because they sinned. Along with most other translations, the TEV also supplies the verb has come.

It is necessary to make clear the pronominal reference at the end of this verse, to make the Jews jealous of them (see RSV "so as to make Israel jealous" and NEB "to stir Israel to emulation"), by adding a reference to those of whom they were made jealous: of them, that is, "of the Gentiles." Paul, then, is saying that God had a purpose in letting Israel reject his message. As a result of their rejection of the Christian message, salvation has come to the Gentiles; and from this fact another result will follow: the people of Israel will be stirred up to jealousy, so that they too will be saved.

The rather complex relationships between the events in the latter half of verse 11 may be rendered as "because the Jews sinned, the Gentiles have come to experience salvation; this happened in order to make the Jews jealous of the Gentiles." It may, however, also be possible to interpret the final phrase of verse 11, to make the Jews jealous of them, as representing result rather than simply purpose—for example, "Gentiles are now experiencing what it means to be saved, and as a result the Jews are jealous of them."

11.12 The sin of the Jews brought rich blessings to the world, and their spiritual poverty brought rich blessings to the Gentiles. How much greater the blessings will be, then, when the complete number of Jews is included!

Following the demands of English discourse structure, the TEV once again makes a pronominal reference explicit (of the Jews is literally "of them"). Moreover, as with the previous sentence, so here also a verb must be supplied from the context (TEV brought; RSV "means"; Goodspeed takes the noun "riches" and transforms it into a verb "has so enriched").

In a number of languages one cannot speak of a noun such as sin "bringing rich blessings." However, sin can be expressed as a cause—for example, "because the Jews sinned, rich blessings have come to the world" or "because the Jews sinned, other people in the world have experienced so many good things."

The Greek word rendered spiritual poverty in the TEV is difficult to translate literally. Elsewhere in the New Testament it occurs only in 1 Corinthians 6.7 with the meaning of "failure" or "defeat." The RSV renders the word by "failure" and the NEB by "falling-off." Goodspeed chooses the word "false step" and Moffatt "defection"; the JB translates by two words "fall and defection." Most commentators see in this word the meaning of "defeat," while others point out that the basic idea in this context is "smaller" or "less." If this last viewpoint is taken, the word may refer either to the small number of Jews who are saved or, as the TEV interprets it, to their spiritual poverty.

As in the first clause of verse 12, there is also a relation of cause and effect between spiritual poverty and the fact of "bringing rich blessings." One may translate, therefore, as "because the Jews were spiritually poor, the Gentiles enjoyed rich blessings" or "because the Jews failed, rich blessings came to the Gentiles."

The KJV represents a rather literal rendering of the last part of this verse: "how much more their fulness?" Paul is arguing from the lesser to the greater, and so the phrase "how much more" must be taken as a reference to rich blessings in the previous line. This then is the logic for the TEV rendering: How much greater the blessings will be.

The meaning of the word "fulness" is also disputed. Some take this as a reference to a time when the Jews will completely do the will of God (see 13.10). However, most commentators and modern translators understand it in the sense of the complete number of Jews who will finally be included in God's salvation (Moffatt "what will it mean when they all come in"; Goodspeed "how much more good the addition of their full number will do"; NAB "how much more their full number").

The final exclamation in verse 12 may be rendered as a strong affirmation in the form "the blessings will even be much greater when all the Jews are included" or "...when the number of those who experience salvation includes all the Jews."

The Salvation of the Gentiles

[13]I am speaking now to you Gentiles: as long as I am an apostle to the Gentiles I will take pride in my work. [14]Perhaps I can make the people of my own race jealous, and so be able to save some of them. [15]For when they were rejected, the world was made friends with God. What will it be, then, when they are accepted? It will be life for the dead!

The section heading The Salvation of the Gentiles may be rendered as passive, "The Gentiles Are Saved," or as active, "God Saved the Gentiles," "The Meaning of God's Saving the Gentiles," or "The Result of God's Saving the Gentiles."

In the next section of this chapter (vv. 13-24) Paul addresses himself directly to the Gentile part of the Roman church. He warns the Gentiles against spiritual pride, as though it were due to their own merit that they have been given God's salvation. He reminds them that they must continue in their faith if they expect to enjoy God's salvation, and how easy it would be for God to include the Jews if they chose to believe.

11.13 I am speaking now to you Gentiles: as long as I am an apostle to the Gentiles I will take pride in my work.

The introductory statement I am speaking now to you Gentiles should indicate clearly that it is what Paul is going to say which is directed to the Gentiles. One may, therefore, need to translate as "in what I am going to say now, this is for you Gentiles" or "my following words are directed to you Gentiles."

Beginning with the words as long as and continuing down through the end of verse 14 is one sentence in Greek. The precise meaning of Paul's words "I glorify my ministry" is difficult to determine. Some commentators take the word "glorify" in the sense of "to give thanks for," but most translators take the word to mean either take pride in (JB "I am proud of being sent"; NEB "I am a missionary to the Gentiles, and as such I give all honour to that ministry") or "make the most of" (Goodspeed; Moffatt "lay great stress on").

The introductory conjunctive phrase as long as should probably not be interpreted in a merely temporal sense, implying that for the time being Paul was an apostle for the Gentiles and he might change his ministry shortly. A more appropriate equivalent in some languages is "inasmuch as" or "since."

In view of the different ways in which the term "glorify" may be interpreted, there are a variety of ways in which the final clause of verse 13 may be translated. What is important, however, is to make certain that a translation of my work will focus upon Paul's "task" rather than upon "what he has accomplished." Paul's pride, therefore, is not in "what he has already done" so much as in "his ministry." Therefore one may translate as "I will take pride in my task" or "I will take pride in the work which I have to do." Following a different interpretation of "glorify," one may have some such translation as "I give thanks to God for the work which he has given me to do." An interpretation such as "make the most of" may be most satisfactorily translated in some languages as "I consider my work very important."

11.14 Perhaps I can make the people of my own race jealous, and so be able to save some of them.

As already pointed out, this verse is a continuation of the Greek sentence begun in verse 13. Perhaps relates verse 14 with the last of verse 13: Perhaps (that is, by taking pride in my work) I can make the people of my own race jealous....

Make the people of my own race jealous is literally "make jealous my flesh," but there is no doubt about what Paul means by the phrase "my flesh"; all scholars indicate that this is a reference to his fellow Jews. Although his primary mission is to be an apostle to the Gentiles, Paul looks upon this calling as a means of reaching his fellow Jews also.

Since a term for save may imply primarily the kind of salvation which only God can accomplish, it may be misleading in the last clause of verse 14 to suggest that Paul himself is able to save some of them. Under such circumstances it may be necessary to say "so that because of me God will save some of them" or "because of what I have done God will save some of them."

11.15 For when they were rejected, the world was made friends with God. What will it be, then, when they are accepted? It will be life for the dead!

Once again Paul argues from the lesser to the greater (see v. 12).

When they were rejected is literally a noun phrase, "their rejection." If it is necessary to indicate who rejected them, then the meaning is "when God rejected them."

11.16

The world was made friends with God is also the translation of a noun phrase "the reconciliation of the world." The Greek phrase "reconciliation of the world" means simply "the world was reconciled (to God)." "Reconciliation" has essentially the same force as the word translated "to be put in a right relation with God"; but it comes from a different area of life and has a somewhat different coloring, which the TEV tries to bring out. Whereas "to be put right with God" comes from the language of the court, "to be made friends with God" comes from the language of everyday life. It is the picture of two persons who were once enemies but have now been brought together and made friends. It is possible that the reconciliation spoken of refers specifically to the uniting of Jews and Gentiles as God's people, but in the context this is not so likely as the other interpretation.

If the clause the world was made friends with God must be transformed into an active expression, then God is the agent, and the world may become "the other peoples in the world"—for example, "God made the other peoples in the world friends with himself" or "God caused the other peoples of the world to be his friends."

In the same way that God must be understood as the agent involved in the verb were rejected, so he is the understood agent of the verb are accepted.

When Paul says it will be life for the dead (literally "life from the dead"), a number of commentators understand him to be saying that the conversion of the Jews will be an eschatological event which will result in the final resurrection. However, it seems that Paul is merely using these words as his way of expressing the greatest blessing imaginable. That is, he is saying that the conversion of the Jews will be such a wonderful event that it can be compared to giving life to the dead.

As in so many instances, the question and answer in verse 15 may need to be changed into a direct statement. But such a statement needs to be emphatic if it is to reflect satisfactorily the stylistic device of question-answer employed in Greek. One may render this expression as "when they are accepted, however, it will most certainly be just like the dead coming back to life."

> [16]If the first piece of bread is given to God, then the whole loaf is his also; and if the roots of a tree are offered to God, the branches are his also. [17]Some of the branches of the cultivated olive tree have been broken off, and the branch of a wild olive tree has been joined to it. You Gentiles are like that wild olive tree, and now you share the strength and rich life of the Jews. [18]So then, you must not despise those who were broken off like branches. How can you be proud? You are just a branch; you don't support the root—the root supports you.

11.16 If the first piece of bread is given to God, then the whole loaf is his also; and if the roots of a tree are offered to God, the branches are his also.

Paul now uses two illustrations to explain the way in which the Gentiles have been brought into the kingdom of God. A number of translations (RSV, NEB,

Goodspeed) connect verse 16 with the previous paragraph, but others (TEV, JB) introduce a new paragraph here. It is certainly legitimate to introduce a new paragraph, since the sentence introduces a new and important idea.

First piece of bread (literally "first portion") translates a technical term used in Jewish religious vocabulary. It refers to the first part of the bread dough that was to be presented as a gift to God, so that the rest could be employed for common use (see Numbers 15.19, 20). So then, the word "holy" (most translations) has the specific meaning of given to God ("holy" appears as offered to God in the next part of the verse).

In view of the necessity in some languages of changing passive to active, one may restructure the first clause of verse 16 as "if anyone gives the first piece of bread to God." Where there is an appropriate term for dough, one may employ it. A reference to the whole loaf may be merely "all of the bread" or "all of the dough." The first two clauses of verse 16 may be modified in certain other ways—for example, "by giving to God the first piece of bread, one really dedicates to him all of the bread" or "...the whole loaf of bread."

The last part of the verse, though using a different metaphor, has the same meaning. It is quite likely, as many commentators point out, that the first piece of bread and the roots of a tree are references to the Jewish ancestors with whom God made his original covenants. Paul is reminding the Gentiles that ultimately they owe their salvation to the Jewish people. Similar to what was suggested in the first half of this verse, the latter half may be translated as "if anyone dedicates to God the roots of a tree, then the branches also belong to him."

11.17 Some of the branches of the cultivated olive tree have been broken off, and the branch of a wild olive tree has been joined to it. You Gentiles are like that wild olive tree, and now you share the strength and rich life of the Jews.

Beginning with this verse 17, the tree metaphor introduced in verse 16 is developed into an allegory which continues through verse 24.

Verse 17 introduces an "if" clause which is continued into the first part of verse 18 in Greek. Since the "if" clause introduces a condition which is true to fact, the TEV changes it to a statement. Moreover, the metaphorical references are made clear for the reader. The wild olive tree (translated literally from the Greek) is identified as the Gentiles---you Gentiles because Paul is speaking directly to Gentile Christians (v. 13)---and "the rich root of the cultivated olive tree" is identified as the rich life of the Jews.

The cultivated olive tree may be translated as "the olive tree that people take good care of." But in reality this refers to a grafted olive tree, that is to say, a tree formed from the roots of a wild olive tree on which have been grafted the shoots of a good olive tree. In a number of languages there are precise ways of talking about such a cultivated tree. On the other hand, wild olive tree may simply be translated as "an olive tree that grew up without being planted," "an olive tree that grew up outside the garden," or, more technically in some languages, "an ungrafted olive tree."

Where the process of grafting is well known there is no difficulty in obtaining a satisfactory equivalent of the phrase joined to it. Where this is not the case, it may be necessary to use some kind of descriptive equivalent—for example, "cause to grow as a part of the cultivated olive tree" or "cause to grow just as though it were a part of the cultivated olive tree." Because of the utter strangeness of such an activity, it may even be advisable in some languages to add some explanatory marginal note which will indicate more precisely what is involved.

It is not always easy to speak of "sharing" the strength and rich life of the Jews. In many cases a more general statement seems to be a more satisfactory equivalent—for example, "you benefit from what the Jews have made possible" or "you greatly benefit from what comes from the Jews." The relation of the metaphor may be preserved somewhat by including it as a type of simile—for example, "you benefit from what has come from the Jews in the same way that the branch of the wild olive tree benefits from the sap of the cultivated olive tree."

11.18 So then, you must not despise those who were broken off like branches. How can you be proud? You are just a branch; you don't support the root—the root supports you.

The verb rendered despise literally means "boast over" (so RSV), and may have the meaning of "think yourself superior to" (JB). The Greek text literally has "do not boast over the branches." The branches referred to are those which have been broken off (see v. 17). The TEV makes this information explicit and changes the metaphor into a simile, those who were... like branches.

If the agent of the process of "breaking off" must be stipulated, it can only be God—for example, "you must not, therefore, despise those whom God broke off like branches."

The question how can you be proud? may be made into a statement: "you must not be proud" or "there is absolutely no reason for you to be proud."

The last part of this verse is handled in a way similar to the first part. You are just a branch does not appear as such in the Greek text, though it is important that this information be made explicit for the English reader.

In translating the term support it is important not to suggest "hold up" but rather "nourish." One may even translate literally "you do not supply sap to the root, but the root supplies sap to you" or "you do not cause the root to be strong; the root causes you to be strong."

[19]But you will say, "Yes, but the branches were broken off to make room for me." [20]This is true. They were broken off because they did not believe, while you remain in place because you believe. But do not have proud thoughts about it; instead, be afraid. [21]God did not spare the Jews, who are like natural branches; do you think he will spare you? [22]Here we see how kind and how severe God is. He is severe toward those who have fallen, but kind to you—if you continue in his kindness; but if you do not, you too will be broken off. [23]And the Jews, if they abandon their unbelief, will be put back in the place

where they were, because God is able to put them back again. [24]You Gentiles are like the branch of a wild olive tree that is broken off, and then, contrary to nature, is joined to the cultivated olive tree. The Jews are like this cultivated tree; and it will be much easier, then, for God to join these broken-off branches back to their own tree.

11.19 But you will say, "Yes, but the branches were broken off to make room for me."

Once again Paul takes up the form of a philosophical argument in which he imagines the objections that his opponents can raise against him (see 2.1).

To make room for me translates the same expression rendered been joined to in verse 17. The word actually means "to graft," that is, to cut a branch from one tree and to join it to another so that it becomes a part of that tree. In order to retain the figure of speech of the original text, one may translate as "in order to be joined to the tree as a part of it."

The immediately preceding section is in the second person singular in the Greek text. However, in order to make it broadly applicable to all the Gentiles to whom Paul is addressing this letter to the Romans, it is often necessary to employ the second person plural. Similarly, in introducing verse 19 one would tend to use the second person plural. However, this will not fit with the use of the first person singular me in the direct discourse. Therefore, one must either change you to "one of you" or change me to "us."

Because of the hypothetical nature of the direct discourse (that is to say, it is not something which has already taken place or is sure to take place), in some languages one must employ a conditional or potential form of the verb rather than merely a future—for example, "some of you may argue," "one of you might say," or "you could respond by saying."

To make room for may be rendered in some languages as "so that I (or we) might have a place," "so that we might take their places," or "so that we might be where they were formerly."

11.20 This is true. They were broken off because they did not believe, while you remain in place because you believe. But do not have proud thoughts about it; instead, be afraid.

They were broken off because they did not believe is literally "by unbelief they were broken off." The TEV changes the noun phrase "by unbelief" to a verb phrase because they did not believe. This restructuring requires that the causative expression (because ...) be placed second in the English sentence. The Greek "by faith you have stood" is dealt with similarly: while you remain in place because you believe.

Have proud thoughts is the same verb which appears in 12.16 (be proud). Have proud thoughts about it is in some languages more readily expressed as "have proud thoughts because of it" or "be proud because you have taken their place."

Be afraid (so Goodspeed; NAB "fearful") is perhaps the nearest English equivalent of Paul's words here. The RSV rendering "stand in awe" (Moffatt "feel awed") is a bit high level for the average English reader and does not convey the full impact of what Paul is saying. On the other hand, the NEB rendering "be on your guard" appears to move in a direction other than what Paul intends in this passage. Nevertheless, in some languages one must make a distinction between fear of something which exists at the time and fear of what may come. It is the second type of fear which is involved at this point, and therefore it may well be rendered by a term which implies "beware."

11.21 God did not spare the Jews, who are like natural branches; do you think he will spare you?

Again there is an "if" clause that assumes the condition to be true to fact. The TEV carries through the force of the Greek construction by rendering the first half of the verse as a statement followed by a question which expects the answer "no." In a number of languages the past conditional, followed by a strong negative statement, may prove to be an excellent equivalent—for example, "if God did not spare the Jews who are like natural branches, he certainly will not spare you."

In some languages the closest equivalent to spare in this type of context is "leave in their places" or "let them go on growing," in which case one would need to say "did not let go on growing the natural branches, which correspond to the Jews."

As throughout this passage, the TEV here identifies the figures of speech (in this case natural branches) with the persons whom they represent (the Jews).

11.22 Here we see how kind and how severe God is. He is severe toward those who have fallen, but kind to you—if you continue in his kindness; but if you do not, you too will be broken off.

In Greek the first sentence in this verse begins with a particle (ide) that is actually a second person singular imperative. However, in such a context this particle serves merely to focus the reader's attention on what is being said. Therefore it is legitimate to translate this particle as a first person plural, Here we see. In other languages the appropriate equivalent may be "but you must pay attention to this," "notice carefully," or "take account of."

In Greek the object of this verb is a noun phrase, "the kindness and the severity of God," which the TEV transforms into a verb phrase, how kind and how severe God is.

In the following sentence the TEV similarly transforms nouns into verb phrases, "severity" to he is severe and "kindness" to he is . . . kind. To be kind may be expressed as "do good to" or "be good to." To be severe in this context may be rendered as "to judge harshly," "to judge with strong words," or "to judge with punishment."

In this type of context who have fallen may be translated as "those who have sinned" or "those who have done wrong." In many languages it is quite difficult to retain the idea of "fallen" as a reference to sinning.

The conditional clause if you continue in his kindness may need to be introduced by some kind of explanatory phrase—for example, "that is to say" or "provided that." The rendering of continue in his kindness involves a number of semantic problems. The persons involved must continue to believe if they are to merit their place (see v. 20). But his kindness refers to God's activity, not to their own. The relation between the two expressions may be indicated in some languages as "if you continue to merit his kindness" or "if you continue to act in such a way that he will be kind to you."

The passive expression you too will be broken off may be made active, with God as the agent. "God will break you off as well."

11.23 And the Jews, if they abandon their unbelief, will be put back in the place where they were, because God is able to put them back again.

In keeping with the demands of English discourse structure, a pronominal reference in Greek (literally "those ones") is made explicit by the TEV: the Jews (see JB and NAB).

The phrase abandon their unbelief (literally, "no longer remains in unbelief") may be rendered as "no longer refuse to believe" or "give up not believing." On the other hand, this may also be expressed positively as "return and believe" or "change and believe."

Will be put back in the place where they were is literally "will be grafted in." See the comments on grafting at verse 17.

11.24 You Gentiles are like the branch of a wild olive tree that is broken off, and then, contrary to nature, is joined to the cultivated olive tree. The Jews are like this cultivated tree; and it will be much easier, then, for God to join these broken-off branches back to their own tree.

Since verse 24 consists essentially of a summary statement of what has preceded, it may be important in some languages to identify this fact by a particle meaning "in conclusion" or "finally."

In this verse also pronominal references have been made explicit: You Gentiles is literally "you" (singular) and the Jews is literally "these ones." Throughout this entire section (vv. 13-24) there is a problem of singular and plural, since Paul is addressing his argument, as it were, to one Gentile. Therefore he speaks of the Gentiles as being "a branch." In contrast, the Jews are referred to as "these ones" and in the analogy they are "branches." It may seem quite anomalous for several branches to be broken out in order for "one Gentile" (me in v. 19) to be inserted. If a plural form of second person is employed ("you" plural) throughout, then quite naturally the reference to Gentiles will be "branches," to parallel the plural branches used in speaking of the Jews.

The branch of a wild olive tree that is broken off is more literally "have been cut off from what is by nature a wild olive tree" (RSV). The Greek phrase "by nature" (kata phusin) is also used in the second part of this verse where it appears with the equivalent of an adjective "natural" in the phrase "the natural ones." In English it is unnatural to speak of any tree as being "an X tree by nature"; we simply say "an X tree." That is why the TEV renders wild olive tree instead of "by nature a wild olive tree" (RSV) or "natural wild olive" (JB). The NEB is ambiguous and sounds odd: "your native wild olive tree."

Contrary to nature (Greek para phusin) is used in formal contrast to the phrase "by nature" (kata phusin). The meaning is obvious: it is contrary to nature for a branch of one kind of olive tree to grow from the trunk of another kind of olive tree.

For God to join these broken-off branches back to their own tree is literally "the natural ones will be joined back to their own olive tree." Once again, God is the understood agent of the passive verb, and "the natural ones" is a reference to the branches that have been broken off the original olive tree. It is unnecessary in English structure to identify these branches as "natural branches," because this is carried by the last part of the verse, to their own tree. Finally, in order that Paul's analogy may be quickly and easily seen, Gentiles and Jews are modified by the phrase are like the branch and are like this cultivated tree.

God's Mercy on All

25 There is a secret truth, my brothers, which I want you to know. It will keep
you from thinking how wise you are. It is this: the stubbornness of the people
of Israel is not permanent, but will last only until the complete number of
Gentiles comes to God. 26 And this is how all Israel will be saved. As the
scripture says,

"The Savior will come from Zion,
and remove all wickedness from the descendants of
Jacob.
27 I will make this covenant with them,
when I take away their sins."

28 Because they reject the Good News, the Jews are God's enemies for the sake
of you, the Gentiles. But because of God's choice, they are his friends for the
sake of the patriarchs. 29 For God does not change his mind about whom he
chooses and blesses. 30 As for you Gentiles, you disobeyed God in the past; but
now you have received God's mercy because the Jews disobeyed. 31 In the same
way, because of the mercy that you have received, the Jews now disobey God,
in order that they also may now receive God's mercy. 32 For God has made all
men prisoners of disobedience, that he might show mercy to them all.

The section heading God's Mercy on All may be changed into a verbal expression "God Shows Mercy to All" or even "God Is Kind to All" (if in such a context "Kind" is the normal equivalent of Mercy).

Paul now brings to a close his discussion of Israel's place in God's purpose. Up to this point he has appealed to the logic of argument, but now he appeals to revelation. His arguments have proved that God has always acted with mercy towards his people, and that Israel must share the full responsibility for its situation. He has shown that Israel's failure has resulted in bringing God's salvation to the Gentiles, and that this will ultimately serve again as a means for bringing God's message to the Jewish nation. But now, apart from argument,

Paul indicates that God has made his secret truth known through revelation that he has given Paul.

11.25 There is a secret truth, my brothers, which I want you to know. It will keep you from thinking how wise you are. It is this: the stubbornness of the people of Israel is not permanent, but will last only until the complete number of Gentiles comes to God.

The opening words of this verse indicate that Paul is introducing a new phase in his discussion: literally "I do not want you to be ignorant." This same expression appears at 1.13; 1 Corinthians 10.1; 2 Corinthians 1.8; and 1 Thessalonians 4.13. Along with other modern translations (RSV, NEB, Moffatt), the TEV transforms a Greek negative statement, "I do not wish you to be ignorant," into a positive one, I want you to know. This is a much more natural way of speaking in English, and it carries better the force of the Greek. Also, the use of the address my brothers indicates a new section in Paul's discussion.

Secret truth is generally translated "mystery" (KJV, RSV, NAB), but several modern translators feel that this is inadequate. Moffatt and Goodspeed translate as "this secret," the JB as "a hidden reason," and the NEB as "a deep truth." This is a favorite Pauline expression, appearing some 21 times in his writings, and so it is important to give close attention to it. Secret truth or "mystery" was a very familiar term in the religious vocabulary of Paul's day. Each of the so-called "mystery religions" had a secret truth which was revealed only to the persons initiated into that particular religion. It was from this fact that the mystery religions were so named. The same term frequently appeared in Jewish apocalyptic literature also, where it was used to describe the secret truth of the way in which God was at work in the world. And this was a truth which, of course, was known only to God's faithful people. So both in Judaism and in the other religions the term denoted a secret truth which was once hidden but had been revealed by God to his people. It is in such a sense that Paul uses the term in this passage and elsewhere. It is rare, however, in present-day languages to find an expression which closely parallels this rather technical concept of "mystery" as found in the context of the New Testament. In general, one must employ some kind of descriptive phrase: "truth that has not been known before," "truth which is just now revealed," or "restricted truth" (in the sense of truth restricted to persons to whom it has been specially revealed).

The sentence It will keep you from thinking how wise you are presents certain difficulties in some languages. First, it may be strange to speak of "a truth keeping you from thinking." Second, how wise you are may be much more readily expressed in some languages as direct discourse. Furthermore, the more natural way of talking about this relation may be that of condition---for example, "If you know this, you will not think about yourself, saying, We are very wise" or "If we know this, we will not say inside of our hearts, We are indeed very wise."

The stubbornness of the people of Israel is not permanent is literally "a hardening in part has come upon Israel." The word "hardening" appears only here and in Mark 3.5 and Ephesians 4.18; the verb "to harden" appears in 11.7

and was discussed there. Translators and commentators differ as to how the phrase "in part" should be related to the rest of the sentence. This phrase appears elsewhere in 15.15, 24 and in 2 Corinthians 1.14. Its force may either be adverbial or adjectival. The TEV understands it in an adverbial sense: the stubbornness of the people of Israel is not permanent. Those who take it as an adjective interpret it in either of two ways: (1) as a reference to a part of the nation, and not to all of the nation (RSV "a hardening has come upon part of Israel"; see also NAB and JB); or (2) as a partial, but not a complete, hardening of the people (Goodspeed "only partial insensibility has come upon Israel"; see also Moffatt and NEB).

In this context stubbornness may be specifically rendered in some languages as "refusal to believe," for this is not stubbornness in the general sense of the term. Then, depending upon one's interpretation of the phrase "in part," one may have one of several different types of expressions: "not all the people of Israel refused to believe," "the people of Israel have not absolutely refused to believe," "the fact that the people of Israel have refused to believe will not always last," or "the people of Israel will not always refuse to believe." In some languages an expression for "refuse to believe" may be expressed as direct discourse—for example, "they declare, We will not believe" or "they insist, We do not believe."

Complete number is the same word discussed in verse 12. There the reference was to the Jewish nation as a whole, but here it is to the non-Jewish world as a whole. Again Paul's belief reflects the thought of Jewish apocalyptic, which assumed that God had not only determined the exact time in which men would be saved but also had determined exactly how many persons would be saved. The complete number should not be translated in such a way as to suggest "all." It is rather "the number that should be," "the determined number," or "the number determined by God."

Comes to God is literally "come in," but the reference is to the coming of the Gentiles to God and his kingdom.

11.26-27 And this is how all Israel will be saved. As the scripture says,

"The Savior will come from Zion,
and remove all wickedness from the descendants of Jacob.
I will make this covenant with them,
when I take away their sins."

This is how relates back to what Paul has previously said, and the following scripture quotation serves to prove the truth of his statement. Paul believes that when the Gentile nations as a whole turn to God, this will also inspire the Jewish people as a whole to do so. Paul appeals to Scripture to support his argument: in verses 26-27a Paul refers to Isaiah 59.20-21 and in verse 27b to Isaiah 27.9. The quotations are fairly close to the Septuagint. The passive expression will be saved may be transformed into an active one—for example, "God will save all Israel."

In a number of languages it is impossible to talk about "removing wickedness" or "taking away sins" other than in the sense of "to forgive." This is essentially the meaning of these expressions in the scriptural context, and lines two and four of the quotation are parallel. The reference to the descendants of Jacob is in Greek literally "Jacob," a familiar way of speaking of the Jewish people.

In order to make clear who is I, it may be necessary to introduce an expression of direct discourse—for example, "and God said, I will make this covenant with them."

11.28 Because they reject the Good News, the Jews are God's enemies for the sake of you, the Gentiles. But because of God's choice, they are his friends for the sake of the patriarchs.

The Greek of this verse is much shorter than the TEV rendering, because there are implicit elements in the Greek which must be made explicit for the sake of English readers. Literally this verse may be rendered something like the following: "As far as the Good News is concerned, enemies because of you, but as far as choice is concerned, friends because of the patriarchs." The TEV takes the phrase "as far as the Good News is concerned" in the sense of because they reject the Good News (NEB "in the spreading of the gospel"). In this context "enemies" must be taken in the sense of God's enemies (see Moffatt, Goodspeed, NEB, JB). "Because of you" is understood to mean "for your sake" (so most translations); and the TEV reflects the demands of English discourse structure in requiring the pronoun "you" to be identified as you, the Gentiles.

There is a potential difficulty in the rendering of the Jews are God's enemies for the sake of you. This might imply that the Jews purposely became God's enemies for the sake of the Gentiles, which is obviously not the case. Therefore, one must translate in some languages: "the Jews are God's enemies, but this turns out to be of help to you, the Gentiles." However, there is no such contrast in the second sentence of verse 28, since at that place there is no adversative relation between the Jews being God's friends and this being for the sake of the patriarchs.

In the second clause "choice" refers to God's choice (see also Goodspeed and NEB). The word rendered friends is not the usual Greek word for "friends"; it means something like "persons who are loved." The RSV, Moffatt, and NAB used the archaic "beloved," while Goodspeed translates "they are dear to him," and JB "they are still loved by God"; NEB has "friends."

For the sake of the patriarchs has a reference either to the promises that God made to the patriarchs or to the covenants he made with them.

The initial phrase, because of God's choice, may be transformed into a verbal expression, "because God chose them."

The final phrase, for the sake of the patriarchs, may need to be somewhat more specific in some languages—for example, "because of the promises God made to the patriarchs" or "because God promised the patriarchs that their descendants would always be his friends."

11.29 For God does not change his mind about whom he chooses and blesses.

The word rendered "irrevocable" by some translations (RSV and NEB) basically means "without change of mind or heart." It is used in this sense in 2 Corinthians 7.10, its only other occurrence in the New Testament. In order to express in English the meaning of "without a change of mind," it is necessary to change the noun into a verb phrase. Both the TEV and Goodspeed render it by God does not change his mind; the JB, assuming that the meaning of the word is "irrevocable," also changes to a verb: "God never takes back his gifts or revokes his choice."

In light of the context, what is the meaning of the phrase "the gifts and the choice of God"? It is possible, of course, to take "gifts" as a general reference to any blessing that God gives, but in the context "gifts" seems to have a more specific meaning. In light of its connection with the word "called," it may best be taken as a reference to those blessings which are bestowed on the persons whom God calls. Since the "calling" comes first and the "blessings" follow, the TEV translates the phrase to mean whom he chooses and blesses.

11.30 As for you Gentiles, you disobeyed God in the past; but now you have received God's mercy because the Jews disobeyed.

The pronominal reference "you" is again made explicit: you Gentiles; and the implied agent of the passive verb (literally "you were mercied") is also made explicit: you have received God's mercy. Finally, the noun phrase ("by the disobedience of these") is changed to a verb phrase, with the pronominal reference explicit: because the Jews disobeyed.

11.31 In the same way, because of the mercy that you have received, the Jews now disobey God, in order that they also may now receive God's mercy.

In Greek this verse is a continuation of the sentence begun in the previous verse, and from the standpoint of translation it is similar to the preceding verse. A literal translation might read: "In the same way these ones are now disobedient because of your mercy in order that they themselves now may be mercied." The TEV reorders two of the major parts of this verse, and makes the participants explicit. The first part of this verse actually appears as the second element in the TEV: "these ones" are identified as the Jews and the object of their disobedience is made explicit, disobey God. The second part of the Greek sentence appears first in the English sentence structure, and the ambiguous phrase "your mercy" is clarified to mean mercy that you have received. Finally, in the last part of the verse, God is identified as the one who gives the mercy: that they also may now receive God's mercy.

The word now (in its second occurrence in this verse) does not appear in some manuscripts; it is omitted by the RSV, the NEB, and Moffatt. The UBS text committee believes that the evidence supports the inclusion of this word and classifies the choice with a "B" rating.

11.32 For God has made all men prisoners of disobedience, that he might show mercy to them all.

In this verse Paul indicates that God's purpose in condemning all men for their disobedience was in order that he might show his mercy to all of them. The phrase made all men prisoners of disobedience is perhaps to be taken in the sense of "made all men prisoners of their own disobedience." The thought is similar to what is expressed in 1.24, 26, 28; but here the purpose of mercy is made explicit.

In some languages to speak of prisoners of disobedience one must use some such expression as "God caused all men to be like prisoners because they disobey" or "As the result of all men disobeying God, they have become like prisoners; God has caused them to be this way."

The final clause of verse 32, that he might show mercy to them all, is an expression of purpose, and it may be necessary to refer again to the main verb if an expression such as prisoners of disobedience is expanded into a clause—for example, "For God has made all men like prisoners because they have disobeyed him; he has done this in order that he might show mercy to all of them."

Praise to God

33 How great are God's riches! How deep are his wisdom and knowledge! Who can explain his decisions? Who can understand his ways? 34 As the scripture says,

"Who knows the mind of the Lord?
Who is able to give him advice?
35 Who has ever given him anything,
so that he had to pay it back?"

36 For all things were created by him, and all things exist through him and for him. To God be the glory forever! Amen.

In some languages it may be necessary to render the section heading Praise to God as "We Should Praise God," "God Ought to Be Praised," or "God Deserves Praise."

Paul's ultimate conclusion is that the understanding of history, and indeed of life itself, is completely within God's power. The form of this passage is that of a hymn of praise to God.

11.33 How great are God's riches! How deep are his wisdom and knowledge! Who can explain his decisions? Who can understand his ways?

The first part of this verse literally reads: "O the depth of the riches and wisdom and knowledge of God" (RSV). This is in the form of an exclamation, but a literal rendering such as this is archaic. It is more natural to begin an exclamation with "how" (see also JB). When this change is made, the word "depth" must be rendered by deep. But if one says "How deep are God's riches," then it may be assumed by the reader that this is something one must dig for. So the TEV translates "depth" by great in the first exclamation and introduces deep in the second, since deep in conjunction with wisdom and knowledge occasions no difficulty for the English reader.

In some languages, however, one cannot translate how great are God's riches, since this would simply imply that God is very wealthy. Even in the form of a strong affirmation, "God has great riches," the reference might be merely to his considerable wealth and not to "the riches of his grace," which is the usual manner in which Paul speaks of God's "riches." Accordingly, the first exclamation must be translated in some languages as "God is indeed very good to all" or "God does indeed show great mercy (or grace)." Similarly, in many languages one cannot speak of wisdom or knowledge as being "deep." In fact, one must say "God is indeed very wise and has much knowledge."

The two questions, Who can explain his decisions? Who can understand his ways?, are also exclamations in Greek. It is possible to retain the form of exclamation (for example, "No one can explain his decisions! No one can understand his ways!"), but the question form is more natural in an English construction of this type. In some languages strong affirmations may be more satisfactory—for example, "no one can explain his decisions; no one can understand his ways."

The words translated explain and understand are actually verbal adjectives in Greek. The first of these terms describes something that cannot be found by searching for it, while the other suggests footprints that cannot be tracked down. Explain his decisions may perhaps be best translated as "explain how he decides." Understand his ways may be rendered as "understand why he does what he does."

11.34-35 As the scripture says,

"Who knows the mind of the Lord?
Who is able to give him advice?
Who has ever given him anything,
so that he had to pay it back?"

Once again Paul introduces scripture to support his affirmation. In verse 34 Paul quotes from Isaiah 40.13 and in verse 35 from Job 41.11. The first of these two quotations is very close to the Septuagint, but the second is apparently nearer the Hebrew. The first quotation emphasizes the fact that God has all knowledge, and the second makes the point that no man can do anything to place God in his debt.

In many languages it is quite difficult to translate Who knows the mind of the Lord? since one cannot readily speak of "knowing another person's mind." It is possible, however, to say "to know how another person thinks" or "to know why a person thinks as he does." Such expressions, therefore, may form the basis for rendering "who knows how the Lord reasons?" or "who knows why the Lord thinks as he does?" This question, as well as the two which follow, may quite naturally be expressed as statements—for example, "no one knows how the Lord thinks; no one is able to give him advice; no one is able to give God anything so as to make God indebted to him."

The question in verse 35 implies putting God under obligation. The closest parallel in some languages may be expressions relating to gift exchange---for example, "Who is able to give a gift to God, so that God will be obliged to give him something in return?"

11.36 For all things were created by him, and all things exist through him and for him. To God be the glory forever! Amen.

The first part of this verse literally reads "for from him and through him and to him are all things." The first of these phrases, "from him," indicates that God is the source of everything, and so is translated by the TEV as all things were created by him. The other two phrases, "through him" and "to him," indicate that God is the one who keeps the created order in existence and that it is moving in the direction that he intends. The TEV renders these last two phrases as and all things exist through him and for him. In the last part of this verse the TEV makes the pronoun "to him" explicit: to God.

The passive construction for all things were created by him may be rendered as "God has created everything." One might be inclined to translate through him as "because of him," but this might suggest "by means of him," which would be essentially the same as the first clause of verse 36, or "for his sake," which would be equivalent to the last phrase of the sentence. A more satisfactory equivalent may be "he sustains all things" or "he keeps all things going." The final phrase, for him, may be expressed as "all things exist for his sake."

The final exclamation To God be the glory forever! may be equivalent to "we must praise God forever" or "God deserves honor forever."

As in a number of other contexts, the term Amen may appropriately be rendered as "this is surely true" or "this is certainly the way it should be."

CHAPTER 12

Life in God's Service

12 So then, my brothers, because of God's great mercy to us, I make this appeal to you: Offer yourselves as a living sacrifice to God, dedicated to his service and pleasing to him. This is the true worship that you should offer. [2]Do not conform outwardly to the standards of this world, but let God transform you inwardly by a complete change of your mind. Then you will be able to know the will of God—what is good, and is pleasing to him, and is perfect.

The section heading Life in God's Service may be transformed into a verb expression, "How We Should Live in Order to Serve God" or "Living in Order to Serve God."

Chapter 12 introduces a marked division in Paul's letter to the Romans. Beginning with this chapter Paul discusses what might be called either practical or ethical matters. But just as the commentators point to the fact that chapter 12 introduces a new division in Paul's letter, they also remind us that there is a close relation between this practical section and the earlier theological section of the letter. The practice of the Christian life grows out of the theology of the Christian life, and so the ethical exhortations occurring in the later chapters are based on the theological viewpoints presented in the earlier chapters. The so-called ethical division of this letter continues through 15.13, where Paul begins to speak of his own personal plans to visit Rome. An overview of these chapters will be helpful before the exegesis is begun.

CHAPTER 12. Verses 1-2 serve as a transition from the argument of the letter to its application. This is indicated by the transitional so then, by the address my brothers, and by the appeal that Paul makes (because of God's great mercy to us). Verses 3-8 discuss the various gifts that God's Spirit has given to the members of the Christian community and encourages the believers to use those gifts in the proper way. The remainder of the chapter, verses 9-21, is controlled by the theme of love and by the motive of what is good.

CHAPTER 13. Verses 1-7, which deal with the Christian's duties toward the state authorities, break the connection between 12.9-21 and 13.8-14. This section is also stylistically different and is similar to the so-called wisdom literature of the Jewish-Hellenistic period. Verses 8-10 are tied closely to 12.9-21, as the catch word love indicates. Stylistically this section is in the form of the giving of laws, and verse 9 quotes from Leviticus 19.18. Verses 11-14 reflect the kind of teaching that was given to new converts, especially at the time of their baptism, which was looked upon as the beginning of their experience in the Christian life. Verses 11-14 have a very definite eschatological appeal.

CHAPTERS 14 and 15. Beginning with verse 1 of chapter 14 and continuing to verse 13 of chapter 15, Paul takes up specific questions, and this material has a form which is distinct from that of the two previous chapters. Chapters 12 and 13 reflect the form of the Old Testament and that of Jewish-Hellenistic literature, but chapters 14 and 15 reflect more the style of apostolic teaching.

This entire section is basically concerned with two groups within the Christian community, those who are weak in the faith (14.1) and those who are strong in the faith (15.1). In 14.1-12 Paul points out the difference between the two groups and at the same time reminds them that they are both joined to the same Lord. In 14.13-23 he attempts to resolve the situation by reminding his readers that Christian freedom should always aim at those things which bring peace and which help strengthen one another (14.19). Finally, in 15.1-13 he brings to the forefront the example of Christ and reminds his readers that it is through him that both Jews and Gentiles have been brought to enjoy God's salvation. The final division of Paul's letter to the Romans begins at 15.14.

12.1 So then, my brothers, because of God's great mercy to us, I make this appeal to you: Offer yourselves as a living sacrifice to God, dedicated to his service and pleasing to him. This is the true worship that you should offer.

The transitional phrase so then may be rendered in some languages as "as a result" or "therefore."

Great mercy (most translations "mercy") translates a plural form in Greek (literally "mercies") and the TEV attempts to bring out the significance of the plural by using the adjective great. The plural may have this intensive significance, but it is also possible that it simply reflects the corresponding Hebrew word in the Old Testament. In fact, this word occurs five times in the New Testament, and in four of them it is used in the plural (Romans 12.1; 2 Corinthians 1.3; Philippians 2.1; Hebrews 10.28), while it is used in the singular only once (Colossians 3.12). In a number of languages great mercy may only be expressed as "the many times that God has shown mercy to us."

I make this appeal (RSV, Goodspeed, Moffatt "I appeal") is rendered "I beg" by the JB and NAB and "I implore" by the NEB. This same verb is also used in 15.30 and 16.17 in a similar way. See also 1 Corinthians 1.10; 4.16; 2 Corinthians 2.8; Philemon 9 and 10. Paul makes three appeals to the Roman Christians; two of them are positive, offer yourselves... let God transform you inwardly, and one is negative, do not conform outwardly. A similar pattern is followed in 13.13-14.

There are a number of ways in which the phrase I make this appeal to you may be rendered in various languages—for example, "I strongly urge you," "I say with strong words," "I beg of you earnestly," or, idiomatically, "I say with my heart open."

Yourselves is literally "your bodies," but in such a context Paul is using "bodies" as a reference to one's entire self (NEB "your very selves"). This is similar to the meaning in 6.13, 19.

The sacrifice that the Christian is to offer is described in three ways: living, dedicated to his service, and pleasing to him.

Dedicated to his service (NEB "dedicated"; Moffatt "consecrated") translates the word rendered "holy" by most translations. As mentioned earlier, the word translated "holy" has as its primary meaning "that which is set apart for

God," but "holy" usually fails to convey this meaning to the English reader. Rather, the idea is one of moral purity. Moral purity is, of course, involved in dedication to God, but it is something which grows out of the "holiness" of the Christian.

The phrase living sacrifice involves a contradiction in terms since a sacrifice is something which is put to death. In some languages the distinction is rendered as "offer yourself as though a killed gift to God while still alive," "give yourself to God just as though you were a sacrifice but still living," or "give your lives to God as though they were a sacrifice." The need for making the contrast between sacrifice and living is especially necessary in languages for which a translation for sacrifice is literally "a killed gift" or "a slain offering."

In some languages it is simpler and more effective to treat dedicated to his service and pleasing to him as being syntactically coordinate with offer yourselves—for example, "dedicate yourselves to serving him and to pleasing him." On the other hand, the relationship to the sacrifice may be made explicit by saying "by offering yourself as a sacrifice, though still living, you dedicate yourself to his service and you are pleasing to him."

This is the true worship (NEB "the worship offered by mind and heart") is taken by some to mean "your rational worship" (Goodspeed; JB "that is worthy of thinking beings") and by others as "your spiritual worship" (NAB; see Moffatt). The meaning of the word rendered true ("rational" and "spiritual") is difficult. Although the etymology of the word may mean "rational," it is misleading. The way in which this word is used elsewhere outside the New Testament suggests that the basic meaning is "that which is in keeping with one's true nature as a person," and the TEV attempts to bring this out by the word true. This seems also to be the basis for the translation of the NEB.

In many languages it is difficult to speak of true worship, especially since worship must generally be expressed by a verb. Furthermore, true in this type of context is not related to the concept of truth as much as it is to the idea of what is fitting and proper. The last sentence of verse 1 may therefore be rendered in some languages as "This is the way in which you ought to worship" or "This is the proper way to worship God." On the other hand, if one understands the underlying Greek expression to refer to spiritual worship, one may translate: "This is the way you ought to worship God in your hearts" or "This is the way to worship God within yourselves."

12.2 Do not conform outwardly to the standards of this world, but let God transform you inwardly by a complete change of your mind. Then you will be able to know the will of God—what is good, and is pleasing to him, and is perfect.

The TEV accurately brings out the contrast between the two verbs that Paul uses, conform outwardly and transform ... inwardly. Some commentators take the position that Paul did not use these two verbs in such a way as to make this distinction, but most commentators assume that Paul did maintain this difference in meaning. The TEV correctly takes the passive voice of the second of these two verbs as a reference to God's action, let God transform you inwardly.

There are a number of ways in which one may render Do not conform outwardly to the standards of this world—for example, "Do not follow the customs of this life," "Do not continue to do what the people in this world do," or "Do not make yourselves like a picture of this world." In many languages the concept of standards is simply "customs" or, more specifically in some instances, "the way in which people in the world think one ought to act."

Let God transform you inwardly may be rendered as "permit God to change your hearts," "let God give you new hearts," or "let God make over your desires." This inward transformation is closely connected in thought by the expression of means, by a complete change of your mind (Goodspeed "your new attitude of mind"; NEB "let your minds be remade"). This is rendered "the renewal of your mind" in many translations. The meaning is that the Christian confession demands that the entire bent of one's mind be changed. The entire clause may be rendered as "permit God to change you inside by giving you a completely new mind" or "...by making your mind and heart completely different."

To know the will of God may be rendered as "to know what God wants" or "to know what God desires."

The final phrases what is good, and is pleasing to him, and is perfect are explanations of what God wants. In some languages this series of explanatory phrases must be introduced by an expression such as "that is to say," "that means," or "namely."

The TEV makes it clear that the adjective pleasing has reference to God (to him, that is, "to God").

Perfect may be rendered "just as it should be" or "what could not be better."

> [3]And because of God's gracious gift to me, I say to all of you: Do not think of yourselves more highly than you should. Instead, be modest in your thinking, and each one of you judge himself according to the amount of faith that God has given him. [4]We have many parts in the one body, and all these parts have different functions. [5]In the same way, though we are many, we are one body in union with Christ and we are all joined to each other as different parts of one body. [6]So we are to use our different gifts in accordance with the grace that God has given us. If our gift is to speak God's message, we must do it according to the faith that we have. [7]If it is to serve, we must serve. If it is to teach, we must teach. [8]If it is to encourage others, we must do so. Whoever shares with others what he has, must do it generously; whoever has authority, must work hard; whoever shows kindness to others, must do it cheerfully.

12.3 And because of God's gracious gift to me, I say to all of you: Do not think of yourselves more highly than you should. Instead, be modest in your thinking, and each one of you judge himself according to the amount of faith that God has given him.

Because of God's gracious gift to me is literally "because of the grace that was given to me." Depending on the context, the word "grace" can be used in the sense of "a (spiritual) gift that God gives out of his grace." It seems quite possible that this is the meaning in the present context, and so the TEV makes this meaning clear (also NEB "the gift that God in his grace has given me"). Once again, a passive ("that was given to me") is transformed into an active, with God as the subject. In some languages the equivalent of this expression of reason is "because of what God has given to me" or "because of the gift that God has given to me."

Do not think of yourselves more highly than you should may be rendered as "Do not think that you yourselves are so high," "Do not think of yourselves with a big head," or "Do not say to yourselves, I am so very big, when you really are not."

Be modest in your thinking appears in a variety of forms: "but think your way to a sober estimate" (NEB); "must judge himself soberly" (JB); "he must take a sane view of himself" (Moffatt); "but to think reasonably" (Goodspeed). The meaning, in any case, is clear in light of what follows: and each one of you judge himself according to the amount of faith that God has given him. Although not stated explicitly, it is clear from the context that Paul has reference to the estimate that each one makes of himself, and so the TEV makes this explicit, be modest in your thinking...each one of you judge himself.

12.4-5 We have many parts in the one body, and all these parts have different functions. (5) In the same way, though we are many, we are one body in union with Christ and we are all joined to each other as different parts of one body.

The thoughts expressed in these verses have already been discussed in earlier passages, but there are a number of problems in translation.

One cannot usually say literally we have many parts in the one body. A more normal expression would be "each one of us has a body made up of different parts" or "the body of each one of us has many different parts." All these parts have different functions may then be rendered as "each part has a different function," "each part has its own use," "each part works in a different way," or "each part is for something different."

Though we are many may be translated as "though we are many different people" or "...distinct persons."

We are one body must be rendered in some languages as "we form one body" or "we are just like one body."

The phrase in union with Christ may be understood as either means or cause—for example, "by being one with Christ" or "because we are one together with Christ."

12.6 So we are to use our different gifts in accordance with the grace that God has given us. If our gift is to speak God's message, we must do it according to the faith that we have.

In Greek verses 6-8 form one sentence, and it is rather complex. It begins with a participle and there is no main verb in the entire sentence. Although a verb is not present in the Greek, the context makes it clear what verb is implicit: we are to use (RSV "let us use them"; NEB "must be exercised accordingly").

Different gifts should be understood distributively rather than collectively, that is to say, each person has a different gift, as is indicated clearly in the rest of this paragraph. Accordingly, one must translate in some languages: "so each one of us should use our own gift in accordance with the way in which God has given it to us" or "each one of us should use the particular gift that God has given to each one."

To speak God's message (NEB "the gift of inspired utterance") translates a single noun that is rendered "prophecy" in many translations. There is no single term that can adequately translate this Greek word. "Preaching" (Goodspeed) comes closer than "prophecy," which focuses the attention on the aspect of prediction, but "preaching" is not completely adequate. The TEV and the NEB place the emphasis on the primary element in this term, that is, the proclamation of God's message.

In some languages it is not easy to relate a term such as gift with an event such as to speak God's message. It may be necessary therefore to indicate somewhat more precisely what the gift consists of: "if God has given us the ability to preach God's message."

The last clause of this verse, we must do it according to the faith that we have, may be rendered as "we must do it with as much faith as we have," "we must do it with all the faith we have," "we must do it in proportion to how much we believe," or "if we believe much, we must do it much."

12.7 If it is to serve, we must serve. If it is to teach, we must teach.

To serve and to teach both translate nouns in Greek; however, in English the verb phrase is much clearer. To serve (RSV "service") is rendered "practical service" by Goodspeed and Moffatt and "administration" by the NEB and the JB. The word itself means simply "service" (see 15.31), and it is doubtful if one should give it the technical and specialized meaning of the NEB and JB rendering. "Administration" would seem to presuppose a more highly organized church structure than was in existence at that time. Moreover, the idea of "administration" focuses attention on an aspect of meaning that is certainly not primary in the word. Where a receptor language possesses a rather general term for serve requiring no grammatical goal, there is very little difficulty in the translation. However, most languages possess no such convenient equivalent. It is therefore necessary in many instances to employ an expression which will be a satisfactory descriptive substitute—for example, "help the congregation," "assist the group of believers," or "be of service to the fellow believers."

It may be necessary to fill out the ellipses in the initial clauses of verses 7 and 8—for example, "If God has given us the ability to help the believers, we should help them; if he has given us the ability to teach, we should teach; if he has given us the ability to encourage others, we should encourage them."

12.8 If it is to encourage others, we must do so. Whoever shares with others what he has, must do it generously; whoever has authority, must work hard; whoever shows kindness to others, must do it cheerfully.

To encourage others is also rendered in a variety of ways: "exhorts" (RSV); "the gift of stirring speech" (NEB); "let the preachers deliver sermons" (JB); "the speaker his words of counsel" (Moffatt). In light of the fact that this gift is mentioned immediately after that of teaching, the work of the preacher is suggested, and the meaning of his role seems to be that of offering encouragement to other believers.

Generously (RSV "in liberality"; Goodspeed "with generosity") is generally assumed to be the meaning of the word that Paul uses, though some see in it the meaning of "with sincerity" (NEB "with all your heart").

Whoever has authority or "if you are a leader" (NEB) are accurate translations of the Greek term that Paul uses here, since it appears that he uses it in a nontechnical sense. "He who gives aid" (RSV) and "he who rules" (NAB) seem to suggest the wrong meaning, while "the officials" (JB), "the office-holder" (Goodspeed), and "the superintendent" (Moffatt) are too highly specialized.

Must work hard should not be rendered in such a way as to imply mere "physical labor." The focus here is upon "exercising authority with diligence" or "doing what he should do with energy" or "...conscientiousness."

The final clause must do it cheerfully may be rendered in some languages as "should do it while smiling" or "should do it but remain happy."

[9]Love must be completely sincere. Hate what is evil, hold on to what is good.
[10]Love one another warmly as brothers in Christ, and be eager to show respect for one another. [11]Work hard, and do not be lazy. Serve the Lord with a heart full of devotion. [12]Let your hope keep you joyful, be patient in your troubles, and pray at all times. [13]Share your belongings with your needy brothers, and open your homes to strangers.

12.9 Love must be completely sincere. Hate what is evil, hold on to what is good.

Though the Greek expressions in this verse are not imperatives, they are used to express obligation and should be so translated in English.

It is very difficult in some languages to say love must be completely sincere. One can speak of people as "loving sincerely" but not of "love being sincere." Hence one may say "when you love you must be completely sincere" or "you must be completely sincere in your loving people." Moreover, it is not easy in some languages to find a term for sincere. In some languages a negative expression is employed—for example, "don't pretend to love."

Hold on to what is good may be rendered idiomatically as "tie yourself to what is good." Since hold on to is in contrast with hate, it may be useful to suggest something of the emotive implications involved—for example, "hold on to in your heart" or "keep firm in your heart."

12.10 Love one another warmly as brothers in Christ, and be eager to show respect for one another.

Love one another warmly translates a verb which appears only here in the New Testament. The verb is used particularly of love within the family relationship, and so the idea of "to love warmly" is expressed by the TEV (see NEB "breed warmth of mutual affection").

As brothers in Christ is literally "by means of brotherly love." The "brotherhood" (as in many translations) referred to is that of the Christian community, and so the TEV renders as brothers in Christ. The first clause in verse 10 is rendered in some languages as "love one another as brothers ought to."

Be eager to show respect for one another (Goodspeed "be eager to show one another honor") translates a difficult Greek expression which may be understood in two possible ways. The meaning may be as the TEV and Moffatt express it, or it may be "let each man consider the other worthy of more honor than himself." It seems that the NEB follows the second possibility, though it is difficult to tell precisely what is meant by the rendering "give pride of place to one another in esteem." Moffatt also sounds unnatural, though he seems to follow the same understanding of the passage that Goodspeed and the TEV have, namely, "be forward to honour one another." Be eager to is equivalent in some languages to "be quick to," "do not hesitate to," or even "be happy to." In one language the equivalent of the entire clause is "be conspicuous in praising one another."

12.11 Work hard, and do not be lazy. Serve the Lord with a heart full of devotion.

This verse, which in Greek continues the sentence begun in verse 9, is translated in a number of different ways. Work hard, and do not be lazy is rendered something like "never flag in zeal" (RSV) by most translations. A literal translation might be "as far as eagerness is concerned, do not be lazy." A translation in line with this more usual type of rendering could be "do not stop being eager" or "do not cease in your zeal." However, if one employs a positive-negative contrast as in work hard, and do not be lazy, it may be necessary in some languages to express the negative aspect first—for example, "do not be lazy but work hard."

With a heart full of devotion (JB "with great earnestness of spirit") is literally "boiling over in spirit." Some take the word "spirit" as a reference to God's Spirit (RSV "be aglow with the Spirit"; Goodspeed "on fire with the Spirit"), but most understand it as a reference to the human spirit (NEB "in ardour of spirit"; Moffatt "maintain the spiritual glow"). In some languages one may say "shine out with the spirit." A similar expression is found in Acts 18.25 and is translated with great enthusiasm by the TEV. In some languages with a heart full of devotion may be "with your whole heart," while in other languages it would be more appropriate to say: "devote yourself completely to serving the Lord."

12.12 Let your hope keep you joyful, be patient in your troubles, and pray at all times.

Let your hope keep you joyful (JB "If you have hope, this will make you cheerful") is literally "rejoicing in hope." The phrase "in hope" means "on the basis of your hope," and this is the basis for the TEV translation. In a number of languages, however, the basis of something may be indicated by a clause beginning with "because"—for example, "because you have hope, keep on being joyful."

The phrase in your troubles may be equivalent to "when you have troubles" or "when others are troubling you."

12.13 Share your belongings with your needy brothers, and open your homes to strangers.

In the expression share your belongings with your needy brothers (NEB "contribute to the needs of God's people") the word brothers is a reference to one's fellow Christians. Share your belongings with your needy brothers may be rendered in some languages as "give to your fellow Christians what they need" or "give what you have to your fellow Christians who do not have what they need."

Open your homes to strangers is a reference to the necessity of exercising hospitality toward Christians who may be traveling from one place to another. In a time when public lodging places were few and often dangerous to stay in, this was an important expression of Christian love. A literal translation of open your homes to strangers may, however, be grossly misinterpreted. A more satisfactory equivalent may be "welcome into your homes Christians who are strangers" or "welcome into your homes as guests those who are traveling."

> [14]Ask God to bless those who persecute you; yes, ask him to bless, not to curse. [15]Be happy with those who are happy, weep with those who weep. [16]Have the same concern for all alike. Do not be proud, but accept humble duties. Do not think of yourselves as wise.

12.14 Ask God to bless those who persecute you; yes, ask him to bless, not to curse.

Ask God to bless (NEB "call down blessings on") is literally "bless." However, in the biblical context it is God who brings blessings on people, and so the translation of the TEV seems nearer to the correct meaning. In some languages one may say literally "pray to God in order that he will bless," "...cause good to come to," or "...that he will favor."

In rendering the verbal expression not to curse it is important that this be understood in the sense of "do not ask God to curse them" or "...to do harm to them." It would be inappropriate if the sense were "ask God not to curse them." One should not imply that God is going to curse them and that the Christian should pray that God would withhold his curse. Rather, the meaning is that the Christian himself refrain from asking God to curse those who persecute the believers.

12.15 Be happy with those who are happy, weep with those who weep.

In verses 9-13 Paul used participles, in verse 14 he switched to imperatives, and now in verse 15 he uses infinitives. However, it is evident that all of these forms are equivalent to imperatives.

Be happy with those who are happy may be rendered as "be happy with others when they are happy." Similarly, weep with those who weep may be rendered as "weep with others when they weep" or "show sorrow for others when they have sorrow."

12.16 Have the same concern for all alike. Do not be proud, but accept humble duties. Do not think of yourselves as wise.

Once again Paul switches back to the form of the participle. Have the same concern for all alike (NEB "care as much about each other as about yourselves"; NAB "have the same attitude toward all"; JB "treat everyone with equal kindness") is taken by a number of scholars to mean "live in harmony with one another" (Goodspeed; so also Moffatt, RSV).

If one follows the interpretation of the TEV, one may employ such renderings as "open your heart to all in the same way," "think about each person in the same way as you think about every other person," or "care for all in the same way." If one follows the interpretation suggested by Goodspeed and others, a type of double negative may be required, "do not live in strife with one another" or "do not have conflicts with one another." In some languages, however, the positive aspect is effectively communicated by certain idiomatic uses—for example, "be dovetailed together" (a figure of speech based upon the manner of joining wood) or "live together like trees in the forest" (who give no evidence of hostility to one another but of harmonious growing together).

The words rendered accept humble duties may also mean "make friends with the lowly" (TEV alternative rendering). The problem is that the noun may either be neuter, humble duties, or masculine, "lowly people." Accept humble duties may be rendered as "be willing to do the small jobs," "be willing to serve others just as though you were a servant," or "be willing to help in little ways." In order to translate "make friends with the lowly," one may need to say "make friends with those who are poor," "make friends with those who are not anybody," "make friends with those whom others look down on," or "be friendly with those whom people do not honor."

17 If someone does evil to you, do not pay him back with evil. Try to do what
all men consider to be good. 18 Do everything possible, on your part, to live at
peace with all men. 19 Never take revenge, my friends, but instead let God's
wrath do it. For the scripture says, "I will take revenge, I will pay back, says
the Lord." 20 Instead, as the scripture says: "If your enemy is hungry, feed him;
if he is thirsty, give him a drink; for by doing this you will heap burning coals
on his head." 21 Do not let evil defeat you; instead, conquer evil with good.

12.17 If someone does evil to you, do not pay him back with evil. Try to do what all men consider to be good.

Do not pay him back with evil may be rendered as "do not do evil to him in return" or "do not be bad to him as he has been bad to you."

The second part of this verse, try to do what all men consider to be good, comes from the Septuagint of Proverbs 3.4.

12.18 Do everything possible, on your part, to live at peace with all men.

On your part may be rendered as "insofar as it depends on you" or "so far as it is possible to you."

12.19 Never take revenge, my friends, but instead let God's wrath do it. For the scripture says, "I will take revenge, I will pay back, says the Lord."

Let God's wrath do it is literally "give place to wrath," but in the present context "wrath" is a reference to God's wrath, and many translations make this explicit (RSV, NEB, JB, NAB, Goodspeed, Moffatt). The scripture quotation in this passage comes from Deuteronomy 32.35. Let God's wrath do it is equivalent in some languages to "let God take revenge," "let God pay him back in judgment," or even "let God condemn him."

It may be awkward in some languages to introduce a direct quotation in a double manner---that is, with the two phrases, for the scripture says and says the Lord. This may be reduced to a single statement in some languages: "for the Lord says in the scripture," "the scripture contains the words of the Lord," or "these are the words of the Lord in the scripture."

In translating I will take revenge it is important to indicate that God takes revenge for what others have done, but not necessarily to himself. In other words, God is not being vengeful in the sense that he retaliates for what people do to him. Rather, he exercises judgment upon those who harm others. Therefore, one may translate "I will take revenge on the evil that has been done" or "I will take revenge on those who have done evil." In some languages the closest equivalent may be "to pay back"—for example, "I will pay them back for how they have caused others to suffer." In other languages one may translate as "I will cause them to suffer in return."

12.20 Instead, as the scripture says: "If your enemy is hungry, feed him; if he is thirsty, give him a drink; for by doing this you will heap burning coals on his head."

The introductory expressions instead, as the scripture says involve considerable ellipsis and these must be filled out in some languages---for example, "do not do that but do as the scripture says" or "instead of taking revenge do what the scripture says." Since the phrase as the scripture says is added as an introduction to the direct quotation, some translators may not feel it necessary to have this type of introductory expression, particularly if the reference to Proverbs 25.21-22 is made clear in a marginal note.

The scripture reference in this verse comes from Proverbs 25.21-22. The imagery of the last clause in this verse is difficult, though all translations seem to prefer to retain the imagery rather than to change the metaphor into a non-metaphor. For by doing this you will heap burning coals on his head is perhaps best taken in the sense of "for by doing this you will make him ashamed."

12.21 Do not let evil defeat you; instead, conquer evil with good.

The translation of this verse is not difficult, though it may be necessary in some languages to fill out certain elliptical elements—for example, "conquer what is evil by doing what is good." This verse is best taken as a summary statement of what Paul has said in verses 17-20.

CHAPTER 13

Duties toward the State Authorities

13 Everyone must obey the state authorities, because no authority exists
without God's permission, and the existing authorities have been put
there by God. [2]Whoever opposes the existing authority opposes what God has
ordered; and anyone who does so will bring judgment on himself. [3]For rulers
are not to be feared by those who do good but by those who do evil. Would
you like to be unafraid of the man in authority? Then do what is good, and
he will praise you. [4]For he is God's servant working for your own good. But
if you do evil, be afraid of him, because his power to punish is real. He is God's
servant and carries out God's wrath on those who do evil. [5]For this reason you
must obey the authorities—not just because of God's wrath, but also as a
matter of conscience.

[6]This is also the reason that you pay taxes, because the authorities are
working for God when they fulfill their duties. [7]Pay, then, what you owe them;
pay them your personal and property taxes, and show respect and honor for
them all.

The section heading Duties toward the State Authorities may be translated as "How One Should Act toward the State Authorities" or "One Should Obey Those Who Rule."

In the Greek there is no transition indicated between this chapter and the previous one. Paul moves directly from a discussion of Christian responsibilities in general to the matter of the specific responsibility of the Christian toward government authorities.

13.1 Everyone must obey the state authorities, because no authority exists without God's permission, and the existing authorities have been put there by God.

Everyone translates a Semitic idiom (literally "every soul"). Paul's viewpoint in these verses expresses the normal Jewish attitude toward government. State authorities (Phillips "civil authorities"; Moffatt "government authorities"; RSV "governing authorities") is more literally rendered by Goodspeed and the NAB as "the authorities that are over him" (see NEB "supreme authorities"). Recently some interpreters have taken authorities to indicate the invisible angelic powers that lie behind the visible state powers. It is true that the word is used elsewhere by Paul in such a sense, but his attitude toward angelic authorities elsewhere intimates that he understands these powers to be more nearly demonic than working for good. Historically, scholars have understood this phrase as a reference to the state authorities of Paul's day (specifically, the Roman government), and there is no valid reason for departing from this viewpoint.

Obligation as expressed by everyone must obey may be more naturally expressed as an imperative in some languages---for example, "all of you should obey" or "all of you obey."

In many languages the state authorities are simply "the rulers," "those that have the power," or as in some languages, idiomatically, "those who have their hands on the stick."

Without God's permission (literally "except by God"; RSV "except from God") is rendered by Goodspeed as "without the permission of God." The second clause of verse 1 may be translated as "no one has power to rule unless God permits him to have it" or "only if God permits a person to rule does he have such power."

The last clause in this verse, the existing authorities..., though translated in a variety of ways, has essentially the same meaning in all modern translations. In some languages this clause may be translated as "if there is a ruler, then God is the one who has made him such," "only God has given power to those who rule," or "those who have power rule because God has made it so."

13.2 Whoever opposes the existing authority opposes what God has ordered; and anyone who does so will bring judgment on himself.

In Greek this verse begins with a particle meaning "so that" (Goodspeed), and this appears in the NEB as "consequently" (NAB "as a consequence") and in the RSV as "therefore." The force of the particle is to introduce a conclusion based on the judgment in the previous verse. However, it is not always necessary to have a transitional particle such as "then" or "hence." The fact that verse 2 is a conclusion to verse 1 is evident from the content itself. Note that there is no particle in the TEV rendering.

What God has ordered (RSV "what God has appointed") renders a noun phrase in Greek ("the thing ordered by God"). Ordered may be rendered in some languages as "put there," "arranged," or "established." It is important to avoid a term which would suggest "command" in the sense of a verbal order.

Anyone who does so is plural in Greek ("those who resist"), but in English discourse structure it is more natural to employ a singular after anyone, whoever, or everyone (v. 1).

Will bring judgment on himself is naturally taken as a reference to God's judgment (see the similar expression in Mark 12.40 and James 3.1); however, this may be a reference either to God's judgment as exercised by the government authorities or to the final exercise of God's judgment at the last day. In the present context the first of these possibilities seems more probable. Accordingly, an equivalent expression may be "will cause the ruler to condemn him," "will cause his own condemnation," or "will cause himself to be punished."

13.3 For rulers are not to be feared by those who do good but by those who do evil. Would you like to be unafraid of the man in authority? Then do what is good, and he will praise you.

By those who do good but by those who do evil represents an abstract noun construction in Greek (literally "not...to good work but to evil"). The reference is to good conduct as opposed to bad conduct (see RSV and NEB), and the TEV expresses this idea of conduct by verb phrases rather than by noun phrases. This first sentence in verse 3 may be expressed in some languages as "For those who do good have no need to be afraid of rulers; only those who do evil must be afraid of rulers."

The man in authority (RSV "him who is in authority") may more literally be rendered as "the authority" (see NEB "of the authorities"); but generally it is better to render this by reference to the one in authority rather than to employ an abstract expression.

The question and response in the second and third sentences of verse 3 can be more idiomatically expressed in some languages as condition and result—for example, "If you would like to be unafraid of those in authority, then do what is good, and those in authority will praise you." As in so many contexts, it may be necessary to use plural expressions rather than singular ones in order to indicate the general nature of such circumstances and relations.

He will praise you is literally "you will have praise from it" (that is, from the authority), and is rendered "you will receive his approval" (RSV) or "you will have their approval" (NEB). The exegetical grounds for rendering the abstract noun "authority" by the man in authority...he is found in the following verse, where this abstract expression is made concrete in the phrase he is God's servant.

13.4 For he is God's servant working for your own good. But if you do evil, be afraid of him, because his power to punish is real. He is God's servant and carries out God's wrath on those who do evil.

For he is God's servant working for your own good is literally "for he is God's servant to you for good" (see KJV). The NEB has essentially the same meaning, except for the use of the plural in place of the singular ("they are God's agents working for your good"; see also Goodspeed). The NAB has "the ruler is God's servant to work for your good"; while the JB states this same meaning in different words: "the state is there to serve God for your benefit." In some instances the most convenient way of translating for your own good may be "in order to help you" or "in order to cause good for you."

His power to punish is real translates a metaphor which is maintained by most translations: "for he does not bear the sword in vain" (RSV). In this verse "the sword" is a symbol of the government official's power to punish, and the adverb "in vain" must be taken with the meaning of "without the power to use it." However, it is doubtful that most readers will see this meaning in the metaphor, and so it is perhaps better either to employ a nonmetaphor or to look for an equivalent figure of speech in the receptor language. The Greek expression "for he does not bear the sword in vain" is rendered in some languages as "it is not for nothing that he has that power." In other languages one may have "he has that power and he uses it" or "he is able to punish and he does." In this way one may indicate clearly that the power is real.

God's wrath is literally "his wrath," but the reference is clearly to God's wrath, and many translations make this fact explicit (JB "they carry out God's revenge"; Moffatt "for the infliction of divine vengeance"; Phillips "to inflict God's punishment"). It is not always easy to render adequately the idea of carrying out God's purpose (or wrath) in inflicting punishment. In some languages this may be equivalent to "may act as God's messengers in causing people who do evil to suffer," or "on God's behalf they judge people and cause those who do evil to suffer." It is normally important to indicate in such contexts as these that punishment is related to official judgment and not to personal revenge or violent retaliation.

13.5 For this reason you must obey the authorities—not just because of God's wrath, but also as a matter of conscience.

For this reason refers back to the grounds of obedience given in the previous verse. God's wrath (see also RSV, Goodspeed, Moffatt) is literally "the wrath," but in light of verse 4 (and in light of the way in which Paul uses the word "wrath" elsewhere in this letter) it is better to take this as a specific reference to God's wrath. However, the NEB appears to try to avoid this conclusion and to make the word refer to the retribution imposed by the authorities. In a sense both of these translations are legitimate. Christians are encouraged to obey the civil authorities so that they will not be punished by them, but Paul definitely looks upon the punishment handed out by the civil authorities as God's wrath on people who do evil. This seems to be the primary focus in the present passage.

In the first part of this verse the authorities is supplied by the TEV as the understood object of the verb obey (Goodspeed "obey them"); most translations do not supply an object to the verb. For Paul the Christian is obligated to obey the civil authorities, not only out of the fear of punishment but for the sake of his conscience towards God. But also as a matter of conscience is rendered in some languages as "but because your heart also tells you to" or "because in your heart you know it is what you should do."

13.6 This is also the reason that you pay taxes, because the authorities are working for God when they fulfill their duties.

This is also the reason is taken by most commentaries as a reference back to the matter of conscience.

That you pay taxes is taken by most commentators and translators as an indicative, though the form may be imperative (see JB "the reason why you must pay taxes" and Phillips "it is right, too, for you to pay taxes"—these seem to be the only translations that interpret this as an imperative).

The authorities is literally "they" in the Greek text but a number of translations make this pronominal reference explicit (see RSV, Phillips, Moffatt, NEB).

Working for God is literally "servants of God." Originally the word "servants" was used of government officials, but later it was used in a wider sense, including priests (see Hebrews 8.2) and servants in general (see 15.16; Philippians 2.25). Most translators prefer to maintain the noun phrase here rather than to transform it into a verb phrase as is done in the TEV.

When they fulfill their duties is literally "as they are constantly giving attention to this very thing." "This very thing" has reference to what precedes (that is, to the general responsibility of rewarding the good and of punishing the evil) and not to what follows (JB "they serve God by collecting taxes"). It is better to render this phrase in a more general way, as most translations do (see NEB "and to these duties they devote their energies"; Goodspeed "devoting themselves to this service"), or to make explicit the reference to what precedes (Phillips "for the good purposes of public order and well-being"). It is advisable not to follow the JB at this place. In some languages this final clause of verse 6 is translated as "when they do their work" or "when they do what they should do."

13.7 Pay, then, what you owe them; pay them your personal and property taxes, and show respect and honor for them all.

It is difficult to know what distinction Paul makes between the two words that he uses for taxes in this verse. Traditionally, the first word is taken to refer to those taxes paid by a subject nation to a nation that ruled over it (see Luke 20.22), while the second word is a more general term, referring to the taxes paid in support of a government (see Matthew 17.25). Some suggest that the first word refers to direct taxes and the second to taxes paid indirectly, but it is doubtful that Paul makes any real distinction. For this reason it is best to select general terms that cover wide areas of meaning. The TEV renders these terms as personal and property taxes, the NEB as "tax and toll," and the JB as "direct tax or indirect." An appropriate equivalent may be "the various kinds of taxes," "the different kinds of taxes," or "whatever kind of taxes there are." The expression for taxes may be closely related to the first clause—for example, "whatever taxes are assessed against you, pay them."

By rendering the last part of this verse literally, many translations intimate that Paul is speaking of two different classes of persons, one to whom respect is due and another to whom honor is due (see, for example, RSV "respect to whom respect is due, honor to whom honor is due"). The style of this sentence in Greek reflects certain special rhetorical features, and to translate it literally may result in a misleading expression. The TEV takes this verse specifically in the context of giving what is due to government officials, whether it be honor or money. Most translations, however, make this verse into a general maxim. See, for example, the NEB: "discharge your obligations to all men; pay tax and toll, reverence and respect, to those to whom they are due." In a number of languages respect and honor must be coalesced into a single expression: "show complete respect to all authorities." In the Greek text the use of the two terms is primarily a means of emphasis, not a technique for making distinctions. The manner in which one shows respect may be expressed quite differently depending upon cultural practices and attitudes—for example, "stoop before," "crouch beneath the seat of," or "sit on the heels before." In some languages one may employ direct discourse: "say to them, You are great."

Duties toward One Another

[8]Be in debt to no one—the only debt you should have is to love one another. Whoever loves his fellow-man has obeyed the Law. [9]The commandments, "Do not commit adultery; do not murder; do not steal; do not covet"—all these, and any others besides, are summed up in the one command, "Love your fellow-man as yourself." [10]Whoever loves his fellow-man will never do him wrong. To love, then, is to obey the whole Law.

Duties toward One Another may be translated as "How People Should Live toward One Another," "How People Should Deal with One Another," or "People Should Love One Another."

Some interpreters see no formal connection between these three verses 8-10 and verses 1-7. For that reason, many look upon these verses as the conclusion to the discussion of the Christian life begun in chapter 12. However, the verb with which verse 8 begins, be in debt, comes from the root of the word used at the beginning of verse 7, what you owe them, and so others look upon these verses as a conclusion to the discussion in verses 1-7.

13.8 Be in debt to no one---the only debt you should have is to love one another. Whoever loves his fellow-man has obeyed the Law.

Be in debt to no one is a very emphatic expression in the Greek text, and its most immediate meaning may be understood to be "Do not be under financial obligations to anyone." It may also be understood in a somewhat broader sense: "Do not be under obligation to anyone." The fact that the second clause refers to a debt of love may suggest that the first clause should also be understood in this broader sense. On the other hand, one may reason that the first clause is to be understood strictly in the sense of financial obligation, while the second clause introduces the broader implications of indebtedness. It may be difficult to combine the concept of financial obligation and the concept of general obligation to love one another. Therefore the second clause may be translated in some instances as "there is only one thing which you must do, and that is to love one another."

One serious exegetical problem in this verse relates to the interpretation of the word translated Law. The TEV (so also Goodspeed and Phillips) takes this as an explicit reference to the Jewish Law, while others understand this as a reference to law in general (see note in JB). In view of the fact that Paul quotes specific commands from the Old Testament in the following verses, it seems better to take it as a reference to the Mosaic Law.

Obeyed (many translations have "fulfilled") is a difficult word to render; the NEB translates as "has satisfied every claim of the law," Goodspeed "has fully satisfied the Law," and the JB "you have carried out your obligations." If the reference is taken to the Mosaic Law, then the idea of obedience seems nearer to the meaning of this term (see Phillips "has obeyed the whole Law").

Fellow-man is literally "the other," a term which is rendered "neighbor" by many translators. The meaning of the word is not "neighbor" in the sense of one who lives nearby, but must be taken in the broadest possible sense, as including all people.

13.9 The commandments, "Do not commit adultery; do not murder; do not steal; do not covet"—all these, and any others besides, are summed up in the one command, "Love your fellow-man as yourself."

The commandments (RSV, NEB, JB, Goodspeed) is literally "for the" (KJV "for this"). This may seem a strange way to begin a sentence, but in Greek this is a normal use of the neuter article "the"; the article may be used in a summary way to refer to a series that follows. In the present passage the series is a list of commandments; in the TEV this information is made explicit for the English reader. The commandments quoted come from Exodus 20.13-15, 17 and the parallels in Deuteronomy 5.17-19, 21.

All these, and any others besides may simply be rendered as "all these commands and all of the other commands" or "all commands, whether these or others."

Are summed up in the one command may be rendered as "are equal to just one command," "are no more than just one command," or "mean just one command."

Love your fellow-man as yourself is a quotation from Leviticus 19.18. The importance of the one command to love is observed by the fact that it is quoted in the New Testament in several places: Matthew 5.43; 19.19; 22.39; Mark 12.31; Luke 10.27; Galatians 5.14; James 2.8. The fact that this command, love your fellow-man as yourself, is in the singular may be quite confusing in some languages. In fact, readers may respond by asking "Which fellow-man?" or "Which neighbor?" It is necessary, therefore, in order to make the statement generally applicable, to employ a plural: "you should love all other people just as you love yourselves" or, in some languages, "each one of you should love his neighbors as he loves himself." In every instance it is any and all fellow human beings, not merely a single neighbor, who must be loved.

13.10 Whoever loves his fellow-man will never do him wrong. To love, then, is to obey the whole Law.

In Greek the first part of this verse is stated in the abstract (literally "love does not do wrong to the fellow-man"), but it is removed from the abstract by the TEV. It is obvious that "love" refers to "the person who loves," and so the TEV makes this specific: Whoever loves his fellow-man will never do him wrong.

The last part of this verse literally reads "love is the fulfilling of the Law." As in verse 8, the TEV here takes "fulfilling" in the sense of "obeying" and the Law as a reference to the Jewish Law. The nouns "love" and "fulfilling" are rendered as infinitives: to love and to obey. The relations between to love and to obey may be variously expressed as means-result and condition-result—for example, "By loving one's neighbors, one obeys the whole Law" or "If one loves one's neighbors, one obeys the whole Law."

[11]You must do this, because you know what hour it is: the time has come for you to wake up from your sleep. For the moment when we will be saved is closer now than it was when we first believed. [12]The night is nearly over, day is almost here. Let us stop doing the things that belong to the dark, and take up the weapons for fighting in the light. [13]Let us conduct ourselves properly, as people who live in the light of day; no orgies or drunkenness, no immorality or indecency, no fighting or jealousy. [14]But take up the weapons of the Lord Jesus Christ, and stop giving attention to your sinful nature, to satisfy its desires.

These verses serve as a conclusion, not only to the immediate discussion of Christian love, but to the entire section beginning at 12.1. All of the exhortations that Paul gives to the Christian life are offered within the context of an eschatological setting.

13.11 You must do this, because you know what hour it is: the time has come for you to wake up from your sleep. For the moment when we will be saved is closer now than it was when we first believed.

You must do this is literally "and this." The force of these two words is to tie Paul's conclusion (vv. 11-14) to what he has previously said. This relation may be expressed in a number of ways. The NAB ("take care to do all these things") and Phillips ("why all this stress on behavior?") go essentially the same route as the TEV, while many other translations merely use a particle or a few particles (RSV "besides this"; NEB "in all this"; JB "besides"; Goodspeed "all this especially"). Moffatt takes "this" as a modifier of the word rendered hour by the TEV and so translates "and then you know what this Crisis means." However, both the grammar and the context indicate that "this" is better taken as a reference to what precedes than to what follows.

The word here rendered hour (used by Paul elsewhere in 3.26; 1 Corinthians 4.5; 7.29) may be a difficult term to translate. Basically the meaning is that of "time," not time as a chronological sequence but as something having a special significance. Goodspeed translates this word by "this critical time" and Moffatt by "Crisis." The NEB renders the entire phrase as "in all this, remember how critical the moment is." The JB has "besides, you know 'the time' has come," with a long note explaining the meaning of "the time." In English the word hour (so TEV and RSV) seems to come nearest to expressing Paul's meaning and eliminates the need for a long theological note. In some languages, however, the word "day" comes closer to expressing "critical time"---for example, "you must do this for you know this is the very day." One must not assume that in such receptor languages "day" is taken any more literally than hour is in English.

In Greek verse 11 is all one sentence and the last part is "for now our salvation is nearer than when we believed." The verb "believed" is an aorist tense and must be taken as a reference to the time in the past when the Roman Christians first became believers. For this reason the verb is best translated when we first believed (see also RSV, NEB, Moffatt, Goodspeed). It is better to maintain the idea of "to believe" than to introduce a non-Pauline expression such as "than it was when we were converted." If an object of the verb is demanded in the receptor language, then "Jesus Christ" is best supplied; one must avoid using a post-Pauline expression such as "than when we first accepted the faith."

Once again a noun, "our salvation," is transformed by the TEV into a verb phrase, the moment when we will be saved. If the passive expression we will be saved must be changed into an active one, then God is the agent: "when God will save us."

In a number of languages the most appropriate general expression for time would not be moment but "day"; hence, "the day when God will save us is now closer than it was when we first believed in Jesus Christ."

3.12 The night is nearly over, day is almost here. Let us stop doing the things that belong to the dark, and take up the weapons for fighting in the light.

As is often done in biblical language, the present evil age is spoken of as night while the time of God's salvation is spoken of as day. However, the metaphor of contrast between night and day is not universal. It may be advisable to change the metaphor to a simile—for example, "it is as though the night were almost over, and the day about to begin" or "it is as though the night was getting light and the day was almost to come."

The change from night to day demands a change in one's way of life. Let us stop doing the things that belong to the dark is literally "let us put off the works of darkness." The verb is aorist and has the force of initiating an action which is not yet begun; therefore, let us stop.... "The works of darkness" means "the things that one does in the darkness." Paul mixes his figures of speech here by speaking of actions as clothing worn at night that one must take off so that he can put on the clothing appropriate for the daytime. Since these mixed metaphors are difficult for the reader to grasp, the TEV translates them as a single metaphor by changing "let us put off" to let us stop doing.

A form of admonition, introduced by let in English, must often be translated as a form of obligation in other languages—for example, "we must stop doing the things that belong to the dark." However, it is not always easy to put across the idea of "the things that belong to the dark." It may, in fact, be necessary to expand somewhat this expression so as to make the reference clear: "the things that people normally do in the darkness of night" or "those evil things which people do in the darkness."

Similar observations may be made with regard to the last part of this sentence. Take up the weapons for fighting in the light is literally "put on (that is, dress ourselves in) the weapons of the light." The verb here is also aorist and has the same force as the previous verb. It is easy to see why "the weapons of the light" is translated as weapons for fighting in the light.

It is not always easy for readers to comprehend exactly what is the significance of the weapons for fighting in the light. Some translators would prefer to use a more neutral expression such as "those things of the light," but the fact is that Paul in several passages uses terms for weapons and frequently employs the analogy of fighting and conflict. Therefore, it is probably more satisfactory to use the expression weapons both here and in verse 14 and to provide a satisfactory series of cross references so that the reader may understand the broader implications of what Paul is trying to say. One can always suggest that this metaphor must be understood in a purely figurative sense by introducing a phrase such as "as it were" or "as it seems"—for example, "we must take up, as it were, the weapons which are used in the light" or "... in the daytime."

13.13 Let us conduct ourselves properly, as people who live in the light of day; no orgies or drunkenness, no immorality or indecency, no fighting or jealousy.

The order of elements within this verse is rearranged by the TEV and certain elements made explicit. Let us conduct ourselves properly (literally "let us walk properly") comes as the second element in the Greek sentence. The NEB handles this clause similarly: "Let us behave with decency as befits the day." "To walk" is a Semitic expression meaning "to live one's life," and since this verb is also aorist, as are the verbs in the preceding sentence, it may also have the force of "let us begin to conduct ourselves properly." In some languages this may be equivalent to "we must begin to live as we should" or "we must begin to behave as we should."

In Greek this sentence begins with an adverbial phrase (literally "as in day") which the TEV understands in the sense of as people who live in the light of day. Since the contrast between light and darkness may not be clear in some languages, it may be possible to say "as people who live in the light and not in the darkness." The contrast with darkness is designed to highlight the moral implications in this context which might be lost by an expression "who live in the light of day."

It is difficult to distinguish in meaning between the Greek words translated orgies and drunkenness. If any distinction in meaning is to be sought, the first denotes both heavy drinking and sexual immorality, while the second relates more strictly to drunkenness. The word rendered orgies is used elsewhere in the New Testament only in Galatians 5.21 and 1 Peter 4.3, while the word rendered drunkenness occurs elsewhere only in Luke 21.34 and Galatians 5.21. Because these terms are essentially synonymous, the real meaning of this type of combination is "all kinds of orgies" or, as in some languages, "all kinds of drunkenness."

The word translated immorality appears elsewhere in the New Testament in a very different sense, but there is no doubt as to its meaning in the present passage. The word rendered indecency occurs more frequently in the New Testament than the one translated immorality, but again these are basically synonymous terms. The word rendered indecency occurs elsewhere in Mark 7.22; 2 Corinthians 12.21; Galatians 5.19; Ephesians 4.19; 1 Peter 4.3; 2 Peter 2.7. In translating this word one may also employ a phrase which will emphasize the wide range of meaning—for example, "all kinds of immorality."

Fighting translates the same word that Paul used in 1.29, while jealousy translates the same word that was used in 10.2 in the phrase "they have a zeal" (TEV they are deeply devoted). The original meaning of the word rendered jealousy was "zeal," but when used with evil connotations the meaning becomes "jealousy" or "envy."

The negative prohibitions in the second part of verse 13 may be expressed as imperatives—for example, "You must not engage in all kinds of drunkenness and immorality; you should not strive with one another and be jealous with one another."

13.14 But take up the weapons of the Lord Jesus Christ, and stop giving attention to your sinful nature, to satisfy its desires.

Take up the weapons of translates the same verb rendered take up in verse 12; the verb actually means "to dress one's self in" (see RSV "but put on the Lord Jesus Christ"). Translating this verb with the meaning of "to take up the weapons of" is arrived at by taking the verb in its extended sense "to put on (armor)." Both the NEB ("let Christ Jesus himself be the armour that you wear") and the JB ("let your armour be the Lord Jesus Christ") follow the same exegesis. Note that in the interpretations of NEB and JB the armor is the Lord Jesus Christ. These are not the weapons which the Lord Jesus Christ gives or which come from him. If weapons is to be understood as armor, it may be possible in some languages to render this word as "defense"—for example, "let the Lord Jesus Christ defend you" or "...be your defense."

Stop giving attention to translates a present imperative, which often has the force of "to stop doing" the action indicated by the verb. The NEB ("give no more thought to") understands the present imperative to have this same force.

Sinful nature is literally "the flesh." Many translations render this term literally, while others limit the word "flesh" to "the bodily appetites" (NEB; see also JB and Goodspeed). It seems better not to understand "flesh" in this limited sense but in the broader meaning of one's nature which rebels against God, that is, one's sinful nature, or, as in some languages, "one's sinful heart," "one's heart which prompts one to sin," or "...which leads one to sin." On the use of the word "flesh" in this sense see 7.5.

To satisfy its desires may be rendered as "to do what your heart wants you to do" or even "to do what you yourselves want to do."

CHAPTER 14

Do Not Judge Your Brother

14 Accept among you the man who is weak in the faith, but do not argue
with him about his personal opinions. [2]One man's faith allows him to
eat anything, but the man who is weak in the faith eats only vegetables. [3]The
man who will eat anything is not to despise the man who doesn't; while the
one who eats only vegetables is not to pass judgment on the one who eats
anything, because God has accepted him. [4]Who are you to judge the servant
of someone else? It is his own Master who will decide whether he succeeds or
fails. And he will succeed, because the Lord is able to make him succeed.

The section heading Do Not Judge Your Brother may require two modifications. First, it may be necessary to employ a term which implies primarily "condemnation" or "judge wrong," and second, Your Brother must often be changed into "Fellow Christians," "Other Christians," or "Those Who Are Also Christians." It is often essential to use the plural in order to make this section apply to any fellow believer rather than merely to one individual, such as would be the case in some languages if Your Brother is translated as a singular.

As already pointed out (pages 232 f), the section of Romans beginning with 14.1 and ending with 15.13 deals with the relationship between those who are "weak in the faith" and those who are "strong in the faith." Many commentators assume that whereas chapters 12 and 13 deal with exhortations to Christian living in general, the present section relates to a specific problem that Paul knew about within the Roman church. But that is not a necessary conclusion, although such a thing is possible. Paul is in Corinth at the time that he writes this letter to the Romans. It may be that he recognizes the existence of a problem in the church at Corinth and deals with it in this letter on the assumption that the same problem exists in Rome also. In any case, nothing is known about these groups ("the weak in the faith" and "the strong in the faith") other than what Paul mentions in the letter itself.

14.1 Accept among you the man who is weak in the faith, but do not argue with him about his personal opinions.

Accept among you (NEB "accept"; Goodspeed "treat... like brothers") is rendered "welcome" by most translations (NAB "extend a kind welcome to"). Paul means that the weak brother must be accepted and made to feel welcome as a member of the Christian community. The same word is used in verse 3, because God has accepted him.

The man who is weak in the faith is the emphatic element in the Greek sentence. From what follows we learn three things about this man: (1) he is a vegetarian (vv. 2, 21); (2) he considers certain days to have special importance (vv. 5-6); and (3) he does not drink wine (v. 21). In choosing a term for weak it is essential to avoid an expression which will indicate only "physical weakness." In some languages it is necessary to employ a negative expression such as "not strong," since this is more likely to convey some element of failure in faith. Other languages may employ an equivalent, though different, term for weak—for example, "those who are soft in their faith." In certain cases it may be necessary to shift the arrangement of semantic components—for example, "people whose faith is weak" or "people whose faith does not stand firm."

But do not argue with him about his personal opinions translates a noun phrase (literally "not for arguments of doubt"). Most translations render this phrase in essentially the same way as the TEV (see Goodspeed, Moffatt, Phillips), while the NEB ("without attempting to settle doubtful points") and the JB ("without starting an argument") appear to understand it in a more general sense. In some instances one may use a translation such as "do not argue with him about what he should or should not do" or "do not argue with him about what he himself should do."

14.2 One man's faith allows him to eat anything, but the man who is weak in the faith eats only vegetables.

On the basis of the previous verse the TEV makes explicit the nature of the man's weakness: he is weak in the faith (also NAB "one who is weak in faith"), though the Greek literally reads "the man who is weak."

In a number of languages the most succinct and meaningful way of saying eats only vegetables is to translate "does not eat meat of any kind."

14.3 The man who will eat anything is not to despise the man who doesn't; while the one who eats only vegetables is not to pass judgment on the one who eats anything, because God has accepted him.

In Greek the verb eat does not have an object (see RSV "let not him who eats"), but the TEV supplies anything as the object (so also Goodspeed and NAB). In the context the contrast is apparently between the person who eats meat and the person who does not, and both Phillips ("the meat eater should not despise the vegetarian") and the JB ("meat-eaters must not despise the scrupulous") make this information explicit.

The word translated despise is a very strong term and means "to count as nothing." Once again Paul reminds his readers, though indirectly, that God's acceptance of a person is based on his own grace and not on what a person does or does not do. For this reason all believers are obligated to accept one another, regardless of their differences of opinion over certain matters. Languages differ considerably in the way in which they express the concept of despise—for example, "look down upon," "say, You are nothing," "are proud against," or "consider one's self far better than."

Pass judgment on may be rendered as "condemn" or "say, You are doing wrong."

In the last clause of verse 3, because God has accepted him, it is important to indicate that the pronoun refers to the one who eats anything.

In translating anything one should avoid a term which implies "everything" in the sense that "he eats too much" or "he eats everything that is available." To avoid this interpretation it is necessary in some languages to employ a double negative—for example, "there is nothing which he does not eat" or "there is nothing which he is unwilling to eat."

14.4 Who are you to judge the servant of someone else? It is his own Master who will decide whether he succeeds or fails. And he will succeed, because the Lord is able to make him succeed.

The commentators point out that in this verse Paul is addressing the man who is weak in faith, but what he says also has application to the man who is strong in faith. Paul uses an analogy from the laws of slavery of his day, according to which the slave owner had absolute rights over his slave, and no one had the right to command another person's slave.

It may be necessary in translating judge to employ a phrase such as "to decide whether the servant of someone else has done right or wrong." However, within this context one may employ a word for judge which primarily signifies "condemn," since this is obviously the inference of the context.

The rhetorical question at the beginning of verse 4 may be changed into a statement: "You should not judge someone else's servant." On the other hand, judgment may be expressed in some languages by quite a different type of expression—for example, "to measure a person."

Succeeds or fails (so also Goodspeed) is literally "stands or falls." What is meant is that the slave owner is the one who determines whether the slave's service is satisfactory or unsatisfactory (see Phillips "it is to his own master that he gives, or fails to give, satisfactory service"). Succeeds or fails may be rendered in some languages as "has done well or not," "has done what he should or not," or "is approved or not."

The word translated servant technically refers to a house slave or a domestic servant and appears elsewhere in Luke 16.13; Acts 10.7; and 1 Peter 2.18. If the receptor language distinguishes between servant and "slave," then servant is the nearer equivalent. It is doubtful that any further distinction should be sought in this term.

He will succeed translates a verb that may be taken as passive (RSV "he will be upheld"; so KJV), but most translations understand it to have an active force as in the TEV. This same verb form appears in Matthew 12.25, where it is given an active force by the RSV ("no city or house divided against itself will stand"). If the verb is taken to be active, Paul is saying "he will stand" (TEV he will succeed), but if the verb is passive, then Paul is saying "God will enable him to stand."

[5]One man thinks that a certain day is more important than the others, while another man thinks that all days are the same. Each one should have his own mind firmly made up. [6]Whoever thinks highly of a certain day does it in honor of the Lord; whoever eats anything does it in honor of the Lord, because he gives thanks to God for the food. Whoever refuses to eat certain things does so in honor of the Lord, and he gives thanks to God. [7]None of us lives for himself only, none of us dies for himself only; [8]if we live, it is for the Lord that we live, and if we die, it is for the Lord that we die. Whether we live or die,

then, we belong to the Lord. [9]For Christ died and rose to life in order to be
the Lord of the living and of the dead. [10]You, then—why do you pass judgment
on your brother? And you—why do you despise your brother? All of us will
stand before God, to be judged by him. [11]For the scripture says,
"As I live, says the Lord,
everyone will kneel before me,
and everyone will confess that I am God."
[12]Every one of us, then, will have to give an account of himself to God.

Most translators and commentators take verses 1-12 as a unit and generally divide it into two paragraphs, though they differ as to where to make the paragraph division. The TEV and the RSV begin a new paragraph at verse 5. The NEB does likewise but has another new paragraph beginning at verse 7. Moffatt, Goodspeed, and the JB make verses 1-12 into a single paragraph. The NAB makes verses 1-11 into a single paragraph and has the next paragraph begin at verse 12.

14.5 One man thinks that a certain day is more important than the others, while another man thinks that all days are the same. Each one should have his own mind firmly made up.

The structure of this verse is similar to that of verse 2; in both verses Paul contrasts the attitude of the man who is weak in faith with the attitude of the man who is strong in faith. In verse 3 Paul referred first to the man who is strong in faith; in verse 5 he refers first to the man who is weak in faith.

Since more than one individual is involved in thinking that one day is more important than another, it is often necessary, instead of one man thinks... to translate "Some people think that a certain day is more important than other days, while other people think that all days have the same value."

It is impossible to state definitely what days Paul has in mind. He may be referring to the tendency of the Jewish Christians to continue to observe the Sabbath day, but it is also possible that he is referring to special days which other groups felt must be observed for religious purposes. For similar passages see Galatians 4.10 and Colossians 2.16.

Although the sense of the last sentence of verse 5, each one should have his own mind firmly made up, is quite evident, it is not always easy to translate such an expression into another language. In some instances this may be done as "each one should be convinced that what he thinks is right," "each one should be sure as to why he thinks as he does," or "each one should be able to say to himself, This is surely what it should be."

14.6 Whoever thinks highly of a certain day does it in honor of the Lord; whoever eats anything does it in honor of the Lord, because he gives thanks to God for the food. Whoever refuses to eat certain things does so in honor of the Lord, and he gives thanks to God.

The expression whoever...does it in honor of the Lord may require some verb of intention—for example, "whoever...does this because he wants to honor the Lord," "whoever...does this in order to show honor to the Lord," or, idiomatically in some languages, "whoever...does this because he desires to lift up the Lord's greatness to all."

Although it is difficult to determine the precise background against which Paul is speaking, as far as translation is concerned this verse is not difficult. The TEV supplies anything as the object of the verb eat; the NEB and JB supply "meat." And the TEV also makes explicit the basis for his thanks to God, namely, for the food.

The two occurrences of the expression he gives thanks to God are introduced in Greek by two different conjunctions. In the first instance, the conjunction gar, which is often translated as "for," and the second case the conjunction kai, normally translated "and." However, gar frequently does not introduce cause but simply suggests another element which needs to be considered. It may, therefore, be more appropriate in most languages to introduce both expressions of giving thanks by the conjunction "and."

14.7-8 None of us lives for himself only, none of us dies for himself only; (8) if we live, it is for the Lord that we live, and if we die, it is for the Lord that we die. Whether we live or die, then, we belong to the Lord.

For himself is rendered "to himself" by some translators. The form is a dative in Greek and so may be translated in either way; but the translator should be conscious of the implications of the two renderings. If one translates "to himself," the implication is that Paul is saying that the believer affects others by his actions (see JB "the life and death of each of us has its influence on others"; Phillips "the truth is that we neither live nor die as self-contained units"). But this seems not to be the emphasis that Paul is making in this verse. The verse must be understood in light of what Paul is saying in verse 8, where he affirms that we do not live in relation to ourselves only but rather in relation to God (see NAB "none of us lives as his own master and none of us dies as his own master").

None of us lives for himself only, none of us dies for himself only states an ideal situation, since the situations are immediately expressed as conditional clauses with if in verse 8, namely, if we live and if we die. Something which is thus potential rather than actual must be expressed in some languages in a modal form indicating an ideal potentiality—for example, "no one of us should live for himself only" or "...just for himself." Since, however, "dying" is a single event rather than an extended process such as "living," and since "dying" is also a future contingency, it may be necessary to change the second clause of verse 7 and say: "if anyone of us dies, he does not die just for himself."

The phrase for the Lord may be rendered simply as benefactive in some languages. In other instances a more explicit relationship must be expressed—for example, "we live in order to honor the Lord" or "we live in order that men may praise the Lord." Similar expressions may be used in speaking about dying in verse 8.

A literal translation of verses 7 and 8, based on the exegesis of "no one lives to himself alone and no one dies to himself alone," is employed widely in some parts of Africa as a confirmation of the efficacy of black magic. That is to say, death is in no sense natural but always brought on by someone else's evil intent. The possibility of this type of interpretation should be carefully avoided.

14.9 For Christ died and rose to life in order to be the Lord of the living and of the dead.

This verse forms a unit along with the two previous verses; it gives the reason why the believers cannot live for themselves but must live for the Lord. He who is Lord both of the living and of the dead must be acknowledged as the Lord of the different groups within the church at Rome. It may not be easy to render a phrase such as the Lord of the living and of the dead. In fact, in some languages this must be rather radically recast—for example, "the one whom both the living and the dead acknowledge as Lord" or "the one whom those who are alive and those who have died say is Lord."

14.10 You, then—why do you pass judgment on your brother? And you—why do you despise your brother? All of us will stand before God, to be judged by him.

As is clearly indicated in the TEV, the words you, then in the first sentence and the words and you in the second sentence are emphatic in the Greek sentence structure. However, the two occurrences of you must be recognized as not necessarily representing the same persons. Accordingly, in some languages one must translate: "Then why do some of you pass judgment on your fellow Christians, and why do others of you despise your fellow Christians?" Pass judgment and despise naturally refer back to the contrast described in verse 3. These questions can be readily transformed into statements: "none of you should pass judgment on your fellow believers, and none of you should despise your fellow believers."

The last part of this verse reads literally "for we shall all stand before the judgment seat of God." The purpose of this standing is clearly that we might be judged by him, and the TEV makes this information explicit (see also Phillips "we shall all be judged one day...by the judgment of God").

14.11 For the scripture says,

"As I live, says the Lord,
everyone will kneel before me,
and everyone will confess that I am God."

For the scripture says is literally "for it has been written" (see 1.17). Once again Paul reinforces his argument by an appeal to scripture; this time the verses quoted are from Isaiah 49.18 and 45.23. The first everyone is literally "every knee" and the second everyone is literally "every tongue." It was quite common for Old Testament writers to refer to one part of the body as functioning in behalf of the entire person and that is what was done here. However, for the English reader it is more natural to indicate that the person himself is doing this action rather than to employ the name for some part of his body.

As in the case of 12.19, there is a problem of a double introduction of direct discourse. There is not only the phrase for the scripture says, but also says the Lord. This may be coalesced in some languages as "for as the scripture gives the words of the Lord," "for as the Lord's words are written in the scripture," or "these are the words that have been written, The Lord says, As I live...."

As I live expresses the surety with which a promise or oath is made. In some languages the equivalent may be "as sure as I am alive, I myself guarantee that everyone will kneel before me," or "I myself can promise you that everyone will kneel before me." As I live is thus to be interpreted as an exceedingly strong affirmation.

An expression such as to kneel does not necessarily communicate the idea of worship or homage. A more satisfactory expression in some languages is "to bow before," "to prostrate one's self before," or even, as in some languages, "to squat before." In a number of languages the most satisfactory equivalent in this particular context is "to worship."

Confess that I am God is literally "confess to God." This phrase is used quite frequently in the Old Testament and the commentators point out that it means essentially "to give praise to God" (see RSV, NAB, Moffatt, JB). However, the content of this phrase in Old Testament contexts is often "to acknowledge that God is God" (NEB "acknowledge God"), and so the TEV translates this phrase by everyone will confess that I am God. In some languages to confess is rendered as "to declare before all" or "to say openly."

14.12 Every one of us, then, will have to give an account of himself to God.

This verse introduces a conclusion drawn on the basis of the Old Testament quotation given in the previous verse. To give an account of himself may be rendered as "to explain to God what one has done and why one has done it" or "to answer to God for what one has done."

Do Not Make Your Brother Fall

13 So then, let us stop judging one another. Instead, this is what you should
decide: not to do anything that would make your brother stumble, or fall into
sin. 14 My union with the Lord Jesus makes me know for certain that nothing
is unclean of itself; but if a man believes that something is unclean, then it
becomes unclean for him. 15 If you hurt your brother because of something you
eat, then you are no longer acting from love. Do not let the food that you eat
ruin the man for whom Christ died! 16 Do not let what you regard as good
acquire a bad name. 17 For God's Kingdom is not a matter of eating and
drinking, but of the righteousness, peace, and joy that the Holy Spirit gives.
18 And whoever serves Christ in this way wins God's pleasure and man's
approval.

14.13

One should beware of translating literally the section heading Do Not Make Your Brother Fall. A more appropriate form may be "Do Not Cause Your Fellow Christian to Sin" or "Do Not Cause Other Believers to Sin."

In the last part of this chapter (vv. 13-23) Paul continues to discuss the subject introduced in the first part, though he approaches it from a different point of view. He has already shown that the matters of differences are insignificant and that each man is in the final analysis responsible to God alone. Now he approaches the matter from the point of view of Christian love. Above all else, Christian love demands consideration for the feelings and consciences of other believers.

14.13 So then, let us stop judging one another. Instead, this is what you should decide: not to do anything that would make your brother stumble, or fall into sin.

Let us stop judging and you should decide translate two different forms of the same verb in Greek. This verb has already appeared five times in the earlier part of the chapter and has been translated in three different ways. In verses 3 and 10 it is translated pass judgment on, while in verse 4 it is translated to judge. Its use (twice) in verse 5 covers a different area of meaning and so is rendered thinks. Its first use in this verse clearly means "to judge" or "to pass judgment on"; but its use in the latter part of the verse is quite different. Whereas the first instance implies a condemnatory judgment, the second instance indicates that the persons involved are to evaluate something and to make up their minds with respect to it. For this reason the TEV renders it as decide (see JB "you should make up your mind").

Let us stop judging one another may be rendered as "we must no longer condemn one another."

The implied subject of the infinitive to do is you, and it should not be given an impersonal construction (NEB "that no obstacle or stumbling-block be placed in a brother's way").

In English it is quite effective to indicate by means of a colon that what follows is the content of what should be decided. However, this is a rather complex construction and must often be replaced in other languages by one of two different forms: (1) a directly subordinate content clause—for example, "instead you must decide to do nothing that would make your fellow believers stumble or fall into sin"; or (2) a form of direct discourse: "instead, this is what you should decide, We will not do anything that will make our fellow believers stumble or fall into sin." In some languages a translation of decide may very well be a form of speaking, "you should say to yourselves," "you should say within your minds," or "your minds should say."

The phrase into sin is introduced by the TEV to qualify what is meant by the stumbling and falling. In a number of languages expressions for stumble or fall may be readily applied to the idea of becoming involved in sin. However, in other languages these terms can only be understood in a strictly physical or literal sense. Therefore it may be necessary to eliminate this figure of speech and to employ a causative form of the verb sin—for example, "cause your fellow believer to sin."

14.14 My union with the Lord Jesus makes me know for certain that nothing is unclean of itself; but if a man believes that something is unclean, then it becomes unclean for him.

My union with the Lord Jesus makes me know for certain translates "I know and I have been persuaded in the Lord Jesus." The TEV takes "I know" and "I have been persuaded" as an instance in which two verbs with similar meanings are used to strengthen one another, and hence the translation know for certain.

In other contexts the phrase "in the Lord Jesus" (see 6.3) would normally be taken with the meaning of (in) union with the Lord Jesus. Both Goodspeed ("as a follower of the Lord Jesus") and the NEB ("as a Christian") take it in this way. However, there are some who see a different meaning in the present context. Several translations take this phrase to mean "on the authority of the Lord Jesus" (NAB; footnote in NEB; see JB "and I speak for the Lord Jesus"). Either of these interpretations is possible, though the meaning of "in union with the Lord Jesus" has stronger support on the basis of similar passages. There is little support for the exegesis reached by Phillips: "as in the presence of the Lord Christ."

My union with the Lord Jesus may be understood as cause—for example, "because I am joined with the Lord Jesus, I know for certain that nothing is unclean of itself." One may follow the lead of Goodspeed or the NEB in this type of rendering and translate as "since I am a follower of the Lord Jesus" or "since I am one who believes in the Lord Jesus."

The term unclean is used purely in a religious sense of that which defiles the worshiper; this is in keeping with the use of this term both in the Old Testament and in other New Testament passages. The translation of the remainder of this verse is not difficult, but it may be helpful to explain what is meant by then it becomes unclean for him. What Paul means is that even though something may not be wrong in itself, if a man believes it is wrong and does it, then he commits a sin against his own conscience.

The term unclean in this context refers to something which may be said to have "negative taboo." That is to say, it is excluded from everyday use because it would defile or make one impure. "Positive taboo," on the other hand, is something which is so filled with "spirit power" that it is dangerous for the uninitiated or the unconsecrated to touch or deal with. Positive taboo, for example, was associated with Mt. Sinai, the covenant box (the ark), the temple, the holy of holies, as well as the vestments and the utensils employed in Jewish ritual. It is generally not satisfactory to translate unclean merely as "dirty" or "not clean," since in most languages there is no relation whatsoever between dirt and defilement. A more satisfactory equivalent for unclean is usually an expression which means "to defile" or even "to make bad." In fact, in some languages the only satisfactory term for unclean in this particular context seems to be a word with the general meaning of "bad" or "harmful"—for example, "there is no thing which, by itself alone, is bad; but if a man believes that something is bad, then it becomes bad for him to do it." One must avoid in the use of a term for "bad" a meaning which would imply "inherently evil," and thus suggest activities which are evil irrespective of circumstances, things such as murder, robbery, covetousness, etc.

14.15 If you hurt your brother because of something you eat, then you are no longer acting from love. Do not let the food that you eat ruin the man for whom Christ died!

This verse refers back to verse 13 and shows the result of causing one's brother to stumble or fall. Because of something you eat is literally "because of food" (see KJV "with thy meat"). This phrase can be misinterpreted as being some physical object which causes harm to a fellow believer. The real meaning here is, of course, "because you insist on eating certain things" or "because you insist that eating certain things is all right."

Then you are no longer acting from love is literally "you are no longer walking according to love." The verb "to walk in" has the same force that it does in 6.4; 8.4; and 13.13. Goodspeed translates by "your life is not governed by love" and the NEB by "your conduct is no longer guided by love." It may be difficult to translate the clause you are no longer acting from love. In some languages some rather important shifts in the semantic structure are required—for example, "what you are doing shows that you do not love him any longer."

The verb translated ruin is a very strong verb and may have reference to eternal destruction. Actually it is not the food that you eat which ruins the man for whom Christ died, but it is the fact that you eat certain foods which causes such a person's ruin. Accordingly, the last sentence of verse 15 may need to be restructured as "just because you eat certain foods, you must not allow that to ruin the man for whom Christ died" or even "...to destroy the person for whom Christ died." However, as in so many contexts of this kind, it may be necessary to employ plurals throughout: "to ruin the people for whom Christ died." Such a shift from singular to plural may apply to this entire chapter.

14.16 Do not let what you regard as good acquire a bad name.

What you regard as good is ambiguous in this passage. Some take this as a reference to Christian salvation; the plural "good things" (TEV good news) is used with this meaning in 10.15. On the other hand, the context seems to imply that what is referred to is the matter of Christian freedom. Paul is encouraging the men who are strong in faith not to let their Christian freedom acquire a bad name from persons outside the Christian community. Acquire a bad name is literally "to be spoken evil of" (Greek blasphēmeō) and is most generally used in reference to the actions committed by nonbelievers.

In English the phrase do not let would seem to imply "permission," but this is not the implication of verse 16. The believers are admonished to act in such a way that they will not cause what they regard as good to be thought of by others as being bad. One may, therefore, translate verse 16 as "Do not cause what you think of as good to be thought of by others as being bad" or "Do not make other people speak of as evil what you think is good."

14.17 For God's Kingdom is not a matter of eating and drinking, but of the righteousness, peace, and joy that the Holy Spirit gives.

The phrase God's Kingdom (or "the Kingdom of God") is used only here in the book of Romans. Elsewhere in Paul's letters it is used in 1 Corinthians 4.20; 6.9,10; 15.24,50; Galatians 5.21; Ephesians 5.5; Colossians 4.11; and 2 Thessalonians 1.5. See also Colossians 1.13. The primary meaning of this phrase is always "the rule of God." That is, the emphasis is always upon the actual kingship or sovereignty of God rather than upon the territory over which he rules. This verse might then be translated: "God's rule in our lives is not related to matters of eating and drinking, but is concerned with righteousness, peace, and joy that the Holy Spirit gives." These qualities of righteousness, peace, and joy describe the believer in terms of his relation to other believers.

It is not at all easy to translate God's Kingdom is not a matter of eating and drinking. In the first place, a matter of is highly generic in meaning and rarely has a close equivalent in languages with entirely different structures. In fact, it may be necessary to radically restructure the form of the first clause of verse 17—for example, "Whether one eats one thing and not another or drinks one thing and not another, this is not what God's rule is all about; rather, it is about righteousness, and peace, and joy." In other languages one may need to say: "When one speaks of God's ruling one does not talk about rules concerning eating and drinking, but one talks about righteousness, and peace, and joy."

In this context righteousness may well be translated as "doing what God requires" or "doing what God says is good." Peace may be understood as "being at peace with God" in the sense of having been reconciled, and joy may be "happiness of heart" or "inner happiness."

That the Holy Spirit gives (literally "in the Holy Spirit"; see RSV) is to be connected with all three of these qualities, and not merely with that of joy. Most commentators understand this phrase in the sense in which the TEV renders it, and many translations make this explicit (NEB "inspired by the Holy Spirit"; NAB "that is given by the Holy Spirit"; JB "brought by the Holy Spirit"). In a number of languages that the Holy Spirit gives is best translated as a causative —for example, "these are what the Holy Spirit causes" or even "we experience these by means of the Holy Spirit."

14.18 And whoever serves Christ in this way wins God's pleasure and man's approval.

Verse 18 serves as a conclusion of the paragraph begun in verse 13. Wins God's pleasure and man's approval may be rendered as "causes God to be pleased and causes men to approve of what he has done."

[19]So then, we must always aim at those things that bring peace, and that help strengthen one another. [20]Do not, because of food, destroy what God has done. All foods may be eaten, but it is wrong to eat anything that will cause someone else to fall into sin. [21]The right thing to do is to keep from eating meat, drinking wine, or doing anything else that will make your brother fall. [22]Keep what you believe about this matter, then, between yourself and God. Happy is the man who does not feel himself condemned when he does what he approves of! [23]But if he has doubts about what he eats, God condemns him when he eats it, because his action is not based on faith. And anything that is not based on faith is sin.

14.19 So then, we must always aim at those things that bring peace, and that help strengthen one another.

This verse is introduced with the same particles that introduce verse 12. Must always aim at translates a subjunctive in Greek, which most translations take with the force of an imperative. Some Greek manuscripts have this verb in the indicative, "we aim at." The UBS text committee gives the reading retained in the text a "D" rating, indicating that there is a high degree of doubt concerning it. The choice between the two readings is difficult, but practically all translators apparently prefer to follow the subjunctive. The tense of this subjunctive is present, and the TEV interprets it to have the force of must always aim at.

We must always aim at those things that bring peace is literally "we must pursue those things of peace." "To pursue peace" is a Semitic idiom which means "to try to live in peace with one's fellow-man." The genitive expression "those things of peace" means those things that bring peace (NEB "the things that make for peace").

We must always aim at those things may be translated in some languages as "we must always try to do those things." Such an expression may be readily combined with the restrictive clause that bring peace, and the first part of verse 19 may then be translated as "we must always try to do what causes peace" or "...causes people to live peacefully together." In some languages the idea of eliminating "strife" may be an effective way of speaking of "peace" in this type of context—for example, "we must always try to do whatever removes strife."

That help strengthen one another is a genitive clause in Greek, which the TEV has translated as a verb expression. The strength referred to is, of course, spiritual strength. The final restrictive clause, that help strengthen one another, may be combined with the preceding as "we must always try to do...what helps one another become strong," "...what causes other believers to become strong," or "...what causes other people to become strong in their faith."

14.20 Do not, because of food, destroy what God has done. All foods may be eaten, but it is wrong to eat anything that will cause someone else to fall into sin.

The phrase because of food may require some amplification in order to indicate that it is the eating of certain kinds of food, not merely food itself, which is involved—for example, "Simply because you think that any kind of food can be eaten, do not therefore destroy what God has done" or "For the sake of being able to eat any kind of food, do not destroy what God has done."

What God has done (literally "the work of God") may be a reference either to the weak brother (v. 15) or in a more general sense to the church, which is the result of God's work through Jesus Christ.

All foods may be eaten is literally "all things are clean," but it should be taken in the specific sense that the TEV employs (see NAB "all foods are clean").

But it is wrong to eat anything that will cause someone else to fall into sin translates a clause which is obscure in Greek. A literal translation is "it is bad for the man who eats through stumbling." Most exegetes understand this as a reference to the man who is strong in faith and who may cause someone else to fall into sin by what he eats. A few take this as a reference to the man who is weak in faith and who by eating injures his own conscience and so causes himself to fall into sin (NAB "but it is wrong for a man to eat when the food offends his conscience"). Most translations are explicit in the way in which they interpret these words, and the NAB is apparently the only modern English translation that follows the second interpretation.

The final portion of verse 20 may be restructured as conditional: "If someone else is caused to fall into sin because of what you eat, then this is wrong."

14.21 The right thing to do is to keep from eating meat, drinking wine, or doing anything else that will make your brother fall.

The right thing to do is literally "it is good." In Greek there is a play on words between the last part of verse 21 (kakon "it is bad") and the first part of this verse (kalon "it is good"). "Good" in such a context describes that which is proper for the circumstances.

In order to relate the right thing to do to the three specific prohibitions, one may in some languages introduce the idea of correctness and follow this with imperatives—for example, "this is what is right: keep from eating meat, do not drink wine, or do not do anything else that will make your brother fall."

Eating meat and drinking wine translates aorist infinitives in Greek, and some take these as a reference to eating and drinking on specific occasions rather than as a general rule of life. They contend that in those situations where eating meat or drinking wine may cause one's brother to fall into sin, the right thing to do is to keep from eating meat or drinking wine; but since these two things are not wrong in themselves, they may be participated in on other occasions without danger of causing someone else to fall.

As noted in verse 13, make your brother fall may be translated as "cause your fellow believer to sin."

14.22 Keep what you believe about this matter, then, between yourself and God. Happy is the man who does not feel himself condemned when he does what he approves of!

What you believe about this matter (Moffatt "your own conviction on the matter"; JB "your own belief"; NEB "if you have a clear conviction") is literally "the faith that you have" (RSV). This is clearly a reference to what one believes about this matter of eating meat and drinking wine.

The first sentence of verse 22 may be rendered in some instances as "whatever you believe about such things is something just for you and God" or "whatever you do in these matters concerns just you and God."

The second sentence, Happy is the man..., is obscure in Greek. Most translators accept the interpretation followed by the TEV (see Goodspeed "he is a happy man who has no fault to find with himself in following the course that he approves"; Moffatt "he is a fortunate man who has no misgivings about what he allows himself to eat"). If this is the correct interpretation, the sentence refers to the man who is strong in faith, while the words of verse 23 refer to the man who is weak in faith. An alternative possibility of interpretation is to take this part of the verse to mean, "Happy who is the man who does not find himself of a divided opinion concerning what he approves and what he knows as a believer he ought to be able to approve." Such an interpretation is valid in light of the context; if it is accepted, the man referred to in this verse is the same one mentioned in verse 23 (he who has doubts about what he eats).

The second sentence of verse 22 may be restructured as conditional: "A man is truly happy if he does not condemn himself when he does what he thinks is right," or "If the man does not say, I did wrong, when he does what he really thinks is right, then he is surely happy."

14.23 But if he has doubts about what he eats, God condemns him when he eats it, because his action is not based on faith. And anything that is not based on faith is sin.

God condemns him is actually a perfect passive tense in Greek (literally "he has been condemned"), which must be taken with God as the agent of the action. When he eats it, though not an actual part of the Greek text, must be introduced in order to explain the circumstances under which the man is condemned. Because his action is not based on faith is literally "because not from faith."

The first sentence of verse 23 may cause difficulties in translation because of the complex relations between clauses, consisting of a substantive clause, a content clause, a principal clause, a temporal clause, and finally a clause of cause. In some languages the final clause may even be followed by still another clause of cause as a restructuring of the expression based on faith. In some languages it may be preferable to combine the clauses about what he eats and when he eats it—for example, "but if a person has doubts when he eats certain kinds of food, then God condemns him," "...says he has done wrong," or "...judges this as wrong." The final clause may be restructured as "because faith did not cause him to do what he did" or "because what he did, did not come from his faith." It is essential in translating a term for doubt to make it clear that doubt is simply about whether or not to eat certain foods—not doubt concerning God himself.

The final sentence of verse 23 may likewise be recast as a conditional: "And if we do anything without faith, then it is sin." In fact, in this context it may be satisfactory to translate faith as "confidence that what we do is right"—for example, "and if we do anything without the confidence that it is right, then it is sin."

CHAPTER 15

Please Others, Not Yourselves

15 We who are strong in the faith ought to help the weak to carry their
burdens. We should not please ourselves. [2]Instead, each of us should
please his brother for his own good, in order to build him up in the faith. [3]For
Christ did not please himself. Instead, as the scripture says, "The insults
spoken by those who insulted you have fallen on me." [4]Everything written in
the Scriptures was written to teach us, in order that we might have hope
through the patience and encouragement the Scriptures give us. [5]And may
God, the source of patience and encouragement, enable you to have the same
point of view among yourselves by following the example of Christ Jesus, [6]so
that all of you together, with one voice, may praise the God and Father of our
Lord Jesus Christ.

The section heading Please Others, Not Yourselves may be more appropriately rendered in some languages as first person plural—for example, "We Should Please Others and Not Ourselves" or, in some instances, "We Should Do What Helps Others and Forget Ourselves."

Verses 1-13 are connected immediately with what precedes and introduce the third section in Paul's discussion of the relation between those who are strong and those who are weak in faith. Some ancient manuscripts have the doxology of 16.25-27 at the end of chapter 14, indicating that some early copies of Romans may have ended with chapter 14. However, in view of the fact that the content of 15.1-13 follows closely on what was said in chapter 14, it is better to conclude that the doxology was not originally placed at the end of chapter 14.

15.1 We who are strong in the faith ought to help the weak to carry their burdens. We should not please ourselves.

It is interesting to note that Paul includes himself among those who are strong in the faith. The words in the faith are not a part of the Greek text as such, but they are included by the TEV to make explicit the meaning of the word strong.

To carry (translated support in 11.18) is used of Jesus carrying his cross in John 19.17 and of believers carrying their cross in Luke 14.27. This verb also occurs in Galatians 6.2. In light of these passages, it is most likely that the verb means more than simply "to tolerate" or "to put up with." It perhaps indicates that those who are strong in faith should be willing to experience self-denial for the sake of believers whose faith is weak.

To carry their burdens seems so natural a metaphor that sometimes translators are not aware that this cannot always be transferred literally into another language. In some instances the metaphor must be changed to a nonmetaphor—for example, "to help the weak to deal with their problems" or "to cause the weak to continue in faith."

We should not please ourselves may be translated as "we should not do just what we ourselves want to do" or "we should not do just what is going to make us happy."

15.2 Instead, each of us should please his brother for his own good, in order to build him up in the faith.

Brother is literally "neighbor," but the reference is to one's fellow Christian, rather than to people in general.

For his own good is literally "for that which is good," but most translators understand this phrase in the same way as in the TEV. For example, Goodspeed has "to do him good" (so also NAB), while the NEB and the RSV have "for his good."

It may be necessary in some languages to make please and for his own good more or less coordinate---for example, "each one of us should do for his fellow believer that which is good for him and that which will please him" or "...cause him to be happy."

In order to build him up in the faith translates a noun phrase (literally "for building up"). Most commentators understand this as a reference to the man who is weak in faith (Moffatt "by building up his faith"; NAB "by building up his spirit"; the JB translates both clauses by "help them to become stronger Christians"). However, the NEB applies this in general to the Christian community ("and will build up the common life"). In light of the context, however, the former interpretation is to be preferred.

This final purpose clause may require some special introduction based on a repetition of, or a reference to, what has just been said—for example, "we should do this in order to cause his faith to become strong" or "we should do this in order that he will become stronger in his believing."

15.3 For Christ did not please himself. Instead, as the scripture says, "The insults spoken by those who insulted you have fallen on me."

In this verse Paul appeals to the example of Christ and to the words of the Old Testament as the basis for the conduct that he hopes to inspire in the persons to whom he is writing. The scripture quotation comes from Psalm 69.9. For the early church the example of Christ and the words of the Old Testament were two authorities which they could not deny.

Christ did not please himself can be translated "Christ did not do what he did just to make himself happy," "Christ did not live just to please himself," or "Christ did not live just for his own benefit."

The scripture quotation presents a number of difficulties in translation. For one thing, some languages do not possess a noun for insult. Also, it is unlikely that languages would speak of "insults by those who insulted." Again, it is rare to talk of "insults falling on someone." Accordingly, this quotation may be restructured in some languages as "what people said when they insulted you has now come upon me" or "people insulted you, but what they said has really insulted me."

15.4 Everything written in the Scriptures was written to teach us, in order that we might have hope through the patience and encouragement the Scriptures give us.

Everything written in the Scriptures may be literally translated as "what was written in earlier times." However, as all commentators point out, the reference is specifically to the Old Testament scriptures, and one should make this information explicit in translating. Otherwise a wrong understanding of the text might result (see, for example, the RSV "for whatever was written in former days").

If the term for Scriptures is essentially a word for "writings," it may be entirely repetitious to have three expressions for writing in the first clause of verse 4, as, for example, "for everything written in the writings was written to teach us." A more satisfactory rendering may be "for everything in the Scriptures teaches us" or "for everything in the Scriptures exists in order to teach us."

The word translated patience is also used in 2.7; 5.3,4; 8.25; and 15.5. This word is generally translated by patience, but in some contexts it has the meaning of "endurance."

Encouragement is used in verse 5. See 12.8, where the phrase "the one encouraging with encouragement" is translated as if it is to encourage others, we must do so.

The meaning of hope was discussed in 5.2.

The expression through the patience and encouragement the Scriptures give us may require some recasting to indicate that the Scriptures are the means of causing us to have patience and encouragement—for example, "because the Scriptures cause us to be patient and they encourage us," "... cause us to have courage," or "... cause us to be steadfast." Encouragement may be translated rather idiomatically as "to stand by him in his heart."

15.5-6 And may God, the source of patience and encouragement, enable you to have the same point of view among yourselves by following the example of Christ Jesus, (6) so that all of you together, with one voice, may praise the God and Father of our Lord Jesus Christ.

In Greek these two verses are one sentence and form a doxology. The introductory expression may God is often restructured as an expression of prayer —for example, "I pray to God," followed by direct discourse, or "I pray that God," followed by indirect discourse.

Paul's literal expression "the God of patience and encouragement" means God, the source of patience and encouragement (NEB "God, the source of all fortitude and all encouragement"). Goodspeed translates this as "God, from whom steadfastness and encouragement come." The source of patience and encouragement is best treated as a causative: "God who causes us to be patient and who causes us to have courage." Note that in verse 4 the Scriptures have already been cited as fulfilling the function of causing patience and courage, but there is no real contradiction here, since it is God who is ultimately responsible for causing believers to be patient and to have courage.

"To think the same thing among one another" is taken by the TEV to mean to have the same point of view among yourselves; other translations take this in the sense of "enable you to live in perfect harmony with one another" (NAB). It is true that the purpose of this exhortation is to encourage the Christians to live in harmony with one another, but that seems to be understood best as the result of having the same point of view among themselves.

May God...enable you to have the same point of view among yourselves may likewise be expressed as a causative: "May God cause you to think the same thing" or "May God cause you to agree among yourselves." It may be more appropriate in some languages to speak of "living together peacefully" as the result of such agreement.

By following the example of Christ Jesus (Goodspeed "in following the example of Christ Jesus"; NEB "after the manner of Christ Jesus") is literally "according to Christ Jesus." By following the example of Christ Jesus is an expression of means, but it is often indicated in languages as cause: "because you follow the example of Christ Jesus." The expression following the example may be rendered as "to do as Christ Jesus did" or "to imitate Christ Jesus."

All of you together translates one word in Greek, which originally meant something like "with one mind" or "of one accord." This word is used frequently in Acts (1.14; 2.46; 4.24; 7.57; 8.6; 12.20; 15.25; 18.12; 19.29), and it seems quite likely that by New Testament times it had become weakened to mean simply "together."

After the expression all of you together it may be not only superfluous but misleading to translate with one voice (Greek "with one mouth"), since if one says "so that all of you together may praise the God and Father of our Lord Jesus Christ," that is certainly equivalent to "speaking as with one voice." In some languages one can say "may praise as if with one voice."

In a number of languages one cannot speak of the God and Father of our Lord Jesus Christ. The use of and in such a phrase would suggest that there were two individuals, not one. Therefore, one must translate "God who is the Father of our Lord Jesus Christ" or "God, the Father of our Lord Jesus Christ" (a construction with apposition). It is possible to interpret this expression in the Greek text as "both the God of our Lord Jesus Christ and also the Father of our Lord Jesus Christ."

The Gospel to the Gentiles

7Accept one another, then, for the glory of God, as Christ has accepted you.
8Because I tell you that Christ became a servant of the Jews to show that God
is faithful, to make God's promises to the patriarchs come true, 9and also to
enable the Gentiles to praise God for his mercy. As the scripture says,

"And so I will give thanks to you among the Gentiles,
I will sing praises to your name."

10Again it says,

"Rejoice, Gentiles, with God's chosen people!"

11And again,

"Praise the Lord, all Gentiles;
praise him, all peoples!"

[12]And again, Isaiah says,
"A descendant of Jesse will come;
he will be raised to rule the Gentiles,
and they will put their hope in him."
[13]May God, the source of hope, fill you with all joy and peace by means of your faith in him, so that your hope will continue to grow by the power of the Holy Spirit.

The section heading The Gospel to the Gentiles may be translated as "The Good News Is Told to the Gentiles" or "The Good News Is Also for the Non-Jews," or "The Gentiles Also Hear the Good News."

15.7 Accept one another, then, for the glory of God, as Christ has accepted you.

In this paragraph Paul generalizes on the principles that he has laid down in the preceding discussion regarding the persons who are weak and those who are strong.

Accept is the same verb that Paul used to introduce the discussion in 14.1. Accept one another may be rendered in some languages as "receive one another into your hearts," "receive happily," or "welcome with kind words."

For the sake of clarity the TEV rearranges the order of the Greek sentence. The phrase for the glory of God in Greek follows after you, but it goes with the imperative accept one another, so the TEV makes this relation explicit. For a discussion of the word glory, see 3.23 and 5.2. Here it is used with the meaning of "praise" (see 4.20). The phrase for the glory of God in this context means "so that people will praise God."

Since the phrase for the glory of God must so frequently be transformed into a clause, "in order that people will praise God," it may be necessary to change the order of clauses in verse 7—for example, "accept one another, then, as Christ has accepted you; do this in order that people will praise God" or "accept one another in order that people will praise God; do this in the same way that Christ accepted you."

Some manuscripts read "us" in the place of you (see KJV), but this is not followed by any modern translations except the NEB. You is the more difficult reading, and the UBS text committee has adopted you and given the reading a "B" rating.

15.8 Because I tell you that Christ became a servant of the Jews to show that God is faithful, to make God's promises to the patriarchs come true,

A servant of the Jews is literally "a servant of circumcision" (RSV "a servant to the circumcised"). See the comments at 2.26. Became a servant of the Jews may sometimes be rendered as "came to help the Jews" or "came to do good for the Jews."

To show that God is faithful (NAB "because of God's faithfulness") is literally "in behalf of the truth of God" (RSV "to show God's truthfulness"). In the

Old Testament "truth" is often used with the meaning of "faithfulness," and it appears that this is the area of meaning covered by Paul's use of the word in the present verse.

In this context faithful is often translated as "to do what one has promised to do." Therefore this clause may be expressed as "in order to show that God would do what he said he would do."

The last part of this verse reads "to make come true the promises of the patriarchs," which the TEV renders to make God's promises to the patriarchs come true (NEB "by making good his promises to the patriarchs"). This is in a sense explanatory of what it means to be faithful. If that God is faithful is translated as "that God does what he promises to do," it may be useful to render the last clause as "that is, to make happen what God had promised to the patriarchs."

15.9 and also to enable the Gentiles to praise God for his mercy. As the scripture says,

"And so I will give thanks to you among the Gentiles,
I will sing praises to your name."

The first part of this verse is a continuation of the Greek sentence begun in the previous verse, and its relation to verse 8 is difficult to define with precision. The TEV understands these words as introducing a second reason why Christ became a servant to the Jews and so introduces the words also to enable to make this relation clear. Most translations follow this same interpretation, though it is possible to connect the first part of verse 9 with the previous verse in a different way. That is, it is possible to understand these words as the object of the verb I tell you and so to translate: "I tell you that Christ became a servant of the Jews to show that God is truthful and has made his promises to the patriarchs come true; (9) while, on the other hand, the Gentiles praised God for his mercy." The latter interpretation is followed by the NAB, but all other English translations follow the same exegesis as the TEV.

Also to enable the Gentiles to praise God is normally expressed as a causative: "and also to cause the Gentiles to praise God."

For his mercy (so most translations) is literally "in behalf of mercy." This may be translated in some languages as "because he is merciful" or "because he shows mercy."

As the scripture says is literally "as it has been written" (see 1.17; 2.24; 3.4,10; 4.17; etc).

I will give thanks to you is literally "I will confess to you" (see 14.11). The same meaning is possible here as in the earlier passage; but in light of the second line of this quotation from Psalm 18.49, and in view of the way in which Paul uses "confess" in this context, "to give thanks" seems to be the meaning here.

If one adopts the interpretation "confess," it may be possible to say "therefore I will confess you as God to the Gentiles." However, if one follows the interpretation give thanks to, there are somewhat more complex problems involved in the phrase among the Gentiles. It may, in fact, be necessary to render this as a clause relating to the subject—for example, "therefore, while I am among the Gentiles, I will give thanks to you" or "therefore, when I am there among the Gentiles, I will give thanks to you."

I will sing praises to your name may require some recasting in order to show the relation between sing and praises and the relation of both to your name —for example, "I will praise you by singing" or "I will sing and in this way praise you."

15.10 Again it says,

"Rejoice, Gentiles, with God's chosen people!"

The scripture quotation in this verse comes from Deuteronomy 32.43. God's chosen people is literally "his people." The word "people," when occurring in the singular, is used to distinguish the Jewish people (that is, the chosen people) from the Gentiles; and "his" is, of course, a reference to God.

The phrase with God's chosen people may require certain special treatment in order to relate it satisfactorily to rejoice: "Join with God's chosen people in rejoicing" or "Rejoice in company with God's chosen people."

15.11 And again,

"Praise the Lord, all Gentiles;
praise him, all peoples!"

This comes from Psalm 117.1; all Gentiles and all peoples are used synonymously in this verse. In Greek the second imperative in this verse is a third person form (literally "let all peoples praise him"), but in English the full force of the form can only be expressed by means of a second person imperative: praise him, all peoples.

In many languages there is no such thing as a third person imperative. It may be necessary therefore to say: "All of you Gentiles praise the Lord; all of you people praise him very much." Or a third person expression of obligation may be employed: "All Gentiles should praise the Lord, and all peoples should praise him very much." All peoples may be translated in some languages as "all nations" or "all tribes."

15.12 And again, Isaiah says,

"A descendant of Jesse will come;
he will be raised to rule the Gentiles,
and they will put their hope in him."

A descendant is literally "a root"; most translators either render literally or by "Scion" (NEB, Moffatt). It is doubtful that either "root" or "scion" conveys much meaning to the modern reader, and so another term must be sought. It is possible that in Isaiah the word "root" had come to be used in a technical sense as a reference to the Messiah, but a more general term seems preferable. It is known that the word "root" was used in a general sense of one's descendants, and descendant seems best suited to the present context.

A descendant of Jesse may be rendered as "someone from the family of Jesse" or "someone from the lineage of Jesse." At this point it may be useful to have some kind of marginal help indicating who Jesse was. At the least, a cross reference at this point is important to indicate that the Jesse referred to here was the father of David.

He will be raised (NEB "the one raised up") is given an active force by most translations (RSV "he who rises"). If this verb is translated with a passive force, it may be necessary to indicate the agent: "God will raise him." In many instances the demands of English structure require that a pronoun be changed to a noun; in the present sentence the opposite is done: the pronoun they of the second line is literally "the Gentiles."

They will put their hope in him is rendered in some languages as "they will hope because of him," "he will cause them to hope," or "... cause them to look forward to with confidence."

15.13 May God, the source of hope, fill you with all joy and peace by means of your faith in him, so that your hope will continue to grow by the power of the Holy Spirit.

As in so many other instances of third person imperative, it may be necessary to introduce verse 13 by an expression of prayer—for example, "I pray that God."

God, the source of hope (so also NAB; Moffatt "the God of your hope") is literally "the God of hope." "Of hope" is ambiguous in this context, and so the TEV makes the meaning of the genitive expression clear. The source of hope may be expressed as a causative: "the one who causes us to hope." In this context it may be more appropriate to employ only the plural "you" instead of "us": "the one who causes you to hope."

Fill you with all joy may be rendered as "cause you to be completely happy," "cause you to feel happy completely in your hearts," or even "cause your hearts to burst because of happiness." Peace also must be understood as the goal of what God has caused: "that God may cause you to have complete happiness and to enjoy peace" or "...experience complete peace." Peace may be expressed idiomatically in some languages—for example, "to sit down in your hearts" or "to hear quietness in your hearts."

"In believing" (RSV) is taken by the TEV to mean "by means of believing," and the object of this belief is supplied: by means of your faith in him. As in so many instances, means may be expressed in some languages by a clause of cause---for example, "because you believe in him." It is perfectly proper to express this faith as "faith in Christ," but within this particular context it seems more fitting to express it as "faith in God."

So that your hope will continue to grow is more literally "so that you may abound in hope" (see KJV, RSV). The verb "to abound" is no longer in current English usage, and so some of the modern English translations restructure by making hope the object of a verb phrase (for example, the NAB "so that you may have hope in abundance"; Goodspeed "so that you may have overflowing hope").

The NEB renders "overflow with hope." The TEV restructures by making hope the subject of the intransitive verb grow, while taking the expression "you ... in hope" as the equivalent of your hope. Moreover, since the tense of the Greek verb "to abound" indicates continuing action, the TEV translates by continue to grow.

In a number of languages one cannot speak of "hope growing." One can, however, "hope more and more," "hope more firmly," or "be more steadfast in hoping." By the power of the Holy Spirit may be interpreted as the means and therefore become the subject of an expression of cause: "so that the Holy Spirit will cause you to have more and more hope."

Paul's Reason for Writing So Boldly

14My brothers: I myself feel sure that you are full of goodness, that you are
filled with all knowledge and are able to teach one another. 15But in this letter
I have been quite bold about certain subjects of which I have reminded you.
I have been bold because of the privilege God has given me 16of being a servant
of Christ Jesus to work for the Gentiles. I serve like a priest in preaching the
Good News from God, in order that the Gentiles may be an offering acceptable
to God, dedicated to him by the Holy Spirit. 17In union with Christ Jesus, then,
I can be proud of my service for God. 18I will be bold and speak only of what
Christ has done through me to lead the Gentiles to obey God, by means of
words and deeds, 19by the power of signs and miracles, and by the power of
the Spirit. And so, in traveling all the way from Jerusalem to Illyricum, I have
proclaimed fully the Good News about Christ. 20My ambition has always been
to proclaim the Good News in places where Christ has not been heard of, so
as not to build on the foundation laid by someone else. 21As the scripture says,

"Those who were not told about him will see,
and those who have not heard will understand."

The section heading Paul's Reason for Writing So Boldly may be translated as "Paul Explains Why He Has Written as He Has" or "Paul Explains Why He Has Written, Without Holding Back Anything."

Paul has now brought to an end the main theological division of his letter. The remainder of this chapter (vv. 14-33) is close in style and in thought to 1.8-17, and may be divided into two sections (vv. 14-21 and 22-33). In these sections Paul turns to consider his own plans, speaking first in general terms of his work as an apostle and concluding with specific mention of his plans to visit Rome.

15.14 My brothers: I myself feel sure that you are full of goodness, that you are filled with all knowledge and are able to teach one another.

As in so many contexts, my brothers may perhaps be best rendered as "my fellow believers," "you who also believe," or "you who are also followers of Christ."

As the TEV indicates, I myself is emphatic in the Greek sentence, as is also the pronoun you (NEB "you yourselves").

All knowledge is the same phrase that occurs in 1 Corinthians 13.2. It may be that the terms goodness and knowledge should be taken in specific relation to the problem that Paul has been discussing. Goodness is then the love which Paul has emphasized in the previous discussion as the only rule of Christian conduct, and knowledge is the understanding of the Christian faith that lies behind this rule of conduct. In a number of languages one cannot speak of being full of such qualities as goodness or knowledge. One may "be very good" or "know completely what should be done," but to be "filled with" these qualities is simply not possible. Therefore one may translate the first clause of verse 14 as "I myself am certain that you yourselves are very good." It may be that a verb such as "to know" or "to have knowledge" must have a goal. In this context the knowledge would be concerning what one should do, and therefore one may say: "you know completely what you should do."

To teach (Goodspeed "to instruct") is rendered "to give advice to" in a number of translations (NEB, NAB, Moffatt; see JB). Paul is not referring to teaching in a formal situation, but in a general sense. He uses this word in a similar way in 1 Corinthians 4.14 (to instruct); Colossians 1.28 (warn); 3.16 (instruct); 1 Thessalonians 5.12 (instruct), 14 (encourage); and 2 Thessalonians 3.15 (warn).

15.15 But in this letter I have been quite bold about certain subjects of which I have reminded you. I have been bold because of the privilege God has given me

I have been quite bold is emphatic in the Greek sentence order. The sentence itself actually begins "but quite boldly I wrote to you." Bold may be expressed in a number of different ways—for example, "openly," "without holding back," "without omitting anything," or "frankly."

About certain subjects (RSV, Goodspeed "on some points") is understood by others to mean "in parts of this letter" (NAB; NEB "at times").

Because of the privilege God has given me is literally "because of the grace which was given me by God" ("grace" is taken in the same sense here that it was in 1.5). Because of the privilege God has given me may also be rendered as "because God has given me the privilege of being a servant...." In some languages the closest equivalent of privilege may be "the wonderful work," "the very special task," or "has honored me by giving me the work of a servant."

15.16 of being a servant of Christ Jesus to work for the Gentiles. I serve like a priest in preaching the Good News from God, in order that the Gentiles may be an offering acceptable to God, dedicated to him by the Holy Spirit.

Servant is the same word used in 13.6.

To work for the Gentiles may be translated in some languages as "to help the Gentiles."

I serve like a priest is rendered in some languages as "I am a priest and I serve" or "I do the work of a priest as I serve in preaching the Good News."

The TEV transforms Paul's expression "in order that the offering of the Gentiles might be acceptable" to read in order that the Gentiles may be an offering acceptable to God. The genitive phrase "offering of the Gentiles" is not something that the Gentiles offer, but it describes the Gentiles as being an offering. In this context the word "acceptable" means acceptable to God.

It may be difficult in some languages to state that "the Gentiles become an offering," but one can say in most instances: "the Gentiles will be like an offering that pleases God" or "...because of which God is happy."

Dedicated (literally "having been made holy") requires an object, to him. On the meaning of the word "holy," see 1.7. Dedicated to him by the Holy Spirit may be transformed into an active expression: "which the Holy Spirit has dedicated to God."

15.17 In union with Christ Jesus, then, I can be proud of my service for God.

In union with Christ Jesus is literally "in Christ Jesus" (see 6.3,9-11).

As in so many contexts, the phrase in union with Christ Jesus may be understood as a causative: "because I am joined with Christ Jesus, I can be proud of my service for God."

I can be proud of my service for God translates an unusual expression in Greek, but it is generally understood in this sense. Proud of my service for God is often rendered in languages as a causative: "proud because I serve God."

15.18 I will be bold and speak only of what Christ has done through me to lead the Gentiles to obey God, by means of words and deeds,

The first part of this verse in Greek is in the form of a double negative statement: "I will not dare to speak of what Christ did not do through me." This is transformed into a strong positive statement by the TEV.

I will be bold and speak may be rendered as "I will speak boldly."

To lead the Gentiles to obey God is a transform of the Greek phrase "for obedience of the Gentiles." The preposition "for" denotes purpose (to lead), while the genitive expression "obedience of the Gentiles" means "that the Gentiles might obey (God)."

In a sense there are two causative relations in the central portion of verse 18: (1) has done through me and (2) to lead the Gentiles to obey God. The first may be expressed in some languages as "what Christ has caused me to do," "what Christ has accomplished by using me," or "what Christ did; he caused me to do it." Similarly, the second, to lead the Gentiles to obey God, may be translated as "to cause the Gentiles to obey God." Putting the two causative expressions together, one may translate as "what Christ did by causing me to lead the Gentiles to obey God" or "what Christ did; he caused me to lead the Gentiles to obey God."

By means of words and deeds is singular in Greek ("by word and deed"), but the plural is more natural in English. The expression of means in the phrase by means of words and deeds must be understood with the verb to lead, not with to obey. This may require a change of word order in some languages—for example, "by words and by deeds I caused the Gentiles to obey God" or "by what I said and by what I did I caused the Gentiles to obey God." It may, however, be more satisfactory to make a break immediately after the phrase to obey God and to begin a new sentence so that words and deeds may also be combined with the expressions power of signs and miracles and the power of the Spirit in verse 19 —for example, "I used words and deeds, strong signs and miracles, and the Spirit caused this by his power." Or, somewhat differently, one may say: "This happened because of the words that I spoke and the deeds that I did, because of the strong signs and miracles that happened, and because of the way in which the Spirit acted so powerfully."

15.19 by the power of signs and miracles, and by the power of the Spirit. And so, in traveling all the way from Jerusalem to Illyricum, I have proclaimed fully the Good News about Christ.

The word signs is used in Romans only here and in 4.11. The word translated miracles taken by itself would most naturally refer to a happening that evokes awe. However, signs and miracles is a set phrase which occurs frequently in biblical literature (some nine times in the book of Acts), and it is not possible to establish any significant difference between the two words.

In the Greek text, the expression of power occurs with both signs and miracles and with the Spirit, but in some languages there is simply no abstract expression of "power." One can, however, reproduce something of the meaning of power by indicating the intensity or strength of some particular event. For that reason in some languages one may translate as "by means of powerful signs and miracles, and by means of what the Spirit did in a powerful way."

In Greek the sentence beginning with and so is continued up to the end of verse 21.

In traveling all the way from Jerusalem to Illyricum is literally "from Jerusalem and around as far as Illyricum." There is some ambiguity connected with the word "around." It may be taken with Jerusalem and mean "from Jerusalem and its vicinity." However, most commentators take it to mean "from Jerusalem (and in territories) around to Illyricum." Illyricum (also known as Dalmatia) was a Roman province northwest of Macedonia, lying on the Adriatic Sea across from Italy.

Moreover, Paul's words are ambiguous from another viewpoint. It is impossible to decide, on the basis of the Greek, whether he is saying that he actually went into the territory of Illyricum or just went as far as its southern and eastern boundary. In light of what is known elsewhere about Paul's ministry, it is possible that he does not state that he actually went into Illyricum, but rather that he reached as far as that territory.

In traveling all the way from Jerusalem to Illyricum may be rendered as "every place I visited, from the city of Jerusalem to the country of Illyricum" or "during all the time that I was going from place to place, from Jerusalem to Illyricum."

I have proclaimed fully the Good News is rendered by some translators as "I have completed the preaching of the good news" (Goodspeed). What Paul means by this is "I have preached the Good News everywhere." The genitive expression "the Good News of Christ" means the Good News about Christ.

15.20 My ambition has always been to proclaim the Good News in places where Christ has not been heard of, so as not to build on the foundation laid by someone else.

As already indicated, this verse is a continuation of the Greek sentence begun with and so in verse 19. Most translations break the sentence at this point and begin a new sentence, as does the TEV.

My ambition has always been translates one word in Greek, a participle. Goodspeed translates as "in all this it has been my ambition" and the NEB as "it is my ambition"; Moffatt renders as "my ambition always being." The NAB seems to press the meaning of this word too far by translating "it has been a point of honor with me." This same verb appears in 2 Corinthians 5.9 (we want to), and 1 Thessalonians 4.11 (make it your aim), but nowhere else in the New Testament.

Many languages have no specific term for ambition, but the expression my ambition has always been to proclaim the Good News may be rendered as "my one desire has been to proclaim the Good News" or "I have always desired just one thing, and that is to proclaim the Good News."

Where Christ has not been heard of (NEB "where the very name of Christ has not been heard") is the meaning of Paul's words "not where Christ has already been named" (RSV). This cause may be conveniently rendered in a number of languages as "where people have not yet heard about Christ" or "where people had previously not known anything about Christ."

Because of the metaphorical use of the expression so as not to build on the foundation laid by someone else, it may be useful to introduce a phrase which will make this into a simile: "so as not to build, so to speak, on the foundation laid by someone else." If this expression of purpose is translated as if it were a statement made by others, its metaphorical significance may be more clearly recognized---for example, "so that people would not say, You have built on a foundation which others have laid down." However, in parts of the world where foundations for buildings are not employed, one can change the metaphor to a nonmetaphor: "so as not to continue the work which someone else has begun" or "so as not to seem to be profiting from something which someone else has started."

15.21 As the scripture says,

"Those who were not told about him will see,
and those who have not heard will understand."

As the scripture says is the same phrase that was used in verse 9 (literally "as it has been written"). The passage quoted is Isaiah 52.15. Paul quotes word for word from the Septuagint and uses the passage to describe the aim of his own missionary activities.

Paul's Plan to Visit Rome

22 For this reason I have been prevented many times from coming to you.
23 But now that I have finished my work in these regions, and since I have been
wanting for so many years to come to see you, 24 I hope to do so now. I would
like to see you on my way to Spain, and be helped by you to go there, after
I have enjoyed visiting you for a while. 25 Right now, however, I am going to
Jerusalem in the service of God's people there. 26 For the churches in Macedonia and Greece have freely decided to give an offering to help the poor among
God's people in Jerusalem. 27 They themselves decided to do it. But, as a matter
of fact, they have an obligation to help those poor; the Jews shared their
spiritual blessings with the Gentiles, and so the Gentiles ought to serve the
Jews with their material blessings. 28 When I have finished this task, and have
turned over to them the full amount of money that has been raised for them,
I shall leave for Spain and visit you on my way there. 29 When I come to you,
I know that I shall come with a full measure of the blessing of Christ.

The section heading Paul's Plan to Visit Rome may be changed into a verb construction, "Paul Plans to Visit Rome," "Paul Writes that He Wants to Visit Rome," or "Paul Says to the Romans that He Wants to Visit Them."

In this section of Paul's letter (15.22-33) there is a noticeable change of style and of tone. Paul now deals with very personal matters and is quite deliberate in the way in which he expresses himself.

15.22 For this reason I have been prevented many times from coming to you.

For this reason is perhaps best taken to refer back to Paul's words at the beginning of verse 20, my ambition has always been to proclaim the Good News in places where Christ has not been heard of. However, for this reason seems to present an anomaly. Why should Paul's desire to preach the Gospel where Christ had not been known prevent him, on many occasions, from visiting the Romans? It may mean that Paul was so busy going elsewhere to preach Christ that it was not possible for him to go to Rome, where obviously some persons had already heard about Jesus Christ.

I have been prevented may be perhaps more satisfactorily rendered in some languages as simply "I have been unable." If this is to be rendered as an active expression, it may be valid to translate "circumstances have many times prevented me." There is no reason for suggesting that God or the devil had prevented Paul from visiting Rome.

Many times is a different expression from the one used in 1.13; the word used here is stronger than the earlier expression. However, it is quite likely that both expressions should be translated in the same way.

15.23 But now that I have finished my work in these regions, and since I have been wanting for so many years to come to see you,

This verse introduces the reason why Paul can now visit Rome; he has finished his work in these regions (where Christ has not been heard of). I have finished my work is more literally "no longer having a place" (see KJV). To translate literally leaves the meaning unclear, and so the RSV supplies a noun phrase to help the reader: "since I no longer have any room for work." The NEB is vague "I have no further scope (in these parts)"; Goodspeed renders "there is no more work for me." I have finished my work may be rendered simply as "I have done what I should do." In these regions may simply be rendered as "here where I am."

15.24 I hope to do so now. I would like to see you on my way to Spain, and be helped by you to go there, after I have enjoyed visiting you for a while.

The TEV and a number of other modern translations rather radically reorder this verse from the form in which it appears in Greek. The NAB represents more nearly than any other modern translation a literal rendering of the Greek text: "as soon as I set out for Spain, I hope to see you in passing." The TEV brings the verb I hope to the beginning of the verse, in order to relate it more closely to what Paul has said in verse 22. As a further technique of tying this verse to verse 22, the words to do so now are introduced. Then the TEV again picks up the idea of I hope (I would like) and connects it with the verb see, as in the Greek text.

I would like to see you on my way to Spain may be translated as "as I am traveling to Spain, I want to stop off to see you" or "instead of going directly to Spain, I want to stop off and see you before going on to Spain."

The verb be helped...to go is used several times in the New Testament in this same sense (Acts 15.3; 1 Corinthians 16.6, 11; 2 Corinthians 1.16; Titus 3.13; 3 John 6); it must have been a frequent expression used in the early missionary work. It may imply a number of different things, such as providing food, money, traveling companions, means of travel, and persons with whom to stay on the journey. The passive expression be helped by you to go there may be rendered as an active: "I want you to help me go there" or "I want you to give me help for my journey to Spain."

In some languages it may be necessary to select an expression for a while which will indicate the approximate amount of time involved. An expression for "several weeks" or "a few months" would probably be the most satisfactory. Something which specifies only "a few days" would not be typical of Paul's ministry; nor would an expression for "several years" be realistic, in view of his plans to go on to Spain.

15.25 Right now, however, I am going to Jerusalem in the service of God's people there.

The participle translated in the service of represents a verb sometimes used by Paul in specific reference to the collection of money for the Jerusalem church (see 2 Corinthians 8.19-20). The related noun is used in this sense in verse 31; 1 Corinthians 16.15; 2 Corinthians 8.4; 9.1, 12, 13. Although this verb may relate to the collection of money for the church in Jerusalem, it seems better to render it by a more general term, as most translations do (RSV "with aid for"; Goodspeed "to take help to"; Moffatt, NEB "on an errand to"; NAB "to bring assistance to"), rather than to make it a specific reference (JB "I must take a present of money"; Phillips "to make a contribution").

God's people is literally "the saints" (see 1.7).

15.26 For the churches in Macedonia and Greece have freely decided to give an offering to help the poor among God's people in Jerusalem.

Although the Greek reads simply "Macedonia and Greece," Paul evidently means by this the churches in Macedonia and Greece. Macedonia was a province immediately north of Greece, the Roman province of Achaia.

The verb rendered have freely decided (RSV "have been pleased"; NAB "kindly decided") is merely rendered "have decided" by some (JB, Moffatt; NEB "resolved"; Goodspeed "determined"). The verb does mean "to decide," but it always implies that a decision has been made because the people were happy to make it. This combination of ideas may be expressed in some languages as "were glad to decide" or "decided with happy hearts."

The word translated offering (RSV, Goodspeed, Moffatt, NAB "contribution"; NEB "a common fund"; JB "a generous contribution") is a word which in other contexts may mean "fellowship" or "sharing." Here it has the specific meaning the translations give it. In some languages to give an offering may be "to give money to" or "to give money as a gift to."

The poor among God's people is literally "the poor of the saints" (see verse 25 and 1.7). The poor among God's people in Jerusalem may be translated in a number of ways: "those who are God's people in Jerusalem and who are poor," "those who belong to God's people in Jerusalem and who are poor," or "the poor who are counted with God's people in Jerusalem."

15.27 They themselves decided to do it. But, as a matter of fact, they have an obligation to help those poor; the Jews shared their spiritual blessings with the Gentiles, and so the Gentiles ought to serve the Jews with their material blessings.

The verb decided is the same verb rendered have freely decided in the previous verse. In some instances the equivalent of freely decided may be "they decided without being commanded to" or "they themselves decided to do it, even though no one had told them that they should do it."

But, as a matter of fact, they have an obligation to help those poor is literally "and they are their debtors." The force of "and" in this context is emphatic (RSV, NEB "and indeed"), and so is rendered but, as a matter of fact by the TEV. In some languages the equivalent may be "in reality, however," "but the truth is," or "but they really (have an obligation)."

"They are their debtors" is transformed by the TEV to read they have an obligation to help (the possessive pronoun "their" refers back to the poor in the previous verse). The expression of obligation may be rendered in some languages as an obligatory mode: "they should help those poor."

The next clause in this sentence literally reads "for if the Gentiles shared in their spiritual things." The "if" clause refers to a condition that is true to fact, and so may be rendered as a statement as in the TEV. "Spiritual things" is best taken in the sense of spiritual blessings (so also RSV); the possessive pronoun "their" refers to the Jews (TEV).

As can be seen in the literal translation, this clause in Greek involves a pseudo-substitute passive construction. Accordingly, "the Gentiles shared in the spiritual blessings of the Jews" may be transformed into an active expression the Jews shared their spiritual blessings with the Gentiles. Spiritual blessings in this context, as in so many instances, is "blessings for their spirits." Within the larger context the entire sentence may read: "The Jews shared with the Gentiles the good things from God for their spirits."

The last clause in this verse contains several problems. First there is the pronominal ambiguity in the Greek text: "they are obligated to serve them." In this "they" refers to the Gentiles, while "them" is a reference to the Jews. Then there is the problem of the Greek phrase "with (or in) their fleshly things." Most translations take the Greek preposition (en) to mean "with" and "fleshly things" (KJV "carnal things") to mean material blessings (so RSV). But the NEB understands the preposition to have the meaning of "in" and so takes "fleshly things" as a reference to the material needs of the Jews: "the Gentiles have a clear duty to contribute to their material needs."

The Gentiles may require further specification, "the Gentile believers"; and their material blessings may be translated as "the things which they have received from God," "the physical things which they have received from God," "the everyday things they have received from God," or "the things necessary for everyday living." The entire clause may be translated: "the Gentile believers, therefore, ought to help the Jewish believers by giving them those things which are needed for everyday life."

15.28 When I have finished this task, and have turned over to them the full amount of money that has been raised for them, I shall leave for Spain and visit you on my way there.

This task (NAB "my task"; Moffatt, NEB "this business"; Goodspeed "this matter") is literally "this" (RSV, JB).

And have turned over to them the full amount of money that has been raised for them is literally "and sealed to them this fruit" (see RSV footnote and KJV). The phrase "this fruit" can easily be understood in the sense of the money that has been raised for them (JB "what has been raised"; Moffatt "the proceeds of the collection"; Goodspeed "this contribution"). The use of the verb "to seal" in this context is admittedly difficult. Perhaps it is best understood from the practice of sealing sacks of grain. If a sack of grain were sealed, the recipient was assured that the grain he received was the full amount that had been placed in the sack. For that reason the TEV renders this verb as have turned over to them the full amount.

And have turned over to them the full amount of money that has been raised for them, may be interpreted as an explanation of this task—for example, "When I have finished this task, namely, turning over to them the full amount of money which has been raised for them." Full amount of money may be "all the money."

I shall leave for Spain and visit you on my way there is literally "I shall go through you to Spain." The JB renders this as "I shall set out for Spain and visit you on the way." This clause may also be rendered as "I will begin my journey to Spain but stop to see you on the way" or "... stop to stay with you for a time on the way."

15.29 When I come to you, I know that I shall come with a full measure of the blessing of Christ.

With a full measure of the blessing of Christ is literally "with fullness of the blessing of Christ." In 11.12 "fullness" is used in the sense of the complete number. In the present context the meaning is full measure (so also NEB) or "full amount." Paul means that he will bring them a blessing from Christ in which nothing will be lacking (Moffatt "a full blessing from Christ"; NAB "with Christ's full blessing"; Goodspeed "with Christ's fullest blessing"; JB "with rich blessings from Christ").

In speaking about the blessing of Christ it is important to indicate that this is a blessing from Christ for the believers in Rome, not merely some blessing from Christ which Paul himself will possess. In order to indicate this, it may be necessary to say: "I shall come and share with you a rich blessing from Christ," "I will come and cause that Christ will bless you fully," or "... completely."

> [30]I urge you, brothers, by our Lord Jesus Christ and by the love that the Spirit gives: join me in praying fervently to God for me. [31]Pray that I may be kept safe from the unbelievers in Judea, and that my service in Jerusalem may be acceptable to God's people there. [32]And so I will come to you full of joy, if it is God's will, and enjoy a refreshing visit with you. [33]May God, our source of peace, be with all of you. Amen.

Although Paul is confident that he will get to Rome, he knows of the dangers that he must face in Jerusalem, and so he asks that the Christians in Rome pray for him.

15.30 I urge you, brothers, by our Lord Jesus Christ and by the love that the Spirit gives: join me in praying fervently to God for me.

In Greek verses 30-32 are all one sentence. I urge you translates the same verb used in 12.1, I make this appeal. It is also used in 12.8 with the meaning of to encourage.

The Greek phrase "love of the Spirit" must be taken with the meaning the love that the Spirit gives (NEB "the love that the Spirit inspires").

15.31

It is not easy to specify precisely how the phrases by our Lord Jesus Christ and by the love that the Spirit gives are to be related to the verb urge. The Greek preposition dia indicates primarily "through" or "by means of," but this does not imply agency. In other words, it would not be correct to say: "our Lord Jesus Christ is the one who causes me to urge you." It would seem that the most satisfactory way of defining the relation in this clause is to consider by our Lord Jesus Christ as stating the underlying basis for Paul's urging the believers at Rome to pray to God for him. Perhaps this can be most satisfactorily rendered as "because of our faith in the Lord Jesus Christ and because of the love that the Spirit has given us, I urge you to pray with me very earnestly to God for me."

Join me in praying fervently (Goodspeed "join me in most earnest prayer"; Phillips "to stand behind me in earnest prayer") is rendered "to strive together with me in your prayers" (RSV). The verb rendered "to strive together with" (RSV) is a metaphor alluding to warfare (note NEB "be my allies in the fight"), but it is best taken figuratively with the meaning of "to join together fervently (in praying)." The NEB ("be my allies in the fight; pray to God for me that...") takes this phrase as describing two actions, but this is not the sense in which the Greek would normally be understood.

15.31 Pray that I may be kept safe from the unbelievers in Judea, and that my service in Jerusalem may be acceptable to God's people there.

The word translated unbelievers (so also RSV, JB, NEB) is literally "those ...who are disobedient" (Goodspeed). The same verb is used in 11.30,31, and is there translated by the TEV with the meaning of "disobedient." In 2.8 the TEV translates it "reject (what is right)." In the present context the meaning of "unbelieving" or of "refusing to believe" seems to be primary. It is a reference to non-Christian Jews. That I may be kept safe from the unbelievers in Judea may be translated as "that those in Judea who do not believe in Jesus Christ may not harm me."

Although the phrase in Jerusalem is literally "into (Greek eis) Jerusalem" (RSV "for Jerusalem"; NEB "to Jerusalem"), the meaning seems best represented by the preposition in.

On God's people (literally "saints"), see verse 25 above and 1.7.

There, though not appearing in the Greek text, is added in accordance with the demands of English grammar.

The second clause of verse 31 may be somewhat altered in the order of its component parts: "and that God's people in Jerusalem may be happy to receive my help for them" or "...what I have done to help them."

15.32 And so I will come to you full of joy, if it is God's will, and enjoy a refreshing visit with you.

The transitional phrase and so may be translated as "and having done this," "and as a result," or even "and then."

As previously indicated, verse 32 is a continuation of the sentence begun in verse 30. It literally begins with "in order that." Paul's expression "enjoy" is rendered by the more natural English expression full of joy (NAB "with joy"; Goodspeed "with a glad heart"; JB "feeling very happy"; NEB "in a happy frame of mind").

If it is God's will is literally "through the will of God." In such a construction the Greek preposition dia ("through") is used in the sense of "the circumstances under which something takes place," and so the phrase would mean something like "through the circumstances made possible by God's will." The JB translates as "if God wills" and Goodspeed translates in the same way as the TEV. If it is God's will must be related to the verb will come, not to the condition of being full of joy. This may require some change in order—for example, "and so, if it is God's will, I will come to you full of joy." In a number of languages an expression of condition normally precedes the result.

The verb enjoy a refreshing visit implies both rest (NEB "enjoy a time of rest"; JB "enjoy a period of rest") and refreshing of one's spirit (NAB "and be refreshed in spirit"). Enjoy a refreshing visit with you may be rendered as "be happy and rested because of my visit with you" or "and my visit with you will cause me to be happy and to become rested."

15.33 May God, our source of peace, be with all of you. Amen.

The third person imperative, introduced in English by the auxiliary may, may be expressed in some languages as prayer: "I pray that God."

In the present context the phrase "the God of peace" means "the God who is our source of peace" (see Goodspeed "God who gives peace") or "who causes us to experience peace."

Since Amen in this context occurs in close proximity to an expression of prayer, it may be most satisfactory to retain the transliterated form, particularly if this is well known and widely used in the receptor-language community.

CHAPTER 16

Personal Greetings

16 I recommend to you our sister Phoebe, who serves the church at
Cenchreae. 2Receive her in the Lord's name, as God's people should,
and give her any help she may need from you; for she herself has been a good
friend to many people and also to me.

The section heading Personal Greetings may be translated as "Paul Greets Various Persons in Rome" or "Paul Sends a Special Word to Some of the Believers in Rome."

This chapter consists primarily of a series of personal greetings, into which have been incorporated a few final instructions (vv. 17-20). It is concluded by a prayer of praise.

16.1 I recommend to you our sister Phoebe, who serves the church at Cenchreae.

Recommend (Moffatt and Goodspeed "introduce") is rendered by most translations as "commend." Letters of "recommendation" were well known in the ancient world and Paul himself alludes to them in 2 Corinthians 3.1.

In some languages there is no technical term such as recommend. It may, therefore, be necessary to use a phrase: "I want to say to you that our sister Phoebe is a fine person," "...Phoebe, who also believes as we do, is a fine person," or "...is to be trusted."

The word sister (like the word "brother") is used in the sense of "fellow believer."

Phoebe is mentioned only here in the New Testament.

Who serves (NEB "who holds office"; Goodspeed "who is a helper") translates a noun (RSV "a deaconess"). It is doubtful that this had become a technical term for an office in the church at the time that Paul wrote, and it is better to use a general term rather than the specific term "deaconess."

Cenchreae was the seaport of Corinth on the eastern side of the isthmus (see Acts 18.18).

16.2 Receive her in the Lord's name, as God's people should, and give her any help she may need from you; for she herself has been a good friend to many people and also to me.

In Greek verses 1 and 2 are all one sentence. "In the Lord" is rendered by the TEV as in the Lord's name (NEB "in the fellowship of the Lord"). In such a context "in the Lord" means "because she belongs to the Lord." The initial phrase receive her in the Lord's name may therefore be rendered as "welcome her as one who belongs to the Lord."

As God's people should (Goodspeed "as God's people should welcome one another") is literally "worthy of saints." On "saints" see 1.7. This phrase could possibly be taken with the meaning "in a way that she should be received because she is one of God's people," but translators and commentators generally take the phrase with the same meaning as in the TEV. Accordingly, one can render this clause as "in the way in which God's people should welcome one another" or "as God's people should receive one another."

Give her any help she may need from you would, of course, include the matter of financial assistance.

Good friend (so NEB) has been translated by the RSV as "helper" and by Goodspeed as "protector." This word appears only here in the New Testament, and though later it is used as a technical term meaning "patroness," it is better rendered in this passage in a general sense. A good friend to many people and also to me may be rendered simply as "she has been very good to many people and also to me" or "she has helped many people very much and has also helped me."

> [3]I send greetings to Priscilla and Aquila, my fellow workers in the service of Christ Jesus, [4]who risked their lives for me. I am grateful to them—not only I, but all the Gentile churches as well. [5]Greetings also to the church that meets in their house.
>
> Greetings to my dear friend Epaenetus, who was the first man in the province of Asia to believe in Christ. [6]Greetings to Mary, who has worked so hard for you. [7]Greetings to Andronicus and Junias, fellow Jews who were in prison with me; they are well known among the apostles, and they became Christians before I did.

16.3-4 I send greetings to Priscilla and Aquila, my fellow workers in the service of Christ Jesus, (4) who risked their lives for me. I am grateful to them---not only I, but all the Gentile churches as well.

I send greetings to is literally "greet." In some languages a translation of I send greetings to may be "I send these special words to" or even "I want to mention."

Priscilla and Aquila are no doubt the two persons mentioned in Acts (see in particular Acts 18; cf. 1 Corinthians 16.19).

"In Christ Jesus" is taken by the TEV in the sense of in the service of Christ Jesus (so also NAB) and by Goodspeed with the meaning of "in the cause of Christ Jesus"; most other translations render literally.

My fellow workers in the service of Christ Jesus may be rendered as "they worked together with me in serving Christ Jesus" or "they joined with me in working for Christ Jesus."

Verse 4 begins "who in behalf of my soul laid down their own necks." The phrase "in behalf of my soul" means for me (RSV "for my life"; NEB and JB "to save my life"); while Paul's remaining words are easily understood in the sense of risked their lives (many translations "risked their necks"). Risked their lives may be expressed in a variety of ways in different languages: "they were in danger of being killed," "they dared to be killed," "they were willing to be killed," or "they were willing to die."

16.5

I am grateful to them may be translated as "I owe them much thanks" or "I thank them very much." In some instances, however, a more figurative expression may be used: "my heart is warmed because of them" or "my bowels groan because of them."

16.5 Greetings also to the church that meets in their house.
Greetings to my dear friend Epaenetus, who was the first man in the province of Asia to believe in Christ.

Verse 5 is a continuation of the Greek sentence begun in verse 3. As this verse indicates, the first Christian places of worship were the private homes of those persons who were fortunate enough to own houses.

It may be difficult to speak in some languages of "greeting a church." One may, however, "greet the members of a church" or "greet the believers who meet as a church in their house."

Epaenetus is mentioned only here in the New Testament. Who was the first man in the province of Asia to believe in Christ translates a Semitic expression ("who is the first fruit of Asia for Christ") which is understood by all commentators in the same sense as in the TEV. A similar phrase is used in 1 Corinthians 16.15.

Since the term first designates a prior event, it may be most naturally translated in some languages as "who, before anyone else in the province of Asia, believed in Christ" or "who believed in Christ when no one else in the province of Asia had believed in Christ."

16.6 Greetings to Mary, who has worked so hard for you.

Nothing further is known of this Mary. There is no justification for identifying her with any other Mary of the New Testament.

16.7 Greetings to Andronicus and Junias, fellow Jews who were in prison with me; they are well known among the apostles, and they became Christians before I did.

Adronicus and Junias are not mentioned elsewhere in the New Testament; they could easily have been husband and wife, or brother and sister.

The word translated fellow Jews (Goodspeed and NEB "fellow-countrymen") is rendered by some to mean "kinsmen" (RSV). However, it is more likely that the broader sense is to be maintained in this passage. Fellow Jews may be translated as "who are also Jews even as I am" or "who, together with me, are Jews."

They are well known among the apostles has been understood by some to mean "the apostles know them well," but a far more acceptable interpretation would imply that these men were counted as apostles and were well known, for example, "as apostles they are well known."

They became Christians before I did is literally "who before me came in Christ." The obvious meaning of this phrase is as the TEV states it.

> 8 My greetings to Ampliatus, my dear friend in the fellowship of the Lord.
> 9 Greetings to Urbanus, our fellow worker in Christ's service, and to Stachys,
> my dear friend. 10 Greetings to Apelles, whose loyalty to Christ has been
> proved. Greetings to those who belong to the family of Aristobulus. 11 Greet-
> ings to Herodion, a fellow Jew, and to the Christian brothers in the family of
> Narcissus.
>
> 12 My greetings to Tryphaena and Tryphosa, who work in the Lord's service,
> and to my dear friend Persis, who has done so much work for the Lord. 13 I
> send greetings to Rufus, that outstanding worker in the Lord's service, and to
> his mother, who has always treated me like a son. 14 My greetings to Asyncritus,
> Phlegon, Hermes, Patrobas, Hermas, and all the other Christian brothers with
> them. 15 Greetings to Philologus and Julia, to Nereus and his sister, to Olympas
> and to all of God's people who are with them.
>
> 16 Greet one another with a brotherly kiss. All the churches of Christ send
> you their greetings.

Nothing else is known, either from the New Testament or from any other source, about the twenty individuals and two families listed in these verses. In this list Paul mentions both men and women. The men are Ampliatus, Urbanus, Stachys, Apelles, Aristobulus, Herodion, Narcissus, Rufus, Asyncritus, Phlegon, Hermes, Patrobas, Hermas, Philologus, Nereus, and Olympas; and the women are Tryphaena (v. 12), Tryphosa (v. 12), Persis (v. 12), and Julia (v. 15).

16.8 My greetings to Ampliatus, my dear friend in the fellowship of the Lord.

In verse 8 in the fellowship of the Lord is literally "in the Lord" (similar to the meaning of "in Christ"; see 6.3, and 9-11).

My dear friend may be equivalent to "my close friend" or "my strong friend," but the phrase in the fellowship of the Lord should not be understood as an expression of cause, as it is in a number of other contexts. In this particular verse it is equivalent to "he is my good friend and is in union with the Lord."

16.9 Greetings to Urbanus, our fellow worker in Christ's service, and to Stachys, my dear friend.

In Christ's service is literally "in Christ" (see v. 3).

16.10-11 Greetings to Apelles, whose loyalty to Christ has been proved. Greetings to those who belong to the family of Aristobulus. (11) Greetings to Herodion, a fellow Jew, and to the Christian brothers in the family of Narcissus.

Paul's phrase "the tested one in Christ" may mean "who has gone through so much for Christ" (JB). Goodspeed moves in this direction by translating "that veteran Christian." However, the word "tested one" may refer to one who has gone through a test and therefore has proved himself (RSV "is approved in Christ"). The TEV understands this phrase in this latter sense: whose loyalty to Christ has been proved. This may be rendered as "who has shown clearly how loyal he is to Christ."

Those who belong to the family of Aristobulus (v. 10) may be understood in the extended sense of "the household of Aristobulus" (NEB). The same judgment may be made with regard to the phrase in the family of Narcissus (v. 11). The Christian brothers (v. 11) is literally "those in the Lord" (RSV), equivalent in some languages to "fellow believers in Christ." The NEB renders this as "who are in the Lord's fellowship" and Goodspeed as "the Christians."

16.12 My greetings to Tryphaena and Tryphosa, who work in the Lord's service, and to my dear friend Persis, who has done so much work for the Lord.

The phrase in the Lord's service is literally "in the Lord" (see vv. 3 and 9); while for the Lord is also literally "in the Lord," and may be taken with the same sense as the previous phrase.

16.13 I send greetings to Rufus, that outstanding worker in the Lord's service, and to his mother, who has always treated me like a son.

That outstanding worker (NEB "an outstanding follower") is literally "the elect one." This is a term which may be applied to all Christians (see 8.33), but in the present context it is used to draw some special attention to Rufus as an outstanding person in the Lord's service. Once again in the Lord's service is literally "in the Lord" (see vv. 2,9,12).

Paul's expression "his mother and mine" is taken by the TEV to mean his mother, who has always treated me like a son (NEB "whom I call mother too"; Goodspeed "who has been a mother to me"). Rufus' mother was not actually Paul's mother and it is clear from the context what Paul means, and so the TEV, along with others, makes this information explicit.

In translating the clause who has always treated me like a son, it is important to avoid the implication that the mother of Rufus had been overbearing. One can render this last clause as "who has helped me just like my own mother would have helped me" or "who has helped me just as though I were her own son."

16.14-15 My greetings to Asyncritus, Phlegon, Hermes, Patrobas, Hermas, and all the other Christian brothers with them. (15) Greetings to Philologus and Julia, to Nereus and his sister, to Olympas and to all of God's people who are with them.

The final phrase with them may be interpreted as "those with whom they associate"—for example, "and all the other fellow Christians who associate with them." The same applies to the last clause of verse 15, who are with them. The two groups of persons identified in these verses may represent persons who met in different homes for Christian fellowship and worship.

16.16 Greet one another with a brotherly kiss. All the churches of Christ send you their greetings.

With a brotherly kiss is literally "with a holy kiss." Paul uses this expression elsewhere (1 Corinthians 16.20; 2 Corinthians 13.12; 1 Thessalonians 5.26), and it occurs in a similar form in 1 Peter 5.14 (literally "with a kiss of love"; TEV with the kiss of Christian love). Evidently the kiss was a manner of sacred greeting among the early Christians; later it became a part of the church liturgy.

In some languages, however, one cannot employ a specific equivalent of kiss, since such would be too closely associated with sexual interest. An equivalent may be "greet one another affectionately," thus employing a general term for the more specific expression of kiss in Greek. Some languages actually employ two quite different terms for kiss, one which identifies kissing on the mouth (which may have sexual connotations) and the other which specifies kissing on the cheek (which denotes greeting). It is the latter form of kissing which should be indicated in this type of context. Though in some languages kissing does not carry overtones of sexual interest, it may be regarded as silly and never something for adults to do. Therefore some other form of appropriate affectionate greeting should be employed.

Final Instructions

17 I urge you, my brothers: watch out for those who cause divisions and upset people's faith, who go against the teaching which you have received; keep away from them. 18 For those who do such things are not serving Christ our Lord, but their own appetites. By their fine words and flattering speech they deceive the minds of innocent people. 19 Everyone has heard of your loyalty to the gospel, and for this reason I am happy about you. I want you to be wise about what is good, but innocent in what is evil. 20 And God, our source of peace, will soon crush Satan under your feet.

The grace of our Lord Jesus be with you.

21 Timothy, my fellow worker, sends you his greetings; and so do Lucius, Jason, and Sosipater, fellow Jews.

22 I, Tertius, the writer of this letter, send you Christian greetings.

23 My host Gaius, in whose house the church meets, sends you his greetings; Erastus, the city treasurer, and our brother Quartus, send you their greetings.

[24 The grace of our Lord Jesus Christ be with you all. Amen.]

The section heading Final Instructions may be rendered as "Paul Tells the Believers at Rome What They Must Do" or "Paul Concludes by Telling the Believers in Rome What They Must Do."

16.17 I urge you, my brothers: watch out for those who cause divisions and upset people's faith, who go against the teaching which you have received; keep away from them.

Watch out for (NEB "keep your eye on"; JB "be on your guard against") is stronger than a translation such as "take note of" (RSV) might suggest.

Those who cause divisions may be rendered as "those who separate people into groups," "those who cause different groups of people to fight with one another," or "those who cause strong differences between people."

Upset people's faith (NEB "lead others astray") may be literally rendered as "do things to cause (people) to stumble." In this context the people who are made to stumble are believers. In some languages it is quite meaningless to talk about "upsetting a person's faith." One can, however, "twist another's faith" or "cause a believer to leave the right road."

Who go against the teaching is a verb transform of the noun phrase "contrary to the teaching" (NAB). Teaching (NEB, Phillips, NAB) or "instruction" (Goodspeed) is a more acceptable term than "doctrine" (RSV, JB, Moffatt). Rather than say go against the teaching, it may be more appropriate to render "talk against the teaching," "teach contrary to the way in which you have received the teaching," or "teach against what you have been taught."

You have received (so NAB; NEB "you received") is literally "which you learned." Several translations make this into a passive construction (RSV "you have been taught"; Goodspeed "you were given").

Keep away from them may be translated in a negative form, "do not associate with them" or "do not go near them."

16.18-19 For those who do such things are not serving Christ our Lord, but their own appetites. By their fine words and flattering speech they deceive the minds of innocent people. (19) Everyone has heard of your loyalty to the gospel, and for this reason I am happy about you. I want you to be wise about what is good, but innocent in what is evil.

Appetites (many translations) is literally "stomach." Although a similar expression is used in Philippians 3.19, it is difficult to define precisely what Paul means by this phrase. Goodspeed rendered it by "base passions" and Moffatt by "base desires," but some commentators understand it in the sense of undue concern with laws about what one can or cannot eat. Something of the parallelism between serving Christ our Lord and their own appetites may be indicated by "For those who do such things are not concerned with helping Christ our Lord; they are only concerned with what they should eat and what they should not eat." One may also say: "...are not thinking about helping Christ our Lord, but are only thinking about what they should or should not eat."

Fine words (NEB "smooth...words"; NAB "smooth...speech") translates a word which appears only here in the New Testament. The reference is to speech that may sound reasonable or "plausible" (Goodspeed). By their fine words and flattering speech may be translated as "They use beautiful words and they flatter people; in this way they deceive."

Minds is literally "hearts," but in Semitic thought the heart was the seat of intellectual activity. In some languages deceive the minds of innocent people may be rendered as "mix up the hearts of people who have not experienced these evils."

Paul uses two different words in verses 18 and 19, both of which are translated innocent by the TEV. The RSV translates the first of these terms by "simple-minded" (so Goodspeed), and the NEB translates the second by "simpletons." Etymologically the two words are different, but they should be translated with essentially the same meaning. The first literally means "inexperienced as far as evil is concerned"—therefore innocent. The second literally means "unmixed," and when followed by the phrase in what is evil, the construction means innocent in what is evil.

Your loyalty to the gospel may be translated as "how strongly you hold to the gospel" or "how well you obey the gospel."

For this reason I am happy about you is rendered in some languages as "therefore you cause me to be happy."

Wise about what is good may be rendered as "wise in knowing what is good." In contrast with this, innocent in what is evil may be rendered as "innocent in doing what is evil" or "innocent as far as doing what is evil is concerned."

16.20 And God, our source of peace, will soon crush Satan under your feet. The grace of our Lord Jesus be with you.

On the expression God, our source of peace see 15.33.

Though generally the phrase will soon crush Satan under your feet can be readily understood, it is possible for some misunderstanding to arise because of the expression under your feet. In some languages this would not express the concept of one's dominance over some object. The meaning is "will destroy Satan and make him subject to you" or "destroy Satan's power and make him subject to you." In some instances an adaptation of this expression may be useful or necessary.

The grace of our Lord Jesus be with you is a prayer, and Paul means "may our Lord Jesus continue to act towards you in grace." He uses similar expressions in 1 Corinthians 16.23; Galatians 6.18; Philippians 4.23; Colossians 4.18; 1 Thessalonians 5.28; 2 Thessalonians 3.18. One may wish to indicate that this is a prayer by rendering: "I pray that our Lord Jesus Christ may continue to show you grace."

16.21 Timothy, my fellow worker, sends you his greetings; and so do Lucius, Jason, and Sosipater, fellow Jews.

Timothy was evidently with Paul when he wrote this letter; he is mentioned in a number of Paul's letters and in several places in the book of Acts (see especially Acts 16.1-3). Nothing definite is known about the other persons mentioned. There is a Lucius mentioned in Acts 13; a Jason is mentioned in Acts 17.5-9; and a Sopater (not Sosipater) is mentioned in Acts 20.4.

Paul evidently dictated this letter as he did other of his letters (see 1 Corinthians 16.21; Galatians 6.11; Colossians 4.18; and 2 Thessalonians 3.17).

16.22 I, Tertius, the writer of this letter, send you Christian greetings.

Nothing further is known of Tertius, to whom Paul dictated this letter. In translating the phrase the writer of this letter, it is important to indicate clearly that Tertius was only one who "copied down this letter" or "wrote down what Paul said"---for example, "I, Tertius, who have written down for this letter what Paul has said, send you greetings as a fellow believer."

"Greet you in the Lord" (RSV) is taken by the TEV and the NEB to mean send you Christian greetings. Goodspeed does something similar: "wish to be remembered to you as a fellow-Christian."

16.23 My host Gaius, in whose house the church meets, sends you his greetings; Erastus, the city treasurer, and our brother Quartus, send you their greetings.

The name Gaius appears several times in the New Testament (Acts 19.29; 20.4; 1 Corinthians 1.14; and 3 John 1), but it is doubtful that the same person is indicated in each case. Gaius is described as Paul's host and the host of the entire church, that is, the one in whose house the church meets. My host may be translated as "the one in whose house I am staying" or "the one who has invited me to stay with him."

The name Erastus appears in Acts 19.22 and 2 Timothy 4.20. The city treasurer may be translated as "the one who keeps the money for the city," "the one who is responsible to pay out money for the city," or "the one who controls the funds of the city government."

Quartus is nowhere else referred to.

16.24 [The grace of our Lord Jesus Christ be with you all. Amen.]

The earliest manuscripts omit verse 24. It is not included in the RSV, the NEB, Goodspeed, the JB, and Moffatt. The NAB likewise omits this benediction, even though it has a verse 24 (the latter part of verse 23 in other translations).

Concluding Prayer of Praise

25 Let us give glory to God! He is able to make you stand firm in your faith, according to the Good News I preach, the message about Jesus Christ, and according to the revelation of the secret truth which was hidden for long ages in the past. 26 Now, however, that truth has been brought out into the open through the writings of the prophets; and by the command of the eternal God it is made known to all nations, so that all may believe and obey.

27 To the only God, who alone is all-wise, be the glory through Jesus Christ forever! Amen.

This final section heading Concluding Prayer of Praise may be rendered as "In Conclusion Paul Prays to God," "Paul Offers Praise to God," or "In Conclusion Paul Praises God."

16.25 Let us give glory to God! He is able to make you stand firm in your faith, according to the Good News I preach, the message about Jesus Christ, and according to the revelation of the secret truth which was hidden for long ages in the past.

In Greek this is all one sentence, and only in verse 27 is it made clear that God is the one addressed and that the prayer is a call to give glory to him. In English, however, it is more natural to introduce this information at the beginning of the prayer, and so the TEV makes the information explicit: Let us give glory to God! This introductory sentence may be translated as "let us praise God" or, as in some languages, "let us lift up God's greatness." In other languages an expression such as this must be translated by a mode indicating obligation or necessity: "we should praise God."

The phrase in your faith is introduced by the TEV to make explicit what is meant by the verb phrase to make you stand firm. The equivalent of make you stand firm in your faith may be "make you believe strongly" or "make you to continue to believe."

In some languages it is not easy to show the relation between the Good News and "standing firm in your faith." One way of indicating this relation may be "this is what I have said as I preached the Good News."

The phrase the message about Jesus Christ is in apposition with the Good News and therefore may be rendered as "the Good News which is about Jesus Christ."

Secret truth is the same word discussed in 11.25. One may also introduce the phrase according to the revelation of the secret truth as being "this is also what the secret truth had revealed."

The clause which was hidden for long ages in the past may need to be set off as a complete sentence---for example, "The secret truth has not been known for many, many generations." The phrase "many, many generations" is one of the ways in which languages can express a long time in human history.

16.26 Now, however, that truth has been brought out into the open through the writings of the prophets; and by the command of the eternal God it is made known to all nations, so that all may believe and obey.

The relation of the writings of the prophets to the process of "bringing out the truth" may be restructured as "but now the writings of the prophets have caused the truth to be known openly" or "...have caused many people to know the truth." Similarly, the second clause in verse 26 may be rendered as "the eternal God has commanded that all nations should know that truth." As in other contexts, eternal God may be translated as "the God who never dies," "the God who always is," or "the God who never ends."

So that all may believe and obey is literally "for the obedience of faith" (see 1.5). If a grammatical goal is required for verbs "believe" and "obey," God may be introduced: "so that all may believe God and obey him."

16.27 To the only God, who alone is all-wise, be the glory through Jesus Christ forever! Amen.

To the only God, who alone is all-wise is more natural in English than the Greek expression "to the only, the wise, God." To the only God may be best expressed in some languages as "to the one God," "to God who alone is God," or "to the only one who is God." The expression all-wise should not be confused with "comprehensive knowledge." It does not mean here that God knows everything, but "God who in everything is wise," or, as in some languages, "... understands completely."

The third person imperative expressed by be the glory must be expressed as first person plural in some languages: "we should praise the only God who alone is all-wise."

Forever, of course, must qualify the manner in which men should praise God.

Through Jesus Christ does not specify the agency for praising, but rather the one who causes such praise to be given to God. In some languages this may be expressed as "this should happen because of what Jesus Christ did." In such an expression "this" must refer to the giving of praise to God.

Amen may either be transliterated or translated—for example, "surely this is true" or "this is indeed so."

BIBLIOGRAPHY

BIBLE TEXTS AND VERSIONS CITED

Bible: A New Translation. 1922. James Moffatt. New York: Harper and Row.

Good News for Modern Man: The New Testament in Today's English Version. 1971. New York: American Bible Society.

King James Version. 1611.

New American Bible. 1970. Washington: Confraternity of Christian Doctrine.

New English Bible. 1970. London: Oxford University Press and Cambridge University Press.

New Testament: An American Translation. 1923. Edgar J. Goodspeed. Chicago: University of Chicago Press.

New Testament in Modern English. 1962. J. B. Phillips. New York: The Macmillan Company.

Revised Standard Version. 1952. New York: Nelson and Sons.

GENERAL BIBLIOGRAPHY

Barrett, C. K. 1957. A commentary on the Epistle to the Romans. Harper's New Testament Commentaries. New York: Harper and Row.

Denney, J. n.d. St. Paul's Epistle to the Romans. The Expositor's Greek Testament. Grand Rapids: Wm. B. Eerdmans Publishing Co.

Dodd, C. H. 1932. The Epistle to the Romans. Moffatt New Testament Commentary. New York: Harper and Row.

Knox, John. 1954. The Epistle to the Romans. The Interpreter's Bible. Nashville: Abingdon Press.

Michel, Otto. 1955. Der Brief an die Römer. Kritisch-exegetischer Kommentar über das Neue Testament. Göttingen: Vandenhoeck und Ruprecht.

Sanday, William, and Arthur C. Headlam. 1905. A critical and exegetical commentary on the Epistle to the Romans. The International Critical Commentary. Edinburgh: T. & T. Clark.

Schmidt, Hans Wilhelm. 1963. Der Brief des Paulus an die Römer. Theologischer Handkommentar zum Neuen Testament. Berlin: Evangelische Verlagsanstalt.

GLOSSARY OF TECHNICAL TERMS

abstract refers to terms which designate the qualities and quantities (that is, the features) of objects and events but which are not objects or events themselves. For example, "red" is a quality of a number of objects but is not a thing in and of itself. Typical abstracts include "goodness," "beauty," "length," "breadth," and "time." See **concrete**.

active voice See **voice**.

adjective is a word which limits, describes, or qualifies a noun. In English, "red," "tall," "beautiful," "important," etc. are adjectives.

adverb is a word which limits, describes, or modifies a verb, an adjective, or another adverb. In English, "quickly," "soon," "primarily," "very," etc. are adverbs.

adversative expresses something opposed to or in contrast to something already stated. "But" and "however" are adversative conjunctions.

agency, agent In a sentence or clause, the *agent* is that which accomplishes the action, regardless of whether the grammatical construction is active or passive. In "John struck Bill" (active) and "Bill was struck by John" (passive), the agent in either case is "John." See **secondary agency**.

allusion in discourse is an implicit reference to another object or event.

ambiguous describes a word or phrase which in a specific context may have two or more different meanings. For example, "Bill did not leave because John came" could mean either (1) "The coming of John prevented Bill from leaving" or (2) "The coming of John was not the cause of Bill's leaving." It is often the case that what is ambiguous in written form is not ambiguous when actually spoken, since features of intonation and slight pauses usually specify which of two or more meanings is intended. Furthermore, even in written discourse, the entire context normally serves to indicate which meaning is intended by the writer.

animate identifies objects which are regarded as alive and normally able to move voluntarily. "Man," "dog," and "fish" are animate objects, but "tree" is not."

aorist refers to a set of forms in Greek verbs which denote an action completed without the implication of continuance or duration. Usually, but not always, the action is considered as completed in past time.

apposition (appositional construction) is the placing of two expressions together so that they both identify the same object or event; for example, "my friend, Mr. Smith." The one expression is said to be the *appositive* of the other.

attribution, attributive An attributive is a term which limits or describes another term. In "the big man ran slowly," the adjective "big" is an attributive of "man," and the adverb "slowly" is an attributive of "ran." Attribution, therefore, is the act of assigning a certain quality or character to an object or an event. See **adjective, adverb.**

benefactive refers to goals for whom or which something is done. The pronoun "him" is the benefactive goal in each of the following constructions: "they showed him kindness," "they did the work for him," and "they found him an apartment."

causative (also **causal relation,** etc.) relates to events and indicates that someone caused something to happen, rather than that he did it himself. In "John ran the horse," the verb "ran" is a causative, since it was not John who ran, but rather it was John who caused the horse to run.

classifier is a term used with another term (often a proper noun) to indicate what category the latter belongs to. "Town" may serve as a classifier in the phrase "town of Bethlehem" and "river" as a classifier in "river Jordan."

clause is a grammatical construction normally consisting of a subject and a predicate. An *independent* clause may stand alone as a sentence, but a *dependent* clause (functioning as a noun, adjective, or adverb) does not form a complete sentence.

components are the parts or elements which go together to form the whole of an object. For example, the components of bread are flour, salt, shortening, yeast, and water. The components of the meaning (semantic components) of a term are the elements of meaning which it contains. For example, some of the components of "boy" are "human," "male," and "immature."

concessive means expressing a *concession,* that is, the allowance or admission of something which is at variance with the principal thing stated. Concession is usually expressed in English by "though" ("even though," "although"). Example: "Though the current was swift, James was able to cross the stream."

concrete refers to the reality or experience of things or events, particularly in contrast to **abstract.** The term "child," for example, is concrete, but "childhood" is an abstraction. See **abstract.**

conditional refers to a clause or phrase which expresses or implies a condition, in English usually introduced by "if."

conjunctions are words which serve as connectors between words, phrases, clauses, and sentences. "And," "but," "if," "because," etc., are typical conjunctions in English.

connotation involves the emotional attitudes of both speaker and hearer (or writer and reader) to an expression (regardless of its specific meaning) and refers to associations and suggestions evoked by the expression which may be quite distinct from the thing named or described. A connotation may be colloquial, vulgar, old-fashioned, intimate, etc.

construction See **structure.**

context is that which precedes and/or follows any part of a discourse. For example, the context of a word or phrase in Scripture would be the other words and phrases associated with it in the sentence, paragraph, section, and even the entire book in which it occurs. The context of a term often affects its meaning, so that it does not mean exactly the same thing in one context that it does in another.

contrastive means adversative.

coordinate structure is a phrase or clause joined to another phrase or clause, but not dependent on it. Coordinate structures are joined by such conjunctions as "and" or "but," or they are paratactically related. See **subordinate structure, paratactic expression.**

dependent clause is a grammatical construction, consisting normally of a subject and predicate, which is dependent on or embedded in another construction. For example, "if he comes" is a dependent clause in the sentence "If he comes, we'll have to leave." See **clause.**

direct discourse See **discourse.**

direct object is the goal of an event or action specified by a verb. In "John hit the ball," the direct object of "hit" is "ball."

discourse is the connected and continuous communication of thought by means of language, whether spoken or written. The way in which the elements of a discourse are arranged is called *discourse structure. Direct discourse* is the reproduction of the actual words of one person embedded in the discourse of another person. For example, "He declared, 'I will have nothing to do with this man.'" *Indirect discourse* is the reporting of the words of one person embedded in the discourse of another person in an altered grammatical form. For example, "He said he would have nothing to do with that man."

doxology is a hymn or other expression of praise to God, typically in a heightened or poetic literary form.

elements are the same as components.

ellipsis (plural *ellipses*) or **elliptical expression** refers to words or phrases normally omitted in a discourse when the sense is perfectly clear without them. In the following sentence, the words within brackets are elliptical: "If [it is] necessary [for me to do so], I will wait up all night." What is elliptical in one language may need to be expressed in another. See **explicit, implicit.**

eschatological refers to the end of the world and the events connected with it. In this connection, the term "world" is understood in various ways by various persons.

etymology is the study of the derivation or history of words. While this can be a helpful study in many ways, it is much more important to know how a word is understood by its users in the actual context of the source language.

euphemism or **euphemistic expression** is a mild or indirect term used in the place of another term which is felt to be impolite, distasteful, or vulgar. For example, "to pass away" is a euphemism for "to die."

event is a semantic category of meanings referring to actions, processes, etc., in which objects can participate. In English, most events are grammatically classified as verbs ("run," "grow," "think," etc.), but many nouns also may refer to events, as, for example, "baptism," "song," "game," and "prayer."

exclusive first person plural excludes the person(s) addressed. That is, a speaker may use "we" to refer to himself and his companions, while specifically excluding the person(s) to whom he is speaking. See **inclusive first person plural.**

exegesis, exegete, exegetical The process of determining the meaning of a text (or the result of this process), normally in terms of "who said what to whom under what circumstances and with what intent," is called *exegesis.* A correct exegesis is indispensable before a passage can be translated correctly. *Exegetes* are men who devote their labors to exegesis. *Exegetical* refers to exegesis.

explicit refers to information which is expressed in the words of a discourse. This is in contrast to *implicit* information. See **implicit.**

figure of speech or **figurative expression** is the use of words in other than their literal or ordinary sense, in order to suggest a picture or image, or for some other special effect. *Metaphors* and *similes* are figures of speech.

finite verb is any verb form which distinguishes person, number, tense, mode, or aspect. It is usually referred to in contrast to an *infinitive* verb form, which indicates the action or state without specifying such things as agent or time.

first person See **person.**

focus is the center of attention in a discourse or any part of a discourse.

generic has reference to all the members of a particular class or kind of objects. It is the contrary of *specific.* For example, the term "animal" is generic, while "dog" is specific. However, "dog" is generic in relation to "poodle."

genitive case is a grammatical set of forms occurring in many languages, used primarily to indicate that a noun is the modifier of another noun. The genitive often indicates possession, but it may also indicate measure, origin, characteristic, etc.

goal is the object which receives or undergoes the action of a verb. Grammatically, the goal may be the subject of a passive construction ("John was hit," in which "John" is the goal of "hit"), or of certain intransitives ("the door shut"), or it may be the direct object of a transitive verb ("[something] hit John").

idiom or **idiomatic expression** is a combination of terms whose meanings cannot be derived by adding up the meanings of the parts. "To hang one's head," "to have a green thumb," and "behind the eight-ball" are English idioms. Idioms almost always lose their meaning completely when translated from one language to another.

imperative refers to forms of a verb which indicate commands or requests. In "go and do likewise," the verbs "go" and "do" are imperatives. In most languages, imperatives are confined to the grammatical second person; but some languages have corresponding forms for the first and third persons. These are usually expressed in English by the use of "may" or "let." For example, "May we not have to beg!" "Let them eat cake!"

implicit refers to information that is not formally represented in a discourse, since it is assumed that it is already known to the receptor. This is in contrast to *explicit* information, which is expressed in the words of a discourse.

inclusive first person plural includes both the speaker and the one(s) to whom he is speaking. See **exclusive first person plural.**

indicative refers to a group of modal forms of verbs in which an act or condition is stated or questioned as an actual fact, rather than a potentiality or unrealized condition. See **imperative, subjunctive, modal.**

indirect discourse See **discourse.**

indirect object is the benefactive goal of the event or action spcified by a verb. In "John threw Henry the ball," the direct object or goal of "threw" is "ball" and the indirect object is "Henry." See **benefactive, direct object.**

infinitive See **finite verb.**

interpretation of a text is the exegesis of it. See **exegesis.**

intransitive refers to a verb which does not have or need a direct object to complete its meaning; for example, "he lives." See **transitive.**

inversion in discourse is to restructure one form into its opposite; for example, to change a passive into an active (as "he was struck by a ball" changed to "a ball struck him").

irony is a sarcastic or humorous manner of discourse in which what is said is intended to express its opposite; for example, "That was a wise thing to do!" intended to convey the meaning, "That was a stupid thing to do!"

linguistic refers to language, especially the formal structure of language.

literal means the ordinary or primary meaning of a term or expression, in contrast to a *figurative* meaning. (See **figure of speech.**) In translation *literal* means following the exact words and word order of the source language.

marginal helps in Bible Society usage are notes, normally occurring on the same page as the text and providing purely objective, factual information of the following types: alternative readings (different forms of the source-language text), alternative renderings (different ways of rendering the source-language text), historical data, and cultural details, all of which may be necessary for a satisfactory understanding of the text.

Notes which are doctrinal or homiletical interpretations of the text are excluded from Scriptures published by the Bible Societies.

markers are features of a discourse which signal some particular structure. For example, words for speaking may mark the onset of direct discourse, a phrase such as "once upon a time" may mark the beginning of a fairy story, and certain features of parallelism are the dominant markers of poetry.

metaphor (metaphorical term) is likening one object to another by speaking of it as if it were the other; for example, "flowers dancing in the breeze." Metaphors are the most commonly used figures of speech and are often so subtle that a speaker or writer is not conscious of the fact that he is using figurative language. See **simile.**

middle voice See **voice.**

modal refers to forms of verbs in certain languages which indicate the attitude of a speaker to what he is saying; for example, wish, hesitancy, command, etc. The various categories of verb forms are called *moods* (or *modes*). In English they are expressed by such auxiliary verbs as "can," "do," "may," "shall," etc. See **imperative, indicative, subjunctive.**

nominal refers to nouns or noun-like words. See **nouns.**

noun is a word that is the name of a subject of discourse, as a person, place, thing, idea, etc. See **proper name.**

object See **direct object, indirect object, semantic.**

paraphrastic refers to **paraphrase**, which is a restatement of the meaning of a passage, usually for the sake of greater clarity. Paraphrase differs from translation in that in paraphrase the writer usually makes radical alterations in the form of the original message, often adding to it extensively, whereas a translator is required to follow more closely the text of the original message.

paratactic expression or relationship **(parataxis)** refers to two or more clauses of equal rank which stand together without being joined by a connective. Example: "I came, I saw, I conquered." See **conjunction.**

parenthetical statement is a digression from the main theme of a discourse which interrupts that discourse. It is usually set off by marks of parenthesis ( ).

particle is a small word whose grammatical form does not change. In English the most common particles are prepositions and conjunctions.

passage is the text of Scripture in a specific location. It is usually thought of as comprising more than one verse, but it can be a single verse or part of a verse.

passive voice See **voice.**

perfect tense For an explanation of this, see page 98.

person, as a grammatical term, refers to the speaker, the person spoken to, or the person(s) or thing(s) spoken about. **First person** is the person(s) or thing(s) speaking ("I," "me," "my," "mine," "we," "us," "our," "ours"). **Second person** is the person(s) or thing(s) spoken to ("thou," "thee," "thy," "thine," "ye," "you," "your," "yours"). **Third person** is the person(s) or thing(s) spoken about ("he," "she," "it," "his," "her," "them," "their," etc.). The examples here given are all pronouns but in many languages the verb forms distinguish between the persons and also indicate whether they are singular or plural.

phrase is a grammatical construction of two or more words, but less than a complete clause or a sentence. A phrase may have the same function as the head word of the phrase. For example, "the old man" has essentially the same functions as "man" would have, or it may have a function which is different from the function of either set of constituents, for example, "to town," "for John."

polemic is a strong argument or disputation, often used in relation to refuting errors of doctrine.

predicate is the division of a clause which contrasts with or supplements the subject. The subject is the topic of the clause and the predicate is what is said about the subject.

preposition is a word (usually a particle) whose function is to indicate the relation of a noun or pronoun to another noun, pronoun, verb, or adjective. Some English prepositions are "for," "from," "in," "to," "with,"

pronominal refers to pronouns.

pronouns are words which are used in place of nouns, such as "he," "him," "his," "she," "we," "them," "who," "which," "this," "these," etc.

proper name or **proper noun** is the name of a unique object, as "Jerusalem," "Joshua," "Jordan." However, the same name may be applied to more than one object, for example, "John" (the Baptist or the Apostle) and "Antioch" (of Syria or of Pisidia).

purpose clause designates a construction which states the purpose involved in some other action; for example, "John came in order to help him," or "John mentioned the problem to his colleagues, so that they would know how to help out."

qualifier is a term which limits the meaning of another term. See **attributive.**

qualitative and **quantitative** are terms which are frequently used in contrast to each other. Qualitative has to do with quality, and quantitative with quantity. Certain words ("great," for example) are sometimes used qualitatively ("a great man") and at other times quantitatively ("a great pile").

recast means the same as restructure. See **structure.**

receptor is the person receiving the message. The *receptor language* is the language into which a translation is made. The *receptor culture* is the culture of the people for whom a translation is made, especially when it differs radically from the culture of the people for whom the original message was written. See **source language.**

redundancy is the expression of information which is entirely predictable from the context. Such information is said to be *redundant.*

reflexive has to do with verbs where the agent and goal are the same person. Sometimes the goal is explicit (as in "he dresses himself"); at other times it is implicit (as in "he dresses"). See **voice.**

relative clause is a dependent clause which qualifies the object to which it refers. In "the man whom you saw," the clause "whom you saw" is relative because it relates to and qualifies "man."

rendering is the manner in which a specific passage is translated from one language to another.

restrictive attributives are so called because they restrict the meaning of the objects which they qualify, while **nonrestrictive attributives** do not. In the expression "The soldiers who were retreating were commanded to halt and regroup" (no commas), the clause "who were retreating" indicates that the command was restricted to a particular class of soldiers, namely, those who were retreating. But in the expression "The soldiers, who were retreating, were commanded to halt and regroup," the same clause (this time set off by commas) qualifies all the soldiers referred to in the discourse and simply provides supplementary information about them.

restructure is to reconstruct or rearrange. See **structure.**

rhetorical refers to special forms of speech which are used for emphasis or to create an effect on the receptor. A *rhetorical question,* for example, is not designed to elicit an answer but to make an emphatic statement.

secondary agency (agent) involves the immediate agent of a causative construction. In the sentence "John made Bill hit the man," John is the primary agent and Bill is the secondary agent. John may also be regarded as *the responsible agent* and Bill as *the immediate agent.* Similarly, in the sentence "God spoke through the prophets," God is the primary agent and the prophets are the secondary agents. They do the actual speaking, but the responsible agent is God. See **agency**.

second person See **person.**

semantic refers to meaning. **Semantics** is the study of the meaning of language forms. *Semantic categories* (or *classes*) group words according to their meaning (objects, events, abstracts, etc.) in contrast to *grammatical categories* (nouns, verbs, etc.). A *semantic domain* is a definable area of experience which is referred to by a set of words whose meanings are in some way related. For example, kinship terms constitute a semantic domain. Similarly, the color terms of a language may be said to form a semantic domain. For **semantic components,** see **components.**

sentence is a grammatical construction composed of one or more clauses and capable of standing alone. See **clause.**

simile (pronounced SIM-i-lee) is a figure of speech which describes one event or object by comparing it to another, as "she runs like a deer," "he is as straight as an arrow." Similes are less subtle than metaphors in that they use "like," "as," or some other word to mark or signal the comparison.

source language is the language in which the original message was produced. For Romans this is the form of the Greek language widely spoken at the time the New Testament was being written (called Koine Greek).

specific See **generic.**

structure is the systematic arrangement of the form of language, including the ways in which words combine into phrases, phrases into clauses, and clauses into sentences. Because this process may be compared to the building of a house or a bridge, such words as *structure* and *construction* are used in reference to it. To separate and rearrange the various components of a sentence or other unit of discourse in the translation process is to *restructure* it.

style is a particular or characteristic manner in discourse. Each language has certain distinctive *stylistic features* which cannot be reproduced literally in another language. Within any language, certain groups of speakers may have their characteristic *discourse styles,* and among individual speakers and writers, each has his own style. Various *stylistic devices* are used for the purpose of achieving a more pleasing style. For example, synonyms are sometimes used to avoid the monotonous repetition of the same words, or the normal order of clauses and phrases may be altered for the sake of emphasis.

subject See **predicate.**

subjunctive refers to certain forms of verbs that are used to express an act or state as being contingent or possible (sometimes as wish or desire), rather than as actual fact. See **modal.**

subordinate structure designates a clause connected with and dependent on another clause. See **coordinate structure, paratactic.**

substitute passive is a form which is passive in meaning, though active in form. For example, in the expression "they received punishment," the subject "they" is really the goal of the activity of the "punishment." The same is true of such expressions as "he got kicked" and "they obtained mercy."

synonyms are words which are different in form but similar in meaning, as "boy" and "lad." Expressions which have essentially the same meaning are said to be *synonymous.*

syntactic refers to **syntax,** which is the arrangement and interrelationships of words in phrases, clauses, and sentences.

taboo refers to something set apart as sacred by religious custom and is therefore forbidden to all but certain persons or uses (*positive taboo*), or something which is regarded as evil and therefore forbidden to all by tradition or social usage (*negative taboo*). For an explanation of these terms, see the comments on Romans 14.14, page 263.

textual refers to the various Greek manuscripts of the New Testament. A *textual reading* is the reading of a particular manuscript (or group of manuscripts), especially where it differs from others. *Textual evidence* is the cumulative evidence for a particular reading. *Textual problems* arise when it is difficult to reconcile or to account for conflicting readings.

third person See **person.**

transition in discourse is passing from one thought or group of related thoughts to another. In written discourse, the use of marks of punctuation and the division into paragraphs help to mark the transitions. *Transitional particles* such as prepositions and conjunctions ("in," "so," "because," "furthermore," "however," etc.) and *transitional phrases* ("in other words," "in the meantime," "at last," etc.) serve a like purpose.

transitive refers to a verb which requires a direct object to complete its meaning. "Hit," for example, is transitive. If one says, "he hits," the question arises, "he hits what?" Many verbs may be either transitive or intransitive, depending on how they are used. For example, "she sings folk songs" (transitive) and "she sings beautifully" (intransitive). See **intransitive.**

translation is the reproduction in a receptor language of the closest natural equivalent of a message in the source language, first, in terms of meaning, and second, in terms of style.

translational refers to translation. A translator may seem to be following an inferior textual reading (see **textual**) when he is simply adjusting the rendering to the requirements of the receptor language, that is, for a *translational reason.*

transliterate is to approximate in the receptor language the sounds of words occurring in the source language. Unfamiliar proper names are usually transliterated in a translation.

verbal has two meanings. (1) It may refer to expressions consisting of words, sometimes in distinction to forms of communication which do not employ words ("sign language," for example). (2) It may refer to word forms which are derived from verbs. For example, "coming" and "engaged" may be called *verbals*, and participles are called *verbal adjectives.*

voice in grammar is the relation of the action expressed by a verb to the participants in the action. In English and many other languages, the **active voice** indicates that the subject performs the action ("John hit the man"), while the **passive voice** indicates that the subject is being acted upon ("the man was hit"). The Greek language has a **middle voice** in which the subject may be regarded as doing something to or for himself (or itself).

GLOSSARY OF BIBLICAL AND HISTORICAL TERMS

Abraham. The earliest ancestor to whom the Jews trace their origin. He was the father of Isaac and the grandfather of Jacob. Abraham is important because it was with him that God made the covenant which distinguished his descendants as the chosen people of God. See Genesis 11.27—25.10 for the life of Abraham.

Adam. The first man and so the ancestor of the human race, according to the biblical account in Genesis 1.26-30; 2.4-25. He is important also because his fall into sin involved all of his posterity (Genesis 3; Romans 5.14-19).

apostle means "messenger." The term refers to each of the twelve men whom Jesus chose to be his followers and helpers, and also to Paul, and occasionally to certain other Christian workers in New Testament times.

Benjamin. The youngest of the twelve sons of Jacob and ancestor of the tribe of Benjamin. For the story of his life, see Genesis 35.16-18 and parts of chapters 42 to 45.

circumcision. The removal of the foreskin of a Jewish baby boy as a sign of God's covenant with the people of Israel.

covenant. The agreement that God made with Abraham and later with his descendants, the people of Israel. The covenant box or "ark" was a box covered with gold in which the people of Israel guarded certain sacred symbols of the covenant.

David. The most famous of the Jewish kings and composer of many of the Psalms. He lived at the beginning of the 10th century before Christ. The story of his life is found in 1 Samuel beginning with chapter 16 and all of 2 Samuel; also 1 Chronicles beginning with chapter 13.

Egypt. A country in northeast Africa, separated from Palestine by the Peninsula of Sinai. It is mostly desert, except for the land adjacent to the Nile river, which flows through it, and this part of Egypt is very rich and productive. In ancient times Egypt was the seat of a powerful empire. The people of Israel emigrated from Egypt to conquer and occupy Palestine.

Elijah. A prophet in the land of Israel in the 9th century before Christ. Elijah left no writings, but he was an impressive historical figure and is frequently mentioned in the New Testament. For the story of his life, see 1 Kings chapters 17 to 19, and 21, and 2 Kings chapters 1 and 2.

Gentiles signifies "the nations" or "foreigners" as opposed to the people of

Israel. From this point of view, the human race is divided into two groups: Jews and Gentiles.

Greeks, strictly speaking, were the inhabitants of Greece, corresponding to the Roman province of Achaia in New Testament times. In the New Testament, the term is used in a wider sense as referring to all those in the Roman Empire who spoke the Greek language and were strongly influenced by Greek culture. Frequently the term Greeks is used as synonymous with Gentiles.

Hebrew. The language in which the Old Testament was written. It belongs to the Semitic family of languages. By the time of Christ, Hebrew had ceased to be the common language of the Jewish people.

Hellenistic refers to Greek culture in New Testament times.

Israel was originally a name given to Jacob (Genesis 32.25-29); but generally, and always in the New Testament, it refers to the people or nation that were Jacob's descendants, that is, the Jews.

Jews. The people of Israel, the descendants of Jacob.

Judaism. The religion of the Jews, particularly as opposed to the teachings of Jesus and his apostles.

Koran. The sacred book of the Muslims. They believe it was dictated to Mahomet by the angel Gabriel and that it is authentic only in the original Arabic language. Therefore the translation of the Koran into other languages is not encouraged.

Law. This term is used in various ways, as is pointed out in the comments in this Handbook. The Old Testament was looked upon as consisting of three parts: the Law, the Prophets, and the Writings; but often the entire Old Testament is referred to as "the Law."

Messianic refers to Messiah. The term is used mainly to describe the prophecies and the hope concerning the coming Messiah (that is, the "Christ").

Mosaic Law. The law which God gave to the people of Israel through Moses. It is embodied in the first five books of the Old Testament, and these books are often referred to as "the Law." See Law and Moses.

Moses. The first great leader of the people of Israel. Under his leadership they left Egypt, spent many years in the desert, and began the conquest of Palestine. During the time they were in the desert, they received the Law. See Mosaic Law.

Mount Sinai. A mountain in the peninsula of Sinai, where Moses received the Law and gave it to the people of Israel.

Palestine. The homeland of the people of Israel. It is often called "the Holy Land."

Palestinian Christians. The Christians living in Palestine in New Testament times, in contrast to those who lived in other parts of the Roman Empire.

patriarchs. The famous ancestors of the Jewish race, particularly Abraham, Isaac, and Jacob, with whom God made his covenant.

prophet. A man who proclaims God's message to men. The term usually refers to the Old Testament prophets, such as Elijah and Isaiah, but sometimes it refers to the prophets of the church.

rabbi, rabbinic, rabbinical. The term rabbi means "master" or "teacher" and refers specifically to a man learned in the Mosaic Law. There were schools of rabbis, and they developed special ways of interpreting the Old Testament Scriptures. As a young man, Saul of Tarsus (that is, the apostle Paul) attended a rabbinical school, and so he was greatly influenced by rabbinic thought.

Sabbath. The term means "rest" or "cessation" from ordinary labor. It is usually employed in reference to the seventh day of the week (Saturday), which in Old Testament times was observed as a day of rest. It is still so observed by most Jews and by some Christians.

Sarah. The wife of Abraham and the mother of Isaac.

Semitic refers to a family of languages which includes Hebrew. Greek belongs to quite another language family, with a distinct cultural background. In view of his Jewish ancestry and training, it is not surprising that some Semitic idioms and thought patterns appear in the Greek writings of the apostle Paul.

Sinai. A desert region east of Egypt and south of Palestine. It is a peninsula bounded by two arms of the Red Sea. See Mount Sinai.

INDEX